Volume I

THE WORD BECOMES FLESH

A Psychodynamic Approach to Homiletics and Catechetics and Meditation

Cycle A

Second Series

CHARLES A. CURRAN
Loyola University
Chicago, Illinois

Counseling-Learning Publications
(Formerly Apple River Press)
Box 285
East Dubuque, Illinois 61025

Printed in the United States of America

NIHIL OBSTAT:

Reverend Thomas G. Doran
Censor Deputatus

IMPRIMATUR:

✠Arthur J. O'Neill
Bishop of Rockford

Second Printing, 1986.

ISBN 0–933138–01–6

CONTENTS

Preface v

FIRST SUNDAY IN ADVENT 1
Homily I 1
Homily II 3
Homily III 4
Homily IV 6

SECOND SUNDAY IN ADVENT 9
Homily I 9
Homily II 11
Homily III 13
Homily IV 16

THIRD SUNDAY IN ADVENT 18
Homily I 18
Homily II 20
Homily III 22
Homily IV 23

FOURTH SUNDAY IN ADVENT 26
Homily I 26
Homily II 28
Homily III 29
Homily IV 31

CHRISTMAS MASS AT MIDNIGHT 33
Homily I 33
Homily II 35
Homily III 37
Homily IV 39

CHRISTMAS MASS DURING THE DAY ... 43
Homily I ... 43
Homily II ... 45
Homily III ... 47
Homily IV ... 50

FEAST OF THE HOLY FAMILY ... 53
Homily I ... 53
Homily II ... 55
Homily III ... 58
Homily IV ... 60

JANUARY THE FIRST—OCTAVE OF CHRISTMAS ... 64
SOLEMNITY OF MARY MOTHER OF GOD ... 64
Homily I ... 64
Homily II ... 66
Homily III ... 67
Homily IV ... 69

SECOND SUNDAY AFTER CHRISTMAS ... 72
Homily I ... 72
Homily II ... 73
Homily III ... 75
Homily IV ... 77

JANUARY 6—EPIPHANY ... 79
Homily I ... 79
Homily II ... 80
Homily III ... 83
Homily IV ... 85

SUNDAY AFTER JANUARY 6—BAPTISM OF OUR LORD ... 88
Homily I ... 88
Homily II ... 90
Homily III ... 91
Homily IV ... 93

Index ... 97

PREFACE

In the following homiletic and catechetical expositions, there are at least *four* for each Sunday and feast. Each one begins with an "ana-gnosis." This is not an ana-logos. That is, it is not intended to be an analogy or simply an example. We have called them "ana-gnoses" rather than analogies, because they are aimed at involving the reader or hearer personally at the level of his own *gnosis* about himself.

Analogy, in the *logos* sense, is too intellectual and remote for what we mean here. The hope is that each person will begin to commit himself and so be talking to himself while he hears or reads. He will thus hopefully be creatively reacting and so giving a homily to himself at the level of his own personal memory and experience.

These presentations are not intended to be all-inclusive. They are only *one form* of communicating the scriptural message. Hopefully their advanced reading may stimulate the reader not simply to memorize them—he or she may do this of course, and, we hope, profitably—but rather, as a result, to move on to his own personal witness and communication with his hearers. They are, therefore, intended basically to be personal stimulants and encouragements starting the reader or hearer on his own personal quest.

One will notice here that the *immediate human meaning* is most often seized upon—not some more complicated and subtle theological conclusion. This is not to deny the latter or its importance. It is rather to draw attention to the basic and rich human elements that are so often central to the scriptural message. The intent too is to initiate a process by which the hearer, or the reader, is allowed to enter into the presentation through its immediate human meaning.

To aid in this, the speaker should simply be himself, speaking in whatever way is most comfortable to him. His natural manner

would therefore usually be more often meditative than dramatic, more conversational than theatrical, allowing for the electronic apparatus to carry his words directly into the ear of the hearer—as in an intimate communication together.

These presentations are all *short;* some are very short. People often seek a short homily or catechetical presentation. But since they are short, further doctrinal and similar material may be added to them, as fits the occasion. Or, more than one may be given.

There is also the allowance for the possibility that later dialogue will extend and develop the embryonic concepts here. In this sense, what happens after words enter the ear is more important than before. This is the "germination" process; that is, seed once entered the soil and embraced by it, germinates and grows there. The entering may be quick—as the acorn enters quickly—but slowly and mysteriously over time, a great oak with powerful branches where birds abide and sing, can result. We have described elsewhere the group dynamic process that, we feel, could aid this.[1]

The model, therefore, is not the mathematics book: problem-solving which arrives at "answers." Our model is the familiar sower who goes out to sow seed. This is our inseminational aim and hope.

These themes are based on a personal approach to homiletics and catechetics, the psychological background of which is explained in detail in a separate volume: *THE WORD BECOMES FLESH: A Psychodynamic Approach to Homelitics and Catechetics* (Theory and Practice).

1. Curran, C. A. *Religious Values in Counseling and Psychotherapy.* New York: Sheed and Ward, Inc., 1969, pp. 231-248.

FIRST SUNDAY IN ADVENT (SERIES A)
HOMILY I

Reading I: *The mountain of the Lord's house shall be established as the highest mountain and raised above the hills, and all nations shall stream towards it.* (Is. 2:2-3)

ANA-GNOSIS

Modern business is constantly striving, in its commercial efforts, to make its product known. In its endeavor to do this, it uses the billboard and other types of neon or illuminated signs wherever it can find space that will attract people's attention. A common form of this is for a company to pick one of the highest spots along a highway, or even in a city, high enough that it towers above most other signs, and big enough that it is as big as, or bigger than, most of them.

We are used to this. A moment's thought can reveal things like this that we know and have seen many times. All this, from a commercial point of view, indicates that a company not only wants business, which of course is true, but also that it is proud of its product and wants people to know its value and to use it.

THEOLOGICAL EXTENSION

Now this kind of commercial common sense is a way of understanding today's Reading from Isaias. The message Isaias represents, not only for the people of his time but for all of us, is first of all the same practical message that commerce represents when it pays a high price for an expensive site and puts there a large sign. It is common sense that if we have a very good product, valuable to mankind, we want to make it known. And so Isaias says, "In the days to come the mountain of the Lord's house shall be established as the highest mountain and raised above the hills, and all nations shall stream towards it." Understandably, therefore, it is so valuable that the message of God, which Isaias here represents, should be made known in the most effective way possible. It is not a misunderstanding of Isaias' image here to say that he would propose renting a billboard, as sometimes religiously motivated people do; or he might want to put his message on television in an expensive presentation; or he might buy space for an ad in a modern newspaper. These would be all modern equivalents of what he is expressing here. All would be ways of expressing that this is an extremely important message, a very important relationship between God and man, and that we must make it known to others.

And so he goes on, "All nations shall stream towards it, many people shall come and say, 'Let us climb the Lord's mountain to the house of the God of Jacob, that he may instruct us in his ways and we may walk in his paths.' " This is the same point today, and one might even see a large sign telling us the same thing, inviting us to come. This is the constant appeal of the commercial advertisement, to try the product, to see how it works. Why? The pragmatic reason is that it hopes that in trying the product, the customers will see that their claim is true, and they will buy it and start to use it. The same conclusion follows here. "Come, let us do this, let us go up to this high place, let's enter the house of God that He may instruct us."

THEOLOGICAL CONCLUSION

So we want to learn first what this remarkable knowledge is about, and then we want to follow it, walk in its ways. This is exactly the mode of our life. One of Cardinal Newman's prayers was, "Oh, God, give me the light to see the truth and the strength to follow it wherever it may lead." This is exactly the same prayer as suggested here by Isaias. It is not enough simply to hear it, to study it, to recite it, to know it. We need God's help not only in the light to see, but in the strength to follow. This is our prayer in the spirit of Isaias.

FIRST SUNDAY IN ADVENT (SERIES A)
HOMILY II

Responsorial Psalm: *Pray for the peace of Jerusalem! May those who love you prosper! May peace be within your walls, prosperity within your buildings!* (Ps. 122:1-9)

ANA-GNOSIS

There is a kind of special security in having something, as we say, "under lock and key." We know the peace that comes from feeling the doors are locked at night, the gates are closed, or the sense that we are protected by the walls of the house. Even as small children there is a sense of peace inside a tent. Or we can all remember, as small children, the peacefulness of getting under the covers, or the kind of special security in putting one's head under the blankets, or even the security of a big box that, as a small child, one could sneak into. We know, too, in fact, thc dangers of this; old refrigerators, and other types of cabinets that have outer locks on them, have sometimes tragically locked children in because of the child's desire for closed places. This suggests how one element of peace is to be behind something closed and locked, and the security that goes with this, and the special peace which follows.

THEOLOGICAL EXTENSION

The Psalmist expresses this same idea of peace by referring to the city of Jerusalem and its gates as the symbol of peace and security. "Now we have set foot within your gates, O Jerusalem! Pray for the peace of Jerusalem," he goes on, "May those who love you prosper, may peace be within your walls and prosperity in your buildings."

Applied to ourselves then, peace is this spiritual enclosure that God puts around us and through which we are protected from wasting and losing ourselves in all sorts of meaningless paths and pursuits. It is kind of like coming home and taking off one's shoes and making sure the doors are locked and the house is secure, and quietly relaxing in bed or in a quiet chair with the busy day done and all the activities quieted; we are secure and at peace.

The Psalmist today is suggesting this same inner peace be with us always, even in the busiest part of the day, or the busiest part of all our activities, and in all the confusion and conflicts that go with daily life. He urges us never to lose this inner spot, these "walls" of our own inner spiritual Jerusalem between God and ourselves.

THEOLOGICAL CONCLUSION

A moment's prayer, a moment's meditation in a chapel or church, if there is one available, is a way, even in very busy days, of finding this peace. It is there for us in our Jerusalem, in our own special place walled off between God and ourselves; we need only to seek it.

And so we say with the Psalmist, "May those who love you prosper! May peace be within your walls, prosperity within your buildings!" These are the walls and buildings of the inner mansion of one's own spiritual world, between ourselves and God.

FIRST SUNDAY IN ADVENT (SERIES A)
HOMILY III

Reading II: *Let us cast off deeds of darkness and put on armor of light.* (Rom. 13:11-14)

ANA-GNOSIS

We are all still disturbed and even shocked as a nation by the rampage that occurred by the blackout not too long ago in New York City. This was all the more upsetting because it had not occurred in the previous electrical failure that had taken place a year or two before. People were then congratulating themselves on the very decent way they had reacted to that first electrical failure and long period of darkness, and so the rampant disorder of the second blackout was all the more disturbing. There was, understandably, a tendency to feel that this was a sign that the world was in for greater confusion and difficulty than it was before, and that big cities like New York are certainly in very bad shape.

One of the first reassurances we get today from St. Paul's epistle to the Romans, and we remember that Rome was a very large city at that time as well as it is today, is that the kind of disorders that happened that night in New York were disorders which St. Paul and the Romans well understood and knew. His analogy is exactly that; "The night is far spent," he says, "the day draws near. Cast off deeds of darkness, put on the armor of light! Let us live honorably as in the daylight, not in carousing and drunkenness, not in sexual excess, lust, not in quarreling and jealousy." So we see he could have put in robbery and looting and any of the other forms of crime or dishonesty. This is a list of what people do in the night and in the darkness without the light. It is evident that they did these things just the same in St. Paul's day in Rome as we experience now.

THEOLOGICAL EXTENSION

The issue, therefore, is not poverty (that is a point and an important one) nor is it being underprivileged. These are all contributing factors, as they always are; but the issue is the darkness that protects us, and gives the impression, at least, that other people will not see what we are doing; that we don't have to face our misdeeds because nobody can arrest us since nobody quite knows or sees who can testify or report us. Darkness gives us this protection.

It isn't simply people in New York City or other cities stricken by darkness who do this. St. Paul is directing his words to all the Romans, and through them to us. We all hide. We all use any excuse we can to pretend that no one will see really what we are doing. Elsewhere the Psalmist raises the same point when he speaks about the man saying, "Who will know what I do? God isn't interested. God won't see." But the answer we well know is that God does see. We know what we do and our own judgment of ourselves, even when we hide it in surpressed guilt, is still there.

So there is no real dark place to hide. We only use this as an excuse and a pretense. This is why, in St. Paul's example here, it is pointed out that we are really children of the light, people of the light. Once we have accepted the faith of Christ, we live twenty-four hours a day in the light. In other words, as we sometimes say, our life is an open book. There is no place to hide and we don't want to hide. We want people to see very genuinely and honestly who we are and what we are and what we do. If we are priests, or sisters, or religiously dedicated people, we want everyone to see that our life has integrity and honesty within the framework of our human weaknesses that we are working against. If we are parents, we want our children to know and understand our genuine openness and honesty and our striving for goodness. If we are young people we want our parents, our friends, our priests and sisters and brothers who teach us, who are concerned for us and love us, to know that basically and fundamentally our lives are open books, ready for the inspection of the light.

THEOLOGICAL CONCLUSION

So there is no darkness, there is no place to hide, there is no blackout in our spiritual lives. There is no way that we can fool God or ourselves. Our Christian faith is a bright light that not only lights up the way of our lives, where we are to go and what we are to do; it lights up ourselves and with that spotlight of our faith upon us we do not fool anybody; but most of all we do not fool ourselves and God.

FIRST SUNDAY IN ADVENT (SERIES A)
HOMILY IV

Gospel Reading: *Be sure of this, if the owner of the house knew when the thief was coming he would keep a watchful eye and not allow his house to be broken into. You must be prepared in the same way; the Son of Man is coming at the time you least expect.* (Mt. 24:37-44)

ANA-GNOSIS

We sometimes read in the paper where a robbery was attempted, but the police had been warned ahead of time so they have the area, as they say, "staked out." They are hidden in cars or appear to be innocent bystanders behind newspapers or other disguises, waiting for the thieves to arrive and the robbery to be in progress before they proceed to arrest the robbers. The newspapers say they were caught "red-handed" as we see pictures of the police going about their business of catching the thieves in the act. It is perfectly obvious that the thieves themselves would never have attempted the robbery had someone tipped them off that the police already knew about it and were ready and waiting for them.

The vast majority of times, however, this doesn't happen. The robbery is usually shocking with surprise.

THEOLOGICAL EXTENSION

Even though we say "be prepared," one might propose that we say "be prepared" for the unexpected. There is a kind of contradiction in terms there. If you don't know what to expect, how be prepared for it! Now this is what our Lord wants us to see about life. We all know this but it is just that we need to keep thinking about it all the time so as not forget it, not to lose sight of it. So Christ repeats it for us too. It is commonplace for one person to say to another about almost any event, "Well you never know what to expect, do you?" That is a true statement of the history and the story and the condition of the way our human life transpires. We never know what to expect; there is no stakeout, no careful preparation to catch the thief in the night. Death will come that way, our Lord tells us, and all sorts of other things can happen that way too.

Therefore, what can we do? When our Lord tells us to be prepared, when He gives us this commonsense discussion today, He says, "Stay awake, therefore, you cannot know the day your Lord is coming." We can stay awake but what does that mean? In simple exchanges together, we often say, "Well, he was asleep at the switch"; "He wasn't paying attention"; "He wasn't watching where he was going"; "Fell asleep at the wheel and had that accident." While we cannot be prepared for the unexpected, we can be prepared for all that life entails. In our Lord's terms, this obviously means to look at life with our eyes wide open, seeing the long view of the future that leads us beyond our present life of seeing the present, and seeing it in terms of what is truly significant for us. This is being awake, this is having our eyes wide open.

It is not so much that going to sleep is in itself bad; most of the time, going to sleep is good if we are in a safe bed and at a place where we should go to sleep. It is dangerous when we go to sleep at times when we should be awake, like when we are driving an automobile. That is the kind of staying awake Christ means for us here.

THEOLOGICAL CONCLUSION

In the responsibility of driving the car of our life, we have to confidently look ahead and be aware of the basic signposts, directives, and guides, that lead us where we genuinely and honestly want to go. This is so not simply in the final end of our life, the beyond of our life, but within the stage-by-stage progress, from day to day and week by week, as one travels to one's final destiny by a series of intervening goals and cities and directives. That is staying awake. That is what we can do. Obviously we cannot be prepared for the unexpected, but we can be awake. We can be alert, and in that sense we can be prepared. "Stay awake, therefore," our Lord tells us, "you cannot know the day your Lord is coming. The Son of Man is coming at the time you least expect."

SECOND SUNDAY IN ADVENT (SERIES A)
HOMILY I

Reading I: *The spirit of the Lord shall rest upon him.* (Is. 11:1-10)

ANA-GNOSIS

The most common and ordinary things about our lives and about ourselves, and those things that are most fundamental to our lives, we often pay least attention to. We may not even notice such things until some more or less serious illnesses occur that makes us aware of them. This can happen, for example, when we notice some questionable thing about ourselves and we go to a hospital or a doctor. By examination, he points out something that we hadn't paid any attention to before; but from then on, of course, we are very observantly aware. Breathing is one of these very simple actions. Many of us go through a good portion of our lives and never think about breathing. Breathing is something we do hundreds of times a day, and we do it easily and smoothly, with little or no thought.

In fact we only consciously think about breathing when someone around us, say, has asthma or some illness of that sort. Then the awareness of breathing becomes very sharp. Most of us, as an ordinary sign of life, think first of all to ask if a person is breathing. Other more complicated signs we think of later, but the most obvious sign of life is the rise and fall of a person's chest and abdomen by which it is recognized that they are breathing. For example, a very ancient test of death was to put a feather near the person's nose and mouth to see if there was any movement in the feather.

The ancients, therefore, had this same deep understanding of how basic breath is. They, like ourselves, probably didn't think that much of it, except in special instances of illness, but the fact is that they came to see breath, and the word "breathing," and all the simple actions that are associated with breathing, as a very central part of life. And so from earliest times we have had an expression like the "Breath of life."

THEOLOGICAL EXTENSION

Now the expression today, "The spirit of the Lord shall rest upon him," is actually that word "breath." If one pronounces *spiritus* in Latin slowly, it is a little bit like the sound of breathing. When we speak even of the Holy Spirit we speak of it in that basic way that the ancients meant it; that is, that it was a special kind of God's breathing with us as we breathe. That is the meaning of the phrase today in Isaias: the spirit of the Lord, the life giving breath, is a special breath from God and therefore, as we breathe physically, God gives us this special kind of life breath. Out of that, then, comes a special kind of understanding of the meaning of life and a special kind of wisdom and decision, not only of taking counsel with ourselves wisely, but being able to help others in a very skilled way that we now call counseling. There is also a kind of courage, a special strength in the midst of difficulties and conflicts, that comes to us. This is basically an inner delight that gives a special richness and meaning to our lives, a special kind of inner breathing, so to speak, a kind of inner life of God that, no matter what our extrinsic circumstances may be, as life changes we keep a peace, tranquility and inner vision and insight of ourselves and others.

For those of us who remember the earlier religious classes of a generation or so ago, this list of Isaias was called the "Gifts of the Holy Spirit" and the delight of the fear of the Lord was called piety. Whether we use that conception of a list of seven Gifts, or whether we see the simple language of Isaias here as meaning a special kind of divine life that breathes in us, it is a wonderful definition of the meaning of faith and the indwelling of the Holy Spirit; or, as we hear it now, the "holy breathing," the "holy breath" of God in us.

THEOLOGICAL CONCLUSION

It is this confidence that Isaias gives us. It is applied here, of course, to the root of Jesse, the family tree of Jesse, the father of

David. So the family tree comes down to Christ, as we know the Messias, our own Jesus, our Lord. But in addition to the description of the Messias as especially possessing in their fullness and perfection these gifts, they extend out to all of us. As we share the Christlife together, we share the divine breathing in Christ that comes to us.

And so, in a certain sense, we have a double life as Christians and a double breathing. When we think therefore of how basic our own breath is to ourselves, as we momentarily sit and consciously think about it, how precious it is, how basic to our lives as we breathe thousands of times every day. We can draw the parallel that Isaais draws for us here that the divine breathing in us is also just as basic even though, in a way, it may appear just as simple and not often consciously observed or thought about. This is the spirit of God in us, the divine indwelling, the divine breathing that gives us a special understanding, a special wisdom, and a special inner peace as we live our ordinary lives of normal physical breathing together. God breathes with us and in us.

SECOND SUNDAY IN ADVENT (SERIES A)
HOMILY II

Responsorial Psalm: *Justice shall flower in his days and profound peace until the moon be no more. May he rule from sea to sea and from the river to the ends of the earth.* (Ps. 72:1-13)

ANA-GNOSIS

There are a number of fundamental things that all of us, members of the human race, desire together. These are things that we seek at our present time in the age of nuclear power and the threat of a nuclear holocaust, and the age of space ship earth, now that we have gone to the moon and seen it with the eyes of television from a far distance. Not only are these things something we desire now with all the special sense of the unity and the meaning of the human person that has come to us, as we recognize ourselves living together on this space ship earth; they seem to be desires that, from the beginning of time as far back as history goes, men have longed for.

One of these things is a reign of peace on earth, and justice and honesty and integrity in a special human way. This is tied up not with elaborate political governments or complicated congresses, but with one man. We know that from time to time history throws up such men or women as great leaders and the nation looks back to them with gratitude. Washington, Lincoln, Roosevelt, names of that sort, quickly come to mind in our history. But there is yet a yearning for a kind of perfect leader and, in the language of the ancients, this perfect leader was thought of as a king. And so one's heart is longing for a king that has a very special gift and grace from God to bring unity and peace to the human race, justice and all the things that, in our human heart, we long for. Behind all the war and crime and delinquency, and the other evils we see around us socially, we seem to yearn for some reign of peace and, therefore, for some great leader to bring it to us. We see evidence of this, for example, in the yearning for a sense of justice, a yearning even in the ancient code of Hammurabi that was discovered long before the time of Christ where, in both the prologue and the epilogue, there is this same description of an ideal, just king.

THEOLOGICAL EXTENSION

We see, therefore, the Psalm today expressing this human yearning. Whether we call it a king, or a president, or some other title, the yearning is for a great leader. And so the prayer says, "O God, with your judgment endow the king as this great leader, with your justice the king's son; he shall govern your people with justice, your afflicted ones with judgment." He shall be a wise king coming from God, God's son, successor to the king. The first part of this is just a simple fulfillment of that prayer of human yearning for a great leader, wise in his judgment, deep in his sense of justice for all. "For justice shall flower in his days and profound peace until the moon be no more." A long period of a peaceful reign is what we all pray for and seek and need. "May he rule from sea to sea and from the river to the ends of the earth."

In the sense of the limited area of where the Psalmist lived, he saw this as including the whole world, and if he had lived today, he would have talked about spaceship earth. All around the globe this rule of justice and peace would come. And so this great ruler shall rescue the poor man when he cries, the afflicted when he has no one to help him. We know how much that yearning exists now, how painful is the awareness that we all have of poverty and suffering and under-privileged throughout the world; and what an overwhelming, joyous fulfillment it is to have a great leader who would have pity for the lowly and the poor.

"The lives of the poor he shall save and indeed then may his name be blessed forever; as long as the sun his name shall remain. In him shall all the tribes of the earth be blessed and all the nations shall proclaim his happiness." The cry of human yearning indeed, isn't it? The cry that we hear as intensely and as strongly today as in the earliest times, as in the code of Hammurabi before the Psalms were written, and in the Psalms themselves the ancient heart of man, and our own modern hearts crying together for this great leader. Now we know that this Psalm is, in a sense, a prophetic Psalm of the coming of the reign of Christ, and of Christ our leader.

THEOLOGICAL CONCLUSION

There is a wonderful reassurance to it, though not the reassurance of a great political leader, for in a certain sense, this becomes an analogy, an example, a symbol. It is rather that if any of these things even partially are to be realized, they are realized because men and women everywhere take up a sense of Godliness in their lives. We feel that the most complete expression of that Godliness is in the teachings and doctrines and practices of our Christian faith. The Godliness, however it would be expressed, is basic to this great reign of peace and justice and unity throughout the world; and this you and I can do something about, in living as totally, as completely, as genuinely and as honestly as we can our Christian dedication.

This, shared and spread by thousands and hundreds of thousands and millions of people, can be the first and most important step in this reign of peace that we yearn for when "Justice shall flower in his days, and profound peace until the moon be no more. May he rule from sea to sea and from the river to the ends of the earth." This is the deepest yearning of the human heart—a yearning for unity and justice. We can begin to bring this about by the integrity and genuineness of our own Christian lives.

SECOND SUNDAY IN ADVENT (SERIES A)
HOMILY III

Reading II: *Everything written before our time was written for our instructions, that we may derive hope from the lessons of patience* *and the words of encouragement in the Scriptures. May God, the source of all patience and encouragement, enable you to live in perfect harmony with one another according to the spirit of Christ Jesus, so that with one heart and voice you may glorify the father of our Lord Jesus Christ.* (Rom. 15:4-9)

ANA-GNOSIS

Sometimes there are special occasions when we want to think of particular words that have special significance in our lives and the lives of those around us. Graduation classes sometimes pick a class motto. Such words are carefully chosen to symbolize something special for that class. When we erect a building of special meaning—religious, civic—we often carve in stone on the outside and on the inside of the building some very special words and phrases that we want to stand for many years. These words or phrases symbolize a particular meaning that this achievement, this period of time, this civic dedication or religious faith, has. Sometimes in special offices people choose mottos as, say, Bishops do. These mottos stand for a particular commitment of their life as a Bishop. Governors sometimes do this, or particular states have such mottos. The United States itself has similar kinds of mottos such as, "In God We Trust."

THEOLOGICAL EXTENSION

Now if we were to be put in a position where we were asked to make up some brief and profound statement about human yearnings and desires, we might chance upon, and choose the quotation from today's Reading from St. Paul to the Romans. We might focus on the exact point of three basic words—hope, patience, and encouragement. St. Paul tells us, "Everything written before our time was written for our instructions, that we might derive hope of the lessons, patience, the words of encouragement in the Scriptures." Hope will come to us from lessons of patience and encouragement that we receive from the teaching of God. But hope we receive ourselves because we have, at the same time, patience; and patience and hope together aid us to have courage when others also encourage us.

Certainly, if we were to ask what is basic to the self-worth in a child, one would answer that he or she needs in themselves to be helped to hope. Now they receive this hope from others. Other people, by giving them a sense of worth and meaning, allow them to be hopeful about themselves, to have hopeful expectancies with regard to themselves, to see a way in which their lives can have significance and meaning and purpose and, therefore, they can feel hopeful. If we have occasion to deal with depressed children, we know that basically they seem to be with little or no hope, and little or no self-regard or self-respect. So hope, in this sense, comes first to us in how others regard us—positively, hopefully—and we then can feel hope about ourselves.

Because we are hopeful we can also be patient. The person who is without hope is also, in a sense, a person without patience because there is nothing to wait for, nothing for which endurance might bring a reward; for unless there is an immediate reward, there is no long term hopefulness that would keep one patient. So the depressed person and the one without hope, is also the person who is impatient. That is why they do precipitous actions, actions often harmful to themselves and others. They can't stand to wait any longer, they want to get something done, they have no patience.

And finally, for both hope and patience to continue, especially when conflicts in life occur as we get older, we need very much the encouragement of others. Basic, of course, is our own courage, our own ability to stand, even if necessary, to stand alone. But we get this courage as adults, to stand alone, because our parents, our brothers and sisters, our friends, those around us when we were children and when we were adolescents, encouraged us. The studies of people of significant success, from the sports to the arts to achievement in writing, show at least one other person who stood out in their memory. Usually it is someone from their early childhood, or adolescence. But it is always someone through whom they received encouragement, and thus were given patience and hope. These three were basic to their achievement.

THEOLOGICAL CONCLUSION

St. Paul gives us a basic source of this encouragement. He says, "May God, the source of all patience and encouragement, enable you to live in perfect harmony with one another. Accept one another then," he says' "as Christ accepted you, for the glory of God." We might, then, paraphrase St. Paul by saying there are these three—hope, patience and encouragement. These are most basic to our relationship with ourselves, to our relationship with

God and our relationship with one another. And these, first of all, we get from others, as we most basically get continually throughout our lives from God. Having hope, having patience, being encouraged—we have courage to live fruitful, rich and religiously significant lives for Christ, for ourselves, and for one another.

SECOND SUNDAY IN ADVENT (SERIES A)
HOMILY IV

Gospel Reading: *When he saw that many of the Pharisees and Sadducees were stepping forward for this bath he said to them, "You brood of vipers, who told you to flee from the wrath to come. Give some evidence that you mean to reform."* (Mt. 3:1-12)

ANA-GNOSIS

We are all familiar with the psychological term "fettish." We know it as an act, object, or ritual of some kind that we carry out to give ourselves artificial reassurance about something. It is sometimes pointed out that adults use cars, as children use toys or particular objects, to give them reassurance. The comic strip character, Linus, and his blanket have made us all aware of this kind of thing which we know to be common among children. But adults, too, have their "blankets," their security symbols, their fettishes. We recognize many of these in our own lives by which we can falsely give ourselves far more meaning than the object warrants, and so it becomes a fettish, rather than something real or genuine.

THEOLOGICAL EXTENSION

Now we can do this with rituals and ceremonies too; and even the Sacraments are not without a fettish aspect from the point of view of our human weakness and our tendency to misuse them. Just the notion that a person repeatedly goes to the Sacraments, as we say, and is very religious in appearance, because he carries out all the external actions of participating in the life of Christ, does not mean necessarily that it is so.

In today's Gospel, when John saw the Sadducees and the Pharisees coming to him for baptism, he felt that they were going to use this as a kind of fettish, as they used many other religious ceremonies. In their desire not to miss out on anything, and to impress the people, they pushed forward. But John had his doubts about them, and about how honest they would be in carrying out anything that his baptism would stand for. He gives us a warning and a caution to make sure we really know what we are doing when we participate in the Sacraments. It is not enough just to receive the Eucharist repeatedly, nor simply to go to Mass, the Eucharistic celebration; nor to do all those other extrinisc things, even when they are so holy as to be Sacraments. They can become a fettish, a self-deception and a fraud. We must make sure that we give some evidence that we mean what we are doing and that we mean to change our lives, to reform ourselves in those things that we know need reforming. We must constantly be working at reforming. If we put a hyphen after *re-*, we get perhaps a better meaning of the word. We must form ourselves over and over again, constantly making ourselves closer to the image of Christ that is unique for us in our lives, with the spirit of Christ guiding us. If we do this, then the Sacraments are real and genuine and significant. They are also, however, capable of being used as fettishes, as symbols of extrinsic reassurance when they are not really evidences of genuine commitment at all.

THEOLOGICAL CONCLUSION

This is what John the Baptist warns against. He warns not only the Pharisees and Sadducees and other people of his time who were formally leaders of their religious people, but all of us. "Who told you to flee from the wrath to come," he says, in that strong language of the stern confronting man that he was—a prophet determined to have people see what this new age of the Messias was about. "Give some evidence that you mean to reform." This applies as well to us. The Sacraments have all the great meaning, infinite help and grace of God in and through them, but we too must do our part in the covenant with God. If we do not, they themselves become, like other material things we have around us, mere fettishes, mere escapes, mere acting out of religious reassurance. That is as Christ elsewhere spoke of some of these people—a whited sepulcher—because its appearance is real but inside it is filled with death-wish and self-deception.

THIRD SUNDAY OF ADVENT (SERIES A)
HOMILY I

Reading I: *Strengthen the hands that are feeble, make firm the knees that are weak. Say to those whose hearts are frightened, "Be strong, fear not, here is your God."* (Is. 35:1-10)

ANA-GNOSIS

When we are young, and even when we are older and adults, but have not really experienced something, it is easy to disregard the difficulties, the handicaps and even the pains and anxieties of other people. The following incident can give us an illustration of this in terms of children. The young woman, a university graduate student, was taking a walk in a new neighborhood. She was a handicapped person needing to walk with one crutch, by reason of a childhood infirmity. Some little children came out, and three or four of them gathered around her and walked along with her. Soon their curiosity was aroused as to why she needed that "stick." One of them, not in cruelty, but in a very genuine desire to help her, pulled the crutch away from her, insisting, "You could walk if you just tried. See! I can walk without that 'stick.'" The young woman had to keep insisting, "No, I will fall if you take this crutch; I have to have it, otherwise I would have to lean on you." One or two of the little children were amazed by this—that they would be so strong that they could hold her up. One even wanted to try it, to take away her crutch and let her lean on him.

Another time this same graduate student was babysitting for a little child, and had taken her to a park. While she was sitting on the bench with the crutch at her side, the little girl quickly grabbed the crutch, ran off, and stood a distance away. She was enjoying having "fun" with what she thought was a kind of an adult toy. There were no other adults or children around, so a pathetically helpless dialogue had to go on between the graduate student and the little child. The graduate student tried to persuade the little child that this was not a toy, but that she had to have it, and she must bring it back; otherwise she could not walk. After intensive persuasion, the little child, perhaps tiring of the "toy," brought it back and, fortunately, mobility and normalcy was restored to the graduate student.

This type of incident reminds us of how easy it is not to understand weakness, not to understand that a person cannot walk, or can only walk with great difficulty, when we ourselves can run and walk and dance and climb with little thought of what it would be like not to be able to do these things. While this is most evident in small children, in more complicated ways we can all have this same indifference, and even cruel inconsideration, because we have never understood, or felt from the inside, what this kind of weakness, suffering and anxiety can mean.

THEOLOGICAL EXTENSION

Today the Reading from Isaias looks at this issue very carefully. He considers both the sense of weakness that we can all have, even though others may not appreciate it; and the great joy that comes when something of strength is restored. So the prayer, "Strengthen the hands that are feeble, make firm the knees that are weak," is appropriate here.

Somewhere in our lifetime we have needed a crutch. Somewhere our hands, by way of some sort of accident, couldn't hold things. Sometimes it happens that we have just been rather seriously ill and our whole body doesn't function well—our hands won't hold things, and our legs and knees won't hold us up. Since somewhere in our adult life, all of us have had an experience like this, we can have real sympathy, real feeling, with others when they are handicapped.

Less common, but still common enough, are the anxieties that can overwhelm people. If we have never really known intense anxiety, or the type of seizure it can bring—near paralysis of the mind and the will, and even the body, that intense anxiety can produce—we might have the same inconsideration as small children. Because we have never known it, we therefore have never understood it. But here, too, the prayer of Isaias today catches this: "Say to those whose hearts are frightened, be strong, fear not, here is your God." In weakness, then, we need God. Those periods of physical weakness, or even psychological weakness of anxiety seizures, remind us of how much we need God, how God does come to save us. All the handicaps and weaknesses and difficulties that we can be heir to have their resolution and their cure and their final feeling in God. "He comes to save you; then will the eyes of the blind be opened and the ears of the deaf be cleared; then will the lame leap like a stag, the tongue of the dumb will sing."

THEOLOGICAL CONCLUSION

We know what a joy it is, when one has been ill, to slowly feel strength coming back and then to feel oneself able to walk or even run again, to hold and grip things with ease as we did before. What a peacefulness! And perhaps even greater peacefulness after a period of anxiety and stress and concern, to see the conflicts resolved and the confusions cleared up.

So we can understand the final beautiful phrase of Isaias: "Those whom the Lord has ransomed will return and enter Zion singing, crowned with everlasting joy. They will meet with joy and gladness, sorrow and mourning will flee." We know this in particular things, in illness and weakness and anxiety. We know that we turn to God in a very special way for strength and comfort. This is true not only in the immediacies of our lives, but in the life beyond this, where a final joy and peace is promised to us in this Reading from Isaias.

THIRD SUNDAY OF ADVENT (SERIES A)
HOMILY II

Responsorial Psalm: *The Lord keeps faith forever.* (Ps. 146:6-10)

ANA-GNOSIS

Life can sometimes give us periods—even long periods—of peace and happiness and joy and enthusiasm, so much so that it stretches out in front of us like a broad valley, rich and green. The beautiful blue skies are inviting as far as the eye can see; or it can be like a broad sweeping highway that entices us to get in our cars and zoom down long distances to promised joys. When life is so open and blooming, particularly when we are young, it is a joy to get up in the mornings and be able to breathe and live. But times can come upon us, particularly when years pass, but even sometimes when we are young, when life is narrowed by anxiety, pain and suffering, failure and discouragement; so narrowed is it, in fact, that we sometimes say we hope we can just make it through the night; we hardly look beyond the dawn. The darkness is close around us, we don't even try to think of the future or even of the next day or week. Just so we get through the night, we say, just so we can make it until the dawn comes.

THEOLOGICAL EXTENSION

This narrowing of our lives is characteristic of the story of all of us. Life can consist of broad vistas, broad sweeps of joy and hope and anticipation, but it can also narrow us so that it is indeed a prayer of thanksgiving and petition that God helps us through the night. This kind of suffering has been known by mankind from the beginning of time, and the Psalmist certainly knows it here. In these times, we have one place to turn always, and that is to God. That is the Psalmist's answer: "The Lord God keeps faith forever." We can be overwhelmed and discouraged with injustice in the world, with hunger everywhere, with the suffering of the handicapped, the sick and the ill. All these thoughts crowd in on us, as they are crowding in on the Psalmist today. We have one refuge for peace and one way to make it through the night of our discouragement and our disturbance and that is the reassurance, "The Lord God keeps faith forever."

THEOLOGICAL CONCLUSION

In a certain sense, there is a desperate state to the human condition wherein there is nowhere else to turn but to God. Sometimes in the middle of the night, when everything else fails, we know that by kneeling down in prayer we make it through the night and through the day; we make it up the hill of discouragement and suddenly, over the top of the hill, the broad vistas loom again—the joyful valley and the blue sky and the inviting green come again into our lives. We know hope and joy and excitement and stimulation again. Our consolation in the nights, when we pray only to make it to the dawn, is this prayer that the Psalmist understood so well, being overwhelmed by the substance of mankind: "The Lord God keeps faith forever." God keeps faith for us.

THIRD SUNDAY OF ADVENT (SERIES A)
HOMILY III

Reading II: *Be patient, my brothers, until the coming of the Lord. See how the farmer awaits the precious yield of the soil. He looks forward to it patiently while the soil receives the winter and the spring rains. You too must be patient.* (Ja. 5:7-10)

ANA-GNOSIS

There is an efficiency and directness and an immediacy of response to mechanical things that, being surrounded by them as we are, may tend to make us impatient with life. We all know the experience of putting coins into a cigarette machine or a soda-pop machine and expecting the immediate rumble of the machine and out comes the cigarette package or the can. Input-output-immediate response! We also know the spontaneous urge to bang the machine, to kick it, to grumble and complain, "What is the matter here." There is the obvious irritation when the machine does not immediately give us our product. We know the same thing when we turn on the ignition of our car and expect it to start immediately. There are many other examples of mechanical efficiency that we are surrounded with that can come to mind when we think about this.

We can all recall an experience that we have had with some kind of apparatus that didn't work, and our immediate irritation with it, perhaps even banging it with our hand, or whatever we did that would reveal our impatience with it. In surrounding ourselves with input-output apparatus that works, or should work if it is any good, we may lose something of the wisdom that is necessary for life. In other words this kind of input-output apparatus, as an environment all around us, makes us and even invites us, to be impatient with life, to want things immediately. We put in the coin—where is the can, where is the cigarette package, where is the object we want? Why keep us waiting? Why do we have to stand around?

THEOLOGICAL EXTENSION

St. James understands this urge too, and so he recalls for us what we all know but few of us experience any longer since we do not live in the country and are not farmers. Real things in life, like the food we eat and basic things similar to that, or real achievements, really worthwhile things that we want for ourselves and others, take a long time. We need to learn patience. Patience goes with hope and hope goes with courage. We must stay at it. We must not simply "put our hands to the plow" and then give up and leave the field looking ridiculous, half-plowed, as our Lord reminds us. We stay at it not only until the field is plowed but until the seed is planted and the harvest comes.

Consequently, rather than turning for an illustration to the common experiences of machines that must work instantly—toasters that must spring up quickly, gas ranges and electric stoves that must turn on immediately, automobiles that must start, apparatus that must give us cans or packages with only a moment's rumble of the machinery—we might look elsewhere in nature to find how things are. Go out to the country again, raise a garden, sow some flowers, do something more natural again.

THEOLOGICAL CONCLUSION

St. James is reminding us that God in nature works slowly and carefully and real things in life take this same form. Genuine achievement is a long-time, constant effort of courage and hope and perseverance. The farmer in the field is a better model for us than all the machinery that surrounds us, as far as the guidance of the way of life is concerned. St. James well knows this and, to those of his own time especially, those who lived in cities, he gives this reminder; and indeed it works just as well for us. "Be patient until the coming of the Lord. See how the farmer awaits the precious yield of the soil. He looks forward to it patiently while the soil receives the winter and the spring rains. You too must be patient."

THIRD SUNDAY OF ADVENT (SERIES A)
HOMILY IV

Gospel Reading: *I solemnly assure you, history has not known a man born of woman greater than John the Baptizer. Yet the least born into the kingdom of God is greater than he.* (Mt. 11:2-11)

ANA-GNOSIS

It is characteristic of our time to marvel, and rightly so, at the greatness of man's inventions, ingenuity, and intelligence. These achievements have been climaxed by man's unbelievable feat of going to the moon—something talked about and yearned for since the beginning of time. We are, of course, in a very special position to admire the marvels that man can produce—from the electric light bulb, to the telephone, to the magic communications everywhere, to rapid travel around the earth.

We cannot help but be overwhelmed by man's greatness and his achievement. In the examinations of the lives of great men we see something of this same thing in their heroic self-discipline, their courage, their sticking to their vocation, to what they have to do. Usually it is this kind of very courageous man that was behind the great achievements of mankind in one way or another. Think of Edison, or of Ford, or of the Wright brothers, or Lindberg, or Einstein. All these names and many others, remind us of people of great dedication.

THEOLOGICAL EXTENSION

In studying the lives of great men in the Bible, we have in front of us today, in the reading from St. Matthew, the life of John the Baptist. Not only was he admired by many people but we see here what a great admiration Christ had for him. So as the other people expounded the heroism of John the Baptist—his courage, his forthrightness, his honesty, his integrity—Christ not only joined this course but re-affirmed it over and over again. He shared with them the magnificence of John's character as a human being and as a man who was leading the way for the coming of the Messias.

Therefore, it is momentarily a little disturbing or perhaps even shocking, but surely surprising, that Christ ends with this great phrase and joint chorus on the virtues and greatness of John the Baptist: "I solemnly assure you, history has not known a man born of woman greater than John the Baptist." This is a most magnificent statement about the life of a great man, that no one is greater or has been greater in the history of mankind. Then there is this momentary shocker: "And yet the least born into the Kingdom of God is greater than he."

We rightly admire the wonders of electricity in the darkness, the power of great lights to light up an enormous field, or lights to make a house brilliant. But even while we are talking about and discussing these things, the sun slowly begins to come up, and right in the midst of all of our admiration for how bright the lights are, it suddenly occurs to us that they aren't bright at all. The sun has totally absorbed the whole area with a light so overwhelming that we can hardly see that the floodlights are on any more, and we can hardly recognize the lamps in the room. We could just as readily turn them off and no one would know the difference.

What we are proposing here is that what Christ is reminding us of, is that these things are magnificent as human achievements in the darkness; but compared to that great light of the sun that comes from God, they are as nothing. This is a clear point that Christ makes here. He wants to hold these people firmly to what John the Baptist's message is about, what his life means, and not simply to a hero-worship which is a form of escaping John the Baptist's real message. His message is that it is the time of the Messias, and that he himself has come to prepare the way for Christ, the Messias, who is now among them. If they really believe and truly admire the greatness of John the Baptist as they say, then they will turn and understand the purpose and meaning of Christ himself, who is there among them and for whom John the Baptist has given his life as a precursor and a prophet.

THEOLOGICAL CONCLUSION

So he asks, "What, then, did you go out to see? A prophet? A prophet indeed and something more. It is about this man that Scripture says, 'I send my messenger ahead of you to prepare the way before you.'" John the Baptist, our Lord reminds us, is a messenger of preparation. Admirable, overwhelming, as great as any man in history; and yet, in a certain sense, like the magnificence of great lights in electricity in the presence of the sun, he pales into nothingness. John the Baptist, in his purely natural courage and heroism is as nothing compared to the least, who by sharing and understanding the life of Christ, shares Christ's divine life with God.

FOURTH SUNDAY OF ADVENT (SERIES A)
HOMILY I

Reading I: *The Lord spoke to Ahaz! Ask for a sign from the Lord, your God. . . . But Ahaz answered, "I will not ask! I will not tempt the Lord!" Then he said: Listen, O house of David! Is it not enough for you to weary men, must you also weary my God? Therefore the Lord himself will give you this sign: the virgin shall be with child, and bear a son, and shall name him Emmanuel.* (Is. 7:10-14)

ANA-GNOSIS

Language is all we have as human beings to express our ideas which grow out of our own experience (if we think about it a moment there is no other place from which language could come). All human beings have a symbol system that we call language. The many languages of the world all do the same thing. They convey experiences and the thoughts that are abstracted from them.

THEOLOGICAL EXTENSION

When the Old Testament writers talk about God, they use language that comes from their human experience. In other words, they talk about God in human terms.

Today's reading shows God weary of man's inability to carry out something simply as a matter of trust. Ahaz symbolizes our own escapisms when he gives a rationalization for his own lack of faith. When he is told to ask boldly for a sign, he answers with what seemed to him genuine humility. But, if we look closely, we see he lacks faith. Thinking himself humble, he says, "I will not ask! I will not tempt the Lord!" We note again the human terms: the Lord is described as not only being weary, but also as being tempted. And because God is weary of man's lack of faith, symbolized by Ahaz, he insists that Ahaz should ask for a sign and a sign will be given. It will be the coming of the Messias, of the Christ, of Emmanuel.

There is striking emphasis here in the Old Testament (and Christ will emphasize the same thing in the New) that it is not enough to pray unless we also have genuine, strong faith. Ahaz symbolizes a tendency in all of us to hesitate to trust God, to have enough confidence in prayer to ask unusual and even great favors. We can share the almost cringing anxiety of Ahaz about tempting God by asking too much. But what we are also saying—perhaps what we are primarily saying—is that we lack the faith to pray for something extraordinary in our lives. We do not believe quite enough, we do not have quite enough confidence in our prayers. Others can pray and receive answers but not us.

The Old Testament tells us that this lack of faith on Ahaz' part (and on our part as well) does not tempt God at all, but makes God weary. In human terms we know how tiresome and frustrating it is when we are encouraging someone to have confidence in himself about accomplishing something, and must watch him continue to held himself back. This makes us weary and the Old Testament writer is applying this same human feeling to God.

THEOLOGICAL CONCLUSION

In summation, we recall that our Lord told us we must knock and we will receive. We must keep after God in the same way the man keeps knocking on the door of the sleeping householder in another New Testament passage. In that passage, the man succeeds in waking the householder; if our prayer is urgent and sincere, it will not weary God. On the contrary, it wearies God when we do not have genuine faith and confidence in prayer.

Our prayer will be answered, although it may not be in the limited way we see. Sometimes, to our amazement, we do get exactly when we want. And, in all cases our prayers are answered; they never go unheard.

The Book of Isaiah is giving necessary guidance on how to pray. It tells us to pray with confidence in ourselves, and in God. We will not tempt God because in his own way, God will answer us. Only our lack of confidence in prayer can weary God. Therefore, as our Lord tells us, "Ask and you shall receive; seek and you shall find; knock and it shall be opened to you."

FOURTH SUNDAY OF ADVENT (SERIES A)
HOMILY II

Responsorial Psalm: *Who can ascend the mountain of the Lord, or who may stand in his holy place? He whose hands are sinless, whose heart is clean, who desires not what is vain.* (Ps. 24:1-6)

ANA-GNOSIS

We know what it is to experience the pangs of guilt, the disturbance of a guilty conscience. Clear as that suffering and pain can be to us, guilt itself is one of the most complicated of human feelings.

At its simplest and most primitive level, it is a form of self-attack. One recognizes that one has done something wrong and our feelings are those of shame and embarrassment. As a purely extrinsic description we can use animals to see how shame can look. For example, dogs slink away when they have behaved unacceptably. They look at us with what we describe as a "hang-dog" look, suggesting some kind of awareness of their wrong-doing. This, of course, may only appear to be communication. We might be seeing a simple conditioned response. The dog knows from previous experience that food, affection and rewards do not go with the rejecting tone of voice. Children at a very early age feel guilt and react in a way not very different from the misbehaving dog. One of our most common admonitions to children, especially when we want them to change behavior is, "Aren't you ashamed of yourself?" And often they are. Guilt, then, helps us learn from our mistakes. The reflex is as basic as touching a hot stove. Because it hurts, we pull away and avoid touching it again.

THEOLOGICAL EXTENSION

Similarly, when a child feels that he has done wrong, he looks at us with sad and sorrowful eyes. This tells us he hurts and it shows recognition of wrongdoing and usually desire to change. We call this constructive guilt. We learned to change many things in our conduct in early childhood and we continue to use guilt in this constructive way.

On the other hand, guilt carried to extreme is one of the most dangerous of the destructive impulses in man. It can cause severe depression, excessive self-attack, deep and sometimes overwhelming discouragement. It can finally lead, as in the case of Judas, to self-destruction. This kind of guilt is dangerous; it is against our faith because we have many assurances from God that our sins are forgiven if we honestly submit our embarrassment and petition for forgiveness to God. Therefore, we avoid destructive guilt while cherishing the guilt that helps us change and do better.

THEOLOGICAL CONCLUSION

The Psalmist today describes the importance of sinlessness before God. With regard to guilt, we know that our hands will be sinless and our hearts clean if we use our shame as a constructive aid to improvement. Specifically, the Psalmist speaks of sinless hands and clean hearts. He could have spoken of sinless hearts and clean hands. Possibly that idea is easier for us to understand. We all know there are times when we have to get our hands dirty. On the practical level, a man working with an automobile sometimes needs to use his bare hands. Gloves impede the sensitive feeling that he needs; so washing dirty hands is inevitable. On a different level, we sometimes get our hands dirty with wrongdoing. Then we must remove guilt as we remove dirt. We must clean ourselves up and go on. We do not dwell on the dirt after it is washed away. If we use guilt for constructive purposes, we have the Psalmist's reassurance that we will "ascend the mountain of the Lord," and "stand in his holy place." Just as we clean up to go to an important banquet or meeting, we want to stand before God with clean hands. It is not that our hands have never been dirty; of course, they have been. But we have washed them. We have washed away the guilt. Once it has helped us change, knowing God's' love and forgiveness, we can stand in a solemn position before God and dare to say "Our Father."

FOURTH SUNDAY OF ADVENT (SERIES A)
HOMILY III

Reading II: *To all in Rome, beloved of God and called to holiness, grace and peace from God our Father and the Lord Jesus Christ.* (Rom. 1:1-7)

ANA-GNOSIS

Events that happened a long time ago, perhaps a hundred or even two thousand years ago, tend by their very distance in time to seem far removed from us. We assume an impersonal and detached attitude toward them. It is hard to feel the immediacy, the excitement that was there when these historical moments occurred. Those who witness such events and record them for us are most often more caught up in the happenings than we are as we read about it today.

Because of this inevitable remoteness, history is, in a sense, dead. However, this need not be so. We can capture the freshness, the excitement of the experienc if we can put ourselves in it, here and now. Film, live drama and television can often take an historical event and make it live for today. Fiction, biography, and autobiography can also make history live. Historical personages can come alive in the immediacy of our own living room or our neighborhood theatre.

THEOLOGICAL EXTENSION

Let us use the simple reading of St. Paul and take away the deadness of something that was said and written two thousand years ago. We want to hear the intense, open, excited, emotional—yet deeply subtle, intelligent man named Paul. We want to recognize him today as humble, holy and yet very conscious of his great burden and dignity as an Apostle, an Apostle to the Gentiles. Therefore, to get this feeling, instead of reading, "to all in Rome," let us leave out Rome and put in the name of our own city. We can go further and consciously put in our own family name, so that we read "to all in the ________________." Now we read St. Paul greeting us in this present moment with the beautiful salutation "To all in ________________, (highly personal locations and/or family names) beloved of God and called to holiness, grace and peace from God our Father and the Lord Jesus Christ."

THEOLOGICAL CONCLUSION

We can consider the message from St. Paul today, as a personal telegram, a letter or a voice over the telephone. We can even imagine St. Paul standing here and greeting us lovingly and personally with this message of grace and peace from God. What more could anyone wish of us? What more blessed thing could we have than God's peace and grace?

FOURTH SUNDAY OF ADVENT (SERIES A) HOMILY IV

Gospel Reading: *When Joseph awoke he did as the angel of the Lord had directed him and received her into his home as his wife.* (Mt. 1:18-24)

ANA-GNOSIS

One of the most disturbing of all human feelings is the feeling that someone is making a fool of us, that someone is "pulling the wool over our eyes." Children can experience this, and it can be a threatening feeling for adults. It is a powerful barrier against trust and confidence and this is particularly true when we are asked to believe in the integrity of the person whom we have come to suspect. There is always the feeling that someone knows about this and is laughing at us behind our back. There is the even more disturbing fact that, at some point, we may be made the laughing stock of the whole neighborhood.

The above description is enough to alert us to the difficulty of believing in something when there is an alternate explanation that could make us look foolish. We do not want to appear naive so we find it difficult to trust under such conditions.

THEOLOGICAL EXTENSION

To appreciate Joseph, we need to consider the whole issue of appearing foolish. Here is a man with a strong faith in a woman and in God. He is faced with a most delicate matter. Nothing is so threatening to a person's dignity than to be fooled in public. And Joseph had good reason to think he would be the butt of many jokes.

Joseph's first conclusion was the one we would expect. Because he loved Mary and did not want to expose her to shame and embarrassment, he would quietly separate from her. As the Gospel describes him, he was an upright man.

THEOLOGICAL CONCLUSION

Now, in today's Reading, we see God leading Joseph to the truth. As a result of his dream Joseph does the indescribably great thing. We marvel at his faith that led him to completely change his human plan without giving into fears of looking foolish, without letting his natural human thoughts prevail. Joseph carried on. The Gospel concludes, "When Joseph awoke he did as the angel of the Lord had directed him and received her into his home as his wife." What a loving and faithful man! He puts his trust in both Mary and God. No wonder then that Joseph is our model of faith and trust. He is, in his own simple goodness, a great man.

CHRISTMAS MASS AT MIDNIGHT (A, B, C)
HOMILY I

Reading I: *The people who walked in darkness have seen a great light; Upon those who dwelt in the land of gloom a light has shown. You have brought them abundant joy and great rejoicing. They rejoice before you as at the harvest, as men make merry when dividing spoils. For the yoke that burdened them, the pole on their shoulder, and the rod of their taskmaster you have smashed, as on the day of Midian. For every boot that tramped in the battle, every cloak rolled in blood, will be burned as fuel for flames.*

For a child is born to us, a son is given to us; upon his shoulder dominion rests. They name him Wonder-Counselor, God-Hero, Father-Forever, Prince of Peace. His dominion is vast and forever peaceful. From David's throne, and over his kingdom, which he confirms and sustains by judgment and justice both now and forever.

The zeal of the Lord of hosts will do this! (Is. 9:1-6)

ANA-GNOSIS

A priest once told the comedian Groucho Marx, "Groucho, I want to thank you for all the joy you have brought into the world." And with the quick repartee for which he was so famous, Groucho replied, "And Father, I want to thank you for all the joy you've taken out of the world."

Now in this quick exchange there are some notions which bear examination; for example, what one means by joy and how one sees religion. These will determine how one interprets the amusing, but at the same time sharp exchange.

If we see joy as immediate pleasure or an exaggerated commitment to physical or material things, then the strictures of religion do limit or take away that pleasure. At least they limit it by making us guilty when we plunge into those kinds of physical joys or material goals. Religion is constantly making us aware of long-term values. It's always putting before us the long view, the ultimate meaning, the ultimate purpose. It's always telling us, "Okay, you can enjoy this for five minutes or an hour or a day or a week, but it will pass away and leave you empty and even more disappointed than before."

Now in this sense religion takes quite a bit of immediate pleasure out of the world. If we follow the injunctions and guidance of religion we hesitate to plunge into immediate and appealing joys. We're cautious about alcohol; we're cautious about drugs; we know they give a temporary euphoria, pleasure and relief from the world and its cares. They provide us with a false sense of grandeur, importance and gaity. If we give in to them we realize that we've violated the injunctions of religion, and, in addition to the headache afterwards and that bang of coming back to earth and reality, we can also have very serious pangs of guilt. So, in this sense, Groucho's quick remark had some real truth in it. The priest representing religion does take this kind of joy out of the world. He at least makes it forbidden from the point of view of religion because of its ability to deceive, disillusion and disappoint us ultimately.

If we mean, though, real and enduring joy, joy that takes us through the lonely, empty periods, the disappointments and the bitter phases of life that could leave us scarred and sour, then religion not only doesn't take it out of the world, but far more even than Groucho or people like him who brought pleasure and happiness to everyone by their shrewd and very human comedy, religion brings joy.

In a certain sense a truly religious man should be a kind of a comedian, someone who doesn't take life, its immediacies, its difficulties and conflicts seriously. A truly religious person should have deep inside an ability to laugh at life. The injunction, "Don't take things seriously" might well be called a religious truth.

We don't have to take the immediate situations of life too seriously even when they seem most tragic, most disappointing and most disillusioning because we never invested too much in them. We always saw them as passing and limited because our eye was always on the beyond.

There's another side, too, to Groucho's remark that points out what often has been the unfortunate experience of people with regard to religion. It has been presented to them, as it may have been to Groucho, as something negative, something always spoiling things, so that whenever a happy occasion occurred and there was some wine or a nice dinner, religion was thought to have said,

"Don't enjoy this now. This is gluttony. This is alcoholism. This is forbidden. This is against the Ten Commandments." One of the unfortunate things about the Ten Commandments, as a norm, is their obvious negation in tone—"Thou shalt not."

THEOLOGICAL EXTENSION

Now to offset this we have to look at the reading from Isaias in the Old Testament and the life of Christ from the New Testament. The "Thou shalt nots" of the Ten Commandments were only the customary form of the time for stating things. But Isaias today tells us, "Upon those who dwell in the land of gloom a light has shone. You have brought them abundant joy and great rejoicing. They rejoice before you as at the harvest, as men make merry when dividing spoils."

Here we see clearly the happiness of a good harvest, the joy, good food and good wine that people use to celebrate. This is certainly a long way from misery or gloom. It is the coming of this long-promised Messias that Isaias is describing who is the light that disperses the gloom. It is not a religion which aims at taking joy out of the world. It is, on the contrary, bringing rich joy into the world. Christ's mission was not to deprive us of joy, to make us miserable and gloomy. He rejoiced in life as we do. But he kept his eyes focused on the Father. He did not limit his joy to the passing pleasures of his worldly life. He did not take them too seriously.

THEOLOGICAL CONCLUSION

Nor should we, if we are Christians. We should, in a very real sense, become comedians. That is to say, put inside our hearts a kind of gaity, a kind of a laughter which will allow us to see the humor in even very serious things of life.

It might be a very funny thing to put above the door of a church but it would not hurt us to see a sign saying, "Don't take things too seriously. Laugh at Life."

CHRISTMAS MASS AT MIDNIGHT (A, B, C) HOMILY II

Responsorial Psalm: R. *Today is born our Savior, Christ the Lord. Today is born our Savior, Christ the Lord.*

1. Sing to the Lord a new song; sing to the Lord all you lands.

2. Announce his salvation, day after day. Tell his glory among the nations; Among all peoples, his wondrous deeds.

Today is born our Savior, Christ the Lord.

3. Let the heavens be glad and the earth rejoice; let the sea and what fills it resound; let the plains be joyful and all that is in them! Then shall all the trees of the forest exult.

Today is born our Savior, Christ the Lord.

4. They shall exult before the Lord, for he comes; for he comes to rule the earth. He shall rule the world with justice and the peoples with his constancy.

Today is born our Savior, Christ the Lord.

(Ps. 96:1-2, 2-3, 11-12, 13. R. Luke 2:11)

ANA-GNOSIS

We have phrases in our language that so vividly catch the exact tone and mood of a situation that they put us right in the center of what they are describing. One such phrase is "dancing in the streets." If someone describing an event were to say, "The people were dancing in the streets," we immediately catch the tone of great rejoicing, that this was an unusually gay, successful, fulfilling event. At the end of World War II, for example all over America people literally "danced in the streets." There was such relief, such joy, such gratitude to God, that at last it was over, that people couldn't simply stay in their homes and dance. Everybody had to get out into the street to show their joy and relief that at last external peace had come to the world.

Nature has a way of doing something like this too. We sometimes talk about trees dancing in the wind. And they do, indeed, seem to dance with a stateliness, a grace, even a joy that can touch us. In seeming to dance, they do indeed bring us moments of exultation. We can recall leafy trees dancing in the summer breeze, gorgeous autumn trees dancing in the winds of October. Even in winter the stark trees sometimes seem to exult in the wind.

THEOLOGICAL EXTENSION

Now this joy is what the Psalmist wants to recall as we now

come to that moment when the Messias is here. The Psalm looks forward to this and says, "Then shall all the trees of the forest exult. They shall exult before the Lord, for he comes."

That, then, is our mood. We're surrounded by lovely, beautiful trees dancing in joy this Christmas. And our joy is the realization that, of all the promises to mankind, of all the hopes, of all the anticipations, nothing is so great, nothing so overwhelming as that God himself should come on earth in the form of a little babe, in total humanity, and become one of us.

This is surely a cause for dancing in the streets, indeed. And in the more pastoral imagery of the Psalms, trees dancing in the wind surely express our joy, our relief, our inner peace this day as we renew the wondrousness, the sense of miraculousness, that indeed it has come about. God *has* become man and dwelt among us.

THEOLOGICAL CONCLUSION

And so there's dancing in the streets and dancing in our hearts tonight as we exult in the coming of our Lord. "Then shall all the trees of the forest exult. They shall exult before the Lord, for he comes."

CHRISTMAS MASS AT MIDNIGHT (A, B, C)
HOMILY III

Reading II: *The grace of God has appeared, offering salvation to all men. It trains us to reject godless ways and worldly desires, and live temperately, justly, and devoutly in this age as we await our blessed hope, the appearing of the glory of the great God and of our Savior Christ Jesus. It was he who sacrificed himself for us, to redeem us from all unrighteousness and to cleanse for himself a people of his own, eager to do what is right.* (Ti. 2:11-14)

ANA-GNOSIS

When we think of animals eating, we recall that they do not eat peacefully. Of course sometimes they may—as cows do grazing or eating at a trough together. But many times animals shove, snarl, push and snap at one another, each one selfishly wanting it all for himself. And while this applies to most animals, we tend to use the phrases "don't hog everything for yourself," or "don't be a pig," when we see someone acting this way.

THEOLOGICAL EXTENSION

Now it may seem a strange kind of meditation on Christmas night to think about "hogging" religion all to ourselves, and being "pigs" in a religious sense. Yet in a very real way, we can act like this if we fail to understand the nature and universality of Christmas.

St. Paul in his letter to Titus begins by saying, "The grace of God has appeared"—this is what we celebrate at Christmas—God's gift of graciousness to us. He, himself, not simply sending a messenger or a prophet as he commonly did in the Old Testament, has come now to us. He is our own, our own flesh and blood. He has dwelt among us and we are his, and he is of us. Then Paul writes, "offering salvation to *all* men." Perhaps in a modern sense we should simply stop with "offering salvation to *all*."

Now here is the point about "hogging," "being pigs" about our religion. It isn't just for us, and we share the selfish gluttony of an animal if we just think it is all our own and we need not share it with anyone else. On the contrary, the very nature of the gift, the grace of Christ's coming, must not simply end with us but go beyond us to others.

St. John tells us that it is not we who first loved God, but God who first loved us. This is the heart of his great gift of coming to us, being a human being exactly like ourselves and yet being God. This is the Christmas grace. But St. John also goes on to tell us that just as God loved us first, so must we love others. So this salvation which comes to us for *all*, is not to be "hogged" just for our own special group or our own special purpose to make us secure or to give us an advantage over others. It is to be carried out to others through us as Christ gave it to us. It is a grace or a gift that we, in turn, should give away.

The message, therefore, is not simply that Christ has come to us on this Christmas night but that, having come to us, through us he should go out to others. We, in turn, are his ambassadors and our love of Christ must be the same as his love of us, going out to all. Our love is not genuinely Christian, Christ-like, if we overlook the universality of his love.

The word "offered" is important too, because "to offer" something is not to force it but simply to make it available. In a sense, Christ has put out a table of great gifts or spiritual food for us. We don't have to eat; he's just offered it. And, in turn, if we bring it to others we can't force them, we can only offer it to them. But at least we must offer it. We must bring it to others.

Our lives are a means of offering salvation to all just as Christ gave it to us. Our behavior, our concern, our engagement with others, our truly going out of ourselves for them is the heart of the nature of Christ's coming to us. We must go out to others as he went out to us. We must leave our own secure place to go to the lost one, to seek others in the wilderness and confusion of their lives. This is our discipleship and our responsibbility.

THEOLOGICAL CONCLUSION

The joy, therefore, of the grace of Christmas night is, indeed, one of profound personal exultation. But we don't "hog" this joy; we're not just "pigs." We carry it out to all others, offering it to them through the Christian meaning and purpose of our lives, so that they can see Christ through us. "The grace of God has appeared offering salvation to all." We, in turn, bring it as much as we can to those who have not yet heard of it effectively or seen it in action. They should hear of it again and see it become real in our lives.

CHRISTMAS MASS AT MIDNIGHT (A, B, C)
HOMILY IV

Gospel Reading: *In those days Caesar Augustus published a decree ordering a census of the whole world. This first census took place while Quirinius was governor of Syria. Everyone went to register, each to his own town. And so Joseph went from the town of Nazareth in Galilee to Judea, to David's town of Bethlehem—because he was of the house and lineage of David—to register with Mary, his espoused wife, who was with child.*

While they were there the days of her confinement were completed. She gave birth to her first-born son and wrapped him in swaddling clothes and laid him in a manger, because there was no room for them in the place where travelers lodged.

There were shepherds in the locality, living in the fields and keeping night watch by turns over their flock. The angel of the Lord appeared to them as the glory of the Lord shone around them, and they were very much afraid. The angel said to them: "You have nothing to fear! I come to proclaim good news to you—tidings of great joy to be shared by the whole people. This day in David's city a savior has been born to you, the Messiah and Lord. Let this be a sign to you: in a manger you will find an infant wrapped in swaddling clothes." Suddenly there was with the angel a multitude of the heavenly host, praising God and saying

"Glory to God in heaven,
peace on earth to those on
whom his favor rests."

(Lk. 2:1-14)

ANA-GNOSIS

Familiar things have a way of becoming so commonplace that we almost ignore them. We certainly tend to overlook them. This is true particularly of the words we use. One of the words that all of us have used innumerable times, and it is most fitting in our Christmas midnight celebration, is, or course, the word that describes where we are and our whole relationship and function. It is a word so familiar that probably hardly any of us have ever thought to look it up in the dictionary and find out its origin and its exact meaning. This is the word "parish"—our parish. We've probably used the word in the last week; we may have told someone we planned to go to our parish for Midnight Mass.

Now let's look for a moment at this word, parish. What did it really mean in its origin? What did people think about when they first started using this word to describe the Christian community?

In Latin and in Italian the word is slightly longer—*parrocchia*.. *Oikia* in Greek is a house or a home. *Para-* as a prefix means to be away from, or outside of or removed from. In this case, it describes being away from one's home. It means to be a traveler, alienated, someone who does not belong. We see then that our familiar word *parish* actually is a place for those who do not belong, who are not at home, who are simply passing through—strangers, travelers. A parish then could be that place Mary and Joseph went to "because there was no room for them in the place where travelers lodged."

THEOLOGICAL EXTENSION

Now we are of a parish too. So, we might meditate briefly about why it should have turned out that Christ who came for us all should have found no place for himself or for Mary and Joseph, should have come to a *para-oikia,* a place where there was no home for him. If we are like that, then what does it mean?

It means that if we are truly committed to Christian values we do not exactly belong in the world. We are always outsiders. We belong to that class of people who are not quite welcome in the places of purely worldly people, of purely worldly things. Why? Because we are people of double vision. St. Paul has told us that we have not here a lasting city. St. Paul proposes, in fact, that all things will pass except love. Love alone remains.

Now it is this vision of everything passing that makes us strangers, that alienates us from a total identity with the world, that has us all in a manner somewhere, out by ourselves.

It is also true that, despite all the appearance of belonging and the artificial warmth of a tavern or an inn, despite all the noise and apparent sounds of happiness that radiated out of those places that had no room for Mary and Joseph and ultimately for Christ, there's a fraudulence there. We can, in truth, be strangers and alone and outsiders even sitting in the middle of such rejoicing. Sometimes on television, particularly on New Year's Eve, we see a crowd of people who've paid high prices at expensive night clubs supposedly to celebrate the coming of the New Year. So often we see people with paper hats on making some effort to appear gay and joyful, yet with long, sad faces. Or we may see them making a heroic effort to appear happy and that is even sadder still. Simply to be in the inn where all the lights are and the music and the dancing, is not to belong or to be happy. One might propose that in the field with Mary, Joseph and the Christ-child there was incomparably greater joy and happiness than in all the noisy taverns and inns that had no place for them.

THEOLOGICAL CONCLUSION

A parish, then, is where we, like Mary and Joseph, come because we have nowhere else to go. It is a place for the alienated, for the outsiders, the non-belongers. And Christ's very birth in that sort of place should, in a very real sense, symbolize the basic meaning of the word "parish" for us. It should recall to us our status as outsiders, as people merely passing through. It should remind us that the only thing that will last is the meaning and purpose brought by that babe far from the noise and clamor of the world.

His message of love came quietly in the manger—far from home, removed—and yet only love will endure.

CHRISTMAS MASS DURING THE DAY (A, B, C)
HOMILY I

Reading I: *How beautiful upon the mountains are the feet of him who brings glad tidings, announcing peace, bearing good news, announcing salvation, and saying to Zion, "Your God is King!"*

Hark! Your watchmen raise a cry,
together they shout for joy,
For they see directly, before their eyes,
the Lord restoring zion.
Break out together in song,
O ruins of Jerusalem!
For the Lord comforts his people,
He redeems Jerusalem.
The Lord has bared his holy arm
in the sight of all the nations;
All the ends of the earth will behold
the salvation of our God. (Is. 52:7-9)

ANA-GNOSIS

We've all seen destruction. In films, television and newspapers we've seen endless pictures of the tragic havoc of World War II—parts of London devastated, French villages destroyed, Italian areas like Monte Casino in ruin, Munich, Dresden and other German cities mostly rubble. We've seen destruction, too, resulting from a hurricane or tornado. Even more personally perhaps, we may have known people who lost the home they lived in and loved for years. Suddenly it became smoking, charred ruins. Either directly or in sharing with others we can all feel what it is like to stand in the midst of destruction.

The greatest temptation is to despair, to give up. When we see all these things we've known—a beautiful house, we'll say, smoked and charred ruins, or stand in the midst of the effects of a tornado and see familiar things scattered all over the place, broken and in ruin—at that moment we all know the surging feelings of despair, of giving up, of saying, "What's the use," and not even trying again.

And yet we've all seen the wonderful restoration that can occur. We've seen those devastated cities of Europe rebuilt new and fresh and modern. We've seen areas devastated by hurricanes or tornados restored and "just like new again." We've known of individual homes rebuilt to the same plan or even made newer and more modern. Then joy returns.

But to bring this about we know there must be hope. To counteract the despair of standing in the midst of ruin, we must have hope. Hope gives people the courage, the inspiration, and motivation to stay in there, to rebuild and finally come to know happiness, joy and fulfillment because in their hope they triumphed over despair.

THEOLOGICAL EXTENSION

Hope is the theme of today's Reading from Isaias. The people are aware of the many times of destruction, of being taken off to captivity, of coming back to a state of devastation and ruin. And they have a sense of joy and happiness when they see things being built again. We know what it's like to walk back again to a home that has been destroyed and to see all the debris and disorder cleared away and a new home fresh and clean beginning to go up. The joists going up into the air and the work going on are symbolic of the achievement of courage and hope. They are an inspiration for all who see it. That's the spirit of Isaias. "Hark! Your watchmen raise a cry . . . for they see directly, before their eyes, the Lord restoring Zion."

It is fitting, I suppose, in this context to recall that Joseph was a carpenter, and that in his early years Christ, too, knew the skills of a carpenter. He was, even as a laborer, someone who built things up.

There is a sense of freshness and newness when we think of a carpenter building a house; the fresh wood, nails, the sound of a hammer, recall happiness, joy, freshness that something new is coming into being. There is the excitement of watching the house grow day by day and week by week until it is finished, and all of a sudden people have moved in. Very soon it is an old familiar house in the neighborhood. But in its construction it symbolizes the accomplishment which hope realizes over despair, when people do not give up, but have the courage to go on.

This is the symbol of Christmas—this kind of hope. For in all the destruction and despair in the world, in all our broken dreams and unrealized plans, in the midst of our temptation to despair about ourselves, Christ builds us up. If there is one word that stands clearly over the symbol of the Babe in Bethlehem, it is surely the word HOPE.

THEOLOGICAL CONCLUSION

Christ builds us up, gives us strength, hope, courage, confidence to start again. We can start over in Christ. All things can become new again—renewed—in Christ. This is what Christmas is for us: despite destruction and tragedy in our own lives and in the world itself—Christ brings us hope.

So we, too, "see directly," as Isaias says. Before our eyes the Lord is restoring the world. He is building up again in hope. This is the image of the Christ-child, and this is our symbol of the meaning of Christmas today and throughout the year.

CHRISTMAS MASS DURING THE DAY (A, B, C)
HOMILY II

Responsorial Psalm: *All the ends of the earth have seen the saving power of God.*

1. Sing to the Lord a new song, for he has done wondrous deeds;
His right hand has won victory for him, his holy arm.

All the ends of the earth have seen the saving power of God.

2. The Lord has made his salvation known; in the sight of the nations he has revealed his justice.
He has remembered his kindness and his faithfulness toward the house of Israel.

All the ends of the earth have seen the saving power of God.

3. All the ends of the earth have seen the salvation by our God.
Sing joyfully to the Lord, all you lands; break into song; sing praise.

All the ends of the earth have seen the saving power of God.

4. Sing praise to the Lord with harp, with the harp and melodious song.
With trumpets and the sound of the horn sing joyfully before the King, the Lord.

All the ends of the earth have seen the saving power of God.

(Ps. 98:1, 2-3, 3-4, 5-6. R. V. 3)

ANA-GNOSIS

Again and again we realize that the most familiar things about ourselves and about things around us—the things we take for granted—are apt to be at the same time most mysterious. But our very familiarity with them tends to hide a great deal of the mystery and wonder which they, in fact, contain. One of these mysteries is our ability to sing. It goes with our ability to laugh. Both these characteristics are peculiar only to human beings. We may speak of a hyena being able to laugh, but we know it's only a mask —he merely appears to be laughing. We may think of birds singing, but really we realize they chirp. They chirp a very fixed sound, which, when different birds chirp together, may seem a little bit like a chorus; but even here we know it is not really singing. Only people can really sing.

Scientists themselves do not understand entirely the mystery of how our vocal chords give us this wide variety of sound and endow some people with such extremely beautiful voices so that they have, even better than any instrument, a perfect pitch and can give us those miracles of operas and beautiful popular songs. How the vocal chords can do this, create this subtlety of sound, scientists do not yet know. Nor do they totally understand the miracle of hearing—how all the small bones of the ear can catch the sound and with it bring to the listener joy, peace and happiness.

THEOLOGICAL EXTENSION

So it is with a sense of wonderment that we greet the hope and joy of Christmas with song. The Psalmist tells us, "Sing to the Lord a new song. Sing joyfully to the Lord. Break into song; sing praise." And then to fill out the wondrous sound of human voices, the Psalmist encourages us to get the help of musical instruments. He says, "Sing praise to the Lord with the harp, with the harp and melodious song. With trumpets and the sound of the horn sing joyfully before the King, the Lord."

Sing all you people. Sing for the joy of Christmas in our hearts. For surely Christmas is something to sing about. It brings hope again. In the midst of the discouragements of the year, the broken plans and hopes and dreams, we start afresh. The spirit of Christmas calls with a song in our hearts.

THEOLOGICAL CONCLUSION

We sing, therefore, this Christmas day as only human beings can sing, knowing the reason for the joy in our heart, knowing the reason for the song. The reason is this child at Bethlehem coming from God; God himself coming into the world for us. No other reason in the history of the human race so much merits a song, so much fills every heart with peace, joy, hope and security.

"Sing joyfully to the Lord, all you lands. Break into song; sing praise," remembering again Christ is coming to dwell among us and be one of us. It is certainly well worth singing about!

CHRISTMAS MASS DURING THE DAY (A, B, C)
HOMILY III

Reading II: *In times past, God spoke in fragmentary and varied ways to our fathers through the prophets; in this, the final age, he has spoken to us through his Son, whom he has made heir of all things and through whom he first created the universe. This Son is the reflection of the Father's glory, the exact representation of the Father's being, and he sustains all things by his powerful word. When the Son had cleansed us from our sins, he took his seat at the right hand of the Majesty in heaven, as far superior to the angels as the name he has inherited is superior to theirs.*

To which of the angels did God ever say,
"You are my son; today I have begotten you?"
Or again,
"I will be his father, and he shall be my son?"
And again when he leads his first-born into the world, he says,
"Let all the angels of God worship him." (Heb. 1:1-6)

ANA-GNOSIS

When we watch a building being constructed, it is apt to seem very confusing. For a large building of fifty stories or so, there is a long period of digging down in the mud; cement is put here and pillars there, and steel pilings put down; if we observe all this we may turn to one another and say, "It is just one mass of confusion, isn't it? You can't make head nor tail of it." But as we watch the building go up through the weeks and months that follow, even though the confusion continues—men over in one corner are doing one thing and men in another are doing something totally unrelated, trucks are coming and going, depositing things in piles here and there—we see that it slowly comes to make sense. Step by step, stage by stage through the careful planning of the architects and engineers a coherent plan is marvelously put together, until finally this gigantic building results.

We've all seen this many times, even, perhaps, in the building of our own home. There is the same disorder and confusion. If we don't understand the architect's plan and know where things are really finally going to fit, we feel the same surprise when we see that people did after all know what they are doing. It wasn't confusion at all, but really was proceeding according to a most careful plan.

THEOLOGICAL EXTENSION

Now, in a sense, Christmas symbolizes this same result. In a very real sense God is the architect of our redemption and the architect of the universe through Christ, just as the Letter to the Hebrews emphasizes today. It emphasizes, too, that this was a process not unlike the construction of a building or a house. When looking at particular statements in the Old Testament from the various prophets and trying to judge them, we can understandably feel confused, much as if we were watching a building going up. Things do not seem to make sense often because one doesn't understand how the placing of certain things over here, seemingly with no relationship to what is going on over there, is in fact in the final plan very carefully related. But if we stay around long enough, or if we understand it as the architects and engineers do, then we'll know this is not confusion but a very carefully planned arrangement, even though at times, it may seem extremely confused and even contradictory.

This can certainly happen when we read segments of the Old Testament, particular prophesies, events, or teachings. But when we bring it all together in and through the New Testament, centering, of course, on Christ and his teachings, then like the completion of a building we see the whole plan come to make sense. So the Letter to the Hebrews tells us this about prophesies coming to final and perfect and complete fulfillment in Christ. "In times past, God spoke in fragmentary and varied ways to our fathers through the prophets." In reading them we can feel the confusion of watching many workmen each doing their own thing in apparent contradiction or indifference to what is going on around them. We know, in fact, that this is not so; we know that there is an architect's plan that is guiding it all very carefully. And so it is with reading the prophets of the Old Testament. "In this, the final age, he has spoken to us through his Son, whom he has made heir of all things and through whom he first created the universe." This Son is the reflection of the Father's glory, the exact representation of the Father's being, and he sustains all things by his powerful word."

Now we get the completed picture: the magnificent edifice that is God's love of mankind. And the Son of God is the strength —the cornerstone—of this magnificent edifice. This is what we rejoice in at Christmas—this sense of the completed building, the magnificent structure of love and care by God for man. When we see a wonderful building, we admire the greatness of the minds of people who can plan in such detail and such care and bring into fulfillment such a magnificent edifice; we rightly are overwhelmed and profoundly impressed. Now then, look carefully at what the incarnation and redemption are all about. Look at the magnificence in which the Old Testament, piece by piece and section by section, built things up and slowly unfolded the promise and meaning and purpose of the Messiah. Then look at how Christ developed in his life—made clearer, more precise and far more wonderful the real intent and purpose of the Messiah. We celebrate with hope and joy this Christmas day the commemoration of that indescribably beautiful and human edifice that God made for us with the coming of Christ his Son.

THEOLOGICAL CONCLUSION

This is the heart of our joy: God brought his work to completion in Christ. He is the fulfillment of the hopes and prophesies. He is greater as the Letter to the Hebrews reminds us, than even the angels. So we, along with them, worship him this Christmas and every day as the marvelous fulfillment of God's plan.

CHRISTMAS MASS DURING THE DAY (A, B, C)
HOMILY IV

Gospel Reading: *In the beginning was the Word; the Word was in God's presence and the Word was God. He was present to God in the beginning. Through him all things came into being, and apart from him nothing came to be. Whatever came to be in him, found life, life for the light of men. The light shines on in darkness, a darkness that did not overcome it.*

There was a man named John sent by God, who came as a witness to testify to the light, so that through him all men might believe—but only to testify to the light, for he himself was not the light. The real light which gives light to every man was coming into the world.

He was in the world, and through him the world was made. Yet the world did not know who he was. To his own he came, yet his own did not accept him. Any who did accept him he empowered to become children of God.

These are they who believe in his name—who were begotten not by blood, nor by carnal desire, nor by man's willing it, but by God.

The Word became flesh and made his dwelling among us, and we have seen his glory; the glory of an only Son coming from the Father filled with enduring love.

John testified to him by proclaiming, "This is he of whom I said, 'The one who comes after me ranks ahead of me, for he was before me.' "

Of his fullness we have all had a share—love following upon love.

For while the law was a gift through Moses, this enduring love came through Jesus Christ. No one has even seen God. It is God the only Son, ever at the Father's side, who has revealed him. (Jn. 1:1-18)

ANA-GNOSIS

All of us know the amusement of a riddle. Children especially delight in riddles. They like to hear them; but most of all they like the power, the fun and the satisfaction of telling riddles to other people, especially to adults. There is a special delight in the child's voice and manner betraying his knowledge of the answer when he tells you the riddle, and especially, if real or acted out, you show him you don't quite understand it.

From the beginning of time, it seems, riddles have existed. Sometimes Greek oracles prophesied in riddles. These prophesies were ambiguous, like pictures, depending on how you see them, looking either one way or another.

We also have other words for this: *puzzle,* for example, which we manipulate with our hands. It may seem deceptively simple but unless we know the secret of the various maneuvers, it is often hard to solve. Or it may be a maze where we have to follow certain lines. There are more complicated words like *enigma,* which catch the more profound sense of mystery. It is a riddle with a far greater extension than we ordinarily think of in the simple word "riddle" itself. There is the less commonly used, but also significant word, *conundrum.* A conundrum is that kind of riddle that has a twist to it, sometimes humorous or confusing, like the silly question, "Why is it wrong to work in the fish market?" and the answer, "Because it makes one sell-fish." You can hear the little child laughing now and saying, "Did you get it?" These sorts of riddles may seem very silly, but they catch the element of ambiguity, that enigmatic quality that, from the beginning of time, always fascinated human beings.

THEOLOGICAL EXTENSION

This fascination involves trying to understand apparent contradictions: two things do not seem to fit, and the satisfaction of the riddle or enigma is to see that they do fit remarkably well. So today in the Gospel of St. John we have a riddle. John testified to Christ by proclaiming, "This is he of whom I said, 'The one who comes after me ranks ahead of me, for he was before me.' " It was this enigmatic quality about the Messiah that made the coming of Christ such a disturbance, such a puzzle. The leaders of the Jewish religious and political situation at the time had their own answers to this Messiah enigma. And a great deal of the conflict between Christ and themselves was their unwillingness to give up their answer, and to accept Christ's answer which, of course, was God's answer, or the true meaning of the enigma. The heart of it is right here: namely, that he who has now come after John the Baptist, was, in fact, before him, since he is God the creator of the universe. Christ is the image of all things made as the Letter to the Hebrews tells us. "This Son is the reflection of the Father's glory, the exact representation of the Father's being and he sustains all things by his powerful word."

Earlier in this Reading from the Gospel of John we get an extension of this enigma: "He was in the world, and through him the world was made. Yet the world did not know who he was. To his own he came, yet his own did not accept him." Man, made by God, did not know God when he was faced by God in his own human form. This is the heart of the riddle or the enigma posed by Christ's existence. And it is not hard to realize why it was so difficult to accept who he really was, because only in the mind of God could so amazing a solution be unfolded. We can be critical of the Pharisees, Scribes and leaders of the political and religious structure of the time, but we also need to have a certain sympathy for them. Only in God's mind could so seemingly unbelievable an idea have been worked out: that God would come on earth himself as a carpenter's son, be born of a woman in a simple outlying manger with no pomp and circumstance, none of the triumphant descriptions of some of the prophesies of the coming of the Messiah.

THEOLOGICAL CONCLUSION

Perhaps no riddle, no enigma, has so puzzled the human race as just how that babe in Bethlehem could have come after John the Baptist and yet have been before him. The world has great difficulty accepting the answer to that riddle, the answer that God gives. Yet this is what we are celebrating today, that the answer to the question, "Who *is* that child?" is "God himself." And if we realize that, if we believe it and let it give meaning and direction to our lives, then, in response to the child's question, "Did you get it?" we can know that, indeed, we have got it.

FEAST OF THE HOLY FAMILY (A, B, C)
HOMILY I

Reading I: *The Lord sets a father in honor over his children; a mother's authority he confirms over her sons. He who honors his father atones for sins; he stores up riches who reveres his mother. He who honors his father is gladdened by children, and when he prays he is heard. He who reveres his father will live a long life; he obeys the Lord who brings comfort to his mother.*

My son, take care of your father when he is old; grieve him not as long as he lives. Even if his mind fail, be considerate with him; revile him not in the fullness of your strength. For kindness to a father will not be forgotten, it will serve as a sin offering—it will take lasting root. (Sir. 3:2-6, 12-14)

ANA-GNOSIS

Modern medicine with its skills and achievements has brought us immeasurable blessings and great help. Many illnesses that were fatal or nearly fatal in other generations, wiping out large numbers of people, are very simply controlled now. And surgery can resolve sometimes quite simply what was a most common cause of death a few generations ago. But one of the by-products and a complicated and difficult issue that the success of modern medicine raises is the quality of life of old people.

We all have a beautiful image of old age: the loving grandfather and grandmother, smiling as the children come to the grandparents' home, greeting them with love and care. Most of us recall wonderful grandparents who did love us, and were a unique part of our childhood, that even our parents could not have supplied.

In the case of children without parents or in institutions, elderly people who volunteer to be their grandparents are extremely effective and helpful. Children and adolescents often relate to these older people much more deeply and with much greater confidence and security and love than to other Staff people, no matter how professionally trained they are. This, of course, is a wonderful picture of elderly people and ideally we would like our parents to come to this kind of old age. We hope they will be happy, secure and physically well, with only minor aches and pains. We wish for them to have a peaceful death with no long, lingering suffering or senility or any of the tragic consequences of old age.

We realize, however, that this often is not true. Old age can bring loneliness, bitterness, a kind of childish misbehavior and an inability to get along with others. It can bring extreme selfishness and, even more tragically, feeble-mindedness and loss of all the powers that this adult man or woman once had. We realize from today's Reading from Sirach that these consequences are not new.

THEOLOGICAL EXTENSION

Sirach, too, was addressing himself to this complicated question of the aged. He describes also something of the tragedies of old age when he describes the father and says, to the son or daughter, "Even if his mind fail, be considerate with him." And from a modern medical point of view we could add many things to that. All people, whatever their age or capabilities, are not without need of our human concern and our love.

This issue of old age is before us all in one way or another. Of great concern to the bishop and priests of a diocese or to the superiors of religious orders of men are the elderly priests. Sisters, especially those originally from a young order, are now faced with very large numbers of elderly sisters who must be cared for. And we all know the problems of a couple raising their own children having on their hands sometimes one or two elderly parents. This situation imposes personal, physical, psychological and financial responsibilities on them.

The answer here is not easy. There is no quick and simple way. What Sirach tells us today is that all our concerns will have meaning in God's eyes. It is an extension, if you like, of the commandment, "Honor thy father and thy mother." But it is reassuring, for Sirach says, "He who honors his father atones for sins. He stores up riches who reveres his mother. He who honors his father is gladdened by children, and when he prays he is heard. He who reveres his father will live a long life; he obeys the Lord who brings comfort to his mother." Of course, equally here we could say *she*. It applies as well to the women in relationship to her father and mother. So we must, as Sirach tells us, be genuinely concerned and deeply touched so that we take upon ourselves something of the burden of the issues of our elderly parents. In doing so we receive God's blessing and get consideration for our own sins and our own weaknesses.

But the burden cannot be totally borne just by the young family raising their own children, which is about the time the burden is heaviest—the children are in high school or college and the parents are already burdened—and all of a sudden, the elderly grandparents in some instances desperately need their help. We know it is too much for one couple now. The government must help; the church must help; society must be concerned as well as the individual. And we need also to look toward our own old age to take on responsibilities for ourselves.

THEOLOGICAL CONCLUSION

But despite the government, despite the church, despite our best intentions to try to take care of ourselves, old age often brings great need and dependency. We are reassured here by Sirach that the man or woman who remembers and is concerned for his or her parents has the blessing of God. "My children," he might say, "take care of your father and mother when they are old, grieve them not as long as they live. Even if their minds fail, be considerate with them; revile them not in the fullness of your strength. For kindness to a father or mother will not be forgotten, it will serve as a sin offering—it will take a lasting root." This is a consolation and should bring us peace if and when these grave concerns about the elderly sometimes seem to overwhelm us in our daily lives.

FEAST OF THE HOLY FAMILY (A, B, C)
HOMILY II

Responsorial Psalm: *Happy are those who fear the Lord and walk in his ways.*

1. Happy are you who fear the Lord, who walk in his ways!
For you shall eat the fruit of your handiwork, Happy you shall be, and favored.

Happy are those who fear the Lord and walk in his ways.

2. Your wife shall be like a fruitful vine in the recesses of your home.
Your children like olive plants around the table.

Happy are those who fear the Lord and walk in his ways.

3. Behold, thus is the man blessed who fears the Lord.
The Lord bless you from zion; may you see the prosperity of Jerusalem all the days of your life.

Happy are those who fear the Lord and walk in his ways.

(Ps. 128:1-2, 3, 4-5. R. V. 1)

ANA-GNOSIS

If we have occasion to plant a garden or put in crops in the spring, we know that many things go into a successful harvest or a beautiful garden of tasty vegetables and beautiful flowers. First of all, there has to be a great deal of planning and care both in how we set up the garden and how we till the soil. If we don't plant the seed properly and keep away the weeds, working at it with great care and concern, generally the harvest will be poor. We know, too, that a garden or a farm can be very carefully tilled and looked after but a drought or a flood may come, or other things may happen over which we, as individuals, have no control, and we have a poor harvest. Sometimes, of course, in a particular year nature is generous; the snow melted at just the right time, and spring rains came, the soil was rich, it was a good summer with not too much sun but enough, and just the right amount of rain; sometimes then people will say "You know, the garden just raised itself," or "The crops just grew by themselves." Now we know that this was not entirely true, that a great deal of care was still expended; but nature, the environment, and the circumstances were all most propitious, and a wonderful harvest resulted. Every single thing that we planted grew and flourished that year.

THEOLOGICAL EXTENSION

Now if we think of a family in this way, as the Psalmist did in saying, "Your wife shall be like a fruitful vine in the recesses of your home. Your children like olive plants around your table," we can see something which may help us. First of all, just as a gardener must care for his plants, we must give a great deal of care in the early years to the training and education of children. Without this care and concern it will be much less likely, just as in a garden, that a beautiful crop and good fruit will result. We know, too, that parents cannot do this alone. The school, the church and the government all must help. They must do their best too, because without their dedicated help children would lack the basic things they need, as seeds growing in the soil would lack basic nutrients.

But the consolation of the farm or the garden image here is that, even when the very best is done, things can happen beyond the control of the farmer or gardener that makes the crop weak and much less fruitful: droughts can come, floods can come, a bad season can come. We must, therefore, be very careful not to blame parents in an exaggerated way. And if we are parents we must be careful not to blame ourselves too much. Like the gardener or the farmer, we must do our very best through the spring and the summer as the plants are growing, especially when they are weak or feeble and have not yet got their roots firmly in the ground. Here much depends on the gardener's care. Just so, parents are most basic to small children, up through the middle years into adolescence; much depends on their care and concern. But there is also much that is mysterious here and we must not bypass it. Parents can only do their very best. But they cannot control the mystery of God's grace or many other circumstances that can mould and influence young people and change their lives for good or ill.

THEOLOGICAL CONCLUSION

So, much like the gardener or the farmer, parents have the responsibility to do well by their children in the early years. But if they come to be good Christian, responsible citizens, as we hope and pray they will, much also came from God's grace and from influences even beyond their parents' control, just as the good harvest is only in part the result of the gardener's or former's efforts. Parents, then, must do their best but realize that, in all sorts of ways, the fruitfulness of their family is out of their hands. And if a bad crop results, one must be careful not to blame them excessively. This, too, can be the result of other circumstances beyond their control. The key is for all of us—parents, those responsible in the school, in the church, and in the state—to do our very best, as a good farmer or good gardener does, and then we must leave it to God and pray.

FEAST OF THE HOLY FAMILY (A, B, C)
HOMILY III

Reading II: *Because you are God's chosen ones; holy and beloved, clothe yourselves with heartfelt mercy, with kindness, with humility, meekness, and patience. Bear with one another; forgive whatever grievances you have against one another. Forgive as the Lord has forgiven you. Over all these virtues put on love, which binds the rest together and makes them perfect. Christ's peace must reign in your hearts, since as members of the one body you have been called to that peace. Dedicate yourselves to thankfulness. Let the word of Christ, rich as it is, dwell in you. In wisdom made perfect, instruct and admonish one another. Sing gratefully to God from your hearts in psalms, hymns, and inspired songs. Whatever you do, whether in speech or in action, do it in the name of the Lord Jesus. Give thanks to God the Father through him.*

You who are wives, be submissive to your husbands. This is your duty in the Lord. Husbands, love your wives. Avoid any bitterness toward them. You children, obey your parents in everything as the acceptable way in the Lord. And fathers, do not nag your children lest they lose heart. (Cor. 3:12-21)

ANA-GNOSIS

It is commonplace when there are difficulties in society, such as crime or vandalism in schools, to find some sort of cause, some scapegoat to blame. In our time we tend to blame the home and lack of discipline in the home. Then we say that this leads to lack of discipline in the school. Many people simply shake their heads and say, "Well, if there were more discipline in the home we wouldn't have this trouble." Now this is very easy to say and, like any such statement, there is, of course, truth in it. But to find out what the truth is and what such a statement really means, and then really to try to carry it out in the home and in school, is no easy matter.

Let us look first at the nature of the word, "discipline." The Latin word *disciplina* doesn't mean rigid obedience, staying in one's place or doing exactly what one is told. Surprisingly, what it really means is directly related to the word "disciple." We all know that a disciple is someone who learns from someone else.

Disciplina, in Latin, means what the disciple or learner learns. Now then, for us to have discipline in the home we must have an atmosphere in which children can learn from their parents. And this gives meaning to the idea that discipline is a valuable experience in childhood. We are not talking about having children march like soldiers rigidly, and do what they're told when their father barks at them or the mother yells orders. On the contrary, that kind of rigid, authoritarian home is often the cause of the very delinquencies and disorders in society that we are lamenting. And the people who talk most about wanting rigid discipline in the home are often critical when such an idea is carried out because it can produce rebelliousness. Real discipline in the home is the atmosphere of loving peace and order into which children naturally, like flowers in good soil, well-watered, grow in ordering themselves and having an inner sense of peacefulness.

THEOLOGICAL EXTENSION

This is the mood in today's Reading from St. Paul's Epistle to the Colossians. He first talks about putting on—almost like garments—kindness, heartfelt mercy, humility, meekness, patience, of bearing one another and forgiving one another for whatever grievances we have against each other as the Lord has forgiven us. These, then, would be the characteristics of the home: a sense of give and take, and a sense of forgiveness and understanding. Paul continues, "Over all these virtues, put on love which binds the rest together and makes them perfect." Now this is the atmosphere—a loving atmosphere of forgiveness and understanding one another—that creates true discipline in the home, an environment in which a child can learn from the older children and especially from the parents.

This atmosphere, then, produces peace. The ancient Greeks had such a respect for order that they called the planetary system the *Kosmos,* which was also the Greek word for beauty. And St. Augustine, in that spirit, defines peace as the tranquility of order. Peace in the home, therefore, is this loving orderliness, that has with it both beauty and this spirit of openness and readiness to learn. This is true discipline.

So Paul continues, "Christ's peace must reign in your hearts since as members of the one body, you have been called to that peace." Elsewhere in the first epistle to the Corinthians he talks about what chaos there would be in the body if the eye refused to see, if the hand or leg resisted and wouldn't move. This happens in illness, in paralysis. When we are sick our organs are undisciplined, they lack order and won't do what we ask them to do. In the normally healthy child, the organs grow in their own discipline, the legs and hands move, the eyes see. And freely growing into our own way of life within the body of Christ, we must learn the orderliness that the organs of the body have naturally. This is the connection, I suppose, between the notion of discipline in the law-and-order sense on the one side, and discipline as learning, on the other: we have to learn as individuals to control ourselves in the same way that the organs of the body do naturally.

Now children must learn this in the home, and this is what we should mean when we say children need discipline in the home. The more they can control themselves in orderly relationship to one another, the more there is of that tranquility of order which St. Augustine called peace and the ancient Greeks called beauty.

THEOLOGICAL CONCLUSION

So when we look at the slogans embroidered here and there and everywhere, calling for or proclaiming "Peace" or "Peace be in our Home" then, in a sense we are also saying, "Discipline," but not rigid, harsh, military orderliness. Rather we mean a loving openness, care and concern, kindness and forgiveness for one another. By such behavior together, like the well-ordered organs of the body, we know peace and love.

"Christ's peace must reign in your hearts," and in our families, "since as members of the one body you have been called to thankfulness." Christ's peace is both the tranquility of order and the beauty which results when the members of his body live together in kindness and commitment of love. That is true discipline and because it brings his peace it should be a goal for all of us.

FEAST OF THE HOLY FAMILY (A, B, C)
HOMILY IV

Gospel Reading: *After the astrologers had left, the angel of the Lord suddenly appeared in a dream to Joseph with the command: "Get up, take the child and his mother, and flee to Egypt. Stay there until I tell you otherwise. Herod is searching for the child to destroy him." Joseph got up and took the child and his mother and left that night for Egypt. He stayed there until the death of Herod, to fulfill what the Lord had said through the prophets,*

"Out of Egypt I have called my son."

But after Herod's death, the angel of the Lord appeared in a dream to Joseph in Egypt with the command: "Get up, take the child and his mother, and set out for the land of Israel. Those who had designs on the life of the child are dead." He got up, took the child and his mother, and returned to the land of Israel. He heard, however, that Archelaus had succeeded his father Herod as king of Judea, and he was afraid to go back there. Instead, because of a warning received in a dream, Joseph went to the region of Galilee. There he settled in a town called Nazareth. In this way what was said through the prophets was fulfilled:

"He shall be called a Nazarene."

(Mt. 2:13-15, 19-23)

ANA-GNOSIS

Modern psychology has made us aware, in a fresh way, of new and subtle aspects of many familiar things about ourselves and others. One of these is the idea of dreams. Dreams have been carefully studied and analyzed in this century, and we know that dreams can tell us a great deal about ourselves. They are broken images that come forward in sleep, almost like disorganized pieces of a jigsaw puzzle. They include part of our experiences, our hopes, our goals, our desires and even part, sometimes, of aspects of ourselves that we do not consciously recognize or look at. So the modern therapist or counselor sometimes uses dreams to help us recognize these aspects of ourselves.

But dreams used this way are simply suggestions that start us consciously on a trail of examining ourselves reasonably. There is no special mystical quality to the dream itself.

We know, too, from the headlines and from television reports that a person may hear, either in a dream or in some kind of trance-like state, a voice that he may readily attribute to God. But this is a very dangerous assumption. We know all too well that disturbed, psychotic people can take a rifle and, on the basis of a voice that they may attribute to an angel of God, kill others and sometimes themselves with a calmness and carefulness that astonishes us. Yet, later, some who survive say sometimes that the voice of God told them to do this, and they may add, "in a dream." This is the dangerous side, of course, of that sort of interpretation of a dream.

THEOLOGICAL EXTENSION

When we look at the text today where, as often happens in the Bible, dreams are given as a part of God's agency, we have to be very careful to see clearly that the dream is defined in the Bible as being used by God. *We* can't define it that way. We know it because the Reading here tells us so; but this is on the authority of the Bible and God's word. We cannot conclude that some dream of our own is God talking to us. This would be to assume blasphemously that we can determine God's' voice to us.

The Bible tells us, "The angel of the Lord suddenly appeared in a dream to Joseph with the command and Joseph got up and took the child and his mother and left that night for Egypt." Now the main point of this Reading is that somehow Joseph understood that it was God's will and, therefore, his own duty, his conscientious responsibility to his child and to his wife, to take them to Egypt and later, in the same responsible way, to return and settle in Galilee because the crisis was over.

Now there is a possible psychological interpretation of this that could fit. One could conceive that rumors of the jealous king, as they do in circumstances such as these, got to Joseph and, thus, in his conscious state he was pondering how serious these rumors were, and how much danger the Christ-child was in. Then in his sleep, in a dream, things vividly crystalized and he saw clearly what his duty was.

We know, for example, that great composers have pondered works of music and have been unable to resolve them and then have awakened from a dream with all the music right in front of them. Some have completed great works in that way. Great scientists have gone to sleep in confusion and awakened in the middle of the night with an exact solution in their mind that managed to resolve their difficulty or problem. So it is not inconceivable then that Joseph might have had conscious knowledge of the danger of Herod and also later that he would have been informed by travelers of the death of this dangerous person, so he could return. He might also have had reason beyond the voice that Holy Scripture calls the angel of God to return to Galilee. Perhaps this was the original home of Joseph and Mary. The point is that it fulfills the criterion of Christ being called a Galilean, when, by way of exception, he was actually born in Bethlehem.

THEOLOGICAL CONCLUSION

We must therefore recognize that when we interpret a dream

we do so wisely by having it correspond to our own reasonableness and to our own sense of duty and the responsibilities which face us. Dreams can then sometimes make vivid and clear a resolution we were unsure of. It is blasphemous however to assume that this dream is the voice of God. We believe this in the case of Joseph only because the Bible affirms it. There is no way we can attribute this to any dream voice that we or others know.

What this account really shows us, though, is Joseph as a model of concern for his wife and child. When it became clear to Joseph what his duty was, he obeyed. He left whatever might have interested him and went to the place where he understood that his duty rquired that he should go. What we have left then, especially in terms of family life, is the image of a most responsible father, a man obedient to God's will when it became vividly clear to him what God wanted. He is an example to us then of how we should respond when it becomes clear to us how God would have us live our lives.

JANUARY THE FIRST—OCTAVE OF CHRISTMAS (NEW YEAR HOMILY)

THE SOLEMNITY OF MARY, MOTHER OF GOD HOMILY I

Reading I: *The Lord said to Moses: "Speak to Aaron and his sons and tell them: This is how you shall bless the Israelites. Say to them:*
The Lord bless and keep you!
The Lord let his face shine upon you, and be gracious to you!
The Lord look upon you kindly and give you peace!

So shall they invoke my name upon the Israelites, and I will bless them." (Nm. 6:22-27)

ANA-GNOSIS

A writer of a generation ago, Hilaire Belloc, made this remark. He said, "There is something of sanctity in good manners." Now, of course, he did not mean pretentious politeness, etiquette for etiquette's sake, or memorizing a book of etiquette and rather artificially and pretentiously acting out those kind of directions. This kind of good manners, we know, is false, misleading, and only betrays the shallowness of the person rather than any depth of meaning. The good manners that Belloc was talking about, those that had something of sanctity in them, are the courtesies and gentle considerations, the thoughtfulness that emerges from the heart of a person. These people seem almost instinctively to know the right thing to do. Basically, the heart of their good manners is consideration for others. At the moment when another person is ill at ease, embarrassed, insecure, or in some way failing, such people of good manners know how to turn that situation to relieve the other person of their embarrassment, to put them at ease and make them feel their own worth. We've all encountered such people.

Contrary to a popular and artificial image, these are not necessarily wealthy people or people of great standing in high society. They may be—sometimes the people of the most gracious, good manners are, in fact, from wealthy, important families—but not necessarily so. Wealthy people can be very crude and artificial too. Sometimes, we find the most sensitive of good manners among very simple people not necessarily educated or rich at all, just ordinary people. But whether they are rich or poor they, in their simple daily relationships with us, manage to put us at ease, make us feel our worth and give us a sense of our dignity and meaning as people. In this sense, then, Belloc's remark is true: there is something of sanctity in good manners.

THEOLOGICAL EXTENSION

Now if we were to sum up in one word what we mean here we could call these people "gracious." It is, therefore, in that context that it is worth reflecting on the line in today's Reading from the Book of Numbers, "The Lord let his face shine upon you and be gracious to you! The Lord look upon you kindly and give you peace!"

It is a wonderful conception to think of God as being gracious. If we add infinite fineness, exquisite thoughtfulness and consideration to all the gracious people we have known in our lives, we come to a description of God. Recall those moments when very sensitive people put us at ease, made us feel our own worth, sometimes when we were small children and other times as adults. Then let us realize that God is this kind of person multiplied to infinity. He is all the fineness, the consideration, the delicacy, the thoughtfulness and concern we have known.

THEOLOGICAL CONCLUSION

So, with very genuine meaning and depth, knowing the wonderful things that graciousness includes, we repeat this prayer: "The Lord let his face shine upon you and be gracious to you! The Lord look upon you kindly and give you peace!"

JANUARY THE FIRST—OCTAVE OF CHRISTMAS

THE SOLEMNITY OF MARY, MOTHER OF GOD
HOMILY II

Responsorial Psalm: R. *May God bless us in his mercy.*

1. May God have pity on us and bless us; may he let his face shine upon us.
So may your way be known upon earth; among all nations, your salvation.

May God bless us in his mercy.

2. May the nations be glad and exult because you rule the peoples in equity; the nations on the earth you guide.

May God bless us in his mercy.

3. May the peoples praise you, O God; may all the peoples praise you!
May God bless us. And may all the ends of the earth fear him!

May God bless us in his mercy.

(Ps. 67:2-3, 5, 6, 8. R. V. 2)

ANA-GNOSIS

Often we use small words to say a variety of common, yet important things. One of these is the simple word "way." We can think of "way" as the direction of something, and we may say to someone, "Tell me the right way to go." He may ask us then, "Where do you want to go?" In other words, the "right way" makes no sense unless we also know where we want to get. And sometimes we use the word "way" in terms of doing something. We say, "Tell me the way to do it," and someone may reply, "This is the right way to do it." In sports particularly, we sometimes hear or say "That's the way to go!" It is normally said when a good play has been made and everyone feels good about it. But it could be interesting to reflect for a moment on this slang phrase, "That's the way to go," and ask "What's the way to go?"

THEOLOGICAL EXTENSION

We might well ask that question at the beginning of a New Year: "What's the way to go?" It's actually quite a question.

The Psalmist, of course, gives us the answer cleanly and simply for today: "May God have pity on us and bless us; may he let his face shine upon us. So may *your way*"—that is, *God's way*—"be known upon earth; among all nations, your salvation." That's the way to go.

What way? God's way. That is, of all the different ways we can go in life or all the different ways we can do something, there is a right way of going and of doing finally, and that is God's way.

The core, then, of our lives, of this year and this day, of all our intentions and of everything we do, is in these lines of the Psalm. "So may your way," says the Psalmist to God, "be known upon earth. Among all nations, your salvation."

The rest simply fills it out and gives us the picture of peace and happiness that we all dream of: "May the nations be glad and exult because you rule the peoples in equity; the nations on the earth you guide." Once God's way is the way to go for all of us, then all these yearnings of the human race for peace, for justice, for some kind of basic security and meaning in life are taken care of.

THEOLOGICAL CONCLUSION

When we cheer one another, then, with "That's the way to go!" let us ask ourselves, "What's the way to go?" and we should answer, "God's way!"

JANUARY THE FIRST—OCTAVE OF CHRISTMAS

THE SOLEMNITY OF MARY, MOTHER OF GOD
HOMILY III

Reading II: *When the designated time had come, God sent forth his Son born of a woman, born under the law, to deliver from the law those who were subjected to it, so that we might receive our status as adopted sons. The proof that you are sons is the fact that God has sent forth into our hearts the spirit of his Son which cries* *out "Abba!" ("Father"). You are no longer a slave but a son! And the fact that you are a son makes you an heir, by God's design.* (Gal. 4:4-7)

ANA-GNOSIS

All of us know the experience of moving from a situation or a relationship where someone is supervising or guiding us to a time when we are on our own. One of the common experiences of this is when we learned to drive an automobile and for the first time we took it by ourselves. There's a great sense of achievement, of independence, and pride. But it is also rather frightening to realize that the teacher is no longer present and we're all alone. We're free indeed and independent, but at the same time totally responsible for everything the car does, every move it makes.

From early childhood on, our parents let us learn to walk and do other things on our own. We've had endless experiences of those first moments when all of a sudden our father or mother or older brother or sister wasn't there and we did it ourselves. Right up through life, depending on the degree of responsibility that our lives give us, we always know those moments when we're in charge. Then we can make the decisions freely, but we also have the responsibilities and obligations that we didn't have before.

THEOLOGICAL EXTENSION

Now it is this idea—this movement from having a guardian or supervisor or guide to being on our own—that today's Reading from Galatians is stressing. The emphasis on the law here doesn't quite indicate the clarity of this point. It begins with, "When the designated time had come, God sent forth his Son born of a woman, born under the law, to deliver from the law those people who were subjected to it, so that we might receive our status as adopted sons." We see the point more clearly if we go back a little bit earlier in the fourth chapter of Galatians starting with, "I mean that the heir, as long as he is a child, is no better than a slave though he is the owner of all the estate, but he is under guardians and trustees until the date set by his father." We see here that it isn't a question of the law as such, but rather the law as an example of a situation where one is under the control of others, just as an heir, until he is twenty-one or eighteen, or whatever the law sets up, doesn't inherit his full authority and freedom; there are legal guardians set up for him. Now this is the idea St. Paul is getting at: namely that, until the coming of Christ, all of us were under a kind of primitive instinctiveness which needed a lot of clearly stated laws to control our basic impulses. But Christ's coming gives us a whole new way of life which is both free and responsible. Now we are on our own. No longer are we simply children running here and there under impulses that we can't quite control and always under supervision because of this immaturity. Now we have the full potential of our maturity in Christ, with the spirit of God guiding us.

THEOLOGICAL CONCLUSION

We all know that if we drive a car or pilot an airplane alone, there's a great sense of freedom and satisfaction in having no supervisor, no one to control us and guide us. But the driving of a car, and even more so the piloting of a plane, is a grave and responsible business.

This is part of St. Paul's meaning too. With the freedom that comes to us as Christians, with this exultation of our nature that we are now sons and daughters and heirs—in Christ—of God, there is also the responsibility and obligation. We must be responsible as adults in contrast to being dependent on a guardian as we were when we were children.

We are the adult heirs of God our Father and with this freedom we must accept a mature, responsible obligation exactly as we might expect from our own child to whom we have given the keys to the car. They are free now to take the car and go where they wish, but they must also be very, very responsible. We are heirs of God in that same way: He gives us the keys, but with them goes our adult responsibility.

JANUARY THE FIRST—OCTAVE OF CHRISTMAS

THE SOLEMNITY OF MARY, MOTHER OF GOD
HOMILY IV

Gospel Reading: *The shepherds went in haste to Bethlehem and found Mary and Joseph, and the baby lying in the manger; once they saw,* *they understood what had been told them concerning this child. All who heard of it were astonished at the report given them by the shepherds.*

Mary treasured all these things and reflected on them in her heart. The shepherds returned, glorifying and praising God for all they had heard and seen, in accord with what had been told them.

When the eighth day arrived for his circumcision, the name Jesus was given the child, the name the angel had given him before he was conceived. (Lk. 22:16-21)

ANA-GNOSIS

Artists, from the earliest times of the Christian church down to our own day, have tried to portray the Christmas scene of Mary and Joseph and the Christ-child. Understandably, to do this challenges the highest and most gifted of artists. We can see by the very way that the shepherds were so impressed and word quickly went everywhere about this mother and child, that something most unusual was evident. St. Luke tells us, "Once they saw, they understood what had been told them concerning this child. All who heard of it were astonished at the report given them by the shepherds." We might get the idea that they found, as in the masterpieces of art, an indescribably beautiful mother and an indescribably lovely child. It seems fitting that it should be so. Somehow we want to think of Mary as God's masterpiece even to the point of being the most beautiful woman God ever made. Understandably then, even the face of this woman would have impressed the simple shepherds. And the child, too, must have had about him a radiance, an intensity that also captivated and overwhelmed the beholders.

THEOLOGICAL EXTENSION

But when we think of Mary as God made her, we move beyond the extrinsic appearance which artists have portrayed endlessly in a wide variety of beautiful mothers of children, and we ask how the character, the deeper elements of Mary were formed.

We must notice then that she's pondering in her heart all these events. And we recognize, among the lines which make up the portrait and meaning of Mary, that sorrow, tragedy, suffering and anxiety all have a place. If we think our lives have difficulties and anxieties and fears, let us look at hers. God so loved her that he wished her life to be deepened and made intense by care and concern, anxiety and suffering, not only for this child who was so mysteriously given to her by God but also for all of us who, having this great mystery of the God-man among us, did not understand. If ever a person understood the meaning of St. John's Gospel, "He came unto his own and his own received him not; He came into the world and the world was made by him, and the world did not know him," it was Mary. This was another of the things she pondered and reflected on in her heart, as St. Luke writes.

THEOLOGICAL CONCLUSION

Poets, as well as artists, have tried to capture the meaning of Mary's life, to paint verbal portraits of the Mother of God. The one thing they return to again and again is the intensity of her own sorrow and pain. Deeply beloved by God, she still suffered because people didn't understand who her son was. Rightly then we can call her the Mother of Sorrows. And we can know, too, that she understands our own fears, sorrows and anxieties because she, more even than we, knows what suffering means.

SECOND SUNDAY AFTER CHRISTMAS
HOMILY I

Reading I: *"From the mouth of the Most High I came forth, and mist-like, covered the earth. In the highest heavens did I dwell, my throne on a pillar of cloud."* (Sir. 24:1-12)

ANA-GNOSIS

When we see the earth parched and crops ruined from lack of rain we can understand the life-giving value rain had for the ancients; it can have much the same meaning for us today. Consequently, a cloud, with its mysterious silent movement was regarded as a great life-force. Water and rain, especially in its delicate form of mist, have been associated for a long time with pictures of God, the source of life. In addition, the majestic eminence of a cloud floating across the sky has led artists to depict God sitting on a cloud. Often, he is in a mist in such a picture. The power of the storm giving rain or light adds magnificence to this image of God. Not only God the Father but Christ too is seen pictured with clouds. The Ascension comes readily to mind. Clouds symbolize the eminence of God and at the same time, the life-giving force of God; they contain rain for the parched and yearning earth.

THEOLOGICAL EXTENSION

We can see then that this image is in today's Reading from Sirach. "From the mouth of the Most High I came forth" is a reference both to the Messiah and to the Paraclete, that is, the Holy Spirit. " . . . and mistlike covered the earth. In the highest heavens did I dwell, my throne on a pillar of cloud." Here are two images put together: the life-giving breath of the Spirit which takes the rather mystical form of mist and the majesty of the cloud with God the Father, Christ, or the Holy Spirit sitting on that cloud on a throne looking down at us.

The chief point of the Reading is the gratitude that the ancient peoples had for the merciful blessing and life-giving meaning of rain and moisture and mist. And, Christ comes to us with this same blessing. The Psalms liken the thirst of men for God to the thirst of the dry earth.

THEOLOGICAL CONCLUSION

Just as God comes on this cloud filled with life and rain to fulfill our thirst, so does the parched earth suddenly become alive with vegetation growing when moisture comes from a cloud. This is how Christ has come to us, enriching our lives with the moisture of his strength, his grace and fulfilling our terrible thirst, our dried-earth need for God. Christ sits on a cloud and his grace rains abundantly on us all.

SECOND SUNDAY AFTER CHRISTMAS
HOMILY II

Responsorial Psalm: *Glorify the Lord, O Jerusalem; praise your God, O Zion. For he has strengthened the bars of your gates; he has blessed your children within you.* (Ps. 147:12-20)

ANA-GNOSIS

The simplest things that have been with man almost since the beginning of time are still the most basic for us. The principle of the wheel comes quickly to mind. Not quite as obvious but still very old and very basic is the bar of a door. All locks are based on the bar; the lock turns a small bar which then holds the door. The most primitive form of this bar principle is a piece of oak that might be held on with a very large bolt and one merely pulls it down and it comes into a strong oak slot and holds. We know that when a door or gate of ancient times was locked this way, opening it required a great battering ram with eight or ten men banging it with all their strength. Even with this force the gate could not always be broken down or the door opened because the solid oaken bar would hold against all that force. Today if we make a smaller steel bar, it is still extremely difficult to bang the door or gate open.

We feel peaceful in a home when the doors are barred or locked. It is not so much to keep people out as it is to have the security that all is safe within the home. In that rare instance when a stranger with evil intent comes, one is warned from the outside as such a person tries to break down the bar or break the lock on the door.

THEOLOGICAL EXTENSION

The inner peace that the bar suggests when we put it down at night or in a modern form, when we put a chain lock on the door, is the peace that the Psalmist suggests, "Glorify the Lord, O, Jerusalem; praise your God, O Zion. For he has strengthened the bars of your gates." The Psalmist is saying that God has brought peace and freedom from anxiety inside us. A bar can only be opened from the inside; a chain can only be unleashed from the inside. The emphasis here is on the inner peace and security that God brings us.

If we need special protection where we live, then the Psalmist is particularly talking to us. We are safe because God is our strength, our protection, our security. More than any bar or chain that we can use, God offers us security, strength and freedom from anxiety.

THEOLOGICAL CONCLUSION

"He has granted us peace in your borders," the Psalmist tells us, "with the best of wheat he fills you. He sends forth his command to the earth; swiftly runs his word!" He told us earlier that all is well: "He has strengthened the bars of your gates; he has blessed your children within you." We know how we feel at night when the house is securely locked. God's peace is infinitely more. It is the peace he brings to us in the inner world of ourselves.

SECOND SUNDAY AFTER CHRISTMAS
HOMILY III

Reading II: *God chose us in him, before the world began, to be holy and blameless in his sight, to be full of love; he likewise predestined us through Christ Jesus to be his adopted sons—such was his will and pleasure.* (Eph. 1:3-18)

ANA-GNOSIS

At times, the understanding of a single word can have grave consequences. One such example stems from the meaning of the word "corn" in the United States. When we say "corn" here in the U. S., there is no doubt that we mean maize or Indian corn. It is what we traditionally eat "on the cob." When the British say "corn," which in its original meaning meant grain of some kind, they meant wheat. It is the farthest thing from our mind to associate wheat with the word "corn," just as it is the farthest thing from their minds to think of Indian corn as we have it here in America.

In World War II, this difference in meaning did cause a grave misunderstanding. By way of cable and other forms of communications, the British had made it known that they were in desperate need of "corn." Of course, they meant wheat. Those in charge of the response did not know the confusion surrounding the word and they filled many ships with Indian corn and sent them to England. Naturally, the whole process proved worthless because they did not need Indian corn! They needed wheat.

THEOLOGICAL EXTENSION

One single word that has caused much difficulty throughout the history of theology, particularly at the time of Calvin and the Reformation itself, is the word that occurs in today's Reading: "predestined" or, as we say theologically, "predestination." As most of us realize, predestination was a doctrine that stated our lives were predetermined by God in an absolute sense.

Now if we read the translation here with the focus on "He likewise predestined us through Christ Jesus to be his adopted sons—such was his will and pleasure," we hear the word "predestined" meaning a rigid, fixed idea of good or bad. It sounds as if we have nothing to do or say about our destiny. It is all in the stars, as we sometimes say with a reference to ancient astrology. But if we look at another translation, a modern translation, we notice that the line is slightly but significantly different. Here it reads, "He destined us in love to be his sons through Jesus Christ, according to the purpose of his will." Now it is not hard to see that, depending on the translator of the ancient text, the word can either be "destined" or "predestined."

It becomes evident that if we leave the "pre" off, we get a much less rigid or fixed conception. And that is exactly what we should understand when we put together all the doctrines of the Old and New Testaments. The emphasis is on our responsibility throughout the Scriptures—by the prophets, by the Evangelists and by Christ himself. There are endless stories which emphasize our responsibility and dignity. The important point is that God gives us our freedom, and if we look carefully we see that freedom and rigid predestination are a contradiction in terms. Here is where the modern translation helps us. "He destined us in love to be his sons through Jesus Christ." We know that something destined in love has to be free. If we were predetermined in an absolute sense we would not be free. The nature of love demands freedom.

THEOLOGICAL CONCLUSION

Just as the word "corn" means different things to Americans and Britishers, so too, the word "predestined" can have two meanings. We can, of course, get a fixed and predetermined conception from the word. But if we hear it as it is meant, we note the important phrase, "destined in love." That is to say, we have a covenant or an alliance with God. A covenant or an alliance is only valid when both parties fulfill their share of the covenant or the alliance; both are free to do so. God has freely loved us and freely destined us in love for glorious fulfillment in and through Christ. But if we are to be loved we must genuinely and freely respond and do our part in the covenant. It is a covenant of love and, therefore, it is a covenant of freedom. We must love God freely as God freely chose to love us by the redemption and his daily graces to us. There is no fixity to it; otherwise, it could not be in love. We are destined in God's plan because he has loved us, but we are free in that we may choose to respond in love.

SECOND SUNDAY AFTER CHRISTMAS
HOMILY IV

Gospel Reading: *He was in the world, and through him the world was made, yet the world did not know who he was. To his own he came, yet his own did not accept him. Any who did accept him he empowered to become children of God.* (Jn. 1:1-18)

ANA-GNOSIS

To look at the question of human freedom, it is helpful to begin with infants. We have seen the infant who nods his head one way to mean "yes" and another way to mean "no" long before he arrives at speech. Then he learns "yes" and "no" among his very first words.

Later on as children and adults, we take satisfaction in knowing "yes" and "no" in a foreign language even if we know nothing else about the language. Why do we learn "yes" and "no?" Because although it seems simple these words express the most profound element of our nature. That is, we can agree to something; we can accept it; we can let it happen with the word "yes" or by nodding our head in a certain way. By the same token, we can disagree, refuse to accept, or refuse to participate with the word "no" or, in our culture, by shaking our head from side to side. Thus human freedom finds its expression in the simple words, "yes" and "no."

THEOLOGICAL EXTENSION

Today, in this magnificent Reading from John, we see how plainly the whole destiny of the human race is summed up in relationship to Christ. First, he is with God and in God and is God from the beginning. "In the beginning was the Word; the Word was in God's' presence, and the Word was God." We believe that God is the perfect being. Because he is the purest of all intelligences, his idea of himself, his Word of himself exists eternally with him. This is similar to our idea of ourselves that we always carry with us. Just as I can conceive of myself, so God conceives his being from eternity. And this is the Word that John expresses here.

The Word became flesh and made his dwelling among us. Now the choice to accept or reject him is before the human race. "He was in the world, and through him the world was made, yet the world did not know who he was." That is, there was no compulsion; he taught who he was but no one was compelled to accept him. In the wording from the previous Reading from St. Paul, no one was predestined to accept or not accept, that is to say, "to know him," to recognize him as God. We are free; the human race must love God but that love demands freedom. We see it now clearly and sharply stated, "To his own he came, yet his own did not accept him." That is, he came through the predicted, promised line of David, the line of the Messiah; he came first to the people who were the carriers of this line to the world. Then he came to all of us. This is a process of history; Christ was not showing preference. He came through a woman of that line to share totally our human nature. He was born of a woman as we are. And, to all he gave a choice.

THEOLOGICAL CONCLUSION

Many of the Jewish line, as we know, did accept Christ. The Christian Church was almost totally Jewish for quite some time; the Jewish customs were the backbone of its liturgy as, in a sense, they still are today. But these Jews had a free choice. There was no predetermination as Jewish leaders at the time of Christ mistakenly thought.

There was to be a great freedom here for all throughout the world to make this choice. And, any who did accept him, he empowered to become "children of God." Those who say "yes" to Christ enter a covenant with God who promises a divine inheritance to those who keep their part of the covenant.

Through Christ, we become children, heirs of God. Magnificent, incomprehensible, mysterious and yet we believe it. It is the cornerstone of our Christian faith and our Christian life. We say "yes" to God, to Christ, and God says "yes" to us, making us heirs with Christian divinity. We are free to say "no" and that is the heart of our capacity to love. We love one another; we are free to say "yes," yet we could have said "no." We love God who truly loves us because he freely came to us and we are free to say "yes" to his coming and thereby love in return. We are among those who did accept him and we are empowered by this acceptance in Christ to become children of God. However, the root of this indescribable fulfillment that is ours is in Christ's willingness to become first one of us. Our response, our willingness to say "yes" to Christ completes the covenant.

JANUARY 6—EPIPHANY (A, B, C)
HOMILY I

Reading I: *Rise up in splendor, Jerusalem! Your light has come, the glory of the Lord shines upon you. See, the darkness covers the earth, and thick clouds cover the peoples; But upon you the Lord shines, and over you appears his glory. Nations shall walk by your light, and kings by your shining radiance. Raise your eyes and look about; they all gather and come to you: Your sons come from afar, and your daughters in the arms of their nurses.*

Then shall you be radiant at what you see, your heart shall throb and overflow. For the riches of the sea shall be emptied out before you, the wealth of nations shall be brought to you. Caravans of camels shall fill you, dromedaries from Midian and Ephah; All from Sheba come bearing gold and frankincense, and proclaiming the praises of the Lord. (Is. 60:1-6)

ANA-GNOSIS

We have seen many times, and some of us have even experienced, the remarkable effect of a spotlight on a stage. We know how the whole stage is dark and all of a sudden a spot hits, following someone out of the wings and across to the center of the stage. We know by the very nature of this arrangement, the light singling this person out of the darkness, that he is the key performer at this moment. We have a phrase, "on the spot," which captures the intense concentration that is on anyone when the spotlight shines out of the darkness and singles out one person in the darkness. This puts a very special emphasis on what this person says or what he does. When everything else is darkness and the spotlight comes down on one person, there is no way we can keep from being fully attentive to that person.

THEOLOGICAL EXTENSION

Now this is the tone of Isaias today: "Your light has come, the glory of the Lord shines upon you." He focuses that light. But the "you" here is not just the people of the Old Testament, it is all of us. Each of us in turn feels the spotlight of God's designation, God's love and grace, upon him or her.

It is interesting to think that we might stand one after the other here in church and, out of the darkness, this spot of light would illumine us, letting everyone else look upon us. But, in a sense, this is what Isaias means. He goes on: "See, darkness covers the earth, and thick clouds cover the peoples; but upon you the Lord shines, and over you appears his glory."

Imagine now, all is darkness, and you are suddenly in the spotlight of God with everyone covered as with clouds looking on you. They are looking on you now, remember, for guidance. Isaias continues: "Nations shall walk by your light, and kings by your shining radiance. Raise your eyes and look about; they all gather and come to you."

The spotlight, therefore, of God's grace, along with the responsibility and dignity and privilege of it, is on us.

The word *epiphany* actually means " to appear out of," just as we would if a spotlight were to shine on us. And our epiphany is exactly this: we stand out, we are on display and others look to us for guidance, direction, example for their lives. It is no wonder then that we are "on the spot." And rightly so, because God's grace illumines us not simply for ourselves, but for others, that others may see and follow and understand and come out of the darkness, led by God's light shining on us. "Nations shall walk by your light, and kings by your shining radiance."

THEOLOGICAL CONCLUSION

Indeed we are "on the spot"—on the spot of God's grace, God's love and God's light, and with the responsibility of using that place in God's light to guide and serve as an example for others.

JANUARY 6—EPIPHANY (A, B, C)
HOMILY II

Responsorial Psalm: *Lord, every nation on earth will adore you.*

O God, with your judgment endow the king, and with your justice, the king's son;
He shall govern your people with justice and your afflicted ones with judgment.

Lord, every nation on earth will adore you.

Justice shall flower in his days, and profound peace, till the moon be no more.
May he rule from sea to sea, and from the river to the ends of the earth.

Lord, every nation on earth will adore you.

The kings of Tarshish and the Isles shall offer gifts; the kings of Arabia and Seba shall bring tribute.
All kings shall pay him homage, all nations shall serve him.

Lord, every nation on earth will adore you.

For he shall rescue the poor man when he cries out, and the afflicted when he had no one to help him.
He shall have pity for the lowly and the poor; the lives of the poor he shall save.

Lord, every nation on earth will adore you.

(Ps. 72:1-2, 7-8, 10-11, 12-13. R. V. 11)

ANA-GNOSIS

One of the ideals we talk about a lot and bring up everywhere is *justice*. We would like to have justice for all peoples. If someone asks us, "What is justice? What do you mean by justice?", we might point to the statues on the courthouses of some of the County Seats—there's this lady with the blindfold over her eyes and the scales perfectly balanced. "Justice is blind," we say, meaning that it plays no favorites. It is fair to us all, rich and poor, powerful and weak, adults and children. There is no exception to justice.

So, in this sense, justice gives us one of the highest ideals of democracy—equal rights. Paralleling this, we must remind ourselves, we have equal duties. Unless we all have duties to other peoples' rights, they have no rights; and unless other people have duties to our rights, we really have no rights either. Justice, then, is really both a sense of our rights and a sense of our duties—fair and square, as we say.

The ancient idea of justice carries this out. Its Latin definition translates as "to each one his own." Even so simple a thing as my driveway, for example, can illustrate the rights-and-duties principle. The law supports my right to have open access to my driveway. It puts up a "no parking" sign. Other people have a duty to recognize my entrance or exit. If anyone parks his car or truck there, I've lost my right. We can carry this principle to the privacy of our homes, to the sanctity of our persons, to our right to freedom from attack, or our right to a good reputation. All these are our rights. Paralleling them, we remember, are our duties. We cannot have one without the other. If I have a right to access to my driveway, then everyone has a duty to recognize that right even when there's no sign there. And I have equal duties toward every other driveway in every city in the world. In justice no one is above the law, not kings, not presidents. We all have rights and we all have duties.

THEOLOGICAL EXTENSION

Rightly, this justice is our ideal; the Psalms hold it up for us. We cannot have peace, of course, unless justice first endures. "Justice shall flower in his days, and profound peace, till the moon be no more." So the ideal to come to realistic fruition—whether we have a king or a president to make and carry out the laws—should be guided by justice. We should pray, as the Prayer of the Psalmist suggests, "O God, with your judgment endow the king, and with your justice, so they shall govern your people and your afflicted ones with judgment," This will bring us peace.

Without such justice, each giving and receiving what is his own, love cannot flourish nor can peace. Constant battles, people violating one another's rights, can give no peace. If I am constantly using other people for myself and they are continually using me for themselves, there's no place for peace or love. These flow from a state of justice where each one is given his own meaning, his own distinction, his own identity, and his own rights, fair and square.

THEOLOGICAL CONCLUSION

From justice, then, peace can follow. And from this, too, if we choose, love can follow. Once I have given you your proper place and your rights, I can choose to love you. Before I do that I may call it love, but I am just using you for my own ends. Justice is basic to peace and love. Se we indeed must pray for all those who have the responsibility of creating and carrying out laws to establish a just society: "O God, with your judgment endow the king, and with your justice, so they may govern with justice and with judgment."

JANUARY 6—EPIPHANY (A, B, C)
HOMILY III

Reading II: *I am sure you have heard of the ministry which God in his goodness gave me in your regard. God's secret plan, as I have briefly described it, was revealed to me, unknown to men in former ages but now revealed by the Spirit of the holy apostles and prophets. It is no less than this: in Christ Jesus the Gentiles are now co-heirs with the Jews, members of the same body and sharers of the promise through the preaching of the Gospel.* (Eph. 3:2-6)

ANA-GNOSIS

The notion of a secret is always exciting. The easiest way to get a child excited is to talk about a secret. "I've got a secret for you," we say, and we see his eyes light up, and he's intrigued and hopes to find out our secret. Hiding things in secret places, playing games that involve secrets, all readily bring to our minds the excitement we knew as small children when we discovered a secret,

THEOLOGICAL EXTENSION

St. Paul today is talking about this kind of exciting secret or mystery. He says, "God's secret plan, as I have briefly described it, was revealed to me, unknown to men in former ages."

The core of St. Paul's ministry is that, like an attorney, he is now trustee of and must carry out God's secret plan. Just as we often make attorneys and other people trustees in wills, God designates Paul as the revealer of his secret plan.

Fittingly, then, this text is given today because the Greek word *epiphany*, which is the feast we are celebrating, while it reminds us also of the coming of the Magi and then the revelation to the Gentiles of the Messiah, also simply means "bringing forth into the open something that might have been secret." So Paul now has his epiphany when he brings to us his special ministry, his special trusteeship, as an apostle of God. His mission, we know, was to announce that we, the Gentiles, in fact the whole human race, are the chosen ones of God. This is God's special secret plan, revealed through Paul: "It is no less than this: in Christ Jesus the Gentiles are now co-heirs with the Jews."

From Paul's time, then, the carrying out of this mission has caused Christianity to be extended all over the world. We see it now long since separated from the original idea that it came from the Jews. One might even propose that in the breadth of this mission we've forgotten and must came back to a very basic point that Paul stresses here. It is obvious of course, but now it is turned upside down because at the time of Paul Christianity clearly was made up almost entirely of Jews. His revelation or surprise, his secret, was that it was also to extend to the Gentiles. We might propose now a reverse surprise, a reverse secret plan recalling that it also extends to the Jews. In the mystery of God's grace and God's plan we must never forget how basic the Jewish people, all their customs and religious practices, are to Christianity. They are "members of the same body and sharers of the promise through the preaching of the gospel." We cannot ever rule out the Jews from this very basic position in our Christian destiny and purpose and meaning.

We must let God's destiny unfold for them. But we must never forget their essential role and let ourselves be tempted to any kind of anti-semitism. That would be attacking ourselves. We are, after all, co-heirs in God's plan.

THEOLOGICAL CONCLUSION

So now, two thousand years after Paul's letter we need to look again at God's secret plan and to realize that while Christianity was opened up to the Gentiles then, we must not forget the other half of the secret: that the Jews were very basic to Christianity because they, too, were co-heirs with Christ, members of the same body, and sharers of the promise through the preaching of the gospel.

This is the epiphany that is revealed, the unfolding of the secret. It should remind us how basic to all our Christian beliefs and practices are those inherited traditions from the Jewish people whom God loved in a very special way and made the source of the coming of the Messiah for all of us.

JANUARY 6—EPIPHANY (A, B, C)
HOMILY IV

Gospel Reading: *After Jesus' birth in Bethlehem of Judea during the reign of King Herod, astrologers from the east arrived one day in Jerusalem inquiring "Where is the newborn king of the Jews? We observed his star at its rising and have come to pay homage." At this news King Herod became greatly disturbed, and with him all Jerusalem. Summoning all the chief priests and scribes of the people, he inquired of them where the Messiah was to be born. In Bethlehem of Judea," they informed him. "Here is what the prophet has written:*

> *'And you, Bethlehem, land of Judah, are by no means least among the princes of Judah, since from you shall come a ruler who is to shepherd my people Israel.' "*

Herod called the astrologers aside and found out from them the exact time of the star's appearance. Then he sent them to Bethlehem, after having instructed them: "Go and get detailed information about the child. When you have discovered something, report your findings to me so that I may go and offer him homage too."

After their audience with the king, they set out. The star which they had observed at its rising went ahead of them until it came to a standstill over the place where the child was. They were overjoyed at seeing the star, and on entering the house, found the child with Mary his mother. They prostrated themselves and did him homage. Then they opened their coffers and presented him with gifts of gold, frankincense, and myrrh.

They received a message in a dream not to return to Herod, so they went back to their own country by another route. (Mt. 2:1-12)

ANA-GNOSIS

We have many different definitions of human nature. We may speak of a man as a "rational animal" and use the degree of his ability to reason to show the human person to be vastly above other animals of the universe. But when we look further at the history of the human race we could also define man as a "contradictory animal." Nothing so marks a person's performance, action, and history as strange, often confusing, contradictions.

One of these is ambition or power. We know that all of us have an urge to find some special meaning and value, success, or achievement, and we have a strong motivation to work for it. As a rule, unless we've been disgraced or depressed or turned away from success and achievement, we work hard for some kind of meaning and purpose. Sometimes people work unbelievably hard for positions of eminence: they amaze us with their dedication and constant struggle through many years to arrive at some special distinction. But the contradiction is that once they've arrived, no matter how simple or how eminent their position, then they are afraid they are going to lose it. They're in a constant state of anxiety worrying how they can keep it. So people who have worked hard to gain money are often worried that they might lose it. The same occurs with jobs or any kind of security we obtain. The minute we have something, we fear that someone else will come along and take our place.

THEOLOGICAL EXTENSION

We see this strikingly emphasized in the picture of Herod. He hears a rumor, and the astrologers corroberate that a special child has been born, a possible king, a possible Messiah of some royal line. He doesn't clearly understand it, but it's enough to make him feel threatened and afraid. As secure as we might think that Herod would be in his position, we know in fact that he is almost panicked, that whoever this royal child is, he will threaten Herod's position. We know this fear reaches such a peak that he gives orders to destroy all the newborn infants in order to make sure he's got the one who might be of the royal line that would threaten him. Joseph, of course, is guided to escape this murderous act of Herod, and the Christ-child is thus saved.

But throughout the history of kings and other people in power this is not an isolated incident. Relatives, even children sometimes, are often sacrificed to the jealousy, fear and anxiety of a king or ambitious person and are slaughtered, put in prison or exiled because of the fear that they might take someone's place in power or eminence.

We need to look at this in ourselves too, because it is there. It doesn't, perhaps, have the far-reaching consequences of the fears of ambitious kings or presidents, but it is there—resentment of others. In our own families or among the people with whom we work or go to school. All these resentments are examples of the same Herod-like fear and self-centeredness that we read about in Matthew's gospel today.

THEOLOGICAL CONCLUSION

We have to look at this carefully lest we cheat and destroy ourselves. The cure for this type of behavior is always a very simple one: we must put our lives in God's hands. We must leave it to God finally to determine what we do and what our final destiny is. We should do our best to develop our one talent or our five, if that's what we have, but only according to God's plan. And we must leave it to God's plan when it is eventually time to divest ourselves from what we have invested in. By refusing to be totally self-seeking we can avoid the tragedy of Herod and the anxiety, contradiction and even the dangers that any kind of position or achievement, even a very small one, can lead us to.

SUNDAY AFTER JANUARY 6—BAPTISM OF OUR LORD
HOMILY I

Reading I: *Here is my servant whom I uphold, my chosen one with whom I am pleased; upon whom I have put my spirit; he shall bring forth justice to the nations. Not crying out, not shouting, not making his voice heard in the street. A bruised reed he shall not break, and a smouldering wick he shall not quench, until he establishes justice on the earth; the coastlands will wait for his teaching.*

I, the Lord, have called you for the victory of justice, I have grasped you by the hand; I formed you, and set you as a covenant of the people, a light for the nations, to open the eyes of the blind, to bring out prisoners from confinement, and from the dungeon, those who live in darkness. (Is. 42:1-7)

ANA-GNOSIS

All of us have dark, depressed moods, and when we're in this discouraged state we can sometimes raise very basic questions about life. We might conceivably say, "What can I really believe in? What is there to hope for?" Now, it is true that we're often down pretty low when we raise questions like this, but they do come at the bleaker moments of our lives.

There are no easy or simple answers to such basic questions. Fundamentally faith is our risk, our trust, our commitment of ourselves to something unseen but hoped for, as St. Paul describes it. It is not a totally convincing argument, but it convinces us enough that we make the act of trust and hope in what we believe in.

THEOLOGICAL EXTENSION

Isaias today in his description of the servant of God. whom we now know to be Christ, shows us vividly the object and purpose of our faith and hope. He presents what the people before the time of Christ were looking forward to: " . . . my servant whom I uphold, my chosen one with whom I am pleased." And this is the one to come to us.

This servant is described as a "covenant of the people, a light for the nations." Therefore, in our dark moods, when we're in a dungeon of discouragement and despair, it is this messianic servant—Jesus Christ—who can bring us out to the light.

But we must believe in this. A covenant has two sides. God sent Christ to us as his side of the covenant. We must believe and hope and give ourselves to that person God sent in order for the covenant to be complete.

Speaking to this person, Christ, the Messiah, God says, "I, the Lord, have called you for the victory of justice, I have grasped you by the hand; I formed you, and set you as a covenant of the people, a light for the nations, to open the eyes of the blind, to bring prisoners from confinement, and from the dungeon, those who live in darkness."

Now we all live in darkness; at some time or other we are all prisoners of ourselves, confined to the dungeons of our own depressions and unhappiness. Christ comes as the light to lead us out of that discouragement, despair and loss of hope. He is the Christ whom we believe in.

But it is a covenant relationship. God has done his part, as Isaias prophesized; he sent Christ the Messiah to become one of us. But just as God did his part of the covenant, we must do ours. We must believe, we must commit ourselves, we must hope. Only then can we be led out of the dungeon of darkness and discouragement of ourselves.

THEOLOGICAL CONCLUSION

What can I really believe in? The answer is: Christ, the Son of God who Isaias foretells is the chosen servant of God for us. "Here is my servant, whom I uphold, my chosen one with whom I am pleased, upon whom I have put my spirit. He shall bring forth justice to the nations . . . A light for the nation to open the eyes of the blind, to bring . . . from the dungeon those who live in darkness." God has committed his Son to us. By our belief, our trust and our hope in his son we will fulfill our side of the divine covenant.

SUNDAY AFTER JANUARY 6—BAPTISM OF OUR LORD HOMILY II

Responsorial Psalm: *The Lord will bless his people with peace*

Give to the Lord, you sons of God, give to the Lord glory and praise,
Give to the Lord the glory due his name; adore the Lord in holy attire.

The Lord will bless his people with peace.

The voice of the Lord is over the waters, the Lord, over vast waters.
The voice of the Lord is mighty; the voice of the Lord is majestic.

The Lord will bless his people with peace.

The God of glory thunders, and in his temple all say, "Glory!"
The Lord is enthroned above the flood; the Lord is enthroned king forever.

The Lord will bless his people with peace.

(Ps. 29:1-2, 314, 9-10 R. V. 11)

ANA-GNOSIS

Nature never ceases to impress us with its beauty, its delicacy, its motion, and sometimes its awesome might. Perhaps, on the sea, more than anywhere else, we witness the vast power of nature. The sea is open, there are no hills, ridges or trees to impede our view. The sky and clouds are clearest there. This is why a storm at sea, an enormous, overwhelming thunderstorm with lightning and reverberating crashes, never ceases to be majestic and profound.

THEOLOGICAL EXTENSION

Sometimes when we lose sight of the greatness of God we need something simple, yet at the same time fundamental, like a terrible storm over water, to catch us up short and make us recognize the unbelievable power of God.

The most extensive hydrogen explosion that man is capable of making releases hardly more energy than a small storm. So if this is true, we must consider the energy of an enormous storm sweeping over the vastness of the ocean. How powerful God is compared to the most powerful thing that man has invented!

The Psalmist writes in this mood today, hoping to impress us with the power of God. He says, "The voice of the Lord is over the waters, the Lord, over vast waters." We can hear the thunder as it sweeps over the sea, the water carrying the sound to our ears. "The voice of the Lord is mighty, the voice of the Lord is majestic. The God of Glory thunders, and in his temple all say 'Glory!' "

When we are watching a storm, particularly at sea or by a lake where we can see and hear the enormous power of it, we might do well to recall the words of the Psalmist and respond in our hearts, "Glory! Glory to God! How magnificent."

It is not God that needs our glory. Rather we need to remind ourselves how glorious God is. We need to remind ourselves how magnificent, how overwhelming God is. If a storm over waters can recall this for us, then it is wise to meditate upon it.

THEOLOGICAL CONCLUSION

The next time we see a storm then, particularly if we are able to view it at sea or in some place which gives us a broad view of its overwhelming power, let us use it as a source for a meditation. And let us recall, as the Psalmist reminds us here, the magnificence, the glory, the awesome power, the splendor and the might of God.

SUNDAY AFTER JANUARY 6—BAPTISM OF OUR LORD HOMILY III

Reading II: *Peter addressed Cornelius and the people assembled at his house in these words, "I begin to see how true it is that God shows no partiality. Rather the man of any nation who fears God and acts uprightly is acceptable to him. This is the message he has sent to the sons of Israel, the good news of peace proclaimed through Jesus Christ who is Lord of all. I take it you know what has been reported all over Judea about Jesus of Nazareth, begin-*

ning in Galilee with the baptism John preached; of the way God anointed him with the Holy Spirit and power. He went about doing good works and healing all who were in the grip of the devil, and God was with him." (Acts 10:34-38)

ANA-GNOSIS

We sometimes speak of diplomacy as the art of compromise. It is also called the art of the possible. Political actions in general are ways by which disagreeing points of view or attitudes or controversial issues are resolved by people trying to see both sides, each one giving in. So it becomes not the ideal or perfect solution but a compromise, what is possible to work out.

THEOLOGICAL EXTENSION

At the time of the apostles, the time of Peter here, like most periods, there was some racism. It was not so much black and white, but Jew and Gentile. Contrary to the anti-Semitism we think of today when the Jewish person is often misinterpreted and misunderstood, the predominant mood then was one of rejection and misinterpretation of the Gentiles. In the very early Church most all Christians were Jews, and we think of Paul as the apostle of the Gentiles, the one who made clear that the Church was universal and not an extension of the Jewish religion and the Jewish people alone. We overlook the fact that Peter, too, took this same stand when later he became involved in a controversy with Paul because he was being diplomatic and trying to appease the Jewish Christian whose sensitivities and background and difficulties he understood and was sympathetic with. This has tended to make us think that Peter did not actually hold the notion of the universal church. Lest we have that idea, we must look carefully to see that, on the contrary, he did. Luke attributes to him here the honor of being the first to convert a Gentile, and conceivably the people at his house, many of whom were also likely to have been Gentiles.

Peter says, according to Luke, "I begin to see how true it is that God shows no partiality. Rather the man of any nation who fears God and acts uprightly is acceptable to him." He makes no compromise here. There is no doubt that Peter is saying that a person of any nation, of any race, is acceptable to God now through the redemption of Christ.

So even though the later controversy between Paul and Peter is very evident and Paul makes a strong record of it, we must not overlook the way that Peter, too, stood for the universality of the Church. If he was cautious later, and this is what Paul challenged him about, it was the caution of diplomacy, of kindness, of compromise. He wanted to make this universal message as painless as he could for the Jewish Christians who, caught up as they were in the confusion of the Old Testament fusing into the New, did not quite see the universal Church as clearly as Peter saw it, while talking to Cornelius. In hindsight, of course, it is very obvious that Christianity was to spread beyond Judaism to the whole world and embrace all peoples. But at the time this was no easy thing for the Jewish Christians to see, and if Peter seemed anxious later not to hurt them excessively, it in no way means he misunderstood the doctrine of the universality of the Church. He has stated it most clearly here, and he was directly responsible for the conversion of Cornelius and possibly others.

THEOLOGICAL CONCLUSION

The issue therefore is not Peter's failure to understand the universality of the Church, but his desire to practice diplomacy, to be cautious, and careful not to hurt others and be unkind. While we understand today the extent of the mission of the Church, we would do well to share Peter's cautious sensitivity to other people.

SUNDAY AFTER JANUARY 6—BAPTISM OF OUR LORD
HOMILY IV

Gospel Reading: *Jesus, coming from Galilee, appeared before John at the Jordan to be baptized by him. John tried to refuse him with the protest, "I should be baptized by you, yet you come to me!" Jesus answered, "Give in for now. We must do this if we would fulfill all God's commands." So John gave in. After Jesus was baptized, he came directly out of the water. Suddenly the sky opened and he saw the Spirit of God descend like a dove and hover over him. With that, a voice from the heavens said, "This is my beloved Son. My favor rests on him."* (Mt. 3:13-17)

ANA-GNOSIS

It is an understandable psychological need when we are guilty and feel sinful to want to wash. It is a way of getting rid of something, not only sin but also responsibility for something. We have the phrase, "I wash my hands of it," taken possibly from Pilate; but for Pilate himself, handwashing was a well-known symbol of the time. Any kind of ceremonial washing has the tone of removing us from a sense of sinfulness.

THEOLOGICAL EXTENSION

This kind of washing or baptism was familiar and practiced by many different leaders, prophets and spokesmen before the time of John. And John preaches this same kind of washing to remove sinfulness. In another reading from Matthew John says, "I baptize you with water for repentence, but he who is coming after me is mightier than I, whose sandals I am not worthy to carry. He will baptize you with the Holy Spirit."

John has no illusions. He knows that his baptism is simply a symbol of forgiveness of sin or sorrow for sin and assumes God's forgiveness if one is genuinely sorry. He also sees clearly that the baptism of Christ is a totally different kind, representing the coming of the Holy Spirit. It is easy then to appreciate his confusion when Christ asks to be baptized. John argues with Christ because, as he rightly maintains, it is he who would receive Christ's baptism of the Holy Spirit. But our Lord has his own intent here: basically to show that he genuinely follows the practices of the Jewish people, and he wants to give us an example. There cannot be any need for repentence in Christ's case. No doubt this, too, is part of John's confusion. But Christ submits to this baptism because he wants to be an example for us in all things. This seems to be the only way to understand it. We should not confuse it, however, with the genuine baptism of Christ himself when he commissions the apostles to baptize, which is the Sacrament that brings the Holy Spirit to us.

Our baptism does take away sin. Its cleansing power restores us to the unity of God through Christ that the human race had lost. It is an outward sign which has the God-given power to make us new internally and through which we will come to the other Sacraments, further signs of God's grace.

THEOLOGICAL CONCLUSION

Christ wants us to understand the importance of extrinsic ceremony for conveying and confirming us in the sacramental life of his Church, so he submits to what may be just an external ceremony. But it is part of his teaching mission as the Messiah, and so he argues with John, and John obediently baptizes him. We have then this example of the humility of Christ to teach us the meaning of the Sacrament of Baptism, so that we will consent to this ceremonial washing and receive the abundance of God's grace awaiting us.

INDEX

Acceptance
—of Christ, 77
Achievement, 23, 24
Advertisement, 2
Ahaz, 26-27
Ambition, 86
Anxiety, 19
—freedom from, 74
—of Ahaz, 27
Architect, 48
Astrologers, 86
Augustine, 60

Baptism, 17, 94
Bar
—of a door, 73
Belloc, H., 64
Belonging, 41
Beyond, the, 34
Breathing, 9
Busincss
commercial, 1

Change, 28
Children
—education of, 57
Choice, 78
Christ
—completion in, 49
—image of, 17
—meaning of, 25
—mission of, 35
—relationship to, 77
Christmas
—universality of, 38
Church
—universality of, 93
Comedian, 34
Compromise, 92
Confidence, 31
—in prayer, 27
Confusion, 48
Conscience
—guilty, 28
Consideration, 64
Contradiction, 51, 85-86
Conundrum, 51
Corn, 75
Counsel, 10
Courage, 15, 23
Covenant, 76, 89
—with God, 17
Crutch, 19

Darkness, 4-5
Death
—preparation for, 7
Dedication, 24
—Christian, 13
Despair, 43-44
Destruction, 43
Dignity
—of Joseph, 31
Diplomacy, 92
Discipline, 58ff.
Discouragement, 21
Dreams, 61
Duty, 81

Edifice
—of Redemption, 49
Education, 57
Efficiency
—mechanical, 22

Encouragement, 14
Epiphany, 80
Escapism, 26
Eucharist, 17
Experience, 26
Exultation,
—of Christmas, 39

Faith, 6
—lack of, 26-27
Fettish, 16
Forgiveness, 29, 59
Freedom, 69, 76, 77

Gifts
—of the Holy Spirit, 10
God, 21
—as architect, 48
—in nature, 23
—wearying of, 27
Grace, 38, 57
Graciousness, 64-65
Guilt, 28, 34, 94

Hammurabi, 12
Happiness, 20, 41
Harvest, 56
Herod, 62, 86
Holy Spirit, 10
Home, 40
Hope, 14-15, 23, 44
—object of, 89
Humility, 26

Image
—of a garden, 56-57
—of Joseph, 63
Indifference, 19
Indwelling
—of God, 11

Jealousy, 86
Jesse, 10
John the Baptist, 17, 24, 94
Joseph, 31, 62
Joy, 20, 33, 36, 44
Justice, 11, 81

King, 12
Kosmos, 59

Language, 26
Law, 68, 82
Leader, 12
Learner, 59
Life, 21, 22
—Breath of, 10
—meaning of, 80
—mode of, 12
—reform of, 17
—spiritual, 6
—wisdom of, 22
Light, 80
—children of, 5
Lock, 73
Love, 41, 78
—of others, 38

Machines, 22
Mary, 70
Marx, G., 33
Medicine
—modern, 53
Message
—of Christmas, 38
—of God, 2
—of John the Baptist, 25
Messiah, 25, 35
Mission
—of Christ, 35
—of St. Paul, 84
Mystery, 46, 51, 83

Narrowness
—of life, 21
Nature, 23, 36, 56, 90
—human, 85
Newman, John Cardinal, 2

Old age, 53

Parents, 56-57
Parish, 40ff.
Patience, 14-15, 23
Peace, 3, 10, 11ff., 74
—external, 36
—in the home, 59
Pharisees, 16-17
Plan, 47-49
—of God, 83
Planting
—image of, 56

Pleasure, 33-34
Poverty, 5
Power, 86
—of God, 91
Prayer, 27
Predestination, 75ff.
Preparation, 7, 25

Racism, 92
Reassurance
—false, 16
Redemption, 48
Reform, 17
Relationship
—to God, 16
—to others, 16
Religion, 33-34, 38
Responsibility, 7, 39, 68, 76
Riddle, 50
Rights, 81
Ritual, 16

Sacraments, 16-17
St. Paul, 30
Salvation, 38
Scapegoat, 58
Secrets, 83
Security, 2, 74
Self-attack, 28
Self-deception, 17
Self-worth, 14
Shame, 28
Sign, 26
Sinfulness, 94
Song, 46
Spiritus, 10
Spotlight, 80
Stranger, 40-41
Suffering, 21

Trust, 31
—lack of, 26-27

Unity, 11
Universality
—of Christmas, 38

Values
—Christian, 41
Vision, 41
Vocation, 24
Voice
—of God, 62

Wakefulness, 7
Way, 66ff.
Weakness, 19
Will
—of God, 62
Wisdom
—of life, 22
World
—identity with, 41

Yearning
—for peace, 11-12

SECOND SERIES

Volume III-2

THE WORD BECOMES FLESH

A Psychodynamic Approach to Homiletics and Catechetics and Meditation

Homilies for the Second Sunday of the Year through the Eighth Sunday of the Year and Homilies for Lent

(Series A)

CHARLES A. CURRAN
Loyola University
Chicago, Illinois

APPLE RIVER PRESS
P.O. Box 3867
Apple River, Illinois 61001

NIHIL OBSTAT:

Reverend Thomas G. Doran
Censor Deputatus

IMPRIMATUR:

✠ Arthur J. O'Neill
Bishop of Rockford

January 1978

Printed in the United States of America

CONTENTS

Preface v

SECOND SUNDAY OF THE YEAR 1
Homily I 1
Homily II 2
Homily III 4
Homily IV 5

THIRD SUNDAY OF THE YEAR 8
Homily I 8
Homily II 9
Homily III 11
Homily IV 13

FOURTH SUNDAY OF THE YEAR 15
Homily I 15
Homily II 16
Homily III 18
Homily IV 20

FIFTH SUNDAY OF THE YEAR 22
Homily I 22
Homily II 24
Homily III 26
Homily IV 28

FIRST SUNDAY OF LENT 31
Homily I 31
Homily II 33
Homily III 34
Homily IV 36

SECOND SUNDAY OF LENT 39
Homily I 39
Homily II 41
Homily III 42
Homily IV 44

THIRD SUNDAY OF LENT 46
Homily I 46
Homily II 48
Homily III 50
Homily IV 52

FOURTH SUNDAY OF LENT 54
Homily I 54
Homily II 56
Homily III 57
Homily IV 58

FIFTH SUNDAY OF LENT 61
Homily I 61
Homily II 62
Homily III 64
Homily IV 65

SIXTH SUNDAY OF THE YEAR 68
Homily I 68
Homily II 69
Homily III 71
Homily IV 73

SEVENTH SUNDAY OF THE YEAR 74
Homily I 74
Homily II 76
Homily III 77
Homily IV 79

EIGHTH SUNDAY OF THE YEAR 82
Homily I 82
Homily II 84
Homily III 85
Homily IV 87

Index 91

*See: "The Word Becomes Flesh: Lent and Easter," Vol. XIII and/or Vol XIII-2, for the Homilies of Passion Sunday, Holy Thursday, Easter Vigil, and Easter Sunday, and for Homilies of the Personages of the Crucifixion.

PREFACE

In the following homiletic and catechetical expositions, there are at least *four* for each Sunday and feast. Each one begins with an "ana-gnosis." This is not an ana-logos. That is, it is not intended to be an analogy or simply an example. We have called them "ana-gnoses" rather than analogies, because they are aimed at involving the reader or hearer personally at the level of his own *gnosis* about himself.

Analogy, in the *logos* sense, is too intellectual and remote for what we mean here. The hope is that each person will begin to commit himself and so be talking to himself while he hears or reads. He will thus hopefully be creatively reacting and so giving a homily to himself at the level of his own personal memory and experience.

These presentations are not intended to be all-inclusive. They are only *one form* of communicating the scriptural message. Hopefully their advanced reading may stimulate the reader not simply to memorize them—he or she may do this of course, and, we hope, profitably—but rather, as a result, to move on to his own personal witness and communication with his hearers. They are, therefore, intended basically to be personal stimulants and encouragements starting the reader or hearer on his own personal quest.

One will notice here that the *immediate human meaning* is most often seized upon—not some more complicated and subtle theological conclusion. This is not to deny the latter or its importance. It is rather to draw attention to the basic and rich human elements that are so often central to the scriptural message. The intent too is to initiate a process by which the hearer, or the reader, is allowed to enter into the presentation through its immediate human meaning.

To aid in this, the speaker should simply be himself, speaking in whatever way is most comfortable to him. His natural manner

would therefore usually be more often meditative than dramatic, more conversational than theatrical, allowing for the electronic apparatus to carry his words directly into the ear of the hearer—as in an intimate communication together.

These presentations are all *short;* some are very short. People often seek a short homily or catechetical presentation. But since they are short, further doctrinal and similar material may be added to them, as fits the occasion. Or, more than one may be given.

There is also the allowance for the possibility that later dialogue will extend and develop the embryonic concepts here. In this sense, what happens after words enter the ear is more important than before. This is the "germination" process; that is, seed once entered the soil and embraced by it, germinates and grows there. The entering may be quick—as the acorn enters quickly—but slowly and mysteriously over time, a great oak with powerful branches where birds abide and sing, can result. We have described elsewhere the group dynamic process that, we feel, could aid this.[1]

The model, therefore, is not the mathematics book: problem-solving which arrives at "answers." Our model is the familiar sower who goes out to sow seed. This is our inseminational aim and hope.

These themes are based on a personal approach to homiletics and catechetics, the psychological background of which is explained in detail in a separate volume: *THE WORD BECOMES FLESH: A Psychodynamic Approach to Homelitics and Catechetics* (Theory and Practice).

1. Curran, C. A. *Religious Values in Counseling and Psychotherapy.* New York: Sheed and Ward, Inc., 1969, pp. 231-248.

SECOND SUNDAY OF THE YEAR (SERIES A)
HOMILY I

Reading I: *The Lord said to me: You are my servant Israel, through whom I show my glory.*
Now the Lord has spoken who formed me as his servant from the womb, that Jacob may be brought back to him and Israel gathered to him; and I am made glorious in the sight of the Lord, and my God is now my strength! It is too little, he says, for you to be my servant, to raise up the tribes of Jacob, and restore the survivors of Israel; I will make you a light to the nations, that my salvation may reach to the ends of the earth. (Is. 49:3, 5-6)

ANA-GNOSIS

We've all known the experience at our birthday or some other special celebration in our honor, where, having received a number of presents, we felt that there were no more gifts. Then we sensed a kind of suspense, a secrecy in the air, and despite the wonderful presents we had received already, and despite the fact that we could think of nothing else that we really would like to have, we felt that there was something more to come. Then with a special smile, a person who loved us particularly said, "Now here's one more thing . . ." And from a pocket or hidden place something not quite as obvious as the other presents, but extremely wonderful all the same, is brought forward.

Spontaneously, almost before we can control ourselves, we say, "Oh that's *too* much!" But, of course, we are deeply grateful and deeply touched that we should mean so much to others that, even above the wonderful gifts they've already given us, they could think of this one more extraordinarily beautiful, fine, lovely present.

THEOLOGICAL EXTENSION

Now this is something of the love God has for us. It is conveyed today in the Reading. First God has given us, the chosen people of the Old Testament, the vocation to be his specially chosen ones and bring to ourselves and others the very special meaning of God in our lives. And so, from Isaiah we have, "It is too little for you to be my servant, to raise up the tribes of Jacob, and restore the survivors of Israel." Even this marvelous vocation, in which Isaiah says, "I'm made glorious in the sight of the Lord and my God is now my strength," is not sufficient. Like the gift that is so special and held back, God wants to give us more. He wants to give us some final thing so that we can almost shout in spontaneous gratitude "Oh, God, that's *too* much!" He goes on, then, to say that he has done too little, that he "will make you a light to the nations, that my salvation will reach to the ends of the earth."

This designates in a special way our vocation in relationship to the vocation of the Jewish people. Their vocation was to bring salvation history to the point of Christ, to prepare the way and make it ready; and our vocation now is to take it and make it living and meaningful to the whole world. Stated another way, our vocation is to show the fullness of God's love for all of us—all his people—so that we are not simply his chosen ones, his special servants to carry his message to the world. But in a very particular way we should radiate divine love and divine light to the world.

THEOLOGICAL CONCLUSION

These images, analogies and poetic descriptions all carry behind them great meaning. Essentially they convey the meaning of God's abundant love, his inexpressibly great love for us in giving us all that we could possibly desire in our divine vocation and then giving us that much more, so much that we are shouting out "Oh, God, it is *too* much." "No," says God to us in the words of Isaiah, "It's too little." Divine love is truly overwhelming.

SECOND SUNDAY OF THE YEAR (SERIES A)
HOMILY II

Responsorial Psalm: *Here am I, Lord; I come to do your will.*
I have waited, waited for the Lord, and he stooped toward me,

and heard my cry. And he put a new song in my mouth, a hymn to our God. (Ps. 40:2, 4, 7-8, 8-9)

ANA-GNOSIS

We all know the experience of waiting and waiting. Buses can be late, trains can be late, airplane flights can be cancelled or late. We've all waited in bus stations, train stations and airports, and been disappointed when the announcement comes that the arrival we are anticipating is late. Sometimes, because of complicated travel arrangements we don't even know when a person we are waiting for is coming, but we go out anyway and wait so that we might be there when he does come. And we've all waited for a telephone call or a letter, or sometimes a visit, anticipating the moment that our friend will come around the bend or will turn in to the driveway.

Almost in proportion to the degree we've waited and longed for, even our disappointment when the plane didn't come on time or whatever, there is the intense joy—sort of a "new song" inside us—when we see the face of the one we've waited for so long. We experience an excitement, sometimes almost ecstasy of that first moment of greeting, of joy and fulfillment when at last they have come.

THEOLOGICAL EXTENSION

The Psalmist wants us to catch this feeling with regard to our prayers, with regard to God. Just as in Advent we awaited the promised One from God, so now we experience the joy of fulfillment. So the Psalmist says, "I have waited, waited for the Lord, and he stooped towards me, and heard my cry. And he put a new song into my mouth, a hymn to our God."

Prayers are often occasions for waiting. We wait and wait and wait. Life, in all sorts of ways, is a waiting. We spend much time waiting—waiting for the thing to happen that we've worked so hard for, that we've looked forward to for so long, that we've yearned for. Then in proportion to how much we yearn and wait and long, there are those wonderful moments or periods when the waiting is fulfilled. Literally we experience this joy like a new song—like the melody that hits our ear, captures our tongue and rings in our mind and our memory. "We can't get it out of our heads," we say. We hear the joy of that new song when our waiting has been fulfilled.

THEOLOGICAL CONCLUSION

We wait for God. In prayer many times we wait for God's answer. It does come. And when it comes, our heart is filled with the joy of a new song. God has arrived, is with us always in love, and now openly has answered our prayers. The Advent period is over, Christmas is here, and we continue to experience it all year round.

SECOND SUNDAY OF THE YEAR (SERIES A) HOMILY III

Reading II: *Paul, called by God's will to be an apostle of Christ Jesus, and Sosthenes our brother, send greetings to the church of God which is in Corinth; to you who have been consecrated in Christ Jesus and called to be a holy people, as to all those who, wherever they may be, call on the name of our Lord Jesus Christ, their Lord and ours. Grace and peace from God our Father and the Lord Jesus Christ.* (1 Cor. 1:1-3)

ANA-GNOSIS

There's a point when something is finished. If it's a machine being repaired or put together, those responsible relax, look at one another and say, "Well, all the pieces fit. It works as it should." If it's an article, a term paper or book, the writer stands back and says, "Well, it's done: all the chapters fit; the ideas have come together." In almost anything there exists this potential for integrity—of things all fitting together, of each part, each person or each idea inter-relating and meshing, doing what it should for itself and others.

At the end of a life, too, we get this same feeling. As we think back over this person's life, sometimes at a funeral or a wake, sometimes months or years afterwards, we recognize a special kind of integrity. All the pieces of their life fit together. Sometimes we say, "It all made sense."

THEOLOGICAL EXTENSION

Today St. Paul uses the word *holy*. He describes us as "you who have been consecrated in Christ Jesus and called to be a holy people." We must realize that *holy* is related to the word "whole" —wholeness or integrity. Holiness is not simply being on one's knees or being pious, or even rather obviously going to church. These things can be deceiving, hypocritical. True holiness is wholeness—it's having all the parts of our lives fit together. What we do for ourselves, what we do for others, what we do for God all makes one piece, all fits.

This is our vocation. This is what being holy is. We see clearly what our goals, our purposes are, what meaning is especially significant for ourselves in our unique vocation from the hand of God, and then discern how this relates to our responsibilities, our love, our genuineness in our relationships with others, and how both of these—love of ourself and love of others—fuse into our love and service of God. This is being holy, and this is finding the holy vocation that St. Paul tells us we are consecrated to. Further, St. Paul reminds us that all who, anywhere in the world, seek God in some way, are seeking Christ. They, too, have this vocation, but we in particular must bring them to the unknown God and unknown Christ they are seeking. We must make this known to them through ourselves and our lives. And to accomplish this we must be holy people. Our lives, in order to be the light that Isaiah said that God has made us, must bear the scrutiny of those seeking the Lord. We must be integrated, we must be holy and whole. Our lives must "make sense."

THEOLOGICAL CONCLUSION

This is our vocation—to have integrity in our lives, each in a unique way. Your life is different from the person beside you. My life is different from yours. Each of us has our own special holiness, and each must find it in the quietness of prayer, thought and meditation. Then, we are assured of God's light and our own holiness. That's the vocation we are consecrated to.

SECOND SUNDAY OF THE YEAR (SERIES A)
HOMILY IV

Gospel Reading: *When John caught sight of Jesus coming toward him, he exclaimed . . . "I saw the Spirit descend like a dove from the* *sky, and it came to rest on him. But, as I say, I did not recognize him. The one who sent me to baptize with water told me, 'When you see the Spirit descend and rest on someone, it is he who is to baptize with the Holy Spirit.' Now I have seen for myself and have testified, 'this is God's chosen One.'"* (Jn. 1:29-34)

ANA-GNOSIS

We spend much of our lives seeking, searching, longing for, trying to find. The Advent season symbolizes this longing and waiting. Christmas recalls those great moments when we find, when we reach what it is we're seeking, when we find that person we've been longing for, or that position or home we've been seeking. Joy is always described as "finding something."

Even the childhood game of hide-and-seek recalls some of the thrill we find in seeking, searching, waiting and finally finding what we're looking for.

THEOLOGICAL EXTENSION

Today's Reading about St. John the Baptist evokes this mood. John the Baptist represents so much the seeking and longing in our lives, sometimes for something right under our nose that we do not recognize. "But as I say, I did not recognize him," he says. Then he has the joy of finding him. Advent is over; Christmas has come and the fulfillment of John's search is present to him and to us all.

"The one who sent me to baptize with water told me, 'When you see the Spirit descend and rest on someone, it is he who is to baptize with the Holy Spirit.'" This is how he was to recognize the one he was to announce, to herald, and to whom he was to turn over his disciples. When he found that one he had a great sense of joy. He says, "Now I have seen for myself and have testified: 'This is God's chosen One.'"

This, in a sense, is the story of our lives too. St. John the Baptist, like all of us, sought someone. And at last, fulfilling his mission, he found his Lord. We know, too, that behind all the other things we seek, all the people we love, all the positions we desire, all the security we look for, there is one person. We have found him. He is Christ, the chosen One. Christmas comes to our lives not just on the 25th of December, but whenever we recognize, as John the Baptist did, that we have found the Chosen One, and we turn ourselves and all those who love us and who might be called our disciples, over to him. John the Baptist did this when he had found the one he sought. So now do we.

THEOLOGICAL CONCLUSION

"Now I have seen for myself and have testified: This is God's chosen One." We can, indeed, say that too. And we, too, give over all that we are and all that we seek to this One behind all longings and all seekings: the Chosen One who is Christ, the Christmas every day of our lives.

THIRD SUNDAY OF THE YEAR (SERIES A)
HOMILY I

Reading I: *Anguish has taken wing; dispelled is darkness. For there is no gloom where but now there was distress. The people who walked in darkness have seen a great light. Upon those who dwelt in the land of gloom, a light has shone.* (Is. 8:23, 9:3)

ANA-GNOSIS

It is often startling to come upon a bird hidden in a bush or a leafy tree, and see it take wing suddenly in front of us. The noise, almost like the muffled sound of a bullet, and the quick movement of the bird, take us by surprise. It is a quick and sudden action.

THEOLOGICAL EXTENSION

This image of a bird suddenly taking flight reminds us of the image used by Isaias in today's Reading for describing how sorrow can leave us. "Anguish," he says, "has taken wing; dispelled is darkness." In something of the same way that a bird takes to flight, a light in a room suddenly disperses darkness. It is the suddenness of the change that grasps our attention. If we have been in a dark room for a while, we know how shocking a sudden light can be, until our eyes become accustomed to it.

It is consoling, therefore, to realize that sorrow often takes flight in much the same way. As light causes darkness to leave the room, or as a bird suddenly flies out of a bush or tree, sorrow too can quickly be dispelled. When we are in a state of sorrow, it seems interminable; sometimes night seems never to end. Or if we are lost in darkness, it seems like we will never find the path again, or the light.

The consolation and the reassurance of today's Reading is that the path will soon be found, and that the light will quickly appear: "Anguish has taken flight; dispelled is darkness. For there is no gloom where but now there was distress. The people who walked in darkness have seen a great light. Upon those who dwelt in the land of gloom, a light has shone. You have brought them abundant joy and great rejoicing." These words are deeply consoling. In our sorrow and sadness, in our losses and failures—in anything that causes us anguish and distress—there is a great light. That great light startles the darkness, makes it fly off. Gloom, anguish, distress, like the flight of a bird, leave us. In the suddenness of a great light we see and understand, and are in joy.

THEOLOGICAL CONCLUSION

Darkness does often seem gloomy and heavy and depressing, in contrast to the joy of light that brightens our heart and our eyes. Happiness is a kind of lightness in our lives. We can be consoled that the darkness and heaviness will be dispersed, and that in their place will be joy and peace. This awareness is captured in the poem of William Cullen Bryant:

> Grass is always greenest after heavy rain,
> And joy is always keenest after days of pain.

One might say that pain and suffering, in their depth and intensity, measure the joy and inner peace when they are dispersed. The deeper the darkness, and the longer one has been in darkness, the sharper and more intense is the light. And so joy and peace are more intense when they come, in proportion as they have been most painful. This is the joy, the hope, and the consolation, as Isaias presents it to us today.

THIRD SUNDAY OF THE YEAR (SERIES A) HOMILY II

Responsorial Psalm: *The Lord is my light and my salvation; whom should I fear? The Lord is my life's refuge; of whom should I be afraid?* (Ps. 27:1, 4, 13-14)

ANA-GNOSIS

We give names to different periods in history. Whether or not these names are always appropriate may be argued, but they are intended to catch the particular characteristic that most people feel about a certain period. In view of this, it is interesting to note that one of the names we have given our own age is "the age of anxiety."

To say that people of our own time are more anxious and worried than those of past ages is difficult to know. The literature that remains, even from fifty or one hundred years ago, is limited in what it conveys, and few people now living remember those times. But by calling our age "the age of anxiety," we at least capture something that touches all of us. Even children are surprisingly worried in our time. They know enough about the destructive power of a hydrogen bomb, for example, to surprise us with their fear. And surely, as adults, this concerns us all.

THEOLOGICAL EXTENSION

When we know anxiety in a personal way it has a unique quality about it that, even when others are not anxious about the same thing, can dominate many aspects of our lives. It helps very little for others to tell us not to be afraid, or that they are not afraid. For when we are caught up in personal fear and anxiety, usually such well-intended reassurance does not help.

We ask then, where we can turn in our fears and anxiety, especially when they are very threatening and all-pervasive, and even make us fear for the future of all mankind. While we obviously can and must help one another, this help is quite limited, at least in some final way. For a final resolution of our anxiety, we need to look beyond ourselves and one another, as we see in the words of the Psalmist today: "The Lord is my life's refuge; of whom should I be afraid." Is this not the answer to "the age of anxiety?" In the end, the only answer to our personal fear, to our being afraid of other people or things, is God.

THEOLOGICAL CONCLUSION

This is the most reassuring answer. As the Psalmist says, "If God is with me, if the Lord is my life's refuge, of whom should I be afraid." These are very sensible answers to fear and anxiety, and all of us, at some time or other, need such answers. We need to be reassured, encouraged, and helped to turn to God when shadows and darkness seem to overwhelm us. In God is our strength and our security; in Him we can be free of fear.

In the prayer just before the receiving of Communion, we say: "Deliver us, Lord, from every evil, and grant us peace in our day. In your mercy, keep us free from sin and protect us from all anxiety." This is a wise prayer and, indeed, the only answer we really have to anxiety.

THIRD SUNDAY OF THE YEAR (SERIES A)
HOMILY III

Reading II: *I beg you, brothers, in the name of the Lord Jesus Christ, to agree in what you say. Let there be no factions; rather, be united in mind and judgment.* (1 Cor. 1:10-17)

ANA-GNOSIS

Perhaps no single experience or change in the Church since the Second Vatican Council has been so surprising and, for some, even so disturbing as the greater openness with which Roman Catholics and Protestants have come to see each other. This change is so dramatic, especially for older people, that when we look back to times when any cooperation between these groups of Christians was considered as almost a denial of one's faith, it is hard to understand how such reversal in attitude could occur. For those who find difficulty, even now, in understanding this, we need to remind ourselves that Christianity, particularly in its direct relationship to the Sacrament of Baptism, was always unified. But we are apt to forget this. Or, stated another way, all Christian churches have recognized this validity of the Sacrament of Baptism in one anothers' churches.

THEOLOGICAL EXTENSION

It is necessary to stress this point in order to remind ourselves that the Catholic Church did not deny the Christian validity and meaning of the Sacrament of Baptism in all Protestant religions. What happened was that, since the Reformation, this validity was not stressed; on the contrary, the tragedy and sadness of division was stressed, with the notion that, somehow, all would return to the Catholic Church as it existed before the Reformation.

But essentially all that Vatican II did was look more closely at the basic concept of Christian unity that the shared Sacrament of Baptism truly represented, and proposed to all of us that we must stress again the conditions of this Christian unity. We always recognized it, but now it became a matter of stress. One of the main reasons for this stress and for this awareness was the slow realization, particularly through the bishops and priests residing in non-Christian areas of the world, of the great scandal and disturbance that all this division in the Christian community was causing. Bishops from Asia and Africa, for instance, emphasized how confusing it was for people to be met by different groups of Christian missionaries who were criticizing one another and disagreeing among themselves; that this was a far greater scandal than any other single thing in the Christian Church.

Vatican II recognized and admitted this scandal, and saw how it was against the prayer of Christ Himself at the Last Supper. St. Paul, in the Reading for today, is stressing this same unity and reminding us of the time in which we are living: that all Churches, symbolized by the World Council of Churches on the one hand, and the openness of Vatican II on the other, have opened their arms to one another. This is not to deny the honest differences that each, in conscience, considers basic; it is, rather, a common opening up to a recognition of what the Sacrament of Baptism always implied—a deep sense of Christian unity that is fundamental to all that we are and do.

THEOLOGICAL CONCLUSION

As we see, St. Paul's injunction for unity is very sharp because he is addressing the same kind of division. This is not at all something new to the Christian community. Something of the same disagreements of the mind and heart have always existed. He says, "I beg you, in the name of the Lord Jesus Christ, to agree in what you say. Let there be no factions; rather, be united in mind and judgment." We, too, need to pray for unity in mind and judgment. It is Christ's will, and it is the meaning of the concept of unity in the Church. It is also the essential point by which the recognition of the Sacrament of Baptism serves as an entrance into the community of Christians.

Thank God now that in our time we are coming to live that unity. We regret the past divisions and disagreements. We pray that, in God's own time, these will be resolved. Unity, of course, does not mean conformity or total identity. Each person must be free to follow the inspiration of the Holy Spirit as he or she is guided by that inspiration.

THIRD SUNDAY OF THE YEAR (SERIES A) HOMILY IV

Gospel Reading: *Jesus toured all of Galillee; he taught in their synagogues, proclaimed the Good News of the Kingdom, and cured the people of every disease and illness.* (Mt. 4:18-25)

ANA-GNOSIS

When we think of the word "Church" now, for most of us it suggests immediately a building such as, perhaps, the Church building, or the parish house, or the school. While the building may actually be quite simple in its construction, we often let our imagination stretch to envision a large brick or stone building, and even a beautiful cathedral such as one finds in Europe. In this sense of the Church, it seems to be something quite stable and fixed, and very real.

Consequently, from this point of view, it has often been somewhat shocking to people that when the Church they had built up and worked so hard to make into a beautiful edifice was gradually taken over by another group of people, perhaps due to a changing neighborhood. Those people who had originally built the Church have moved out to the suburbs and perhaps started to build another Church. This may readily cause one to wonder how long this will continue. It is interesting to realize that until comparatively recently in the United States, the areas where we now live were not areas where Catholic Churches, at least, were actually built. Instead of this, there was the notion of a moving Church: for example, a priest or a minister on horseback who came only on weekends and conducted the religious service in someone's home, or some other suitable place. Instead of a fixed and stable building, that Church was a moving person who went from place to place and gathered together the Christian community.

THEOLOGICAL EXTENSION

This image of a moving Church reminds us that Christ did not build any Church, in the sense of a material edifice, anywhere. He was closer to the notion of what would have been called, in the early days of our country, a circuit rider, than a Church builder.

Today's passage from the Gospel brings this home to us: "Jesus toured all of Galillee; he taught in their synagogues, proclaimed the Good News of the Kingdom . . ." wherever he could find a suitable place where people would listen to him. We recall, for instance, in another context, that he anchored a boat a little way out in the lake so that he could be seen by everyone, and that was "Church." Like the old-time circuit rider, he went from place to place and assembled the Church community around him and taught them.

We can become too secure in constructing our buildings and setting up our institutions which, while necessary and important up to a certain point, may mislead us. We all enjoy, for example, the excitement of moving from a makeshift structure to a lovely, solid Church which is the result of the united effort of everyone in the parish; this, too, can be a fine symbol of prayer. But its danger is that it can anchor us far too deeply in material values. In light of that, it is perhaps a good thing in the history of the Church that new people move into a neighborhood and everything is changed. The Church must really always be on the move, for if it becomes too stable, it can atrophy.

THEOLOGICAL CONCLUSION

The image of Christ in today's Gospel as someone always on the move, always teaching where he could find people interested in hearing, seems more truly the picture of the Church, rather than stable and solid buildings, no matter how wonderful and magnificent they may be.

FOURTH SUNDAY OF THE YEAR (SERIES A)
HOMILY I

Reading I: *They shall do no wrong and speak no lies;*
Nor shall there be found in their mouths a deceitful tongue;
They shall pasture and couch their flocks with none to disturb them. (Zep. 2:3, 3:12-13)

ANA-GNOSIS

We constantly think and talk about right and wrong, good and bad. We are very aware of the question of evil, and we ask ourselves "What is sin? What makes something sinful?" This is a subtle and complex issue but it can be helpful if we in some way reduce evil or sin to one basic concept.

THEOLOGICAL EXTENSION

From earliest times in the Old and New Testaments, as well as in philosophical writings, there has always been the realization that the heart of everything that is evil is a lie. Christ said it perhaps more sharply than anyone else when he called the symbol of all evil, Satan, the "father of lies." The prophet in our first Reading catches this idea, too, with great clarity. Describing the goodness of these people, he says, "They shall do no wrong, and speak no lies: Nor shall there be found in their mouths a deceitful tongue."

If we look more carefully at why a lie is at the heart of evil, we can see easily the tragedy of this duplicity. If a man is boastful and a liar he is evil first of all and most viciously toward himself. In lying to others he creates a false world—a world of his own making, not God's. And in so doing, he exalts himself, deceives himself, in fact, into acting as if he believed he were a god.

All evil has this self-deception in it. Thomas Aquinas, the great philosopher-theologian, makes the point, though, that if a man were actually saying something that *could* come into being and *might* actually happen, that he would not be boastful or lying. He would be a prophet, a visionary, a man of great foresight and wisdom. Lying means what he says will never come into being; it is pure deception, not only of others but oneself. Therefore it is tragically disillusioning, embittering and self-defeating. This is not the same as prophecy, though generations of well-meaning people have confused the two. How many genuine prophets have been disparaged by their own friends and acquaintances, called liars and blasphemers, only to be proved right years later? Christ himself was accused of these kinds of boastful exaggerations and blasphemies when those around him could not accept the profound truth that he was teaching. We have to be very careful, then, that what you call lying and deceit really is such.

How do we tell? We try to discern whether what the person is saying has some basis in the world God made, in the potential of things around us. Then this may not be a boast, but a vision. Visions have a foundation in reality. Lies don't. We make them up ourselves, and in doing so we make gods of ourselves. This is what sinfulness is all about.

THEOLOGICAL CONCLUSION

So the prophet tells today that goodness is inextricably bound to truthfulness. Lying and deceit have no place in the lives of the people of God. If we are truly his people we must renounce deception of others and of ourselves, so that we, too, shall do no wrong, speak no lies, nor have in our mouths a deceitful tongue.

FOURTH SUNDAY OF THE YEAR (SERIES A)
HOMILY II

Responsorial Psalm: *The Lord keeps faith forever, secures justice for the oppressed, gives food to the hungry. The Lord sets captives free.* (Ps. 146:6-7, 8-9, 9-10. R. Mt. 5:3)

ANA-GNOSIS

During the first half of this century kidnapping, particularly the kidnapping of an adult, was rare enough that we didn't think much about it. We had, of course, dramatic cases of kidnapping, such as that of the Lindberg child, but the infrequency of kidnapping made that case startling. Very recently, however, in conjunction with the hijacking of airplanes, the whole notion of making people captive and holding them for ransom has returned again with a vengeance. The phrase so familiar in Biblical times of "captives" rings true again. We recall the prayer for the freeing of captives and even the idea that religious orders would dedicate themselves to giving their lives in ransom for people taken captive. Very recently the Holy Father himself offered himself as a ransom for people held captive.

This holding people for ransom was very common in early days, and it is returning again in a way that, even with all our modern police and weaponry, we don't yet know quite how to handle. But it was such a common idea during the writing of the Old and New Testaments that it recurs as an image.

Now when we see the relief on the faces of those released from a hijacked airliner, when we know the joy and gratitude for their safe deliverance, we sense again what it means to "set captives free."

THEOLOGICAL EXTENSION

This emotion is evoked by the phrase in today's Psalm: "The Lord sets captives free." Imagine for a moment how you would feel—trapped, closed in, aboard a captured airliner, not knowing how or if you would be released. This is very much how our lives would have been without the saving grace of God. But through his loving intervention we, the captives, are set free, relieved, exhilerated, joyful.

The Psalmist reminds us of this reality. We have only to read the newspaper headlines to have fresh examples of what captivity and, hopefully, the joy of release can mean. To recall this is yet another way of reflecting on our redemption through Christ.

THEOLOGICAL CONCLUSION

The Psalmist's message is one of redemption, one of great joy for all of us. We can hope, we have been ransomed, the Lord has set us free. We are released from captivity through Christ.

FOURTH SUNDAY OF THE YEAR (SERIES A)
HOMILY III

Reading II: *Brothers, you are among those called. Consider your own situation. Not many of you are wise, as men account wisdom; not many are influential; and surely not many are well-born. God chose those whom the world considers absurd to shame the wise; he singled out the weak of this world to shame the strong. He chose the world's lowborn and despised those who count for nothing, to reduce to nothing those who were something, so that mankind can do no boasting before God. God it is who has given you life in Christ Jesus. He has made him our wisdom and also our justice, our sanctification, and our redemption. This is just as you find it written, "Let him who would boast, boast in the Lord."* (1 Cor. 1:26-31)

ANA-GNOSIS

One of the visions held dear throughout the two hundred years of United States history is that of an opportunity for the ordinary person to make something of himself or herself. This vision is still powerful here and elsewhere on earth, and no promise that Communism or any new form of government can offer is as dramatic and effective as this American promise.

We know it has not been a totally empty promise. Many of our ancestors who came searching for that opportunity found fulfillment. Many people who worked hard and diligently and were honest and genuine did get a great deal from America. But we know also there's another side to that story. For all those who did realize their dream there have been vast numbers who did not see that promise fulfilled, often through no fault of their own. They were and are trapped in ghettos, inner-cities or small country villages, dust bowl areas with no harvest. For them the promise was bitter because, even with their best efforts, no fulfillment came.

And we must realize that, while we can hold up this ideal of material success we need to become realistic about the limits of what one can achieve even in America. We are beginning to see that to make these achievements possible, we have perhaps overused the natural resources of our country, and future generations will pay a great price for what we too freely and greedily used up too quickly. All this remains to be seen, but we well know that questions of energy, conservation and pollution all suggest some of these grave possibilities.

THEOLOGICAL EXTENSION

This is a time, then, to return to the meaning of success we find in the Gospel, to the meaning and purpose of life given to us by the Gospel. And despite our reverence for the American ideal that we can all potentially be president or a success of some kind, this is not the Gospel's message at all.

In the Parable of the Talents we are told simply to look at what we have. If we have one talent, then we work simply and honestly and genuinely with that one. This is our vocation and our purpose. If we have two, we put those to work. If we have five, we must look carefully at the burdens and responsibilities and gravity of our special gifts. We have the obligation to work much harder. This is a very different notion than the idea that every child born in a log cabin or a mansion can be president. It is rather looking genuinely at ourselves, finding out who we are as God has made us, and then working simply and honestly to achieve what to most people perhaps are very simple goals, very simple fulfillments, but which are our real purpose and meaning in life.

St. Paul repeats this in his letter to the Christian community at Corinth. He says, "Not many of you are wise, as men account wisdom; not many are influential; and surely not many are well-born." It is not our Christian vocation to be richly endowed necessarily. In those instances when it happens—the five talents given by our Lord, for instance—then those people have grave obligations. But for most of us, our life goals are quite ordinary and simple. But this in no way makes them less holy, less significant or, ultimately, less sublime. This is the consoling message of St. Paul: that God uses the simple people, the one-talented, the two-talented, to confound the pride that can go with five talents. He says, "God chose those whom the world considers absurd to shame the wise. He singled out the weak of the world to shame the strong. He chose the world's lowborn and despised, those who count for nothing, to reduce to nothing those who were something, so that mankind can do no boasting before God."

Even Christ was looked down on. He came from a little town of Nazareth, and "What good can come out of Nazareth?" was one of the snide remarks he heard. He was often thought to mix with a low class of people—fishermen, tax collectors, sinners. He didn't really fit in or mix with the gifted leaders of his time at all. And this may easily be the case with us too.

Consequently, in our anxiety to procure material welfare for everyone—and this is right and should be done; people should be liberated from stark poverty, misery and suffering; Christians must work towards this—in focusing *only* on that, we can falsely hold up only a materialism that the middle class and the rich have already found disillusioning and embittering. We are not doing the poor any favor by proposing to them goals and values which, when they get them, will be sour in their mouths or dry like ashes on their tongues.

THEOLOGICAL CONCLUSION

So today's Reading reminds us to accept our simple life in its ordinary way, to understand that it is our Christian vocation. We must live it to the very best of our ability, giving ourselves as instruments of God through Christ's grace to others, for it is in this way that the world knows Christ in each generation.

"God it is who has given you life in Christ Jesus. He has made him our wisdom and also our justice, our sanctification and our redemption. This is just as you would find it written, 'Let him who would boast, boast in the Lord.' "

We are, indeed, great, magnificent, and most gifted, but only *in Christ,* not in materialism or special worldly talents.

FOURTH SUNDAY OF THE YEAR (SERIES A)
HOMILY IV

Gospel Reading: *Blest are they who hunger and thirst for holiness; they shall have their fill.* (Mt. 5:1-12)

ANA-GNOSIS

Generally when we think of ourselves as being blessed, we have in mind all the blessings we have received. We think of what we have; during the celebration of Thanksgiving, for example, we thank God for a rich table filled with good food, or at Christmas or our birthday we're very aware of the gifts we've received from those who love us. We often connect being very blessed only with what we have received, with how much God has given us. Even in the prayer which we sometimes say before meals, "Bless us, O Lord, and these thy gifts which we have received from thy bounty, through Christ our Lord," we are again suggesting that blessings and being blessed are associated with what we have. So we thank God for these gifts.

THEOLOGICAL EXTENSION

Now it is interesting to reflect on the Beatitudes we read today, this magnificent, classic description of goodness and holiness in life and of the real meaning and purpose of our lives and how we should live them. For in them, blessing and blessedness are not associated with what we have received, but with what we do not have but are striving for.

The key line, therefore, that best catches this tone is, "Blest are they who hunger and thirst for holiness; they shall have their fill." We are blessed then, not by what we have, by our full tables at Thanksgiving for instance, but by what we are seeking—a life of holiness with God.

It is when we are hungry and thirsty that we are most vividly aware of what we do not have, and in this awareness we are blessed. It is most helpful to us then, when we are discouraged, when we feel we have failed, to realize that we are blessed, that God is blessing our hungering and thirsting after the holiness of a Christian life, even when we don't seem to be succeeding too well.

The core of our Christian hope and confidence is based on our assurance of God's blessings, not only in the things he has given us, but also in his unfailing support of our efforts to bring justice, peace, dignity and human liberation of all people. We know that our hunger and thirst is not in vain.

THEOLOGICAL CONCLUSION

The heart of the beatitudes then is that we are blessed even in what we do not have yet. It is this blessing of our efforts towards holiness that gives us the courage and confidence to continue when we might feel that it's no use. This is even a greater blessing than all those we generally recognize when we thank God for the blessings, the gifts, we've received.

FIFTH SUNDAY OF THE YEAR (SERIES A)
HOMILY I

Reading I: *Then you shall call, and the Lord will answer, you shall cry for help, and he will say: Here I am! If you remove from your midst oppression, false accusation and malicious speech; If you bestow your bread on the hungry and satisfy the afflicted; Then light shall rise for you in the darkness, and the gloom shall become for you like midday.* (Is. 58:7-10)

ANA-GNOSIS

Some days of the year are unusual—they begin dull, heavy, dark and grey. It seems as if we are in for continuous rain or gloom. Then, surprisingly, almost without our being aware of it, the sun comes out and the gloom has disappeared; the darkness has gone; the greyness is dispersed. We look up and we see a delightful blue sky, light clouds, and the sun. We're suddenly filled with joy and delight. Now this doesn't happen often, but when it does happen, we generally remember it because it is so unexpected.

THEOLOGICAL EXTENSION

This is the image of the prayer that we have today. Prayers are often answered in the same surprising way that a grey, dull day is suddenly filled with sunlight. Sometimes when we least expect it, when we've almost given up hope, astonishingly our prayer is answered.

One way of having prayers answered, our Lord has told us, is to pray continually with faith and confidence and not to give up: "Seek and you will find." We recall, too, the man who was asleep and was awakened by the persistent neighbor. Our Lord gave us this story to illustrate continuous confidence in prayer and not giving up.

But our Lord also told us that it was not enough simply to pray. Prayer has a great deal to do with the way we live and what we do. The Reading today from Isaiah emphasizes this for us. He raises the question: Do we really want our prayers answered? What is the best way when we pray to work for an answer?

We know we must pray consistently, confidently and faithfully, not giving up. But Isaiah tells us quite a bit more that we need to do if we truly want our prayers answered. He says, "Then you shall call, and the Lord will answer. You shall cry for help, and he will say, 'Here I am.' When? What is it that puts us in a position of real assurance of God's answer? What gives us this special position?

"If you remove from your midst oppression." That's the first thing Isaiah tells us. Some oppressions, some dishonesties, some inconsiderations, we can't do anything about directly. They are local affairs, government affairs, or affairs that the Church or large social organizations have to work for, with our small, but important, support and help. But other dishonesties and oppressions, inconsiderations and injustices—all the little, mean, hurtful things that go on around us—we *can* do something about. Isaiah tells us that this is the way to have our prayers answered—to look around and see an injustice or an oppression, see something unfair and do something about it. Removing oppressions, then, is the first condition.

Then "false accusation and malicious speech" is next. Much unfairness, much oppression and dishonesty comes from malicious speech, quick judgments from gossip, from a genuine failure to look at the facts and deal with them sincerely. One way, therefore, to put ourselves in a position of getting an answer to our prayer is to watch our own tongue and to help offset the evil effects that dishonesties, prejudices and oppressions that gossipy, distorted tongues produce.

Then Isaiah says, "bestow your bread on the hungry and satisfy the afflicted." He means this within the limits of our responsibilities and obligations to those close to us and ourselves. We must genuinely be concerned with the poor, those who have less than we, and show our concern whenever possible by our own donation. We must show a real concern for the sick among us, for the handicapped, for the underprivileged, for the special child or adult who is mentally handicapped in some way. All these concerns bring answers to our prayers.

THEOLOGICAL CONCLUSION

If we live this way, then Isaiah reassures us, "Then light shall rise for you in the darkness; and the gloom shall become for you like midday." In other words, in the prayerful sense it will be one of those glorious days that begin grey, dull and depressed and suddenly becomes glorious, filled with sunlight. God's light will enter our lives because we are concerned for others while we are praying.

FIFTH SUNDAY OF THE YEAR (SERIES A)
HOMILY II

Responsorial Psalm: *The Lord dawns through the darkness, a light for the upright; he is gracious and merciful and just. Well for the man who is gracious and lends, who conducts his affairs with justice.* (Ps. 112:4-9)

ANA-GNOSIS

Often we have encounters with service people or government or agency workers which turn out less than satisfactory. We usually get what we went for—a check, a paper signed, a repair made or whatever—but we frequently come away angry, frustrated, and resentful.

Why? Because very often, while we succeed in obtaining what we went for, the person we had to deal with made us feel almost nonhuman. We were humiliated, embarrassed, hassled, and we left completely upset with the treatment we received. This feeling of resentment is not uncommon or unjustified. All too frequently when we ourselves are in a similar position of relative power, we treat the people who come to us in their need with inconsideration and thoughtlessness. Then we cover it over for ourselves by saying, "Well, I did my job, didn't I? I did what they came for. They got what they wanted. I don't know what they're complaining about." But they are complaining, and rightfully.

THEOLOGICAL EXTENSION

The Psalmist today ties three words together that we don't think about enough. Usually when we think of the word *justice,* we recognize that it contains everything that we legitimately have a right to. The service given us can be just. If there's some kind of charity in it, something beyond justice, something given that, in a sense, we couldn't strictly demand, then we can add the word *mercy*. The person who served was not only just, but merciful; he gave more than we could legitimately claim. We tend to think that this is all that we need.

But notice that the Psalmist adds *gracious*. First of all he applies it to God. This is a word we do not think enough about in relationship to God. It is very common for us to hear that God is just and God is merciful, and that we should be just and merciful in imitation of God. But the third attribute, which we need very much, is graciousness. The Psalmist says, "The Lord dawns through the darkness, a light for the upright. He is *gracious* and *merciful* and *just*."

So if we are to live our lives in imitation of God, it is not enough that we be just. It is not enough even that we be merciful. When people are interviewed after they have gone to some government, private, or Church agency for aid, aid which perhaps is not absolutely due to them in justice, which is a kind act of mercy, they often say that they wish they didn't have to go through the treatment they received. When people go to outpatient clinics and hospitals, they often say, "I just was treated so badly. They gave me the medicine. Physically they did what they should have done, but they treated me terribly. I felt ashamed and humiliated."

Now, for people to experience this kind of treatment, even where there are justice and mercy, is wrong—because, as we see here, there is a third word to describe God which must describe us also, and that is *gracious*. If anything is needed to make life far more pleasant among us, it is that we need to imitate God's graciousness as well as his justice and his mercy.

The Psalmist confirms this by saying that "the man who is gracious and lends; who conducts his affairs with justice, shall never be moved. He shall have an everlasting remembrance." We know this is true. The thing that we recall most vividly in our remembrance of someone is, even above his justice and mercy, his graciousness. And graciousness is never so deeply appreciated as when it is shown under circumstances where the other person feels already humiliated, ashamed or inferior. Here justice and mercy should be clothed in graciousness. This is the greatest gift of all.

THEOLOGICAL CONCLUSION

God, then, is not only just, not only merciful towards us, but he is gracious. In our relationships with our neighbors, with those around us, let us be the same, reflecting as we do in the Lord's prayer that we ask God to treat us as we treat others. Our own treatment by God, then, hinges not simply on our justice or even on our mercy, both of which are very important, but equally on our graciousness. God, the Psalmist, tells us "is gracious and merciful and just." So must we also be.

FIFTH SUNDAY OF THE YEAR (SERIES A) HOMILY III

Reading II: *As for myself, brothers, when I came to you I did not come proclaiming God's testimony with any particular eloquence or "wisdom." No, I determined that while I was with you I would speak of nothing but Jesus Christ and him crucified. When I came among you it was in weakness and fear, and with much trepidation. My message and my preaching had not the persuasive force of "wise" argumentation, but the convincing power of the Spirit. As a consequence, your faith rests not on the wisdom of men but on the power of God.* (1 Cor. 2:1-5)

ANA-GNOSIS

In the history of sports it is a fact that teams with successful records often played in a rather undramatic and prosaic way. They made no special plays, but rather depended on unspectacular and quite simple plans and systems. Characteristically, in football we describe such a team as "five yards and a cloud of dust," (catching, of course, the old days when fields were grass and dust rather than artificial turf). The point was that there was nothing spectacular about what such a team did, but step by step they moved from one end of the field to the other and piled up scores. In baseball, Casey Stengel is said to have recalled a team that didn't play outstandingly well, didn't hit many home runs or do anything you might expect—they were very tiresome to watch—the only thing they did was beat you.

This experience in sports, where the exciting teams, week after week, often do not win nearly as many games as the steady, but unspectacular, team, recalls a truth that goes beyond sports to life. If we ask why these teams win even though they don't seem to play spectacularly, the answer is that they are teams well drilled in basics. They can be counted on to do these things well play after play, day after day, so that when the season is over, their record year after year is surprisingly better than teams that may have much better players and, in particular instances, play in a much more effective and dramatic way.

This certainly applies to life. A genuinely good life, a genuinely responsible life, is not necessarily very dramatic or, to outside appearances, spectacular. It is a day by day performance in which the words *duty, responsibility, caring,* and *graciousness* come in. By themselves these are not particularly dramatic. But they are the basics of a Christian life. And most basic of all is our realization that whatever we do and whatever we are it is God and the Spirit of Christ working through us, and not something we do uniquely or totally in and through ourselves.

THEOLOGICAL EXTENSION

This is what St. Paul is stressing for us. Christian life is not necessarily outstanding. He makes it very personal when he talks about his own sense of fear and trepidation and weakness. He doesn't see himself as any great dramatic character at all, no matter how spectacular he seems to us now. His inner view of himself, then, was much like our view of ourselves. We see ourselves often as weak, anxious and insecure; we're not dramatic, spectacular heroes or heroines, not people who accomplish great feats of history. St. Paul did not see himself as that either, but he gave us a basic conception through his own life of the way to live our own Christian lives. We need not be dramatic or spectacular. We might not stand out brilliantly. We don't, in sports' terms, have to make the fantastic, last minute play that wins the game. But we need to have, day by day, a steady "five yard and a cloud of dust" way of living.

THEOLOGICAL CONCLUSION

We rest in our faith on the power of God, St. Paul tells. That should be enough. Like St. Paul, then, we need only open ourselves to God, to allow him into our lives every day, be gracious, kind, merciful and just as he is, and we needn't worry about the dramatic quality of our existence. It is our consistent practice of good Christian living that is important. Like the teams who succeed by their steady accomplishment of the basics of their sport, so we will be successful men and women of Christ if we concentrate on living out the basic values given us by our Lord.

FIFTH SUNDAY OF THE YEAR (SERIES A)
HOMILY IV

Gospel Reading: *Jesus said to his disciples: "You are the salt of the earth. But what if salt goes flat? How can you restore its flavor? Then it is good for nothing but to be thrown out and trampled underfoot.*
"You are the light of the world. A city set on a hill cannot be hidden. Men do not light a lamp and then put it under a bushel basket. They set it on a stand where it gives light to all in the house. In the same way, your light must shine before men so that they may see goodness in your acts and give praise to your heavenly Father. (Mt. 5:13-16)

ANA-GNOSIS

Whenever we sit down to dinner we almost immediately reach for the salt. After we have said our prayers, adjusted our napkin and tasted the main course, we either reach out for the salt or we say, "It's salted enough." Some people are so sensitive to their need for salt that they don't even taste the food. Sometimes to the irritation of the person who prepared it, they put salt on it before they even try it.

What does the salt do? Why do we reach out spontaneously for it? What does it offer to the taste? This is hard to answer. There's an intangible quality that salt gives to foods, a sublety that is difficult to put into words. It's based on a sense of taste that we all share, but we can hardly describe it. We taste it and appreciate it, not through the sense of sound or through words that we might read, but through something on our tongue.

This subtle, intangible thing that salt brings to food is not only very precious but also somewhat unstable. Salt can lose this special flavor, and then it's not worth much. Perhaps chemically it will melt snow so we can throw it on the ground for that, but mostly we throw it away.

But the fact is that salt does bring a subtle, intangible extra something to our meals, and that has made it valuable and precious to us.

THEOLOGICAL EXTENSION

Our Lord has called us "the salt of the earth." How does that apply to what we know about salt and the familiar experiences we have with it as it flavors and seasons our food?

One way of thinking about it is that all human relations have a certain substance, goodness, naturalness and value to them without question. All human relations are good in their normal process. What the Christian life adds to this is a kind of fineness of feeling, a kind of regard and graciousness—as the description of God in the first Reading says—that makes it something very special. So when we experience a genuinely Christian relationship together it is not essentially different from other relationships, but it has a special touch, a special taste, a special flavor, a special quality. And in this openness of deep regard and love for one another we create an atmosphere that causes people who are not Christian to yearn again and again for this experience. One might call this a kind of *redemptive* regard or love that we have for others. We so appreciate their worth that they sense in us, almost like in a mirror, a reflection of their worth.

St. Paul asked the question: "Do you know what a great price you were purchased for?" This question is a redemptive question. If we answer, as Christians, "Yes, we do appreciate our value," then we are also saying we appreciate the value of every other person because all were redeemed by Christ; all people are precious.

Now this is the kind of subtle flavor that we, as Christians, have in any relationship in which we enter—a sense of the unique worth of every person we relate to since we are all redeemed by Christ. If we lose this regard for others, the salt has lost its flavor. There is nothing special about us or our relationship to others. It's just the same as everything else. But if we hold this sense then we have something uniquely precious that can come from no one else.

We know that when salt was discovered by the West it became so valuable that caravans and new routes to the East were devised to bring more and more salt. It was so precious that the word *salary* comes from it because salt was used as a form of wages. Now this is what our Lord is telling us that we are to the world. What we bring, like salt, is difficult to describe! we can only experience it. But once experienced, this deep Christian regard for each person's unique worth in Christ, is like salt with its delicate and sensitive flavor. The world yearns for it and seeks it. This is our special meaning to others. But it can be lost. It will be lost if we lose our vision—the vision of Christ's redemption of us and its worth to us.

THEOLOGICAL CONCLUSION

As salt, then, we must continue to add this subtle, intangible but extremely important ingredient to all our relationships. We must continually be aware of Christ's redemptive work in and through our lives. Otherwise we become as useless as salt which no longer flavors things, which no longer fills the purpose for which it was intended.

FIRST SUNDAY OF LENT (SERIES A)
HOMILY I

Reading I: *The Lord God formed man out of the clay of the ground and blew into his nostrils the breath of life, and so man became a living being.*
Then the Lord God planted a garden in Eden, in the east, and he placed there the man whom he had formed. Out of the ground the Lord God made various trees grow that were delightful to look at and good for food, with the tree of life in the middle of the garden and the tree of the knowledge of good and bad. (Gen. 2:7-9, 3:1-7)

ANA-GNOSIS

We often remember important events in history by stories which are basically true but which, in the process of being told or because of the truth they convey, have elements in them that are not historically accurate. Historical research may prove them to be wholly fictitious, yet often these stories survive and are repeated through many generations. Yet each time they are repeated someone comes forward with the observation that there is evidence that part of the story is not precisely true.

Then why are they repeated? They are repeated because they catch a mood or important aspect or point of that historical circumstance. The story catches this so well that people keep repeating it even knowing that it is not entirely true.

We've probably run across the story about President Lincoln being told during the Civil War, that General Grant was drinking quite a bit, though, of course he was the most successful Union Army general. Lincoln is reported to have said, "Find out what kind of whiskey he's drinking and let's send barrels of it to the other generals."

Lincoln denied that he ever said this, and investigation of General Grant's life in greater detail seems to indicate that he was not an alcoholic at all, the rumor that he was a heavy drinker having come from a letter written by a resentful member of his staff. But the story endured, not because it was true, but because it caught the main concern of Lincoln and everyone else for the preservation of the union. They wanted the war to be carried quickly and successfully to a conclusion. This was the important thing—that General Grant was successfully able to do this.

THEOLOGICAL EXTENSION

This example and others we can think of developed embroidered details, which while not exactly realistic, captured the tone of the event. They continue to be repeated because they illustrate so clearly the real mood of the historical period.

Keeping this in mind we can better understand the passage from the Book of Genesis today. We must recognize that this recitation of events about the first sin of Adam and Eve against God, their first act of disobedience or rebellion, has to have been developed later when men looked back at the beginning of the world and tried to determine the reason for man's divided state. We know that we yearn for a place of perfect happiness and security. This place could be called *Eden,* the actual Hebrew word for pleasure or material happiness and fulfillment. But we know that somehow or other on earth we don't have it. We can propose that we have it; we simply have this frustrated longing which will never be fulfilled. Or we can propose that God wanted us to have it and, in fact, did give it to us at one time, but we, through our own sinfulness, lost it. We continue to lose it now in proportion to the degree to which our will is separated from God's and to the degree to which we refuse to submit to God's will for us. The source of our separation is our own desire to pit our will against God's. The details simply serve to illustrate this willfulness so we can better understand it and come to terms with it. We do not achieve happiness by denying God's plan for us. He wants us to have happiness, to have peace of mind and inner security, but he wants us to see that the path to these things is not through our own selfishness. What will bring us to our real purpose is to submit humbly and openly to God's will. To be distracted from understanding this by arguing over the historical veracity of the story is to miss the entire point.

THEOLOGICAL CONCLUSION

Its details, like those of the Lincoln/Grant story, are not of primary importance. They may help us visualize the point the writer is trying to make. What is most important here is to realize how we find inner peace and contentment—Eden in a material and spiritual sense. This is what the Book of Genesis teaches us. God wishes this for us. But we can only achieve it by completely giving ourselves to God's will in the best way we can, not by deceiving ourselves and following our own will in our lives.

FIRST SUNDAY OF LENT (SERIES A)
HOMILY II

Responsorial Psalm: *Have mercy on me, O God, in your goodness; in the greatness of your compassion wipe out my offense. Thoroughly wash me from my guilt, and of my sin cleanse me.* (Ps. 51:3-4, 5-6, 12-13, 14, 17)

ANA-GNOSIS

Sometimes in an otherwise familiar situation we encounter an unexpected difficulty which leaves us confused and disoriented. Afterwards when we discover what we couldn't find or what we overlooked, of course it all seems very simple. But in the anxiety and pressure of the moment we can feel quite lost. We may overlook a very simple thing that may be the remedy for our situation.

Recently a man was telling me of such an incident. He was out driving in a borrowed car and hadn't paid much attention to the details of the dashboard except to be able to start the car and run it. He was driving at night and a sudden rainstorm came up, an intense storm that literally blinded him. Searching for the windshield button in the familiar place, he couldn't find it. He got more and more anxious and almost panicked because the rain was so intense. Driving with one hand and frantically reaching all over trying to find the right button, he finally realized how dangerous his situation was and pulled over to the side, lit a match and carefully looked over the the panel. He found the button he sought, but not where he'd thought it would be at all. Once he found it, his problem was solved, the windshield wiper worked smoothly, and he was no longed confused or panicked. The difficulty was that when he was panicked and confused he couldn't find the simple remedy to his problem.

THEOLOGICAL EXTENSION

Life has a lot of this confusion in it. We can find ourselves in a mixed up state of danger and personal confusion not unlike a sudden rainstorm that has the driver all mixed up. If we can quickly call on God's forgiveness, call on the sacrament of reconciliation and restore ourselves to the peace of God, we will be all right. Then we can see clearly. But life can sometimes confuse us to the point that we forget or fail to find this obvious point, that if we can reach and believe in God's forgiveness, then we have solved our painful and difficult confusion.

We, too, need to cleanse or wipe clean the confusion in our vision of ourselves and others. The Psalmist tells us this. He says, "Have mercy on me, O God, in your goodness; in the greatness of your compassion *wipe out my offense.* Thoroughly wash me from my guilt, and of my sin cleanse me." God's forgiveness is the source through which our vision is restored so we can see clearly where we are going in our lives.

If we fail to seek God's forgiveness or if, in our confusion, we don't even know to look for it, we can be left with terribly painful anxieties of guilt and confusion.

THEOLOGICAL CONCLUSION

We ask God, therefore, to give us back the joy of his salvation and a willing spirit to sustain us. We acknowledge our offenses and our sins. We turn to God because essentially our cleansing comes from him. "A clean heart create for me O God, and a steadfast spirit renew within me." God can clear our vision and give us the proper orientation for our lives. We need only to turn to him, as the Psalmist did, acknowledging our sinfulness and asking for forgiveness.

FIRST SUNDAY OF LENT (SERIES A)
HOMILY III

Reading II: *Through one man sin entered the world and with sin death, death thus coming to all men inasmuch as all sinned. If death began its reign through one man because of his offense, much more shall those who receive the overflowing grace and gift of justice live and reign through the one man, Jesus Christ.*

To sum up, then: just as a single offense brought condemnation to all men, a single righteous act brought all men acquittal and life. Just as through one man's disobedience all became sinners, so through one man's obedience all shall become just. (Rom. 5:12-19)

ANA-GNOSIS

Life is sometimes compared to a cave. It is a fitting comparison. In our lives we slowly realize that we're in the center of something confusing, dark and unclear. We grope for knowledge, we go to school, we study, we learn, we ask questions; and this is, in a very real sense, like groping our way out of a cave. When a particular solution dawns on us we often say, "I begin to see the light." "I'm not as lost as I was." All of this suggests that we are coming out of a cave.

Also we know that in going into a strange cave with many passages, twists and turns, a very wise way to explore is to start with a string and let it fall as we go so at some point we can turn around and follow the string out. In other words, the way out is the way we came in.

THEOLOGICAL EXTENSION

Now when we apply this conception to life, we begin with a basic realization of sinfulness. The fact of sin is all around us. It is one of the first memories we have as a child. We recall early memories not only of goodness, but of wrongfulness. We know guilt and shame early in our lives. We are born in the middle of this cave of confusion and darkness that we call sinfulness.

When we try to ask about how sinfulness came into the world before we were born, it is not unlike asking ourselves why we were in the particular town we were born in. We know it's because our father and mother decided we were going to be born there. We had no say about it. Now much the same is true of our finding ourselves in sin. The father of the human race determined our sinfulness, as our parents determine in large measure the situation that we are born into. We are born into sin because our parents, Adam and Eve, gave us this state of sin.

The glory is that the same thing that brought us into sinfulness takes us back out, like the cord that guides us back out of the cave. In the same way that we got in the state of sin through our parent's choice against God, Christ's act of redemption gives all of us the opportunity for salvation. We have the consequence of Adam's sinfulness, but we also have the consequences of Christ's redemption since we all belong to a common human family. This is the point of what St. Paul says. "To sum up then: just as a single offense brought condemnation to all men, a single righteous act brought all men acquittal and life. Just as through one man's disobedience all became sinners, so through one man's obedience all shall become just."

THEOLOGICAL CONCLUSION

Christ gives us a free choice about our part in his redemption. He respects our free will just as God respected the free will of Adam and Eve. Redemption is not automatic for us, but something we must turn to Christ for and work in Christ to achieve. We're free to accept Christ's redemption. It's available to us; St. Paul assures us of that. If we choose redemption we will follow Christ out into the light of God's presence.

FIRST SUNDAY OF LENT (SERIES A)
HOMILY IV

Gospel Reading: *Jesus was led into the desert by the Spirit to be tempted by the devil. He fasted forty days and forty nights, and afterward was hungry. The tempter approached and said to him, "If you are the Son of God, command these stones to be turned into bread."* (Mt. 4:1-11)

ANA-GNOSIS

Perhaps one of the more disturbing changes that has occurred in the Church since Vatican Council II has been the way that our traditional image of Church people has changed. From childhood on for many of us it had been almost second nature to have great respect for bishops, priests, sisters and brothers, all who represent the Church. Consequently, it was and is a painful thing to have the weaknesses, inefficiencies and ineffectiveness of the Church and of Church people pointed out. It's somewhat like finding, as we become adults, stories and evidences of weaknesses in our parents. We know they are human like ourselves, and yet it's almost as if we don't want to hear anything that hurts our idealized image of them. We have the same idealized image of Church people, dedicated as they are, and it is hard and painful to see weakness and have to accept it.

The positive side of this, however, is that unless we honestly and willingly look at what is wrong, in the Church or in our lives, we will be in danger of not correcting it. One must recognize that something is wrong or inadequate or ineffective before one can take any steps to change it. Therefore, we have to see the Church as having two aspects. One is the awesome power that it represents in standing for God in our lives. "As the Father sent me, I also send you," said Christ. But this YOU that Christ sends to us, is a very human YOU, just as we are, filled with human imperfections. The reassurance of the ideal of the Church is that at some basic point Christ is with the Church and will be with us in the Church for all days.

But this does not change both the evidences of weakness in the Church and the need for reform and change. The Church must constantly reform itself in its humanity, constantly perfect its mission.

THEOLOGICAL EXTENSION

One way of understanding today's Gospel is to see its relation to the Church, and to the power given to the Church to stand for Christ in our lives. As the extension of Christ in the world, the humanity of the Church can be easily put into just such tempting situations as Christ faced in the Gospel today.

To turn stones into bread, of course, is to have power over materiality. The Church, to do its work in the world, has become a very powerful, wealthy and important social and political organization. The danger is how easily Church men and women can misuse this materiality. That's the first temptation that the Church, in its human side, must face and constantly work against.

Then there is the temptation of status, importance and power themselves. Because Church people represent Christ in our lives we honor them in a very special way, and fittingly so. "He who hears you, hears me," said Christ. We give them authority and power in order that they be effective. Here again, though, there is a danger of misuse of authority and power. The second temptation suggests this to us, that the Church, indeed, has miraculous power and an awesome commission from Christ; yet it may misuse its authority, prestige and dignity. Christ's resistance of this temptation gives a model for the Church in its human personality to renounce this temptation also.

Finally political intrigue and maneuvering are, perhaps, most outstanding among all misuses of the Church as we look back through history. It's so easy for Church people to take over political power, to have control, to manipulate and maneuver with other governments, to get lost in secularity and lose their real mission and purpose. St. Paul is constantly calling us back to the essential message that he came to preach Christ, and Christ crucified and nothing else. But it's so easy for Churchmen to have lost this. We only have to recite from memory great names in history who were Church men, but who were more well-known for political intrigue, maneuvering and dishonesty than for anything related to the love and service of God. This is the third temptation that the Church, in its human agency, is cautioned against. We must serve only God and not give ourselves over to secularity, to human power and maneuvering. Once the Church is simply a city, a political structure, even if it has the glorious title of St. Augustine's City of God, unless it is truly dedicated in all its work to the things of God, it becomes a tragic political corruption. And Church men and women lost in politics, whether Church politics or secular politics, are shadows of the glorious, substantial images representing Christ that they were called to be and should be.

THEOLOGICAL CONCLUSION

These temptations affect us all, and by looking at them we see that the Church must be constantly reforming itself. The Second Vatican Council with the phrase *aggiornamento* of Pope John, highlights this need. But it's a constant concern, not only for Church men and women, but for all of us who are part of the Church. We need to recognize our weakness and temptations to help overcome the confusions and disorders which this story foretells will be the lot of the Church in its humanity.

We can be reassured that at no time will Satan finally overcome the Church, no more than he did Christ. Christ has assured us of his constant, essential presence in the Church despite all its human and sometimes glaring weaknesses. With his aid we need not fear facing the temptations, for he can help us renounce them.

SECOND SUNDAY OF LENT (SERIES A)
HOMILY I

Reading I: *The Lord said to Abram: "Go forth from the land of your kinsfolk and from your father's house to a land that I will show you.*

"I will make of you a great nation and I will bless you;
I will make your name great, so that you will be a blessing.
I will bless those who bless you and curse those who curse you.
All the communities of the earth shall find blessing in you."

Abram went as the Lord directed him and Lot went with him. Abram was seventy-five years old when he left Haran. (Gen. 12:1-4)

ANA-GNOSIS

One of the inevitabilities of life is growing old. We all do it. When we're young, we can't wait until we grow up. Even when we're comparatively young adults, there's a certain anxiety to "get settled," and so be a little older. But somewhere it dawns on us personally that we are growing old. For the young to hear this is meaningless, but for the middle-aged and those older it's a very vivid realization.

With growing old comes the anxiety that we might not have value any longer. There's much peace and contentment in the notion of retiring, having our ease. These are positive thoughts about growing old. But the great fear of old age—and it's becoming more prominent all the time in modern retirement—is that, somehow, having lost our daily work, we will be useless, we won't have any value to ourselves or other people.

Now this fear has to be faced directly as we grow old. There is no way of avoiding it or putting it off because it is real. We all know some old people demonstrate this feeling. They feel themselves worthless, of no good to anyone. This tragedy we must avoid. We can avoid it best by realizing that our vocation doesn't cease at retirement, or when we are middle aged or young. God calls us daily to a unique way of life. God has meaning and purpose and intention for our lives, even into long old age.

THEOLOGICAL EXTENSION

Perhaps the most dramatic example of this in recent history is Pope John XXIII. The story goes that he was elected because he was so old——in his seventies and people in the Vatican thought he would just be a transitional Pope until they got things worked out for a younger man. We know that he proved to be one of the most farsighted, revolutionary, and, in a real sense, youngest Popes in history. His vision, his awareness of the need for change, his realism, his humor, his humanity, flooded the whole world. No Pope in modern times has proved so human and such a rich personality. His blessing for the church is immeasurable. Yet we realize he was a very old man when he was elected.

Now this is the reassurance of God's word for us today. In setting up this whole new destiny for the people of God, Abram, the father of God's people, was not called to this vocation until he was 75 years old, almost identical with Pope John. The Reading tells us, "Abram went as the Lord directed him . . . Abram was 75 years old when he left Haran." Now most of us think 75 is very old, and yet here we find a man who left virtually everything he was familiar with and started on a whole new mission, because God called him. It sounds as if he were 20 or 25 years old. Pope John did the same. He didn't disavow a vocation to be Pope because he was too old. He accepted God's will, as Abram did, and carried out a magnificent, meaningful vocation.

Think of the tragedy for all of us if Abram, the father of the Chosen People and of the whole biblical destiny, had said he was too old for what God was calling him. Consider, in modern times, what the Church and the world would have lost, if Pope John had said he was too old. We see now clearly that we're never too old to be called by God to a rich, meaningful vocation.

Old people have much to give. Children and adolescents especially understand the richness of old age, and often cling to it. For many people their grandparents were far more significant in their lives, far more influential, despite all the gratitude and honor they hold for their parents. Their grandparents made the first deep influences in their life. Old age therefore, has much to give—much wisdom, much depth of understanding of the meaning of life, much humor, much that we all need.

THEOLOGICAL CONCLUSION

We needed Abram in the Old Testament. Thank God he followed God's will. We needed Pope John in our own time; and thank God he did not think himself too old. We need all our old people in the richness of their vocations to which God is calling them.

SECOND SUNDAY OF LENT (SERIES A)
HOMILY II

Responsorial Psalm: *Upright is the word of the Lord, and all his words are trustworthy. He loves justice and right; Of the kindness of the Lord the earth is full.* (Ps. 33:4-5, 18-19, 20, 22)

ANA-GNOSIS

Quite frequently when we remark to someone about his fine family or her successful career, the person to whom we are speaking will reply, "Well, you know, God has been good to me."

Interestingly, too, we note that children, adolescents and young adults almost never say this. It is an expression we associate with people in middle and old age. It seems that a real appreciation of God's goodness to us, the kindness of God, doesn't come to us in early years. Probably we are too involved in securing immediate goals to get quite the whole picture. Somewhere in middle age, though, as we look back, sufferings, sorrows, disappointments and failures level off, and we see how many times these were, in fact, blessings in disguise. We see the finger of God, the handwriting of God more clearly as we look back from middle age or old age.

THEOLOGICAL EXTENSION

The Psalmist is no doubt speaking from middle age when he writes, "Of the kindness of the Lord the earth is full. Upright is the word of the Lord and all his works are trustworthy. He loves justice and right." We grow to appreciate how kind God is as the years go by. And we grow to see that even those things that were painful and disappointing in earlier years had a subtle, even profound wisdom about them. They were, indeed, blessings for us.

THEOLOGICAL CONCLUSION

We can say with the Psalmist, "Of the kindness of the Lord my life is full. And we can say, when people compliment us, praise us, or in some way show respect, admiration or even possibly envy, "Well, you see, God has been very, very good to me. He has been very kind indeed. My life has been full of the kindness of God."

SECOND SUNDAY OF LENT (SERIES A)
HOMILY III

Reading II: *Bear your share of the hardship which the gospel entails . . .*

God has saved us and has called us to a holy life, not because of any merit of ours but according to his own design—the grace held out to us in Christ Jesus before the world began is now made manifest through the appearance of our Saviour. He has robbed death of its power and has brought life and immortality into clear light through the gospel. (2 Tim.. 1:8-10)

ANA-GNOSIS

Sometimes when we receive an extremely gracious consideration or gift, or when someone has done a very thoughtful thing for us, we are apt to say spontaneously, or feel the need to say, "Oh, you shouldn't really have done this for me. I don't know why you went to all this trouble. I didn't really deserve it at all."

And we mean this. We feel very deeply grateful in our awareness that someone is extremely considerate of us. The person may say back, "Oh, yes you did. I really appreciate over all these years how much what you've done really amounted to. I want to show you its great value in my eyes by a return gift." Again we may feel quite surprised, and still not able to see that what we had done was that much.

Sometimes, however, we realize that the gift a person has given us or what he may have done for us is not truly due to any merit on our part. A child who may have felt that he wasn't too good before Christmas or his birthday, may be flooded with joy to realize that, even if he was bad, his parents still loved him. Somehow you have the feeling that children sometimes misbehave —certainly adults sometimes do—almost to get this proof of unconditional love. They want to know that someone still loves them even after they've done shameful or embarrassing or failing things. And there is a deep reward and fulfillment when we haven't truly merited something that someone has done for us even though we may say, "You shouldn't have done this. I didn't really deserve it." There is perhaps an even greater sense of our worth and our meaning when someone says, "Well, it doesn't matter whether you deserve it or not—I just love you and that's why I did it."

THEOLOGICAL EXTENSION

Now this is why God did, and does, all the things he does for us. St. Paul stresses this today when he says "God has saved us and has called us to a holy life not because of any merit of ours but according to his own design."

God loves us unconditionally. Sometimes when we are deeply caught up in guilt and a sense of our own unworthiness or even worthlessness, we need to remind ourselves of this. Guilt is good when it is constructive. When it moves us to change to do better, to have genuine concern for others and for God then it is good. But when guilt leads to our forgetting and, therefore, denying God's unconditional love for us, no matter what we have done or not done, then such guilt is fraudulent and self-deceptive and wrong. We are right when we say we don't deserve it, but that doesn't make God stop loving us.

THEOLOGICAL CONCLUSION

This is St. Paul's point. We need to remind ourselves of this so we don't get too concerned about our failures and inadequacies. No matter what we have done or not done, we can never merit or deserve God's love. He does what he does for us not because we have earned it, but because he loves us. Here again as St. Paul presents it: "God has saved us and has called us to a holy life, not because of any merit of ours but according to his own design." We are right when we say we don't deserve it, but we must not let our guilty feelings interfere with our hearing God's reply: "I did it because I love you."

SECOND SUNDAY OF LENT (SERIES A)
HOMILY IV

Gospel Reading: *As they were coming down the mountainside Jesus commanded them, "Do not tell anyone of the vision until the Son of man rises from the dead."* (Mt. 17:1-9)

ANA-GNOSIS

Seminary training for priests, and religious preparation for sisters, is quite familiar to us. People go away from their homes, from their usual circumstances of work and daily life, and for a period of time—as long as four or five years sometimes—live a very special life that trains them for the work that they will have to do. With the coming of the married diaconate and other forms of religious dedication and service, this kind of training is not nearly so possible and people stay in their own homes and continue with their own work, but it still remains an idea, wherever possible, to take people away for a comparatively long time and give them a very special life.

THEOLOGICAL EXTENSION

There is a hint of this idea in the gospel of Matthew today. We see Christ taking the apostles and disciples aside and spending time with them. We know that they left their daily work, followed him and were with him, and that they had a way of life together.

In today's Gospel we also see a very special picture of the deep religious experience which Jesus gave to those he chose to lead his Church. He gave them these experiences to sustain them through the anxieties and insecurities of the days to come. In just such a way, seminary training for priests should provide them with a depth of religious experience and understanding of their faith that they can draw on as they go out to minister to the people of God and meet challenges, anxieties and insecurities of their own.

In sharing this experience of the Transfiguration Christ shows great love for the disciples. He is preparing them for the tasks ahead of them and giving them the knowledge that will enable them to complete these tasks. We sense the preparation and training that seem to be behind all this in his last direction, as they were coming down the mountain. He said, "Do not tell anyone of the vision until the Son of Man rises from the dead." That is, keep these things in your hearts and dwell upon them. They will sustain you later when you must carry on the mission of bringing God's Kingdom to completion.

THEOLOGICAL CONCLUSION

This is the spirit of the seminary, which then explains and justifies the expense, the faculty, buildings, and the long period of time that this training involved. Christ was concerned for his leaders, that they not simply be educated and understand but that they have a deep and rich spiritual life to stay with them through all the years of their priesthood. The seminary experience of a priest should give him the foundations of deep, religious experience on which he can rely and on which he can build further a strong spiritual life despite the anxieties and insecurities which may befall him.

THIRD SUNDAY OF LENT (SERIES A)
HOMILY I

Reading I: *In their thirst for water, the people grumbled against Moses, saying, "Why did you ever make us leave Egypt? Was it just to have us die here of thirst with our children and our livestock?"* (Ex. 17:3-7)

ANA-GNOSIS

There is a story told about twin boys, one an optimist and the other a pessimist. Their father was telling a rich friend who owned a department store and a farm about these two boys and about how totally different they were. One was never unhappy with anything. No matter how bad it was, he seemed always able to find some good side of it. The other, no matter how good things were, always seemed to find something to complain about. So the friend said, "Well, I'll make a bet with you that we'll be able to do something that the complaining boy will have to be satisfied with and the optimistic boy will have to complain about." The father replied, "All right, but I've never seen it happen before." They took the complaining, pessimistic boy to the toy department of the friend's store and said, "Now, you play with any toy you want here and then you pick out the one you like best and you can take it home with you. We'll leave you here for a while and then we'll come back." As they were going down in the elevator the friend said, "Certainly now the boy must be happy with all those wonderful toys. You see how his eyes lit up, and the lady in charge of the department is there to keep him company and show him how to work all the toys." They took the other boy out to the farm and put him in the hot, smelly barn filled with manure and heavy with flies. They said, "Now, we're going to leave you here all by yourself and we'll come back in an hour and let you out. In the meantime you're going to have to stay in this stinking place all by yourself." So again they went out and the friend said, "That boy has got to find something to complain about in that horrible place."

When they went back to the department store the pessimistic boy was sitting in the middle of the room not having played with anything. He was crying, and said that there were just so many toys he didn't know which one to play with or which one to pick out to take home. The father said, "See. That's the pessimist for you."

Then they went to the farm, and even before they got to the door they heard somebody singing and whistling. The other boy was shoveling away, cleaning out the barn. The friend said, "Now how could you possibly have found anything happy in a stinking, filthy place like this?" The boy said, "You see all that horse manure? There has to be a pony around here somewhere." And whistling again, he went back to his work.

That little story illustrates a common human situation—some people find anything miserable and other people have a wonderful way of finding even the most miserable situation hopeful and potentially good.

THEOLOGICAL EXTENSION

The Reading from Exodus today shows God's people to be rather like that pessimistic little boy despite all their blessings. After all God had relieved them from the captivity they were in, he gave them guidance through Moses, and he had shown them in countless ways that he loved them and yet they had their share of complainers. So when it looked like there wasn't water around, despite all the blessings and even miracles they had witnessed, they started to complain.

"Why did you ever make us leave Egypt?" they asked Moses. They blamed him; they were "made to leave," they didn't go on their own. The grumbler, the complainer, the pessimist seems often to blame other people for his or her own circumstances. Somebody else made him do it, someone else was responsible. So here Moses is being blamed for the plight of the Israelites. "Was it just to have us die here with our children and our livestock?" You can hear the exaggerated moaning of the pessimistic complainer.

But God heard their prayers and their discouragements. Even though he had given them every reason to trust him, he again answered their prayer and gave them water. God understood their weakness just as he understands ours. He knows we lose heart quickly, that we are not very courageous, and he knows we soon give way to complaint before long. The heartening thing for us to realize is that despite our pessimism, he loves us anyway, just as he loved the Israelites he was trying to bring to the Promised Land.

THEOLOGICAL CONCLUSION

Like the Israelites, like the little boy in the toy department, we can find ourselves blaming others for our situations, complaining and finding fault with our circumstances despite our many blessings. But this response on our part does not stop God from trying to reach us, from trying to bring us to joy and faith and hope in him. Even at our most desperate, God hears our prayers, he does not ignore our despair or our anxiety but continually tries to bring us closer to him. The knowledge of this alone is certainly cause enough to give us hope.

THIRD SUNDAY OF LENT (SERIES A)
HOMILY II

Responsorial Psalm: *If today you hear his voice, harden not your hearts. Come, let us bow down in worship; Let us kneel before the Lord who made us. For he is our God, and we are the people he shepherds, the flock he guides.* (Ps. 95:1-2, 6-7, 8-9)

ANA-GNOSIS

Some images, examples and analogies are so familiar, we've used them so much, that they lose their meaning for us. They become such commonplaces that we don't realize that their original intent may be quite different from the way we think of them today.

THEOLOGICAL EXTENSION

One of the most common of all the examples of our relationship with Christ and our relationship with God in the Old Testament is that of sheep and shepherd. What is misleading about this is that we see sheep nowadays contentedly grazing on farms, usually behind fences, secure and peaceful. Our image of sheep is of a very safe animal. We can hardly associate sheep with danger, fear or anxiety now. The word "sheep" calls to mind a sense of peace and tranquility.

But this familiar modern image is very misleading. We totally misunderstand the idea that God is our shepherd and we are his sheep, as the Psalm tells us today. We constantly need to remind ourselves that the method of raising sheep in the Old Testament and at the time of Christ was very different than the one we're familiar with now. There were no farms and safely fenced off places then. It was much more like the unfenced grazing land of the Old West in our own country a century ago, where cattle simply wandered long distances to find grazing ground, and were branded so that they could be distinguished later on. At the time of the Old Testament and of Christ, sheep did much the same thing except that, unlike herds of cattle in the West, sheep are more readily prey to other animals, particularly wolves, and as a consequence, a shepherd had to go with them and stay with them all the time. The shepherd did two things: he guided them to grazing ground and back again, and he had to protect them from the wolves. Now all this is a part of the Biblical image.

We recall that Christ makes a profound distinction between the shepherd who stays because the sheep really belong to him, and protects them from the wolves even when he is in danger of losing his own life, and the one who simply ran away because he was tired and he had no interest in protecting them. And we see, therefore, that the image of God guiding us as a shepherd is not a peaceful image in itself. Sheep were often in condition of great danger and difficulty. They had to follow and stay close to the shepherd in order to receive guidance and protection. The sheep who wandered away and got lost was not only lost in the sense that he didn't know where he was going any longer, but he was also in great, grave danger from wolves, of being devoured.

So the sheep-shepherd image, far from promoting the concept of tranquility, points out how complicated our lives are, how dangerous they are, how filled with conflict and difficulty they are, and how much we need God's guidance and protection.

THEOLOGICAL CONCLUSION

Sheep without a shepherd can be lost—they can wander aimlessly and even lose their lives if left on their own. So, too, can we if we do not stay close to our Shepherd. God is there to guide us and protect us through the struggles and difficulties of our lives.

He cares, he is interested and he will not desert us. So let us rejoice as the Psalmist suggests:

"Come, let us bow down in worship; let us kneel before the Lord who made us. For he is our God, and we are the people he shepherds, the flock he guides." He is our security no matter what dangers or confusions we encounter in our lives.

THIRD SUNDAY OF LENT (SERIES A)
HOMILY III

Reading II: *Now that we have been justified by faith, we are at peace with God through our Lord Jesus Christ. Through him we have gained access by faith to the grace in which we now stand, and we boast of our hope for the glory of God. And this hope will not leave us disappointed, because the love of God has been poured out in our hearts through the Holy Spirit who has been given to us. At the appointed time, when we were still powerless, Christ died for us godless men. It is rare that anyone should lay down his life for a just man, though it is barely possible that for a good man someone may have the courage to die. It is precisely in this that God proves his love for us: that while we were still sinners, Christ died for us.* (Rom. 5:1-2, 5-8)

ANA-GNOSIS

It's common for people when they know important or famous persons to talk about them often in their conversation. Sometimes this gets to be such a habit that we call it "namedropping." That is, whether they know such people or not, there are certain columnists, writers or conversationalists who drop these names casually, giving the impression that they mix with these powerful, important, famous people all the time.

Now we usually find this excessive habit of namedropping, of claiming relationship or friendship with famous people, irritating and a little bit of a nuisance if it's done too much. But, positively, we know that we are all proud when we, in truth, have the friendship and the confidence of some famous or great person. Those who have known the President from boyhood or adolescence take great pride in letting it be known that they have been a friend of the President for all these years. People come to Rome from the birthplace or childhood home of the Pope and they receive a special welcome because he has known them since his childhood or from when he was a young priest.

We are all pleased when we learn that the President of the United States has his high school football team as his special guests at the White House, or we were pleased when Pope John had a number of the simple peasants who were his family friends to the Vatican and gave them very special honors.

All of us yearn for some kind of friendship or importance like this, and it's good to ask ourselves, "Do we have such friends or such a friend?" Most of us answer, "No, we don't know the President or the Pope. We don't know anybody of any real importance. We don't even know a Hollywood movie star." We can't really do any namedropping; we don't know any famous persons, and thus we feel we have no one whose friendship we can boast about.

THEOLOGICAL EXTENSION

We are wrong when we say that. We have to back up and rethink our lives. St. Paul reminds us that we are wrong when he says, "Now that we have been justified by faith, we are at peace with God through our Lord Jesus Christ. Through him we have gained access by faith to the grace in which we now stand, and we boast of our hope for the glory of God." We have a most important person, says St. Paul, the most important person in the history of mankind who is and was and will be our closest friend. We are distinguished even beyond being friends with the Pope or the President or a King or any other famous person. We are friends of and have a special access to God through our friend, our most distinguished friend, Jesus Christ. This, says St. Paul, we can honestly and truthfully boast about.

That doesn't mean negative, arrogant or fraudulent boasting. It means that we can take great pride in this, as people take great pride in being friends with the President or the Pope. We know that they go to the White House or the Vatican and get a special reception or access. St. Paul assures us that we have this same sort of special entrance to God, in the grace of God through Christ, through our friend Jesus Christ.

THEOLOGICAL CONCLUSION

So, indeed, we can be namedroppers not only of Christ but of all the Apostles and Saints. In Christ they are all our friends, more famous really, greater and more significant than any other friends anyone in the would could have. We do know important people. We have the friendship of God our Father and Christ. What more important, valuable friends could we possibly want?

THIRD SUNDAY OF LENT (SERIES A)
HOMILY IV

Gospel Reading: *Many Samaritans from that town believed in him on the strength of the woman's testimony: "He told me everything I ever did." The result was that, when these Samaritans came to him, they begged him to stay with them for a while. So he stayed there two days, and through his spoken word many more came to faith.* (Jn. 4:5-42)

ANA-GNOSIS

One of the surprises for the ordinary soldier in World War II was that women were officers in the Army and Navy. The soldier had to learn quickly that he must salute them exactly the same way that he saluted men officers. He had to obey them just as he did his male officers or he was subject to punishment or charges of disobedience. This surprised many and was not easy for them to accept. Thirty or so years later we are subject to the further surprise that we have now women at West Point and Annapolis. And many other jobs are at last opening up for women which were traditionally held only for men. Chief Engineers of tunnels and construction jobs sometimes turn out to be women rather than the common stereotype of the middle aged man.

THEOLOGICAL EXTENSION

Now the time of Christ was even more clearly a time when women were expected to stay off to themselves in the home, quite removed from outside activity. Therefore, we must recognize how shocking Christ's conversation with the woman at the well seemed, how odd the confidence he put in her, making her a disciple, in a sense, to go and represent him in the next city. Yet she did this most effectively. We overlook the dramatic quality of today's reading if we ignore the degree to which Christ violated in the most extreme way all the customs about keeping women in their place, keeping them removed. He called them, as well, to participate in bringing God's word to all people.

THEOLOGICAL CONCLUSION

The story reminds us, therefore, that as our own time unfolds a greater potential for women to participate in all sorts of areas and activities, that Christ led the way in this. He was perhaps the most radical representative of what we are calling Women's Liberation. We must remember this when we may be tempted to deny opportunities to any of God's people. He chose *all* people. No one should be refused a chance to serve him in whatever particular vocation is appropriate to them.

FOURTH SUNDAY OF LENT (SERIES A)
HOMILY I

Reading I: *The Lord said to Samuel: "I am sending you to Jesse of Bethlehem, for I have chosen my king from among his sons."* (1 Sam. 16:1, 6-7, 10-13)

ANA-GNOSIS

A Secret Service officer who worked in the White House for many years as a personal guardian of the Presidents describes in his autobiography an incident where he and President Wilson were out walking. Wilson was a very small man, and the Secret Service man was tall, strong, handsome and distinguished. On this walk they passed by a ditch where two immigrants were working and the older one was saying to the younger one, "See what a great country this is. The President of the United States is such a fine big, tall man. What a wonderful country to have a President so distinguished and imposing as that."

The young man, who had been studying for his citizenship and, therefore, knew about the President, said, "Well, actually, it's the little guy who's the President, not that big fella. He's just the Secret Service guard."

And without hesitating or changing his tone in the slightest, the older replied, "See, what did I tell you? What a wonderful country this is that a little, puny guy like that can be President."

THEOLOGICAL EXTENSION

Now, this incident, true or not, highlights how misleading appearances are. Sometimes the most important people hardly impress us at all, until we discover who they are and what they know and what their achievements have been. Oftentimes people who look very much like we might imagine kings, private detectives or cowboys to be are simply good actors. And the real people whose roles they are taking appear very different.

This is the theme today. The handsome man, Eliab, seems fit to be the king. Certainly Samuel thought so; as Jesse and his sons came to the sacrifice, Samuel looked at Eliab and thought, "Surely the Lord's anointed one is here before him."

Well, we know the contrary was true. The Lord said to Samuel, "Do not judge from his appearance or from his lofty stature, because I have rejected him. Not as man sees does God see, because man sees the appearance but the Lord looks into the heart."

God's chosen one, David, was out in the field. He wasn't even thought important enough or significant enough by his own father to be brought in. Yet this insignificant boy, the shepherd in the fields, became the great David, so famous for all time.

We know of many similar instances in history. Often even the parents of the child do not recognize his future greatness. Many times people are not only surprised at the later significance of someone they knew, but often they had so rejected that person that they hardly want to admit his greatness years later.

God reminds us, therefore, throughout the Old and New Testaments, that his ways are not man's ways. We must adapt ourselves to, trust and abandon ourselves to, this mystery in our own lives and in the lives of others. This is why any intervention in God's plan for human life is a most profound, difficult and dangerous question. Who knows what, in God's plan, this puny little infant of a child is going to be? Who knows what miraculous unfolding may emerge? If we think of all the weak, apparently inadequate, children who have proved to be great blessings to the human race, we see how faulty our human judgment is. It is faulty most of all because so often it is based on extrinsic appearance.

THEOLOGICAL CONCLUSION

The Reading today, then, reminds us of this basic truth. As the Lord said to Samuel: "Do not judge from his appearance or from his lofty stature because I have rejected him. Not as man sees does God see, because man sees the appearance but the Lord looks into the heart." We must never forget this whenever we are tempted to pass judgment, particularly on children or the young.

FOURTH SUNDAY OF LENT (SERIES A)
HOMILY II

Responsorial Psalm: *The Lord is my shepherd: there is nothing I shall want.*
The Lord is my shepherd; I shall not want.
In verdant pastures he gives me repose;
Beside restful waters he leads me;
He refreshes my soul. (Ps. 23:1-3, 3-4, 5, 6. R. v. 1)

ANA-GNOSIS

Simple basic things of nature never lose their deep, rich significance for us. They have a power, a soothing quality, that almost nothing man makes can match. Oftentimes in the spring or summer or fall when the weather is nice we find a special, indescribable peacefulness in just sitting on the ground. So the joy of a picnic is often just in simply being with nature, being close to the ground, stretching out and feeling the earth and the grass. To feel nature close at hand brings us a sense of peace and security we rarely find elsewhere. A flowing stream gets to the very heart of our being and gives us a special kind of peace. So picnics remain, generation after generation, one of the really satisfying things that people can do together. Even though often the food is very simple, and really all they do is get close to nature again and talk together, still a picnic can occasion this feeling of deep abiding peace.

THEOLOGICAL EXTENSION

The Psalmist knows this feeling too—and this tells us how much like ourselves these people were. He knows the joys of picnics beside a stream and sitting in a rich, verdant pastureland, just enjoying nature. He reminds us that, as we have this directly from God's hand, to enjoy nature is a sure way of appreciating how much God loves us and how soothing his presence is. For if nature gives us this peace and nature is God's handiwork, how much more peace have we directly from God. Certain it is that we can go into the fields and contemplate in them the beauty and grandeur of God. We can go on picnics and enjoy again the restfulness of nature. But we needn't have this with us always to feel close to God. We can come to him in the peacefulness of prayer, in moments of quiet contemplation, in a visit to a nearby chapel.

THEOLOGICAL CONCLUSION

He is there for us in nature, as the Psalmist recognizes, but he is also there wherever and whenever we open ourselves up to him and choose to rest in the security of his love.

FOURTH SUNDAY OF LENT (SERIES A) HOMILY III

Reading I: *There was a time when you were in darkness but now you are light in the Lord. Well, then, live as children of light. Light produces every kind of goodness and justice and truth. Be correct in your judgment of what pleases the Lord. Take no part in vain deeds done in darkness; rather condemn them. It is shameful even to mention the things these people do in secret; but when such deeds are condemned they are seen in the light of day, and all that then appears is light. That is why we read:*
Awake, O sleeper,
arise from the dead,
and Christ will give you light." (Eph. 5:8-14)

ANA-GNOSIS

It is common for people who are sorry for what they have done in the past, for their way of life, to say, "I was just so blind I couldn't see anything." Or they may say, "I was in the dark, I didn't know where I was going," or "I just had to wake up to what was happening to me." These are familiar phrases, and they catch exactly the human conceptions and feelings that we hear today in this Reading from Ephesians.

THEOLOGICAL EXTENSION

The essence of this kind of blindness in our lives, of being in the dark, of not being awake and seeing things as we should, is the failure to have the light of Christ guiding us. If we have these feelings about ourselves, a sure cure comes from exposing them to the light of Christ. When we feel lost, blind, groping for the right way to live out our lives we need to reflect on our actions in the light of Christ, seeing them as extensions of his own ministry and teachings. The light brought into the world by Christ's life and love will show us whether our actions conform to his or not.

"Take no part," says St. Paul, "in vain deeds done in darkness, rather condemn them. It is shameful even to mention the things these people do in secret. But when such deeds are condemned they are seen in the light of day, and all that then appears is light, Christ's light."

His light, his life is the remedy for our blindness, the remedy that wakes us up and makes us see things as they really are. That is why we read:

Awake, O sleeper,
arise from the dead,
and Christ will give you light.

THEOLOGICAL CONCLUSION

Indeed this is so. Christ is our way of coming awake to ourselves and others, of seeing as we should, of no longer being blind and foolish, but seeing clearly and being wise.

FOURTH SUNDAY OF LENT (SERIES A)
HOMILY IV

Gospel Reading: *"It was no sin, either of this man or of his parents. Rather, it was to let God's works go forth in him. I must do the deeds of him who sent me while it is day. The night comes on when no one can work. While I am in the world I am the light of the world."* (Jn. 9:1-41)

ANA-GNOSIS

Perhaps few things are so disturbing to our faith and God's goodness and kindness and love of us and our world as to see a severely handicapped person, especially a small, severely handicapped child. It's hard to keep from saying, "Why should God allow such a thing?" It's difficult not to question the wisdom of God in this handicap. It pulls at our heartstrings and spontaneously causes us to wish God would not ever face us with such handicapped people. In fact, sometimes we avoid them because we find it so difficult to share the awareness of their handicapped state.

THEOLOGICAL EXTENSION

Now, the blind man today in this Reading is a severely handicapped person. Blindness removes from a person one of the greatest of all human joys: to see. The blind man cannot see colors which would allow him greater access to the beauty of nature, of other people, of the human face and human body, of a thousand other things which those of us who can see take for granted. A blind person's inability to share in what seems to most of us so essential is not easily accepted and understood. Blindness, like other handicaps, brings with it suffering and pain, if not physical, then emotional. Parents, relatives and friends, all those who love such a person, suffer with them in this.

But their suffering, as Christ points out, is through no fault of their own. He makes this very clear, opposing a popular idea of the time that it was some sort of punishment for sin. We tend to feel this too. We have a kind of guilt, a kind of self-consciousness or shame around a handicapped child or person. But Christ emphasized, "It was no sin either of this man or of his parents."

Then what was it? And how, then, can we understand any handicap, even the most severe?

Christ's answer is "rather it was to let God's work show forth in him." Handicapped people, then, are special windows through whom we can see a particular quality of God.

Perhaps one of the most tragically handicapped person is one born without arms. Yet, and many of us have seen this, that person can learn to write and do many things with his feet. He goes through high school and college, sometimes as an honor student. He does all this without arms. We can cite many other examples of the amazing achievements, ingenuities, and great love of handicapped people we have known. We know how much real blessing they bring when they are loved and respected as coming from the hand of God.

THEOLOGICAL CONCLUSION

This is the point today. Through such people Christ's work becomes known, God's light comes into the world. Christ, who is God's light, shines in a particular way through the handicapped person. Let us appreciate, then, handicapped persons and realize that they are in a special way showing forth the wisdom and the wonder and the light of God. They have something special to teach us about life and about God's love for all.

FIFTH SUNDAY OF LENT (SERIES A)
HOMILY I

Reading I: *Thus says the Lord God: O my people, I will open your graves and have you rise from them, and bring you back to the land of Israel. Then you shall know that I am the Lord, when I open your graves and have you rise from them, O my people! I will put my spirit in you that you may live, and I will settle you upon your land; thus you shall know that I am the Lord. I have promised, and I will do it, says the Lord.* (Ez. 37:12-14)

ANA-GNOSIS

Almost all of us, especially the adults, have loved ones who have died. We've gone from time to time to the cemetery and "visited" them there, as we say. And there we are as close as we can be naturally and in our limited humanity to the ones we love. Their remains are there in the ground near us. There's always a deep feeling, almost like a childhood fantasy, of yearning. We find ourselves wishing that, only for five minutes perhaps, that beloved person could come up out of the grave and sit beside us and talk. How wonderful it would be if that grave would just open up.

Sometimes the thoughts and memories that came to us beside the grave of a loved one are so rich and vivid, that when we leave, it does seem as if we've had a visit again. It seems almost as if the grave did open up and that person came forth and was sitting there talking with us. Surely that is our deepest yearning and hope for all those we love.

THEOLOGICAL EXTENSION

The Christian promise of the resurrection fulfills this hope. It reassures us that this will be so, that in the mysterious way of

God, that person—not the remains there in the ground, but that real person whom we knew and loved—will be with us in some way in God again.

In the Old Testament, Ezekiel the prophet tells us the same thing: "Then you shall know that I am the Lord, when I open your graves and have you rise from them, O my people! I will put my spirit in you that you may live." This is our hope as we sit by the graves of those whom we love, or even now, as we think how much we yearn to see them and be with them again. In the resurrection God's spirit and God's light will open up the graves and bring us together again.

THEOLOGICAL CONCLUSION

This is the hope and the meaning of the resurrection. The people of the Old Testament, as Ezekiel tells us, shared this same hope and yearning. And they, like ourselves, have been given the promise of the fulfillment of this yearning. "Thus says the Lord God: O my people, I will open your graves and have you rise from them . . . I have promised, and I will do it, says the Lord." The Lord God keeps his word. We have great reason for our hope.

FIFTH SUNDAY OF LENT (SERIES A)
HOMILY II

Responsorial Psalm: *With the Lord there is mercy, and fullness of redemption . . .*
I trust in the Lord; my soul trusts in his word.
More than sentinels wait for the dawn, let Israel wait for the Lord.
(Ps. 130:1-2, 3-4, 5-6, 7-8)

ANA-GNOSIS

When we are discouraged and depressed, when we've suffered a disappointment or failure, or when we are extremely conscious of our limits, our inadequacies, it is easy to think that other people do not have these same discouragements or weaknesses or this sense of loss or failure. We feel that we are unusual and everybody else has a much freer, easier, much more hopeful and blessed life.

When we think about this realistically, and when we talk with others and they share their inner feelings and reactions, we find, sometimes to our surprise, that they are very much like us.

It's almost as if we were to propose that other people experienced life with all daylight and no darkness, as to suppose that others do not have discouragements, failures and inadequacies too. Indeed they do. When we read autobiographies of great people we find them surprisingly like ourselves in all these conflicts and confusions. All of us know periods of joy, happiness, and fulfillment, but all of us also know discouragement, failure, and a sense of our own weakness and inadequacy. We all know the light of day and the dark of night.

THEOLOGICAL EXTENSION

This the Psalmist stresses for us today. And, despite our inner darkness, he stresses that we must hold up our hope and our confidence in God. "I trust in the Lord; my soul trusts in his word."

We may know from experience or we can easily imagine the dreariness of being a military sentinel marching back and forth, so many paces one way, so many paces another, all night long. The Psalmist picks this image to symbolize vividly the weariness of life and the long, long, tiresome business that can discourage us while we are waiting for things to change, when everything seems dark and somewhat overwhelming. Will the night ever end? Will the dawn come? But the Psalmist counsels, "More than sentinels wait for the dawn, let Israel wait for the Lord." Why? "For with the Lord is kindness, and with him is plenteous redemption. And he will redeem Israel from all their iniquities." Like the sentinel, we wait for God's light to dawn in our lives, knowing through faith and trust that the sun indeed will come, no matter how weary we may be. No darkness is ever so great in our lives that the sunlight, the dawn of God's blessing and grace and love will not light it up again.

THEOLOGICAL CONCLUSION

Our discouragements are not unique. Others, too, feel the weight of their failures, their inadequacies, their limitations. And to all of us the Lord promises that this discouragement is not ultimate. If we wait in hope and trust in him, he will bring us through the bad times, whatever they may be, into the dawn of his light.

Just as the morning light comes to the sentinels on guard, so God's mercy and kindness will come to us.

FIFTH SUNDAY OF LENT (SERIES A)
HOMILY III

Reading II: *Those who are in the flesh cannot please God. But you are in the spirit, since the Spirit of God dwells in you. If anyone does not have the Spirit of Christ, he does not belong to Christ. If Christ is in you, the body is indeed dead because of sin, while the spirit lives because of justice. If the Spirit of him who raised Jesus from the dead dwells in you, then he who raised Christ from the dead will bring your mortal bodies to live also through his spirit dwelling in you.* (Rom. 8:8-11)

ANA-GNOSIS

Sometimes very simple expressions that we use, even when we use them without thinking, contain deep truths. When we are very tired we are apt to say, "I just feel dead." We sometimes use this, too, for times we don't have any fineness of feeling or reaction. We are without any enthusiasm, without any excitement. Another expression connoting this dismal feeling is, "It was a dead loss." Here again, "dead" suggests this waste of ourselves, lack of reaction, lack of real significance.

THEOLOGICAL EXTENSION

Now St. Paul catches that tone here today when he talks not simply about our final death, but about these dead feelings that we can have. The reason, he says, is that we are too much tied to our pure physical reactions, our pure animal selfishness, our carnality.

He says, "Those who are in the flesh cannot please God, but you are not in the flesh; you are in the Spirit." The Spirit, then, is the opposite of that dead feeling. When we feel a dead loss to ourselves and others then it is because we have lost our sense of the real meaning of life. We've lost the Spirit of life.

Sometimes we say, "You have to get into the spirit of the thing." Someone might say, "The whole thing is a dead loss," and another person might reply, "You have to get into the spirit of the thing. It won't be a dead loss if you get into the spirit of it." That's essentially St. Paul's point here.

But we need the realization that he means not just "spirit," but "The Holy Spirit." He means getting God's purpose and meaning into our lives and living in and through this divine spirit of grace in us. He goes on to say, "If Christ is in you, the body is indeed dead because of sin, while the spirit lives because of justice." If we get into the spirit of something, if we get into the real Spirit of life, we're out of the deadness of formality, out of the "dead loss" of selfishness that is essentially sinfulness. This is a kind of daily resurrection. From feeling ourselves a dead loss we suddenly get into the spirit of things and come alive again.

THEOLOGICAL CONCLUSION

The same spirit that brings this life to Christ brings it to us. "Then he who raised Christ from the dead will bring your mortal bodies to life also, through his Spirit dwelling in you." So when you feel dead, when you feel life is a dead loss, get into the Spirit, get into the Spirit of life. Reach out for the Holy Spirit in your life in and through Christ. This is the answer to those anxieties and fears that cause us to think we and our life are a"dead loss." We need to get into the Spirit of things, to feel new life and a resurrected Spirit in us.

FIFTH SUNDAY OF LENT (SERIES A)
HOMILY IV

Gospel Reading: *I am the resurrection and the life: whoever believes in me, though he should die, will come to life; and whoever is alive and believes in me will never die.* (Jn. 11:1-45)

ANA-GNOSIS

Often when one person tells another something quite difficult to accept, unexpected, unusual, the person who hears him is apt to say, "You must be kidding." The other person, wanting to make very clear that he is not joking and that this is really so, at some point says, "You'd better believe it!"

Now this exchange does bring forward something very basic about the way we relate to something difficult to accept. Our first reaction is to disbelieve. But finally, sometimes because of another person's sincerity or our own common sense, we realize that it is so convincing that we'd "better believe it."

THEOLOGICAL EXTENSION

Now something of this human exchange applies and even, in a sense, is necessary to understand the fantastic event, almost unbelievable event, that today's Reading reveals for us. Though we may first react to this with confusion, our Christian faith and our common sense and our whole grasp of Christ's life, tells us: You'd better believe it.

Both Martha and Mary, deeply loving Christ and deeply loved by Christ, begin with the same disbelief. They can't quite believe that Christ means a particular miracle in which their brother will come back to life. Mary repeats, understandably, the general belief that the resurrection will eventually occur. But Christ makes it very clear that he's not talking about some future resurrection, but rather a particular act is going to occur to reassure us of this future resurrection. That act will be the coming to life again of his friend Lazarus.

When he describes Lazarus's death he also tells us that this particular death means something beyond the death itself. Jesus said plainly, "For your sakes I am glad I was not there, that you may come to believe." There was a purpose beyond Lazarus's actual death in his dying. Just as there was a special purpose to the blind man's blindness, so Lazarus's death would have far-reaching consequences.

But when told of his imminent resurrection no one can quite believe it. The temptation is to say, "You must be kidding." No one had claimed in himself complete power over life and death. For a person to claim this exact power, that he himself had this power and was the center of the resurrection of all mankind, was almost incredible. But through his actions Jesus' answer comes back firm and clear: You better believe it.

Christ says firmly: "Your brother is going to arise again." "I know he will rise again," Martha replied, "in the resurrection on the last day." Jesus told her, "I am the resurrection and the life. Whoever believes in me, though he should die, will come to life.

And whoever is alive and believes in me will never die. Do you believe this?"

This question is not only addressed to Martha, but to all of us. Do *you* believe this? We might first react with: "You must be kidding."

But deep within ourselves we know he is not kidding. It is true. We had better believe it.

There is no way in the face of this claim, "I am the resurrection and the life," that we can simply think of Christ as a good man whom later his followers made into a kind of God figure. If this statement is true, then it is the statement of a person with divine powers here and now. And the point of this miracle, as Christ makes clear, is so that all may believe that it is through him that the ultimate resurrection for all of us occurs.

THEOLOGICAL CONCLUSION

Lazarus's death, then, has a very special meaning, a teaching purpose, that his resurrection will show. Despite all the fantastic circumstances here which may make our first reaction: "You've got to be kidding," and our subsequent reaction to look for reasons why it must not be so, why it must just be an exaggeration, or a series of analogies, the evidence is so sharp and clear that there can be no doubt. In fact, we see that when this story got around it was the beginning of the end for Christ's earthly life. Those in authority were so threatened by this act that they began to move against him.

The process leading to the crucifixion and death of Christ soon began.

Yet in raising Lazarus his message is not one of death but one of life. Through Christ we have the way to eternal life. He is not kidding. We would do well to believe it.

SIXTH SUNDAY OF THE YEAR (SERIES A)
HOMILY I

Reading I: *If you choose you can keep the commandments; it is loyalty to do his will. There are set before you fire and water; to whichever you choose, stretch forth your hand. Before man are life and death, whichever he chooses shall be given him. Immense is the wisdom of the Lord; he is mighty in power, and all-seeing. The eyes of God see all he has made; he understands man's every deed. No man does he command to sin, to none does he give strength for lies.* (Sir. 15:15-20)

ANA-GNOSIS

"Let me be free!" We've all heard that, perhaps even said it ourselves. It's one of the most common pleas of our time. Faced with an age of computers, highly sophisticated technological advancements, and increasingly complex social structures, we find freedom from all these demands and restrictions extremely desirable. Everywhere we turn there are white lines, red lights, forms to fill out, regulations to comply with, and taxes to pay. To call for freedom from this overly demanding society in which we find ourselves is to seek a breath of fresh air in a stuffy, smoke-filled room. We may feel ourselves being suffocated; freedom, like fresh air, is enormously desirable.

THEOLOGICAL EXTENSION

We know, however, that just to be free is not the end. The question is: what does one do with one's freedom? Which do we choose, good or bad? What do we do, the right or the wrong? Do we choose to do things that are helpful to ourselves and others, that will relate us to God, or do we do things injurious to others and ourselves, that cut off our relationship with God? There is more to freedom than just having it. We need it, yes; but beyond that we have a great responsibility to use our freedom well.

The book of Sirach assures us that ultimately we are free, God has left us free to make the choices that matter. "If you choose you can keep the commandments. . . . There are set before you fire and water; to whichever you choose stretch forth your hand." The stress here is on our free choice. We can do what we choose. Society may bind us by all sorts of restrictions and modern conditions may hem us in or demand things of us, but God does not. This is essentially what Sirach tells us today. We are free in God's eyes. Even society cannot so bind us that our basic freedoms are gone. These we must fight for with what strength we have against governmental and mass industrial forces, because God has left us free to do what we choose to do. How we use our freedom is our responsibility. Just as we know we are free to do the wrong thing when driving a car, perhaps causing a tragic accident, we know we are equally free day after day to do the right thing and use the car wisely and well. It is up to us.

THEOLOGICAL CONCLUSION

This is the freedom God grants to us. "The eyes of God see all he has made; he understands man's every deed. No man does he command to sin. To none does he give strength for lies." He knows what is happening, but he doesn't determine it himself. He leaves that choice to us. "Before man are life and death, whichever he chooses shall be given him." We can choose death impulses, destructive impulses for ourselves and others, or we can choose life for ourselves and others with God. We are free to choose.

We do not say, "I want to be free." In fact we are free. What do we do with our freedom? This is the important question for all of us.

SIXTH SUNDAY OF THE YEAR (SERIES A) HOMILY II

Responsorial Psalm: *Happy are they who follow the law of the Lord! . . . Be good to your servant, that I may live and keep your words. Open my eyes, that I may consider the wonders of your law!* (Ps. 119:1-2, 4-5, 17-18, 33-34)

ANA-GNOSIS

Modern superhighways in and around the nation's large cities are immensely useful for getting us where we want to go quickly. They eliminate the slow movement, traffic light after traffic light, or trudging through narrow commercial streets. But, especially if we're in a strange or somewhat unfamiliar area, they require a lot of concentration and awareness on our part if we want to get where we hope to go. All around us we see signs and guideposts to help us, but we need to be paying attention, keeping our eyes open, or we'll miss the one we need and may end up miles out of our way before we can get back to where we want to go.

THEOLOGICAL EXTENSION

"Keep your eyes open. Pay attention to the signs. If you don't, you'll get lost." Familiar enough to all of us who've driven or ridden on a modern freeway. But equally important words to us if we are to live our lives according to God's will. The Psalmist certainly knew this. He asked God, in fact: "Open my eyes that I may consider the wonders of your law. Instruct me, O Lord, in the way of your statutes, that I may exactly observe them. Give me discernment, that I may observe your law and keep it with all my heart." That's exactly what we do on a highway: discern the guideposts placed there for our benefit, make sure we get in the right lane so we can turn off at the right place, and follow each sign—doing what it directs.

In the Old Testament God's signs and directives were found in the law. It contains a series of wise and learned spiritual guideposts for his people. And by following those guideposts, like the signs on a superhighway, we get where we want to go. Understandably, of course, we may have our doubts. The signs may seem unclear or odd to us. We may not wholly understand them at the time. But by placing our faith in God we go ahead and follow his signs. And ultimately we will get where we wanted to go. We won't get lost.

THEOLOGICAL CONCLUSION

God has given us these guideposts, but we must keep our eyes open. In the fast movement of life, in the twists and turns that we can get into, becoming perhaps absorbed by watching the traffic around us, we can fail to see the guidepost, the signs, and we can fail to make the right response to get us where we want to go. We use our freedom wisely, then, by keeping our eyes open and by being alert to the signs that guide us where we want to go.

So we pray with the Psalmist, "Open my eyes, that I may consider the wonders of your law! Instruct me, O Lord, in the ways of your statutes." Help me see the guideposts, the signs, so that I will make the right turns and will end up where I want to go.

SIXTH SUNDAY OF THE YEAR (SERIES A)
HOMILY III

Reading II: *There is, to be sure, a certain wisdom which we express among the spiritually mature. It is not a wisdom of this age, however, nor of the rulers of this age, who are men headed for destruction. No, what we utter is God's wisdom: a mysterious, a hidden wisdom. God planned it before all ages for our glory. None of the rulers of this age knew the mystery; if they had known it, they would never have crucified the Lord of glory. Of this wisdom it is written:*

> *"Eye has not seen, ear has not heard, nor has it so much as dawned on man what God has prepared for those who love him."*

Yet God has revealed this wisdom to us through the Spirit. The Spirit scrutinizes all matters, even the deep things of God. (1 Cor. 2:6-10)

ANA-GNOSIS

There's a lot of concern these days about being mature. "Psychological maturity" is a goal for most every person we meet. Simple physical maturity is easily achieved. The passage of time accomplishes that for us. But what about being mature persons on the whole? That's a more challenging question.

But let us ask, in what does real psychological and spiritual maturity consist? What do I do, what do I choose or where do I go to get this? Popular answers are not clear, although many popular columnists and writers are very glib with their answers. Even serious psychological studies do not reveal absolute answers, Despite the term "psychological maturity," no one in modern psychology really knows exactly what constitutes "maturity." All kinds of controversies and disagreements occur once one tries to pin it down or describe exactly how one gets to be "psychologically mature."

THEOLOGICAL EXTENSION

The way to maturity is not easily attained in our age. Certainly it was not in the time of St. Paul. Yet he tells us that wisdom is found among the spiritually mature of God's kingdom. The way to maturity is through the Lord's wisdom, a mysterious wisdom, not earthly knowledge.

St. Paul does not mean necessarily that the men of his and our age are all foolish. He simply means that in the end they are often shortsighted. In using their freedom in a purely earthly fashion they may trap themselves into virtual slavery—slavery to a social system or, even worse, to alcoholism or drug addiction. Then those people become greater slaves as a result of their free choices. Theirs is a self-defeating freedom. Had they been guided by the wisdom of God, they would have remained truly free. This is the heart of what St. Paul is saying.

The wisdom of God and the spirit of God guide us and keep us free. They even lead us to greater freedom and ultimately to maturity. St. Paul says, "God has revealed this wisdom to us through the Spirit." To trust him is to take a positive step toward real maturity.

Of course, we want to be mature. We want to be real adults, not simply physically adult. We want to avoid childishness, infantilism and adolescent regression. How do we get it then? The answer here which St. Paul gives us is to follow the ultimate wisdom of God and the guidance of the Spirit. Since this is mysterious, even with regard to ourselves and to what really is the best for us, we must make an act of trust and commitment to the Spirit. We need to open ourselves up to his guidance however it may come to us. In this way we become wise and mature.

THEOLOGICAL CONCLUSION

"There is, to be sure," says St. Paul, "a certain wisdom which we express among the spiritually mature. It is not a wisdom of this age." Psychology can help us, philosophical concepts can help us; these are not to be disregarded. But from an ultimate point of view, with regard to our lives and their ultimate purpose, it is our faith and our faith commitment to the guidance of the Spirit that finally leads us to where we want to go. The responsible living out of this commitment of faith makes us truly mature.

SIXTH SUNDAY OF THE YEAR (SERIES A)
HOMILY IV

Gospel Reading: *Jesus said to his disciples: "Do not think that I have come to abolish the law and the prophets. I have come, not to abolish them, but to fulfill them."* (Matt. 5:17-37)

ANA-GNOSIS

When we hear a person speaking his own native language, or someone who is an expert in that language, it is always astonishing to hear the ease, the flow, the rhythm and accuracy with which they speak. This is particularly apparent if we, as students, have been struggling to learn to speak that language. In order to learn to speak it we have to learn grammar, constructions, and particular words. These are rather painfully, and with great difficulty, put together. When we first try to compose paragraphs, every sentence has one or two mistakes in it, and it seems a very difficult, if not impossible task.

When we contrast the rules of grammar, the details of construction, and all the minutiae of the laws of grammar with the living, fluid, rich, warm speech of an educated expert, the contrast seems truly like night and day. We, the learners, are caught up in the law, caught up in all sorts of details and minute applications, and constantly anxious about making mistakes. The educated expert never makes any of these mistakes; he speaks with an ease, a fluency, a rhythm, and accuracy that astonishes us.

THEOLOGICAL EXTENSION

The fluency of the native speaker is ideal, but it is not immediately achievable. And the same idea is found in our Lord's words today. He is not telling us that all details and minutiae, the guideposts and laws, the wisdoms of the Old Testament are to be done away with. It is true that elsewhere he tells us that the whole of the law and prophets is summed up in the loving of God and ourselves and our neighbors. But he means here that when love flows expertly from us in the Christian life, imbued by the Spirit and with the guidance of the Old and the New Testament, then we are like the native or very accomplished speaker. Our whole life then flows with rhythm, warmth, security and ease in a most deeply Christian and loving way. He points out that this does not do away with or change all the detailed demands of the law of the Old Testament. The expert speaker does not do away with the laws of grammar, the proper constructions, the agreements of adjectives and nouns, and myriad of other things which he is carefully observing as he speaks. It has become so much a part of him, so much a part of his living self, that this whole expression is himself.

It is rather like St. Paul elsewhere said when he remarked, "I live now, not I, but Christ lives in me." The expert who has learned a foreign language has, in fact, developed a living self in that language. This living person speaks with such ease that he doesn't violate the grammar at all. The Gospel of Love lived out as Christ would have it lived, does the same thing: it fulfills, not abolishes the law.

THEOLOGICAL CONCLUSION

Jesus said to his disciples, "Do not think that I have come to abolish the law and the prophets. I have come not to abolish them, but to fulfill them. Of this much I assure you: until heaven and earth pass away, not the smallest letter of the law, not the smallest part of a letter shall be done away with until it all comes true." Love certainly is the heart of the Christian gospel, but it does not do away with the essential wisdom of the Old Testament understood in the light of the New. Like the expert speaker in a language, the Christian does not break the laws but fulfills them in the living, rhythmic warmth of his life.

SEVENTH SUNDAY OF THE YEAR (SERIES A)
HOMILY I

Reading I: *The Lord said to Moses: "Speak to the whole Israelite community and tell them: Be holy, for I, the Lord, your God, am holy." "You shall not bear hatred for your brother in your heart.*

Though you may have to reprove your fellow man, do not incur sin because of him. Take no revenge and cherish no grudge against your fellow countrymen. You shall love your neighbor as yourself. I am the Lord." (Lv. 19:1-2, 17-18)

ANA-GNOSIS

Do you recall that, when you go to the dentist, the assistant, before the dentist begins to work, turns on the water in the bowl by the chair? If we think about this at all, we realize that it is in preparation for the possibility that we may have to spit some blood as a result of what the dentist does. Yet it is done in such a matter-of-fact way that we aren't really threatened at all. And even what the dentist does, though occasionally it may hurt, we accept because we know his intention is to help us. He does not hurt us because he wants vindication or revenge; he simply wants to do us good.

THEOLOGICAL EXTENSION

One of the most difficult things that we have to do, with children or adults, is to reprimand them, to confront them, to show them that they have done wrong, and to help them see that they should change their behavior. It is hard because often when somebody does something wrong we get angry. They have frustrated us or they have caused something to fail. Because this threatens us, we are spontaneously angry.

But anger does not often work effectively as a corrective measure, nor does it help us to behave in a holy manner, as the Lord exhorts us to do today. When Leviticus says, "Though you may have to reprove your fellow man, do not incur sin because of him," he is cautioning us against commiting a further wrong in our reproof. The danger is that we may release our anger not in a constructive way, but as a personal, vindictive, vengeful attack on the person who has erred. This would be sinful. It would not do the other person much good, and it would be very harmful to ourselves.

We can be helped by the example of the dentist. By long tradition we see dentists as people who help other persons sometimes by hurting them. But his attitude is one of concern for the person's welfare. He is commiting no sin by his probing of our teeth, even though we may not enjoy it. We understand why he does it and, in fact, even appreciate it. The concern, almost impersonal, of the dentist can be a hint for us when we need to confront someone or reprimand him. If we do it in a calm, dignified manner, not allowing our anger or our own frustrations to encourage us to attack them personally and vindictively, then we are following the Lord's commands. We are not incurring sin; we are in fact, helping someone else.

THEOLOGICAL CONCLUSION

We must, then, control our own anger before we can effectively reprove someone else. If we do not, our "correction" will not help but will only make them defensive and hostile. Usually they will attack us back and will not accept or profit by the correction at all. If we know we may cause pain, let us try to imitate the dentist here, and not allow our personal feelings to defeat the possibility that our correction might do some good. Not many of us would accept a correction given as a part of an attack on ourselves. If we can control ourselves, then, we can reprimand some one, do them some good, and remain without sin. We can be holy as our Lord has commanded us.

SEVENTH SUNDAY OF THE YEAR (SERIES A)
HOMILY II

Responsorial Psalm: *The Lord is kind and merciful.*
He pardons all your iniquities,
He heals all your ills.
He redeems your life from destruction,
He crowns you with kindness and compassion.
(Ps. 103:1-2, 3-4, 8, 10, 12-13)

ANA-GNOSIS

Traditionally when our thoughts turn to the love we received in our youth, we have recalled especially our mothers. They were noted for tenderness, open affection and deep caring. Fathers, too, of course, entered our thoughts, but not usually at the first impulse. Their role in generations of children's lives became more evident as children grew and sought the stability, quiet guidance and love that their fathers would give. In more recent years we have seen that certain aspects of love need not be associated specifically with a man or a woman. In fact, a child can receive all the benefits of love traditionally associated with one parent from the other. But this was not always acceptable, nor can we expect the Psalmist in an age far removed from ours to see the world as we see it now.

THEOLOGICAL EXTENSION

There is a real value, then, in exploring just what he meant by the compassion of a father. What particular aspects of love does he wish to recall here?

Compassion means much the same as *sympathy*. They both call to mind the idea of sharing deep feelings together. Parents who deeply love their children share their feelings. They know, deep down, how their children are feeling and understand these feelings. They are there for their children to depend on, even when the children may not have acted like the best children in the world.

All these things are a part of the compassion of a father the Psalmist recalls today. And they are a part, too, of God our Father's love for us. He cares very deeply for each of us, he is there to support us whenever we need him, and he heals and pardons us when we fall short of being the best people we could be. In him we find all the aspects of love we so need, and especially, today, the compassionate love which shares our concerns, our cares and our burdens.

THEOLOGICAL CONCLUSION

Love comes to us in many ways—each showing us only a part of God's infinite love for all of us. Let us take time, then, to celebrate today one aspect of his boundless love—the compassionate care and support he gives us, so often through our parents, and traditionally, through our fathers .

SEVENTH SUNDAY OF THE YEAR (SERIES A)
HOMILY III

Reading II: *Are you not aware that you are the temple of God, and that the Spirit of God dwells in you? If anyone destroys God's tem-*

ple, God will destroy him. For the temple of God is holy, and you are that temple. (1 Cor. 3:3-23)

ANA-GNOSIS

We are all deeply impressed by the greatness, the size, the magnificence of architectural wonders of the world. The great medieval cathedrals, particularly the cathedrals of Europe, stand out as monuments of man's achievements and God's glory. They are among the most brilliant of the works that have come from the hand of man. It took great commitment and dedication to bring these temples into being, and still thousands of people every year visit them and pray in them.

Of the great medieval cathedral in France, Chartres, Kenneth Clark says, "It's very construction was a kind of miracle." The chroniclers describe how people came from all over France to join in the work, how whole villages moved in order to help provide for the workmen. The building required hundreds of masons, not to mention a small army of glassmakers who were to provide the hundred and seventy huge windows with stained glass.

This effort demonstrates the extreme significance for the people of that time which the cathedral of Chartres had. It stood for many of the aspirations and the ideals and the goals of mankind.

The people of the Old Testament had this same conception and this same spirit. They, too, had a magnificent temple. For the building of the temple, the Old Testament tells us that Solomon assigned 70,000 men to bear burdens and 80,000 to quarry in the hill country, and 3,600 to oversee them. This is very similar to all the workmen coming from all over France to dedicate themselves to the building of Chartres. And for the Jewish people this temple of unbelievable splendor and magnificence was their one reassurance of stability and security after all their years of wandering. And so they placed great confidence in the temple and clung to its stability.

THEOLOGICAL EXTENSION

Our Lord, seeing this excessive materialism in their exaggeration of the physical temple, constantly reminded them that even this unbelievably magnificent, overwhelming temple would pass away. He also made the very strong point that beyond material temples and physical reassurance, they, themselves, were temples of the Holy Spirit. So St. Paul reminds the Corinthians when he writes, "Are you not aware that you are the temple of God, and that the Spirit of God dwells in you?" In other words, great as Chartres is, great as that temple of the Old Testament was, there is a far greater thing which is simply YOU. Just as we might admire the great cathedral of the Vatican, St. Peter's, or as we might stand in awe of Notre Dame in Paris, of Chartres, we should turn and look at one another, realizing that despite the magnificence of the temples and cathedrals men have made, each of us is a far more magnificent cathedral honoring God. We are churches, we are temples, we are cathedrals—each one of us. It is our regard for ourselves and one another that is a far greater honor to God than purely material temples. We are more magnificent cathedrals than anything that man can make no matter how glorious, because we are from the hand of God. St. Paul tells us " . . . the temple of God is holy and you are that temple."

THEOLOGICAL CONCLUSION

Cathedrals are great and wonderful. But each one of us is more magnificent and holy. We stand more totally for God in the world than any great cathedral ever could. Let us remember that every day. Keeping ourselves aware of it should help us act more like our Lord when we deal with other people.

SEVENTH SUNDAY OF THE YEAR (SERIES A) HOMILY IV

Gospel Reading: *"You have heard the commandment, 'You shall love your countryman but hate your enemy.' My command to you is: love your enemies, pray for your persecutors. This will prove that you are sons of your heavenly Father, for his sun rises on the bad and the good, he rains on the just and the unjust. If you love those who love you, what merit is there in that? Do not tax collectors do as much? And if you greet your brothers only, what is so praiseworthy about that? Do not pagans do as much? In a word, you must be perfect as your heavenly Father is perfect."* (Mt. 5:38-48)

ANA-GNOSIS

We all like to be loved. All of us like to be popular, to feel ourselves wanted; we like to be greeted by others warmly and feel we belong. It gives us a wonderful sense of meaning and value to be greeted warmly, to be liked and loved, to be appreciated. And in these circumstances we naturally love too. In a setting where people like us and care for us we can, without effort really, have the same loving regard and kindness for them. In fact it's almost impossible to conceive of a person being truly loved and appreciated not being himself a loving, appreciative person in return.

THEOLOGICAL EXTENSION

The hard bit is loving those who don't really seem to love us at all. And this Christ challenges his disciples to do today. What is there, after all, of the love of God in our love if we are simply responding to the way people like, care for and appreciate us. It doesn't take any special love of God for that. We will respond naturally to that because we like to be liked. We like them because they like us. What Christ requires is that we go beyond all this and love those who seem to us inimical, hostile, opposed, who seem not to regard us positively or with respect, but even with disdain, disregard and hostility. To approach these people in open love is a very different and a very difficult thing. We do it as an expression of our conviction not that other people love us, but, more importantly, that God loves us. Being sure of God's love, we have the strength to be loving and to turn ourselves outward and open ourselves even to those who are hostile and inimical to us. We can see, therefore, that to go out to someone who is resistant and negative, is itself a deep expression of our confidence and faith in God's redemptive love of us. If we feel our own intrinsic worth, we can withstand the rejection of these people. We can be secure enough in God's love to be confident enough to love them without demanding a return of our care and affection. Certainly their returned love would be wonderful, but if they do not respond we are not excused from continuing to love them. We have God's love to sustain us in the face of those who disdain or reject us. Nothing anyone does can deprive us of that.

THEOLOGICAL CONCLUSION

Christ urges those who would follow him to go beyond their ordinary good impulses to respond with love to those who love us. If they can love those who do not return their love they reach something of the way God loves all. Just as the rain falls and the sun shines on the unjust and the just alike, so God's love goes without distinction, unsparingly to all. Loving this way we imitate God's love. And to give us the courage to do so he gives us the assurance that we have been loved first by God and he will always continue to love us.

EIGHTH SUNDAY OF THE YEAR (SERIES A)
HOMILY I

Reading I: *Zion said, "The Lord has forsaken me; my Lord has forgotten me." Can a mother forget her infant, be without tenderness for the child of her womb? Even should she forget, I will never forget you.* (Is. 49:14-15)

ANA-GNOSIS

A small child, we know, has many mysterious fears. Fear of the dark is very common. For some time a child may not go into a room alone to go to sleep unless there is a light burning. Fear of being alone is frequent. Even to have to sleep in a bed alone causes the child to pad down the hall to his parents' bedroom, usually in the middle of the night.

Being lost or left is often a great fear to a child. In one instance a small child exaggeratedly clung to his mother and was afraid to leave her. He wanted to have her around constantly. She could hardly go out of the room without taking him with her. When it was worked out through the skill of play therapy, it turned out that his fear came from a rather small event. Once or twice when they had been downtown, the mother, because he was behaving so badly, had told him if he didn't stop misbehaving she was going to leave him. She hadn't thought much about it. Her own mother may have even said that to her, and she just repeated it to get the child to behave better. But apparently this had buried itself very deeply in the child's awareness, and from then on he began to fear that she was going to leave him. As he got it worked through, it cleared up and ceased to cause the panic that it had before.

But many of these fears seem to stem from a more basic fear of annihilation, a fear of going into nothingness, a fear of being totally destroyed. Now this seems to be behind the mystery of these childhood fears. The child attaches to a particular experience—darkness for example, or being lost—this far more profound and fundamental fear that seems to be part of our human nature.

THEOLOGICAL EXTENSION

Now, if we have this fear, we have it throughout our lives; it is part of our human nature. We merely mask it over by greater assurance as we grow older and are no longer afraid of particular things that might harm us. We get confidence in our ability to handle them. But we never lose this fundamental, primitive, anxiety that we'll simply be wiped out, we'll be annihilated, we'll have no value.

It is this fear which takes many subtle forms throughout life that Isaiah recalls for us here now. He puts it into terms of that early childhood fear, saying "Zion said, 'The Lord has forsaken me; my Lord has forgotten me.'" Here is the anxiety of a child, that his parent has left him, that he's all alone now. Isaiah saying, "Can a mother forget her infant?" reminds us that when we had these childhood fears our mother was always there. When we went down to the bedroom in the middle of the night our parents always took us in and reassured us and comforted us. Isaiah recalls this for us. Then he goes on with the profound reassurance that, in that rare instance where our parents or loved ones might forget, it will not happen with God. "Even should she forget, I will never forget you," he quotes God.

This is a profound reassurance against all our fears. It tells us that there is no place, no time, no circumstance, no sin, no guilt so enormous that can cause God to forget us or reject us. God will always be there to calm us, console us and restore us to meaning and significance.

THEOLOGICAL CONCLUSION

In our deepest fears and anxieties, then—for adults these center around death, illness or the loss of our powers and our meaning in life—even if those closest to us, symbolized by our mother here, were to forget us, God will never forget us. In God there is no way we can be overcome by our fears or be destroyed.

EIGHTH SUNDAY OF THE YEAR (SERIES A)
HOMILY II

Responsorial Psalm: *Rest in God alone, my soul. Only in God is my soul at rest; from him comes my salvation. He only is my rock and my salvation, my stronghold; I shall not be disturbed at all.* (Ps. 62:2-3, 6-7, 8-9)

ANA-GNOSIS

When we think of the human person we often think of the great differences between humans and other animals. We always point out a person's ability to reason, his vastly superior intelligence, and other things which a child or adult can do that are totally beyond the capacity of even the most powerful or most intelligent of the animals.

One of the things we are apt to overlook in this comparison is the capacity that a human person has to hope. Animals have almost no capacity to hope. That is, put in a circumstance where their immediate guides by way of instinct for coping with a condition are removed, animals quickly die. They have no sustaining power within them to keep them working at a way out, when, in the immediate situation, all of the familiar ways are blocked. They do not have, in other words, the virtue or the ability to hope. And so they have very little power to keep striving against something that is blocking them in their familiar ways of doing things.

THEOLOGICAL EXTENSION

In fact, one might propose that hope, as a sense of confidence in God under any circumstances however overwhelming—this idea of "I can overcome in God"—is peculiar to the Old and New Testaments. Other civilizations have never had hope in such an intense form. Among the Greeks, for example, hope was considered sinful. They felt it totally misled people. Since the gods predetermined a person's life, there was no way he could change anything, and, therefore, hope was simply an illusion leading to despair.

It's in the Old Testament—here we see it in the Psalms—and in the New, that we have learned that powerful capacity to keep going with a strong inner confidence no matter how much difficulty or conflict looms ahead. No matter how great it appears to be, we can, with God's help, overcome it.

The Psalmist says, "Only in God be at rest, my soul, for from him comes my hope. He only is my rock and my salvation, my stronghold; I shall not be disturbed." Part of our inner peacefulness, then, or our inner rest and security, despite all the conflicts around us and our apparent failures and inadequacies, is our sense of hope. We have put ourselves in God's hands, and so we hope. This hope leads us beyond all despair, beyond all loss of courage, beyond all immediate defeat or guilt, to the security that, in the mystery of God, whatever it is we seek will come to be.

THEOLOGICAL CONCLUSION

In this sense, then, the center of our peacefulness is God, not simply as our strength or protection, but also our hope. "Only in God be at rest, my soul, for from him comes my hope. He only is my rock and my salvation, my stronghold. I shall not be disturbed." I will not be disturbed because, at the root of my being in God, I have hope.

EIGHTH SUNDAY OF THE YEAR (SERIES A) HOMILY III

Reading II: *Men should regard us as servants of Christ and administrators of the mysteries of God. The first requirement of an administrator is that he prove trustworthy. It matters little to me whether you or any human court pass judgment on me. I do not even pass judgment on myself. Mind you, I have nothing on my conscience. But that does not mean that I am declaring myself innocent. The Lord is the one to judge me, so stop passing judgment before the time of his return. He will bring to light what is hidden in darkness and manifest the intentions of hearts. At that time, everyone will receive his praise from God.* (1 Cor. 4:1-5)

ANA-GNOSIS

One of the nicest things we can say about someone is that such a person has good judgment. We mean he has good common sense, is very practical, is a good person to rely on when we want something done, and particularly when there is a choice of various things, means, persons or complicated relationships to be handled or resolved. When we fall back on a certain person, the reason we give is usually, "He has very good judgment. I can rely on his judgment."

Evidently, then, judgment and the ability to judge are very necessary in our lives. Before we can do anything we have to pass many judgments. We decide how and with what means we are going to do it, whether we need help or can do it alone, if we need help, whose we will seek. These are all judgments. And this ability to counsel with ourselves and others and then make a wise decision or judgment is one of the highest abilities that we have as human beings. So it is great praise for someone to tell us, "You have very good judgment." He is complimenting our ability to weigh alternatives and make decisions on a myriad of small details which will add up to larger, more far-reaching decisions.

THEOLOGICAL EXTENSION

Since judgment seems so necessary and even praiseworthy, it is a bit puzzling then to encounter the words of St. Paul telling us to refrain from judgment. How do we get these two together: that we are not to judge others and we're not to pass judgment, and yet we have to make a thousand different judgments to be a person of good judgment, which is obviously a virtue and something very Christian.

Clearly, Paul is talking about final and fixed judgments. He means labeling or categorizing a person in a final way. He is talking about phrases like, "He is no good. He never was any good and he never will be any good." We've all heard that said. Sometimes, tragically, we've heard parents speak of their children that way, or we've heard children speak of their parents. It is very easy to judge people that way because of a series of things they have done that seems to add up to something permanent and absolute in their lives. It is this tendency, to take the place of God and make final judgments about the lives, the meaning, the significance and the character of other people, that Paul warns us against.

There is that same danger of judgment about ourselves. A person at a point of extreme guilt or discouragement—perhaps Judas always stands out as a salient and terrifying example of this—can make that same absolute, permanent, and final judgment against himself, finally saying, "I am no good. I never was and never will be." This is a blasphemous statement if I put myself in the place of God and make a final judgment about myself that I have no right to make.

Paul is stressing this then: we don't pass judgment on others. Even a court of law, one of our best human means of trying to make a good judgment, cannot rightly make a final judgment on anyone. Even Paul does not regard it ultimately as having any final significance. All that matters, he points out, is the way God sees us and the way God judges us.

We must watch our tongues lest we appear to make final judgments of others and appear blasphemous because we are taking the place of God. No one can say, because God in his mercy does not say, that this person is no good and never will be any good. The redemption of Christ speaks against this. Such a person is always open to the grace of God.

What we need to do for ourselves and others, then, is to hope and pray, and not make any final judgment of how good or bad they are.

THEOLOGICAL CONCLUSION

St. Paul counsels us, "It matters little to me whether you or any human court pass judgment on me. I do not even pass judgment on myself. Mind you, I have nothing on my conscience, but that does not mean that I am declaring myself innocent." The Psalmist elsewhere prays that God will reveal to us the hidden things of our lives. Many things we do not consciously see at the moment we may be doing wrongly to ourselves or others. Therefore, just because I feel I am innocent I can also be wrong about that. Our final norm, then, is to wait for the light of God to bring forth the intentions of the hearts. "At that time," says St. Paul, "everyone will receive his praise from God." That judgment is the only one that matters.

EIGHTH SUNDAY OF THE YEAR (SERIES A) HOMILY IV

Gospel Reading: *Jesus said to his disciples: "No man can serve two masters. He will either hate one and love the other or be attentive to one and despise the other. You cannot give yourself to God and money. I warn you, then: Do not worry about your livelihood, what you are to eat or drink or use for clothing. Is not life more than food? Is not the body more valuable than clothes?"* (Mt. 6:24-34)

ANA-GNOSIS

A father I know related a story of his family's vacation planning. He had asked everyone to come with ideas of where they wanted to go and what they wanted to do. Well, it turned out that they came up with an enormous variety of contradictions. One wanted to go skiing in July, another wanted to go swimming in Alaska and so on. And as soon as it seemed that everyone agreed that it might be nice to go to a lake and fish and swim, suddenly one of the children would get the notion that it might be much nicer to explore a desert somewhere.

We know that children often have not had sufficient experience to know that you can't go north-south, that you can't take a trip in all directions and in all seasons of the year, that if you wish to go skiing, then you are limited to places where there is snow. Since it's not easy to find snow except rarely in America in July, then you are not likely to go skiing. If you want the sun and a place where you can swim, with the exception of a few warm climates in winter, generally you have to wait for summer to do that.

This simply expresses what we all know well, that we can't have things both ways. We can't leave from Chicago enroute to San Francisco and make a stopover in New York. That's not the way life works.

THEOLOGICAL EXTENSION

No man can serve two masters. No man can go north-south. Thus, if our life has to have norms, goals and directions—and it surely does even when we say we don't have such directions, we are still going somewhere—then obviously the first and most important thing, as with the children and their vacation, is to decide exactly what it is we want. If we want skiing, then that, in large measure, predetermines that we will want a winter vacation.

So Christ is telling us to sharpen our goal direction. He tells us that people who have no clear Christian faith are always running after all sorts of things. What he says to us is that we need to see the heart, the essential basic goals of our lives, and having chosen it, all the other things will organize themselves around it.

Our goal, Christ urges us, is to let God be the king of our lives. He knows all that we really need, so if we seek first his kingship over us, then everything will gather around and organize itself around our choice of him. God will see to that.

THEOLOGICAL CONCLUSION

Consequently, excessive worry about the future is pointless. Conscientiously doing what needs to be done is one thing, but constant preoccupation with things which are out of our hands is something else. Let us concentrate on going God's way today, on making him our one goal. "Enough, then, of worrying about tomorrow. Let tomorrow take care of itself. Today has troubles enough of its own."

If we know the direction we are going in, if we let God be our top priority, then we will be able to resolve our contradictions and lessen our worries, for we can trust God not to let them overwhelm us. When he is our king, we can trustingly live each day to the fullest, and confidently let tomorrow take care of itself.

INDEX

Accusation
  —false, 23
Age
  —of anxiety, 10
  —old, 39
Anger, 75
Annihilation
  —fear of, 82
Answer
  —to prayer, 23
Anxiety
  —age of, 10
Appearances, 54 ff.
Aquinas, T., 16

Baptism, 11
Beatitudes, 21 ff
Blessings, 20, 47
Blindness, 57, 59
Bryant, W. C., 9

Captivity, 17, 47
Carnality, 64
Cave, 35
Change
  —in the Church, 11, 36
Choice, 36, 39
Christ
  —light of, 57
Christianity, 11 ff.
Church, 13
  —as moving, 13-14
  —change in, 11, 36
  —misuse of, 37-38
  —unity in, 12-13
Clark, K., 78
Community
  —of Christians, 11 ff.

Compassion
  —of a father, 77
Confidence, 63, 84
  —in prayer, 22-23
Confusion
  —of life, 34

Darkness, 8-9, 21
Death, 64
Deception, 16
Dignity, 38
Disbelief, 66
Division
  —among Christians, 12
Duty, 27

Eden, 32
Evil, 15
Experience
  —religious, 44

Faith, 22
  —commitment to, 72-73
Fear, 82
Forgiveness, 34
Freedom, 68, 70, 72
Friendship
  —with Christ, 51
Fulfillment, 18
  —joy of, 3

Gift, 1, 42
Goal
  —of life, 88
God
  —as shepherd, 48-49
  —love of us, 43
  —plan of, 55

Graciousness, 25, 27
Guidepost, 70
Guilt, 35

Happiness, 9, 32
Holiness, 5, 21
Hope, 61, 84
—Christian, 21
Humanity
—of the Church, 37-38

Ideal, 18
Image
—of salt, 28
—of sheep, 48
Imitation
—of God, 25
Integrity, 4

John the Baptist, 6
Joy, 9, 21
—of fulfillment, 3
Judgment, 55, 85
Justice, 21, 24-25

Kidnapping, 16-17

Law, 70, 73-74
Lazarus, 66
Lies, 15
Life, 27, 35, 63
—as a waiting, 3
—Christian, 27, 29
—dangers of, 49
—purpose of, 19, 21
Light
—of Christ, 57
Lincoln, A., 31
Longing, 6
Love, 43, 74
—of enemies, 80
—of God, 2, 56, 77
—redemptive, 29

Materialism, 20, 37, 78
Maturity, 71
Mercy, 25
Merit, 43

Nature, 56

Openness, 11
Oppression, 23

Pessimism, 46 ff.
Plan
—of God, 55
Pope John XXIII, 40
Power, 37
Prayer, 3, 22
Pride, 19
Promise, 18
—Christian, 61

Ransom, 17
Redemption, 17, 36
Relationship, 69
—Christian, 29
—with others, 25-26
Responsibility, 5, 27
Resurrection, 61
—of Lazarus, 66

Sacrament
—of Baptism, 11
—of Reconciliation, 34
Salary, 29
Salt
—as image, 28 ff.
Salvation, 36
Satan, 15
Scandal
—among Christians, 12
Self-deception, 16
Selfishness, 64-65
Service, 25
Sheep
—as image, 48
Sin, 35, 59
—of Adam and Eve, 32
Sorrow, 8
Speech
—malicious, 23
Sports, 26
Stengel, C., 26
Striving, 21
Success, 19
Suffering, 9, 59
Sympathy, 77

Talents
—Parable of, 19

Temple, 78
Temptation
—of Christ, 36 ff.
Transfiguration
—of Christ, 44-45
Trust
—in the Spirit, 72

Validity
—of Baptism, 11
Values
—material, 14
Vatican II, 11-12, 36, 40
Vision, 16, 30
Vocation, 2, 19
—to holiness, 5

Waiting, 3
Weariness, 63
Wholeness, 5
Will
—of Christ, 12
—of God, 70
Wilson, W., 54
Women
—role of, 52
Worth
—sense of, 43
—unique, 43

SECOND SERIES

Volume IV-2

THE WORD BECOMES FLESH

A Psychodynamic Approach to Homiletics and Catechetics and Meditation

Homilies for the Second Sunday of Easter to the Eleventh Sunday of the Year

(Series A)

CHARLES A. CURRAN
Loyola University
Chicago, Illinois

APPLE RIVER PRESS
P.O. Box 3867
Apple River, Illinois 61001

NIHIL OBSTAT:

Reverend Thomas G. Doran
Censor Deputatus

IMPRIMATUR:

✠ Arthur J. O'Neill
Bishop of Rockford

March 1978

Printed in the United States of America

CONTENTS

Preface v

SECOND SUNDAY OF EASTER 1
Homily I 1
Homily II 3
Homily III 5
Homily IV 7

THIRD SUNDAY OF EASTER 10
Homily I 10
Homily II 11
Homily III 13
Homily IV 14

FOURTH SUNDAY OF EASTER 17
Homily I 17
Homily II 18
Homily III 20
Homily IV 21

FIFTH SUNDAY OF EASTER 24
Homily I 24
Homily II 26
Homily III 28
Homily IV 29

SIXTH SUNDAY OF EASTER 31
Homily I 31
Homily II 33
Homily III 34
Homily IV 36

SEVENTH SUNDAY OF EASTER 39
Homily I 39

Homily II 41
Homily III 42
Homily IV 44

ASCENSION 47
Homily I 47
Homily II 49
Homily III 50
Homily IV 52

PENTECOST SUNDAY 55
Homily I 55
Homily II 57
Homily III 59
Homily IV 62

TRINITY SUNDAY 64
Homily I 64
Homily II 65
Homily III 67
Homily IV 68

CORPUS CHRISTI 71
Homily I 71
Homily II 72
Homily III 74
Homily IV 76

NINTH SUNDAY OF THE YEAR 78
Homily I 78
Homily II 79
Homily III 80
Homily IV 82

TENTH SUNDAY OF THE YEAR 85
Homily I 85
Homily II 87
Homily III 89
Homily IV 90

ELEVENTH SUNDAY OF THE YEAR 93
Homily I 93
Homily II 95
Homily III 97
Homily IV 98

Index 101

PREFACE

In the following homiletic and catechetical expositions, there are at least *four* for each Sunday and feast. Each one begins with an "ana-gnosis." This is not an ana-logos. That is, it is not intended to be an analogy or simply an example. We have called them "ana-gnoses" rather than analogies, because they are aimed at involving the reader or hearer personally at the level of his own *gnosis* about himself.

Analogy, in the *logos* sense, is too intellectual and remote for what we mean here. The hope is that each person will begin to commit himself and so be talking to himself while he hears or reads. He will thus hopefully be creatively reacting and so giving a homily to himself at the level of his own personal memory and experience.

These presentations are not intended to be all-inclusive. They are only *one form* of communicating the scriptural message. Hopefully their advanced reading may stimulate the reader not simply to memorize them—he or she may do this of course, and, we hope, profitably—but rather, as a result, to move on to his own personal witness and communication with his hearers. They are, therefore, intended basically to be personal stimulants and encouragements starting the reader or hearer on his own personal quest.

One will notice here that the *immediate human meaning* is most often seized upon—not some more complicated and subtle theological conclusion. This is not to deny the latter or its importance. It is rather to draw attention to the basic and rich human elements that are so often central to the scriptural message. The intent too is to initiate a process by which the hearer, or the reader, is allowed to enter into the presentation through its immediate human meaning.

To aid in this, the speaker should simply be himself, speaking in whatever way is most comfortable to him. His natural manner

would therefore usually be more often meditative than dramatic, more conversational than theatrical, allowing for the electronic apparatus to carry his words directly into the ear of the hearer—as in an intimate communication together.

These presentations are all *short;* some are very short. People often seek a short homily or catechetical presentation. But since they are short, further doctrinal and similar material may be added to them, as fits the occasion. Or, more than one may be given.

There is also the allowance for the possibility that later dialogue will extend and develop the embryonic concepts here. In this sense, what happens after words enter the ear is more important than before. This is the "germination" process; that is, seed once entered the soil and embraced by it, germinates and grows there. The entering may be quick—as the acorn enters quickly—but slowly and mysteriously over time, a great oak with powerful branches where birds abide and sing, can result. We have described elsewhere the group dynamic process that, we feel, could aid this.[1]

The model, therefore, is not the mathematics book: problem-solving which arrives at "answers." Our model is the familiar sower who goes out to sow seed. This is our inseminational aim and hope.

These themes are based on a personal approach to homiletics and catechetics, the psychological background of which is explained in detail in a separate volume: *THE WORD BECOMES FLESH: A Psychodynamic Approach to Homelitics and Catechetics* (Theory and Practice).

1. Curran, C. A. *Religious Values in Counseling and Psychotherapy.* New York: Sheed and Ward, Inc., 1969, pp. 231-248.

SECOND SUNDAY OF EASTER (SERIES A)
HOMILY I

Reading I: *The brethren devoted themselves to the apostles' instruction and the communal life, to the breaking of bread and the prayers. A reverent fear overtook them all, for many Wonders and signs were performed by the apostles. Those who believed shared all things in common; they would sell their property and goods, dividing everything on the basis of each one's need. They went to the temple area together every day, while in their homes they broke bread. With exultant and sincere hearts they took their meals in common, praising God and winning the approval of all the people. Day by day the Lord added to their number those who were being saved.* (Acts 2:42-47)

ANA-GNOSIS

An interesting and even surprising development in recent years is the growth of small communities of people sharing a house or houses or sometimes a farm and living a common life together. These are usually young people; very often they are young married couples with small children. Sometimes there are married and unmarried couples together and, more rarely, a group of older people may share this life with them. What is surprising is that this is a reversal from the ordinary tradition in America that each one has his own private family and property. Here are groups of people, sometimes as many as twenty, even sometimes a hundred or more, who have decided on quite a different way of life—sharing all their goods together, often eating together, and usually sharing a common philosophy of life or life values.

THEOLOGICAL EXTENSION

This should, however, not necessarily surprise us even as much as it does. We see in the Reading from the Acts of the Apostles that this is exactly what the early Christians did, probably for the same psychological reasons, namely that they shared a fresh sense of a new way of life, new concepts of how to live together, new concepts of genuinely loving and regarding and respecting one another. It seemed natural for them to want to share, even as a rather large family, this life together, and not exclude anyone or even to break up into individual families. This is often the thinking of young people who go off into this type of community living. They want to support one another in groups without narrowing off, as they would see it, into individual blood-related families.

We notice that in the Reading from the Acts of the Apostles this communal life is stressed very strongly. They gave themselves to instruction together, to the communal life and the breaking of bread. Those who believed shared all things in common. They would sell their property and goods, and divide everything on the basis of each one's needs. So do many who live in the communes we encounter today. In some instances, when the communes survive, they become quite remarkable, productive groups after four or five years of living together. Whether they exist as an economic enterprise such as a farm, or whether they have members who hold outside jobs and share their resources with their community, what they are doing could be in the spirit of the Gospel. Many religious orders from the time of St. Francis or earlier developed these same conceptions, and the vow of poverty is a symbol of one way of carrying this out in particular religious orders. We also know that Protestant communities, particularly the Amish and groups of that sort, live out this same idea and exist today. We can go to them to see the prosperous farms and the remarkably simple and very effective life that these people live together.

All this suggests that communal life can endure and also that it is a very effective way for individual groups of people to preserve a sense of common values, having in groups what as individual families they might not have nearly so fully or effectively.

So whatever these small communities emerging now, particularly among young people, eventually develop into, what we have to see is that it is nothing new. We need to remind ourselves that, different as it may appear to us at the moment, it is within the whole Christian tradition from the very earliest times, as we can see from the Acts of the Apostles.

Of course there are real difficulties in sharing property and living together, each according to his needs and each to what he can give, because there are often people who take advantage of this so that it becomes unfair. It demands a very deep commitment on the part of everyone—husband, wife, children, the whole community—each one to do his share, so there is a fair sharing of burdens and responsibilities as well as advantages.

It is still, however, a very workable ideal, and one that is deeply Christian from its beginnings. Such communities should not meet with our discouragement or rejection, but with our prayer and encouragement. We can often see, in them, God's will working for a way of relating which is also, historically, very Christian. They call for an extension of the family, not simply including blood relatives, but encompassing a much broaded notion of family including many more people with the same intensity that we now associate with the very small family. This is Christianity at its very heart. Our Lord made the point that anyone who follows his word is closer to him than a brother, sister, father or mother. This same love is at the heart of any Christian commune.

THEOLOGICAL CONCLUSION

We should not, then, turn away from the idea of communal living. It is deeply Christian in its roots. Rather we need to encourage the concept of "family" that it witnesses to, and in our own lives try to live out this ideal.

SECOND SUNDAY OF EASTER (SERIES A) HOMILY II

Responsorial Psalm: *Give thanks to the Lord for he is good, his love is everlasting.*
The stone which the builders rejected has become the cornerstone.
By the Lord this has been done; it is wonderful in our eyes.
This is the day the Lord has made; let us be glad and rejoice in it.
(Ps. 118:2-4, 13-15, 22-24)

ANA-GNOSIS

The sun is shining, the birds are singing. It's going to be a good day right from the start. We know it the minute we pull up the shade and look outside. And we carry this optimism, this happiness to all our daily activities. We go through our day full of hope and promise.

There are other special days too—birthdays, weddings, moves —days that we have looked forward to for ages. Some of us can recall waking up and realizing, "This is the day I'm to be married." Some remember waking up and saying, "This is the day I'm going to graduate from school," or "This is the day I'm going to be ordained," or "This is the day I'm going to start my new job." These days promise something very joyful, rich and significant. They stand out in our memory as very special days.

What we need to do, however, is to think about all the other days—those days when we pull the shade and see snow, ice or rain. Some days we're not feeling too well, we don't respond with joy, but rather, we groan when we even have to get out of bed. We may even say afterwards, "I should have stayed *in* bed."

How do we deal with such days? How do we deal with the dark and empty days of life? They are also there in good number.

THEOLOGICAL EXTENSION

But the Lord made every day, as the Psalmist reminds us here. God has sent the rain, the snow and the cold as well as the sunshine and warmth. So God has made every day—the nice days and the dull days—all for us.

"This is the day the Lord has made," no matter what day it is, no matter how dull and dark, no matter how depressing, no matter how hard. So "Let us be glad and rejoice in it." In that particular day. Not because the sun is shining, not because we are feeling great, not because everything is going our way, but just because it is another day that God has made, made for us. Let us rejoice and be glad to have that day.

It's easy enough to be happy and joyful when the sun is shining and things are going well. But, now, here is a way of revitalizing ourselves in the dark days, in the depressed days, in the days that are not necessarily going well. We should renew our confidence that God made that day, too, for us. Behind the surface of the rain or the depression or the bad way things are going, God is there for us always in his love and mercy.

THEOLOGICAL CONCLUSION

So let us follow the Psalmist, and no matter what the day is or how it may seem to us, let us remember, "This is the day the Lord has made"—this one, good or bad—"let us be glad and rejoice in it."

SECOND SUNDAY OF EASTER (SERIES A)
HOMILY III

Reading II: *There is cause for rejoicing here. You may for a time have to suffer the distress of many trials; but this is so that your faith, which is more precious than the passing splendor of fire-tried gold, may by its genuineness lead to praise, glory, and honor when Jesus Christ appears. Although you have never seen him, you love him, and without seeing you believe in him, and rejoice with inexpressible joy touched with glory because you are achieving faith's goal, your salvation.* (1 Peter 1:3-9)

ANA-GNOSIS

One of the most complimentary things we can say about a person is that he or she is "refined." And in that expression, "refined," we bring together a whole series of outstanding, distinguished attributes and qualities. A refined person is basically very sensitive and cultured, a person of most delicate and perceptive awareness about life, particularly about people. He is not simply a person of good manners, though he is that; nor is he simply of cultivated taste, though he is that too. There is a quality beyond all that which we ought to look into more deeply.

When we look at the word *refined* carefully we recognize that it commonly applies to a piece of jewelry. Gold and silver are refined. But when we think a moment more as to how gold and silver have been refined, we realize that it is done by an intense fire, an intense heat.

The Psalmist much earlier speaks of a person being like silver, seven times refined. That is, the silver is heated in an intense heat and then allowed to cool, then heated again and allowed to cool seven times in order that all the dross, all the impurities, all those things that are inadequate and unworthy of the silver at its best, may be drained away. Gold is refined in much the same way.

Now those pieces of silver or gold have most extraordinary value because, as we say, "They are most refined."

THEOLOGICAL EXTENSION

Now when St. Peter speaks here of suffering he uses it in that same tone that the Psalmist does. What he is saying to us is that if we really want to be "very refined" as persons, it is not simply a matter of going to school or of studying books of etiquette or even just relating in kindness to one another; it also involves suffering. "You may for a time," Peter tells us, "have to suffer the distress of many trials." Why? "This is so that your faith which is more precious than the passing splendor of fire-tried gold, may by its genuineness lead to praise, glory and honor when Jesus Christ appears."

The genuine gold stays in the fire and is not drained off. The dross, the unworthy particles, are drained off by the intense heat. A genuine Christian stays in suffering and his faith is refined through deep personal suffering. This is what Peter's Letter is telling us: we will become more genuinely Christian, more truly refined as Christians as we bear willingly in faith the sufferings and trials of life.

This gives a quite different purpose to the point of our life. Rather than pain, suffering and trial being seen as something to be avoided and feared, to be depressed and discouraged about, here St. Peter is telling us that it is the most constructive means possible to make us truly refined persons. But he means this in a far deeper sense than merely worldly refinement. It will refine our faith to the point of true integrity and genuineness if we bear our trials, trusting in God's mercy and care for us. God, through Jesus, gave us a new birth, Peter tells us. Let us trust that mercy, then, so we may emerge refined.

THEOLOGICAL CONCLUSION

True refinement, then, has a quality only brought about by bearing hardship and suffering with integrity and genuineness. A Christian bears his trials with this aim in mind. These trials drain off the dross from our lives. They provide the cleansing fire that makes us truly refined.

SECOND SUNDAY OF EASTER (SERIES A)
HOMILY IV

Gospel Reading: *"Peace be with you," he said again. "As the Father has sent me, so I send you."* (John 20:19-31)

ANA-GNOSIS

One of the rewards of Vatican II and its aftermath was the discovery by Protestants and Catholics alike of how many things, as Christians, they have in common. They have come to understand more clearly the Mass, now that it is in English, and have come to see that it is not that greatly different from religious ceremonies that they have which commemorate the Last Supper. In many other ways, too, they have come to appreciate our prayers and hymns, as we have come to understand in a far deeper and more respectful way their prayers and their hymns. But we have also noted the differences. And perhaps no difference is sharper than our focus on what we did call the Sacrament of confession or penance and what we now call, in a more apt way, the Sacrament of Reconciliation. I'm sure it has often occurred to all of us that Protestant denominations do not have a formal, separate counterpart to confession, while we, as Catholics, hold it so tightly and venerate it so greatly.

THEOLOGICAL EXTENSION

When we look today at the text we see the heart of what the Sacrament of Reconciliation is about. We see that it is intended to bring peace again into our soul by bringing together our guilt, our sense of sinfulness and our relationship with God reconciling them. The text here is very clear: "At the sight of the Lord, the disciples rejoiced. 'Peace be with you,' he said again. 'As the Father has sent me, so I send you.' "

Now let's stop here and look very carefully at this. Peace comes to us through one another, but not simply as human beings. We can get a certain peace that way, but it is not this special peace of God. In natural communication we get peace through confiding and sharing our guilts and our conflicts with another. Christ extends this natural structure to grant us God's peace using the same idea. And so he says "as God has sent me to you" . . . so I send you to everyone else. You can bring God's peace to them, reconciling them not simply with themselves and with you, but by reconciling them with God.

Now, why did Protestants not hold onto this Sacrament? Because they understood it, as many people have, as simply an act of blasphemy. How could human beings dare to forgive other people's sins and, therefore, act in God's place? This, of course, is what the people around Christ wondered too. You remember that when he first said that he forgave a man's sins, he then had to work a physical miracle to show them that he was acting with God's power. So it seemed to Protestant Christians that the priest was assuming the right to forgive sins *himself*. We must be fair here and acknowledge that many of the confusions over indulgences and other things that occurred at the time of the Reformation certainly could be interpreted as an abuse and a misuse of many of these spiritual practices and elements in the Church. Reformers saw it that way, and they felt the only way to correct that abuse, which they felt gave priests arrogant power to assume God's right over people, was to do away with any authority that priests might have over sin.

I think in all this we are wisely now, after Vatican II, saying with the Scriptures, "Let the dead bury the dead." Let us look clearly here at the Bible's authority of the forgiveness of sins. Protestant Christians believe deeply in the Bible and, therefore, they believe deeply in these passages. If they see them, as we do, as not assuming the authority of God over sin, but as a designation by God to Christ and Christ to the priest, then this is not blasphemy or the taking of the authority of God into our own hands, but rather simply obeying God's designation as his ambassadors to forgive sin.

Let us go on now with the Reading. Jesus first said, " 'As the Father sent me, so I send you.' Then he breathed on them and said, 'Receive the Holy Spirit.' " It is the Holy Spirit who is forgiving sins, not the priest or the agent in human form. "Receive the Holy Spirit. If you forgive men's sins, they are forgiven them. If you hold them bound, they are held bound." This is what Scripture says. Christ, commissioned by God, commissioned others to forgive sin. This is the only possible justification for the Sacrament of Reconciliation.

THEOLOGICAL CONCLUSION

So when we go to the Sacrament of Reconciliation, to another human being like ourselves, it is not that this person has some magic power; it is not that this person is in any way superior. We are not believing in any human power of the priest or any magic; we are believing in God's word in the Scripture: "Receive the Holy Spirit. If you forgive men's sins, they are forgiven them." This is what constitutes the heart of the Sacrament of Reconciliation, believing in God's word in the Holy Scriptures. We go to another human being who is so designated by the Church and we believe that through him, through his office, the Holy Spirit will forgive our sins. The authority and power of God, coming to us through the natural communication with another person forgives our sins and reconciles us again with our Lord.

THIRD SUNDAY OF EASTER (SERIES A)
HOMILY I

Reading I: *On the day of Pentecost Peter stood up with the Eleven, raised his voice, and addressed them: "You who are Jews, indeed all of you staying in Jerusalem! Listen to what I have to say: Men of Israel, listen to me!"* (Acts 2, 14, 22-28)

ANA-GNOSIS

All of us admire courage. When we know a person who has done a courageous act or a number of things that are very courageous, we can so admire and respect him that we can almost think that he is different from us. It's easy to think that such people are born courageous and have never really known the fear or anxiety that most of us experience. When, in fact, we know such people, however, and they tell us truthfully and simply about themselves, we discover that true courage has a great deal of fear and anxiety in it. But somehow the fear has been overcome. One saying that captures this idea is that "courage is fear that has said its prayers."

THEOLOGICAL EXTENSION

When we look at the character of Peter we get a whole series of pictures of him. We know that at the time of Christ's Last Supper and agony before the crucifixion, he is portrayed as boastful at first and then pitiably afraid, even afraid of the accusations of a servant girl in the courtyard. Even at the time of Christ's appearance after the crucifixion, he and the other Apostles were huddling together in a room for fear. Now here's a picture of a man who is not a courageous leader at all, but a man of great anxiety and fear. And yet, when we look today, we see a man of great courage standing in the midst of the whole assembly. "He stood up and raised his voice and addressed them: Listen to me! Men of

Israel, listen to me!" Then he goes on to delineate the exact credentials of Christ: "Jesus the Nazarene was a man whom God sent you with miracles, wonders and signs as his credentials. These God worked through him in your midst as you well know."

They had all witnessed and seen this; it was no secret but a common understanding. He clearly delineates the crucifixion itself: "He was delivered up by the set purpose and plan of God; you even used pagans to crucify and kill him. God freed him from death's bitter pangs however, and raised him up again. For it was impossible that death should keep its hold on him." Courageous words, challenging words, confronting words. And yet this is the same fearful, anxiety-ridden man who denied Jesus, now speaking out in clear and unmistakable tones.

Consequently, courage is not something that is different from fear and anxiety. Courageous people are not of a different breed or a different blood, as we might think if we admire their courage. Peter is the same person who fearfully denied that he had anything to do with Christ on the night of Christ's arrest. He is the same fearful man who huddled behind locked doors after the crucifixion. But now fear has said its prayers. The miracle of faith is evident as it is full grown now in Peter. He is ready to stand courageously for the Christ he committed himself to, the Christ he believed in, hoped in, and loved. We know that he stayed in this loyal commitment until he himself was crucified, a witness, to his courage, his faith and his love of Christ.

THEOLOGICAL CONCLUSION

Peter is a remarkable man in that sense because we know how afraid and fearful he was. We know, too, how courageous he became and continued to be until the end of his life. He is an inspiration to us because he is not so very different from us. He faced his fears with the Lord's help and overcame them. With the Lord's help we, too, can do the same.

THIRD SUNDAY OF EASTER (SERIES A)
HOMILY II

Responsorial Psalm: *Lord you will show us the path of life.*
I bless the Lord who counsels me; even in the night my heart exhorts me. I set the Lord ever before me; with him at my right hand I shall not be disturbed. (Ps. 16:1-2, 5, 7-8, 9-10, 11)

ANA-GNOSIS

When we have occasion to help a person with his school lessons, he often wants help in mathematics. And one of the things we can be asked to help with in mathematics is the equation. We can carefully explain that an equation is a set of relationships in which all sides are equal to each other. For example: as two is to four, so is four to eight. This, we say, is an equation. That is, as it relates to one situation (two is to four), so it will relate to another situation (in this case, four is to eight): the equation holds.

THEOLOGICAL EXTENSION

Now what we see in today's Psalm as we compare it with what Peter is saying in the Acts of the Apostles is a similar kind of equation. When St. Peter speaks of this Psalm he applies it directly to Christ: "David said of him, 'I set the Lord ever before me; with him at my right hand I shall not be disturbed.' " And he goes on to recite the Psalm in basically the same words that the 16th Psalm gives us.

But when we hear it in the 16th Psalm itself, it is directly applied to ourselves. And so we say, therefore, "My heart is glad and so rejoices. My body, too, abides in confidence; because you will not abandon my soul to the nether world, nor will you suffer your faithful one to undergo corruption."

Now that's an equation. Namely, as Peter says this happened to Christ in relationship to God, so the Psalm now tells us this will also happen to us. In other words, as Christ is to God, so are we to God. That's the equation. Because Christ was confident and secure and totally abandoned himself to his Father, God did not abandon his soul; he could abide in confidence. The equation then is that as we imitate Christ in abandoning ourselves to God and doing his will—as two is to four, so four is to eight—then we can be assured of the same confidence and reassurance and support that he received. "You will show me," says the Psalmist, "the path of life, fullness of joys in your presence, the delights at your right hand forever."

THEOLOGICAL CONCLUSION

As Christ is in God, so will we be in God. We will be, too, at God's right hand. We share in the sonship of Christ to the extent that we are like him. That's the equation. As two is to four, four is to eight. As Christ is to God, insofar as we are Christ-like in our lives, we, in turn, will be to God.

THIRD SUNDAY OF EASTER (SERIES A)
HOMILY III

Reading II: *In prayer you call upon a Father who judges each one justly on the basis of his actions. Since this is so, conduct yourselves reverently during your sojourn in a strange land. Realize that you were delivered from the futile way of life your fathers handed on to you, not by any diminishable sum of silver or gold but by Christ's blood beyond all price; the blood of a spotless, unblemished lamb chosen before the world's foundation and revealed for your sake in these last days. It is through him you are believers in God, the God who raised him from the dead and gave him glory. Your faith and hope, then, are centered in God.* (1 Peter 1:17-21)

ANA-GNOSIS

With state lotteries becoming more and more common, we are all getting familiar with the dramatic experience of the people who have a ticket that, as the drawings go by, becomes more and more valuable. It runs a high percentage of possibly winning the final lottery sweepstakes. We know how exciting and intense that final drawing can be. These people, as the ticket gets more and more valuable, generally put it in a bank vault or safe deposit box or keep it guarded in some very special place. And if a child were to ask a parent or a relative why he was so worried about safeguarding that ticket, of course the answer would be, "I have to keep that ticket safe because if I win that prize, the ticket is the way I redeem it. It's the reason that I can offer that I am the true winner." So we speak, then, about "redeeming" something with such a ticket.

THEOLOGICAL EXTENSION

Now this kind of modern usage of "redeeming" something and gaining a prize is exactly what St. Peter is saying about Christ. He points out that we did not receive this way of life through some diminishable sum of silver or gold, but by Christ's blood beyond all price. "It is through him that you are believers in God," says Peter, "the God who raised him from the dead and gave him glory." *Through him.* In other words, our ticket to redemption is Christ. Our relationship with and our engagement in Christ and his way of life is what will bring us to redemption. As we keep his word, so he, then, will validate our claim.

As lottery participants are most concerned and anxious for safeguarding their claim to the winning ticket, so we must recognize the extreme preciousness of our engagement with Christ and his way of life. He is our ticket. So St. Peter tells us, "Your faith and hope, then, are centered in God." And they are centered in God because, as he says earlier of Christ and his redemption, "It is through him you are believers in God." We must continually recognize his ultimate value to our lives, as it is through his love and our sharing in it that the true prize is ours.

THEOLOGICAL CONCLUSION

How often we acknowledge that "Christ is our redeemer" without ever really seeming to realize how precious this makes him. We often concentrate more energy on our lottery tickets than we do on him. Let us remind ourselves again, as Peter has done today, that it is because of Christ that we are believers in God and it is through him that we will be redeemed unto eternal life. He is far more precious than the redemption of any earthly prize.

THIRD SUNDAY OF EASTER (SERIES A)
HOMILY IV

Gospel Reading: *Then he said to them, "What little sense you have! How slow you are to believe all that the prophets have announced! Did not the Messaih have to undergo all this so as to enter his glory?* (Lk. 24:13-35)

ANA-GNOSIS

In the age of television, newspapers and magazines we are a

very informed people. It is rare to meet someone who, when a great event has occurred, doesn't know about it. Sometimes a person has been away on a trip in some far-off place, but even there it is rare that he would not have heard, perhaps on a radio, some information of such an event. But when he is ignorant of the event, invariably the phrase is, "Where have you been? How could you possibly not know what's happened?"

THEOLOGICAL EXTENSION

Now when we look at the time of Christ and the period immediately after his death, we realize, of course, that there were no radios, televisions, or even newspapers, but a startling event was still extremely well-known, even though Jerusalem was a very large city. Yet we see in today's Reading that the events surrounding Jesus's crucifixion were well known, just as elsewhere St. Peter speaks about these events being known to everyone to whom he is talking. The Gospel speaks of Jesus joining these men and asking them what they were discussing. And they stopped talking and one of them, Cleopas, asked him, " 'Are you the only resident of Jerusalem who does not know the things that went on these past few days?' He said to them, 'What things?' They said, 'All those that had to do with Jesus of Nazareth.' "

Now we see here that, despite the lack of television and all our modern communications media, this experience of Christ—his life, his death, and even now the evidence of his resurrection—is widely known in this very large city of Jerusalem. These men are astonished at Christ when he portrays to them the simplicity of not seeming to know what went on. And they literally say to him, "Where have you been? How could you be the only person in Jerusalem who doesn't know this?"

But even though they know about the event, they don't quite see how things fit together. And they seem to say, as we often do in those circumstances, "But it doesn't make sense. How could it have happened that way?" And our Lord then replies to them, "What little sense you have! How slow you are to believe all that the prophets have announced!" Even though they "know" it, they cannot quite believe it! They have said that not only did this man die, but there is evidence now that the tomb is empty. He had foretold, and all the prophets have foretold, not only the coming of the Messiah, but this extreme closeness between the Messiah and God. He had even foretold his resurrection. But now they said, "It doesn't seem to make sense." And Christ said back, "How senseless indeed you are."

THEOLOGICAL CONCLUSION

Some things, in other words, only make sense in faith. Here we have a unique situation in which God becomes man and demonstrates for us all, finally, not only to those thousands of people in Jerusalem who knew all those events and were following them carefully, his divinity. Christ rises from the dead. Yet we can know it as a conviction, as a way of life, only by our faith. And it is difficult. Yet nothing else makes sense. There is the empty tomb and there is evidence now of Christ's Resurrection and his appearance not only to the disciples, but to many others as well.

The only sense it makes is to believe that Christ is the Son of God, resurrected now for us.

FOURTH SUNDAY OF EASTER (SERIES A)
HOMILY I

Reading I: *On the day of Pentecost Peter stood up with the Eleven, raised his voice, and addressed them: "Let the whole house of Israel know beyond any doubt that God has made both Lord and Messiah this Jesus whom you crucified"* (Acts 2:14, 36-41)

ANA-GNOSIS

The idea of representation is very familiar to all of us. We have all either been representatives of some group or some cause, or we have elected others to be our representatives. We have, of course, in our system of government, the House of Representatives. And even children recognize that in a group we have one or two who speak for us or present our viewpoint or the requests of our whole group. It makes good sense because even as many as fifteen or twenty people can't too readily share ideas. It's simpler to have one or two elected by them, to stand for them. Captains, for example, stand for athletic teams even though there are only five or nine or eleven members.

THEOLOGICAL EXTENSION

This idea of representation permeates the New Testament, particularly the Acts of the Apostles, when it refers to the relationship of the Christians to the Jewish people, especially what Peter calls "the House of Israel." The House of Israel represents all of us in the long period of promise and waiting for the coming of the Messiah. It even represents us when we might prefer that it didn't. "Let the whole house of Israel know beyond any doubt," says Peter, "that God has made both Lord and Messiah this Jesus *whom you crucified."* He wraps it up in a very sharp statement. The act of crucifixion was accomplished by a group who stands for and represents all of us in our weaknesses and propensities away from God. Just as they were given the promise of the Messiah not only for themselves but for us "who are still far off whom the Lord our God calls," as Peter says, so they represented us in the crucifixion.

We must now see that we should be represented as well in their sorrow when they said, "What are we to do, brothers?" They were deeply shaken, and we need to be deeply shaken as well. And we need to follow them, our representatives, in turning now to a total commitment to Christ. Those who accepted his message, the Acts of the Apostles tells us, "were baptized; some three thousand that day."

THEOLOGICAL CONCLUSION

We all understand that we are re-presented in others. We pick one or two or three and they present themselves for all of us, and what they say and agree to, and what they sign, binds us all. Their acts are the acts of all of us. This was so for the House of Israel, and it was true of the three thousand baptized. They also represent us in their sorrow and in their awareness of turning to Christ. As they represent us in this act of total commitment, we, too, renew our commitment, our faith as the children of promise, as those who have seen the promise fulfilled. Though we may have been "far off" then, the Lord has called us, and we respond as the people did who were baptized in Christ's name.

FOURTH SUNDAY OF EASTER (SERIES A)
HOMILY II

Responsorial Psalm: *He guides me in right paths for his name's sake. Even though I walk in the dark valley I fear no evil; for you are at my side, with your rod and your staff that give me courage.* (Ps. 23:1-3, 3-4, 5, 6 ,R.v. 1)

ANA-GNOSIS

It happens to all of us that we can, with the best of intentions, want to do something that will be worthwhile, successful and valuable to ourselves and others, and somehow, almost imperceptibly, we find ourselves in a situation that is so mixed up, confused and snarled we are defeated, we have failed, and we don't quite know what happened. Very often we shake our heads and say, "How did I get myself into such a mess?"

This tendency towards "messing up," towards entangling ourselves in some hopeless situation, this tendency towards self-defeat, if we aren't very careful, works almost like the law of gravity, dragging us down all the time. Modern psychologists, trying to explain what mankind has dealt with from the beginning of time, have brought up the idea of death here. They propose that these entanglements can be a death-wish: that while we all have strong urges to life and, therefore, to achievement and creative success and fulfillment, we have, almost like an inner law of gravity, another force that pulls us toward destruction and death. There is comfort and security in death that is always weighing down on us and pulling us down. Therefore, just to plan something creative, something innovative, just to make a leap out that has a life force to it, is not enough. If we are not careful and aware, this new promise of achievement, success, and meaning will find itself defeated. We will find our lives "messed up," and we'll shake our heads and say, "How in God's name did I get into such a mess?" The answer is that, not looking carefully at the force of this pull of death in us, we have been led to failure and defeat because we were not constantly alert.

THEOLOGICAL EXTENSION

The Psalmist is dealing with this same conception when he speaks of God as our shepherd. He says, "He guides me in right paths for his name's sake. Even though I walk in the dark valley, I fear no evil." Another, perhaps even more familiar, translation is: "Even though I walk through the valley of death." The phrase "valley of death" catches more sharply this modern idea of the pull of death. Walking through the valley of death is, in a sense, the way we live. Defeat is constantly possible and we never totally escape the valley of death; we must constantly push towards life. But these life forces are not easily achieved. Still, the Psalmist gives us a means for overcoming this death force when he recalls, "For you are at my side, with your rod and your staff that give me courage." Walking in this predetermined valley of death, then, we need guidance and help or the death-wish will snarl us up. If we forget that we need God's help, his guidance and counsel, then we will end up in defeat, overcome by the forces of the "valley of death." But if God is at our side with his rod and staff, and we are aware of him, calling upon him, then we will have the courage to keep at creative urges and goals and plans, and we will achieve them.

THEOLOGICAL CONCLUSION

God is there to guide us for his name's sake. We have only to call on his strength to help us persevere and succeed in those things which we undertake in his name.

FOURTH SUNDAY OF EASTER (SERIES A)
HOMILY III

Reading II: *If you put up with suffering for doing what is right, this is acceptable in God's eyes. It was for this you were called, since Christ suffered for you in just this way and left you an example, to have you follow in his footsteps.* (1 Peter 2:20-25)

ANA-GNOSIS

It is common that a person can be made responsible for, or blamed for, something that he or she did not do. We have all been in that situation personally, and it can even be more broadly social and cultural when one generation or one group or class of people is blamed for something that they, as individuals, had no part in and in no way approved. When prejudice is discussed, for example, we often hear people sincerely express their resistance. They say, "I've never been prejudiced against people," and they mean it; they are sincere. They can give very real and honest examples to show that they, individually, were not prejudiced. So they state, "I don't see why I should be blamed, or my generation or group should be blamed, when I didn't do anything like this myself and have never shared any of those attitudes and, in fact, resist them."

THEOLOGICAL EXTENSION

Now the Epistle today from St. Peter helps us see that we cannot always escape this responsibility even though we, personally, may not be guilty. Sometimes we have to bear responsibility for evils we did not commit, just as Christ took others' sins upon himself. So St. Peter tells us, "It was for this you were called." We are called to put up with suffering for doing what is right just as Christ did. Peter says, "He did no wrong; no deceit was found in his mouth. When he was insulted he returned no insult." Yet he was blamed for many things. He took upon himself the responsibility of the evil of mankind even though he had no part in it.

Now if we take prejudice as an example of this, we can see, therefore, that in following the footsteps of Christ, the issue is not whether we personally have done any prejudicial acts or feel prejudice or superiority or hostility, or whether we unjustly condemn others for their color or background or religion. We can be totally innocent of this; yet in imitation of Christ we need to take on the burden and responsibility of what others have done. It is not enough for us, therefore, to say, "We have not done this." No, Christ did not do any of these things individually either, but he took on the burden of suffering for evil, and so must we. It is in doing this that we fulfill our Christian vocation in its most complete form. "If you put up with suffering for doing what is right, this is acceptable in God's eyes." Why? Because it was for this you were called, since Christ suffered for you in just the same way, and left you an example to have you follow in his footsteps.

THEOLOGICAL CONCLUSION

We bear the burden, therefore, of the evils of the human race. We take the responsibilities of them upon our shoulders and bear them and try to make amends for them, not necessarily because we as individuals have committed that particular wrong, but because, in following the footsteps of Christ, we bear the burden, like he did, of all the wrongs and evils of mankind. We also bear the privilege and the blessing and vocation to strive to overcome them in and through Christ.

FOURTH SUNDAY OF EASTER (SERIES A)
HOMILY IV

Gospel Reading: *I am the gate. Whoever enters through me will be safe. He will go in and out, and find pasture. The thief comes only* *to steal and slaughter and destroy. I came that they might have life and have it to the full.* (Jn. 10:1-10)

ANA-GNOSIS

When we read, or see a film, about a robbery of a bank or a well-guarded house, we are often left with astonishment and even admiration at the skill and ingenuity with which the thieves managed to break in. By contrast, we notice the ease with which the owner of a bank or the clerk turns a few knobs and opens the vault door. But in a robbery, access usually comes through difficult means, dynamiting and blasting, coming up through the sewer or through the ceiling or wall. It takes great effort and ingenuity and skill. And when police or civil authorities talk about some of these skilled thieves they often say that these people were so intelligent, so ingenious that, had they chosen a normal profession in life, they would have been great leaders and very successful people. There is, then, a strange contradiction, that with all their special gifts, intelligence and skills they somehow choose this perverse way to life in which they often end in prisons and in disgrace when their lives might have been so rich in honor and fulfillment. Their lives, too, might have been immeasurably simpler, as it is a great deal simpler for a man to open the vault by the combination of the door than it is to work all night dynamiting and digging to rob the vault.

THEOLOGICAL EXTENSION

Christ uses the familiar concept of his own day—as bank vaults would be for us today—when he refers to the sheepfold, and he makes the same point; that the gate is there and he who comes through the gate comes through simply and obviously. But to climb over a high fence or try to get in some other way is not only thievery, but is much more difficult. In the Epistle today Peter says, "We follow in the footsteps of Christ. In just this way Christ left you an example to have you follow in his footsteps." To follow in someone's footsteps is a great deal easier in high snow or in a thick underbrush than to plow through the snow or make our way through the underbrush ourselves. Similarly it makes sense to follow a four-lane highway rather than try to prove the strength of our car by driving across an open field. Now this is what Christ is telling us: the gate to the sheepfold or the entrance to the vault or the path through life is available for us if we follow in his footsteps. If the bank attendant opens the vault for us, it is simpler. If the person who has the key to the door opens it, it is simpler. And so, in a very real sense, to go through Christ, who is the gate, is to be helped immeasurably in simplifying the complexities and difficulties of life. We have, therefore, not to give in to this contrary urge in us, to take the difficult thing just for the sake of difficulty when there is a well-trodden path, an open gate that we can simply go through to arrive where we want to go.

THEOLOGICAL CONCLUSION

"I am the gate. Whoever enters through me will be safe. He will go in and out and find pasture." This not only is wise in the Christian sense, but it sensible in common sense. If there is a well-trodden path, a way to God which will help us overcome or avoid difficulties, let us take it. Let us use the gate that he is so we may come to share in God's kingdom with him. It is a good deal wiser than, like thieves, trying to break into the kingdom all by ourselves.

FIFTH SUNDAY OF EASTER (SERIES A)
HOMILY I

Reading I: *In those days as the number of disciples grew, the ones who spoke Greek complained that their widows were being neglected in the daily distribution of food, as compared with the widows of those who spoke Hebrew. The Twelve assembled the community of the disciples and said, "It is not right for us to neglect the word of God in order to wait on the tables. Look around among your own number, brothers, for seven men acknowledged to be deeply spiritual and prudent, and we shall appoint them to this task. This will permit us to concentrate on prayer and the ministry of the word.* (Acts 6:1-7)

ANA-GNOSIS

Of all the changes that have occurred since Vatican II, one that has produced much discussion and even controversy has been the change in the lives of the Sisters. The process of change has caused many of them to be no longer simply teachers of English, Math or Chemistry in our parochial schools, but rather to be more directly engaged in the ministry of the word: in religious instruction, in religious activity, in direct pastoral concerns. They are now functioning in a pastoral way in parishes and hospitals, on campus and in schools. This change has been compounded by the fact that we have fewer religious vocations now than before, with the result that we have needed many more lay teachers in the schools to take the Sisters' places. It is a great compliment to the Sisters' effectiveness that so many people wish we still had them in the schools even though so many excellent lay persons have come forward to serve in their places. Still, many people question why these Sisters should have changed the plan of their lives when they seemed so important and so necessary in teaching the secular subjects in parochial schools.

THEOLOGICAL EXTENSION

In the Reading today we see that the early Christian community faced somewhat the same issues, and they, too, made an interesting choice. They found that a great deal of charity was necessary, what we would call social work or Catholic Charities, because there were widows now in the community as well as orphans, and they needed to be taken care of. This was becoming a more and more complicated process as "in those days the numbers of the disciples grew." There was the division between those obviously of Jewish origin who spoke Hebrew, and those of non-Jewish origin, who spoke Greek, and some felt they were being neglected in favor of others.

But, important and basic as all this is, the whole Christian community unanimously decided that those who were especially called to a religious administration of the word—ministry of the word—should not be spending their time on these things. "And so the Twelve assembled the community of disciples and said, "It is not right for us to neglect the word of God in order to wait on tables."

Now something of this is reflected in the decision of those Sisters who choose to leave the parochial schools and go directly into pastoral work rather than to be nurses or teachers of secular subjects. Now we must respect their right to make this decision because we see how profound and basic their argument was in the early Christian community itself. The Sisters were raising no new issue.

When we deal with the spiritual works of mercy we mean counselling the doubtful and instructing the ignorant. Instructing the ignorant can be interpreted two ways: it can be thought of as giving *all* instruction—Mathematics, History, English, Literature; or it can be thought of much more exactly as instructing people in God's way, in the meaning of Christ's life and word and teachings—the ministry of the word. We cannot fault those Sisters who have chosen to interpret it this second way. In the early Christian community the Apostles made the same interpretation and the proposal was unanimously accepted by the community. There seemed to be no doubt in the minds of the early Christian people that when people were trained and called in a special way, as many Sisters now are, having very thorough logical and religious training, then they should be giving all their time to that work.

THEOLOGICAL CONCLUSION

So while we may well regret their diminishing numbers in schools, and we may wish we had enough Sisters to restore again their position in the parochial schools of a generation or two ago, on the other hand, it is a great event to see more and more lay people participating in this work, making it their own commitment and vocation. At the same time the Sisters and Priests are able to give greater and greater direct concentration to the ministry of the word.

In today's Reading we have a background understanding for this movement. The Apostles said, "It is not right for us to neglect the word of God in order to wait on tables." They had a special vocation which required direct involvement in the ministry of the word. They were unanimously supported by their community in choosing to leave the waiting of tables to others. So we should support the Sisters who move into new areas of direct pastoral ministry. The issue is certainly not new, and perhaps we can grow as Christians by initiating the understanding and acceptance shown bby the early Church to those who first chose to be involved in the direct ministry of the word.

FIFTH SUNDAY OF EASTER (SERIES A)
HOMILY II

Responsorial Psalm: *Exult, you just, in the Lord; praise from the upright is fitting. Give thanks to the Lord on the harp; with the ten-stringed lyre chant his praises.* (Ps. 33:1-2, 4-5, 18-19)

ANA-GNOSIS

Cartoons are both a source of amusement and often a shrewd judgment on the subject being portrayed. Cartoons in the daily paper and weekly magazines often slyly and sometimes with exaggerated humor, and even with deep feeling, point out crucial issues and deep concerns of all of us. And the drawings, by exaggeration and cariacture, often make a powerful and profound appeal or teach a significant lesson. The cartoonists do this by vastly exaggerating some characteristic. The simplicity of the early Americans in contrast, supposedly, to the wily cultivated superiority of the cultured European, evolved into the figure of the simple, but shrewd and ultimately powerful, Uncle Sam. Now we all know when a cartoon portrays the tall, gaunt figure that he's talking about us as Americans.

Another exaggerated simplistic picture portrays the clergyman or "good" person as a rigid, rather sour, sad-faced person. The clergyman is often drawn as someone who always is pointing the finger, a kind of a kill-joy, a depressing figure that people don't really want around when they are having a real celebration. If that figure is around, then everything is artificial and people are solemn and pretentiously well-behaved. We know this caricature of the minister or the priest quite well from not only cartoons but from television, movies and plays. Wherever it is, we find this exaggerated tone of solemnity and a fraudulent atmosphere devoid of joy and humor.

THEOLOGICAL EXTENSION

Now wherever this exaggerated caricature has come from, it is tragically inappropriate. Today the Psalmist, writing years before Christ, tells us that a good person should always be singing, always joyful, delightful to be around. There could never be a more exaggerated, misleading view of goodness than to see it as something sad, solemn and rigid. "Exult, you just, in the Lord; praise from the upright is fitting. Give thanks to the Lord on the harp; with a ten-stringed lyre chant his praises." In other words, goodness is happiness, is joy, is singing. To love God and genuinely to be upright is to be singing all the time in God's love, not only in one's heart but extrinsically. If we are giving the impression with our lives that Christians are dour, sad, rigid people then we are contributing to a tragic misconception, and we need to reflect on the Christian quality of our own lives. If we were living them as the Psalmist suggested and with the love that Christ urged, we would find that our likeness in cartoons would reflect a joy, a happiness, a fulfillment that is now absent.

THEOLOGICAL CONCLUSION

"Exult, you just, in the Lord; praise from the upright is fitting." To be good is to sing, to be happy, to be filled with joy to know that God's hand is guiding us. And so guided and so taken care of, our life should be one of happiness and joy and of God's melody. If it is not, then let us try to discover why it is not and ask Christ to help us find the joy that he intends for us.

FIFTH SUNDAY OF EASTER (SERIES A)
HOMILY III

Reading II: *You, however, are "a chosen race, a royal priesthood, a consecrated nation, a people he claims for his own to proclaim the glorious works" of the One who called you from darkness into his marvelous light.* (1 Peter 2:4-9)

ANA-GNOSIS

The airplane, particularly the jet plane, has changed the modern world. Trains and automobiles have been of great utility, but neither has the spectacular swiftness of the jet plane. In a jet we can leave the United States and, in five or six hours be in Europe or some other faraway place. It's startling when we realize the distance we have traveled so rapidly. Perhaps, though, the most startling contrast jets permit us is the experience of leaving the cold and a five- or six-inch snowstorm in Ohio or Minnesota or some northern state and, in two hours, landing in Miami, Florida in brilliant sunshine and 80 degree temperatures. It's almost a shock to experience the difference.

We can compare this, of course, with other experiences. We know what it's like to be out at night in the cold and have someone welcome us into a warm, lighted room. We also know the startling contrast of being in a tunnel for a long time and then suddenly coming out into the light. We are almost blinded by the difference we experience.

THEOLOGICAL EXTENSION

Now all these contrasts help us appreciate the point that is being made by the first Epistle of St. Peter which we read today. He uses the simple contrast of coming out from darkness into brilliant, marvelous light. What St. Peter wants us to see by this contrast is the difference between the coldness, the darkness without Christ that our lives would be, and the marvelous light, the warmth, the fulfillment, the richness that is ours in and through Christ. With Christ as the center, the cornerstone of the building of our life, then it is solid, it is secure, it is lasting. Without Christ it is unstable and weak; it will topple. Without Christ we are in darkness, in the cold. With Christ we come in out of the cold, we come into marvelous light.

THEOLOGICAL CONCLUSION

The light is ours, St. Peter tells us, if we accept Christ as the center of our lives. Without Christ we are in the dark, we don't know where we are going. He gives us the direction we need to get to where we want to be. When we are in the dark about life, Christ provides us with a marvelous light which will bring us to understanding, to clarity and to goodness.

FIFTH SUNDAY OF EASTER (SERIES A)
HOMILY IV

Gospel Reading: *Jesus said to his disciples: "Do not let your hearts be troubled. Have faith in God and faith in me. In my father's house there are many dwelling places; otherwise, how could I have told you that I was going to prepare a place for you?*
I am indeed going to prepare a place for you, and then I shall come back and take you with me, that where I am you also may be. You know the way that leads where I go." (Jn. 14:1-12)

ANA-GNOSIS

When people are separating, when one is going on a long journey and is going to be apart for a rather long time, there's understandably a desire to say something consoling or reassuring. When we are leaving someone or they are leaving us, we want something to remember them by. We want some phrase or some action that we can hold onto and keep with us as a reassurance and a consolation during the long period of separation. So it is understandable that at some point the person who is leaving tries to say something very special, something that sums up the meaning of people's lives together just before they leave.

THEOLOGICAL EXTENSION

Now this is the spirit and the mood of the Gospel today. Christ is saying something to the disciples and to all of us that we can take with us and hold during this long period of separation before we see him again. He means to console and reassure us as he gives us his last statement here to hold onto: "Do not let your hearts be troubled. Have faith in God and faith in me." This is the essence of our lives. We must not let ourselves be overwhelmed and we must keep our faith in God in and through Christ. He goes on: "In my father's house there are many dwelling places; otherwise how could I have told you that I was going to prepare a place for you." It recalls to us the early days of our country when a man left Great Britain or Ireland or the continent, reassuring his wife and children, "Don't worry now. It'll be a while but we'll have a wonderful home in America." Finally, then, our Lord says: "I am indeed going to prepare a place for you, and then I shall come back to take you with me, that where I am you also may be. You know the way that leads where I go." How confident, how sure he is that we know what we should do. And he promises that he will be back and will bring us to that place that he is now preparing for us.

This is a very simple reassurance. One might almost say, having heard it so often, that it runs the danger of becoming banal and so trite that we dismiss it. And yet if we put it in the setting of someone leaving and wanting to say the most consoling thing that he can to reassure those he is leaving behind during his departure and the following separation, what could be more beautiful than what Christ has said?

He promises this because he is certain that we know the way. And when the disciples are confused about this way, as we can readily be, Christ reassures them, "I am the way, the truth and the life, no one comes to the Father but through me. If you know me, you know my father also." There we are. We are in the family of God. Christ reassures us that through him we can be confident of a loving welcome and protection and warmth by God our father.

THEOLOGICAL CONCLUSION

Banal and trite as it may seem because we have heard it thousands of times, we can renew its freshness and richness if we hear it in the appropriate setting. Then we can take heart because Christ's promise gives meaning and purpose to our lives until we are reunited with him.

SIXTH SUNDAY OF EASTER (SERIES A)
HOMILY I

Reading I: *Philip went down to the town of Samaria and there proclaimed the Messiah. Without exception, the crowds that heard Philip and saw the miracles he performed attended closely to what he had to say. There were many who had unclean spirits, which came out shrieking loudly. Many others were paralytics or cripples, and these were cured. The rejoicing in that town rose to fever pitch.* (Acts 8:5-8, 14-17)

ANA-GNOSIS

We are all familiar with the opening of a new store, the special gifts, entertainment, and perhaps premiums that are offered for all those who attend the opening day. Each of us has received advertisements that tell about a free 30-day offer, or a free gift for trying a new product. Even some banks offer gifts to encourage people to start new accounts.

In other words, in all these cases people are faced with something new, unknown, of unrecognized worth, and so they need a special lure to bring them to try it. Of course, once you have tried the product, you don't get that premium any more. The company believes that the product is so good that once you have used it you will become confirmed and convinced and will continue to support that product. But the premium satisfies a psychological need; it gives the person a reward for trying something new which otherwise he would not risk trying.

THEOLOGICAL EXTENSION

Now when we read today in the Acts of the Apostles about the early Church and the work of Philip in the town of Samaria, we see that he performed unusual miracles: "Philip went down to Samaria and there proclaimed the Messiah. Without exception, the crowds that heard Philip and saw the miracles he performed, attended closely to what he had to say." Now, if we were describing this today we would no doubt leave out that line, "and saw the miracles." We would write, "Without exception the crowd that heard Philip attended closely to what he had to say." Now without intending to be disrespectful to the miracles, signs and wonders that accompanied much of the early mission of the Church, we can see them as filling something of the same psychological need that premiums now fill for new products first going to be marketed. The miracles attracted peoples' attention. They dared to try something unfamiliar, to trust it, and they began then to know its true value in their lives. The miracles, then, like the premiums, served a purpose.

So if we ask why, now, there are far fewer miracles, granting that there are still some, the answer could very simply and truthfully be that they are no longer needed. Miracles were needed at a time when the whole doctrine of Christ and the Christian community were new. Understandably, human nature needed a special appeal to attract attention to its doctrine and to enable people to commit themselves to it and to live by it. But once this is established, as in the use of premiums, there is no longer any need for this special appeal. Now the people knew the value and meaning of Christ and lived in his way and continued to be convinced of his truth.

THEOLOGICAL CONCLUSION

Miracles were there to help persuade people in the beginning because Christianity was new and unknown. But once Christianity became well-known, as in the western world it soon did, then gradually spreading over the globe, enough people saw its wisdom and truth to accept it without needing to be convinced by miraculous happenings. Now, instead of miracles bringing people to Christ, God counts on our conviction, our way of life, our example in our words and lives to bring others to the Church. Stated another way, we are now a mature church of convinced and confirmed faith. Christ is no longer unknown, but he must be known better now in and through us, through our lives and works. This is the great compliment and responsibility that God gives us: Christ becomes known through us now, and not as much by signs and wonders as he was before.

SIXTH SUNDAY OF EASTER (SERIES A)
HOMILY II

Responsorial Psalm: *Let all the earth cry out to God with joy. . . . Hear now, all of you who fear God, while I declare what he has done for me. Blessed be God who refused me not my prayer or his kindness!* (Ps. 66:1-3, 4-5, 6-7, 16, 20)

ANA-GNOSIS

In an age which finds some people in a constant striving for more headlines and glaring publicity, we find comparatively few people dominating the media continually, while the vast majority we never hear from at all. We often speak of the "silent majority," and in fact, most of us belong to it. We are those who never make the headlines and are never invited to talkshows, and very often we have very different values, goals and standards than those people we read about so often. Yet we don't often realize we are not alone unless a nationwide poll calls it to our attention. We may think that everyone else feels just the way the publicity seekers do.

A recent type of headline maker has been the "born-again Christian." And, as we suspect all publicity seekers, we can't help but suspect a politician who suddenly "finds Christ" and writes a best-selling book, or a man who has made a fortune on pornography suddenly saying he's "found Christ." We cannot help but be cynical and wonder if it is just another new fad for them. This we cannot judge; we must leave it to God.

What we must realize though is that, whether or not these publicity seekers are telling the truth, there have, in fact, been many people we've never heard of who have found noticeable meaning and significance in their lives, have changed their lives, or have lived simple, but very rich, lives in and through Christ.

THEOLOGICAL EXTENSION

So just because the aura of fraudulency and publicity seeking may now be around there "re-born" people, we should not neglect the fact that knowing Christ does profoundly change our lives. This is what the Psalmist reminds us of now when he says, "Hear now, all you who fear God, while I declare what he has done for me." He sounds like one of these publicity seekers who has found Christ. But as we see, he is not out for his own notoriety. This is the statement of an ancient, prayerful man, aware of his sinfulness, who knows in his heart what life would have been without God, and what it now is with him.

We can say this of ourselves too. We can leave out all the publicity and all the blare and all the talkshow banality and look very simply at our own lives. We can all say, then, with rich testimony, "Hear now, all you who fear God, while *I* declare what he has done for *me*."

Just a meditation of a few minutes, or an hour or a day spent in recollection or in retreat, brings to us again the sharp realization of all we have received from God. How different our lives are because Christ is in them! This is not a talkshow or a best-seller or a lot of blaring publicity of reform. This is the quiet meaning of Christ in our own lives. Indeed, he has done enormous things for us.

THEOLOGICAL CONCLUSION

So we can say with the Psalmist, "Blessed be God who refused me not my prayer or his kindness.' How often, in fact, do we say, prefacing our story of some wonderful thing that has happened, "Thank God, this happened to me. It was the answer to a prayer." We're not on a talkshow; we're not writing a best-seller, we're speaking from our heart, and we really mean it when we declare the wonders he has done for us. We share with the Psalmist this spirit of deep joy at the evidence of God's wonderful love for us.

SIXTH SUNDAY OF EASTER (SERIES A)
HOMILY III

Reading II: *Venerate the Lord, that is, Christ, in your hearts. Should anyone ask you the reason for this hope of yours, be ever ready to reply, but speak gently and respectfully. Keep your conscience clear so that, whenever you are defamed, those who libel your way of life in Christ may be disappointed. If it should be God's will* *that you suffer, it is better to do so for good deeds than for evil ones.* (1 Pt. 3:15-18)

ANA-GNOSIS

It's one of the contradictions of human nature that sometimes the only way a person can approach something that he or she is genuinely interested in or genuinely attracted by, is to start by criticizing it, attacking it, finding things wrong with it. This is true of persons also. We can be very attracted by a person, and yet have an urge to criticize them, and even to appear very negative towards them. We all know the charming, oft-repeated theme in which the little boy teases or pulls the pigtails of, or chases after, a little girl, appearing to annoy her. Yet most of the time that little girl is his favorite.

This childhood scene reveals something that carries on throughout life. Often we are unable to face openly and directly what we really care about. We must do it negatively, hostilely, even in a very critical or unjust way at first. It is only when this does not succeed in totally alienating us or making us enemies of another person that we then grow to realize and acknowledge how much we care for this other person. We've seen many movies and plays, and we even may know particular instances of our own relatives and friends, where people have begun a courtship by being very angry, hostile and resentful of one another. The man may sometimes have behaved in an almost unbearable way the first time he met the woman that he later married and lived a whole life with in love. Sometimes it is the woman who rejects the man, and years later, in laughter and amusement, they tell about how hostile they were to one another for quite some time before they began to realize that, in fact, they really loved one another.

THEOLOGICAL EXTENSION

Now all this is enough to set the atmosphere for our under standing of what St. Peter is saying today about people who are often interested in our faith and in our Christian way of life. They often begin by inquiring, but sometimes the inquiry is negative and even hostile. They may repeat to us sometimes ridiculous, sometimes exaggerated accusations, and these may be so defaming and so shameful in their form, that they could motivate us to quick anger and resentment and cause us to attack them in return.

But St. Peter is advising us not to do it that way at all because, behind all this there can genuinely be a real concern even though, like the little boy pulling the girl's hair, or the beginning of a courtship that starts in a vicious quarrel, these people can only show their interest in our Christian way of life by negation and even vicious criticism and attack. So St. Peter tells us, "Should anyone ask you the reason for this hope of yours, be ready to reply, but speak gently and carefully." Be careful of anger and the urge to attack back, especially when something unjust has been said. "Keep your conscience clear, so that whenever you are defamed, those who libel your life in Christ may be disappointed. If it should be God's will that you suffer, it is better to do so for good deeds than for evil ones."

Now there is a great deal of common sense in all this. If we can forestall our urge to attack back, to be very angry and hostile, to be ungracious or disrespectful when someone has defamed our Christian way of life or even our personal behaviour in some very unjust way, often we can recognize what is really the beginning of their deep interest in us and in our way of life. And we all know stories, the same as those of hostile early courtship and subsequent marriage, in which some of the deepest and most committed Christians have been people who began with horrible distortions and misunderstandings of what Christ was all about.

THEOLOGICAL CONCLUSION

It is important, therefore, that we follow this caution of St. Peter and not attack our critics in meanness, hostility and bitterness. We must remain always, as he says, "speaking gently and respectfully," so that through our gentleness and our respect for them, they can get beyond their distortion and their antagonism, and begin to see the true and genuine way of Christian life. This is what will lead them to the meaning of Christianity for themselves.

SIXTH SUNDAY OF EASTER (SERIES A)
HOMILY IV

Gospel Reading: *A little while now and the world will see me no more; but you see me as one who has life, and you will have life. On that* *day you will know that I am in my Father, and you in me, and I in you. He who obeys the commandments he has from me is the man who loves me; and he who loves me will be loved by my Father. I too will love him and reveal myself to him."* (Jn. 14: 15-21)

ANA-GNOSIS

The phrase, "a little while," can mean many different things. When someone says, "Wait here a little while, I'll be right back," we know that a little while means only a few minutes. But from another point of view, if we think of how quickly life passes, a little while can really be a lifetime. And if we think of the hundreds of thousands of years that it took the universe to be formed, we can say even that hundreds of years might be thought of as "a little while." Anyone reading a history book finds that in three or four paragraphs a whole century may be covered. So one page covering "a little while," can mean hundreds of years.

Now the idea of how relative time is, is perhaps one of the most vivid realizations of life. Everyone who grows older, and especially as they move into old age, reminds us and needs to keep reminding us of how short life is. Until we are old we just can't seem to grasp this. Older people are constantly saying,"It seems just like yesterday," and when we are young we think that's just a phrase. But when we get older we realize that is exactly true, that it does seem just like yesterday, even though it was 20 or 30 or even 50 years ago. "A little while," as we see, is a very relative term.

THEOLOGICAL EXTENSION

Now stated here, as Christ states it, we can see how short the time is of our separation from him. This "little while" that he tells the Apostles that he will be gone and then he will be with them and they with him, is also true of us. "A little while now and the world will see me no more. But you see me as one who has life, and you will have life." So while the world—those who have no faith and no understanding of Christ insofar as his physical presence is not here—may dismiss him as a historical character 2,000 years ago, you and I have his presence with us, and in "a little while" we will be with him again. "A little while," in this case, is the way elderly people see their lives, a very brief period, even though it may have been 70 or 80 years.

So Christ reassures us, "A little while now and the world will see me no more, but you see me as one who has life, and you will have life. On that day you will know that I am in my father, and you in me, and I in you." Now until that time, what do we do? We show our love by doing our very best to follow his guidance and his direction. He goes on to tell us, "He who obeys the commandments he has from me is the man who loves me. And he who loves me will be loved by my Father. I too will love him and reveal myself to him."

THEOLOGICAL CONCLUSION

So, indeed, life is "a little while." It seems astonishingly short once it is past. It seems long to children, but to those who have lived a "long" life it seems, as it approaches its close, to be a very little while. That is the short time between our birth and our coming into the fullness of our Christian meaning, if we honestly and sincerely follow in his way. To do this indicates that we love him, and if we do he reassures us, "I too will love you and reveal myself to you."

SEVENTH SUNDAY OF EASTER (SERIES A)
HOMILY I

Reading I: *After Jesus was taken up into the heavens, the apostles returned to Jerusalem from the mount called Olivet near Jerusalem, a mere Sabbath's journey away. Entering the city, they went to the upstairs room where they were staying: Peter and John and James and Andrew; Philip and Thomas; Bartholomew and Matthew; James, son of Alpheus; Simon, the Zealot party member, and Judas, son of James. Together they devoted themselves to constant prayer. There were some women in their company and Mary, the mother of Jesus, and his brothers.* (Acts 1:12-14)

ANA-GNOSIS

We are now getting accustomed to a whole series of changes that have been emerging in the Church since Vatican II. One of the interesting things about these changes is the degree to which they are not totally new, but in some ways resemble the early Church soon after the resurrection and ascension of Christ.

For a long period in history we tended to think of men and women in the Church as functioning in separate and even unrelated ways. The Sisters were off in convents, hospitals and schools for girls or women, while the Priests and Brothers were directly involved in parish work and activities. We rarely thought of them as functioning together.

Sisters and Religious Women had all their prayers and activities totally separate from the prayers and activities of Priests. We were so used to all this that we hardly even thought about any alternative. One never saw, for example, a group of Priests saying their prayers of office or the breviary with a group of Nuns. On the contrary, the Sisters were in one chapel at one end of the property and whatever Priests might be around would be completely down at the other end. They virtually never functioned together.

Since Vatican II this has changed. We've seen Sisters increasingly getting into pastoral work, becoming very active in parish work and as assistants and associates in hospitals, not simply as nurses but as pastoral counselors and ministers of the word.

THEOLOGICAL EXTENSION

This involvement in ministry and in prayer groups by men and women together, even men and women religious, is not in any sense new. It is exactly what also occurred in the early Church. We see a clue to this fact here in the casual description of how the disciples functioned after the resurrection and ascension of Christ. The Reading from the Acts of the Apostles tells us, "After Jesus was taken up into the heavens the Apostles returned to Jerusalem from the Mount called Olivet near Jerusalem . . . together they devoted themselves to constant prayer." But they were not alone, not isolated, because "there were women in their company and Mary, the mother of Jesus, and his brothers."

Elsewhere, we realize, Paul mentions women assisting him, even traveling with him, and he indicates that the other Apostles had this kind of aid from women also. St. Paul, in fact, mentions a whole series of women by name to whom he owes a great debt for the help and assistance they have given him.

Consequently, even though it might seem strange to us now to see men and women functioning much more directly together in the ministry of the Church, it is definitely a part of the spirit of the early Christian Church. It is, also, the spirit of our age. Since World War I more and more women have been functioning with men in offices, factories and in the professions. They work side by side as persons of mutual respect, authority and recognition. So the Church, too, must follow this mood and give women, in every way, their rightful place, their rightful authority and their rightful significance, and reward and recognize their rights, exactly as it has always rewarded and recognized men.

THEOLOGICAL CONCLUSION

Doing all this, we see, we will not be doing something totally new or absolutely radical. Rather, in some ways, we are returning to the way in which men and women prayed together and worked together in the early Church.

SEVENTH SUNDAY OF EASTER (SERIES A)
HOMILY II

Responsorial Psalm: *I believe that I shall see the good things of the Lord in the land of the living. The Lord is my light and my salvation; whom should I fear? The Lord is my life's refuge; of whom shoudl I be afraid?* (Ps. 27:1, 4, 7-8)

ANA-GNOSIS

All of us know the feeling, especially as adults, of wanting to get away from it all. We have all felt "fed up." In other words, things can just pile up on us until we have to escape, we have to get away. Sometimes this involves taking a trip; sometimes it involves just not going to work, staying home; sometimes if the home is what piles up on us, it involves going somewhere, even just for a shopping trip for a day. But whatever our means of getting away, insofar as it's effective, it refreshes us, it gives us a whole new view. We come back with new energy and new enthusiasm, and we can take up where we left off, refreshed and renewed.

We know, however, that many times when people seek to get away, especially if they use alcohol or dope or something similar, or if they just go somewhere and spend a lot of money, they haven't really succeeded in refreshing or helping themselves. They very often come back after this effort to get away in as bad a state as they were in before.

THEOLOGICAL EXTENSION

What we know from our experience in prayer is that one of the most effective ways to renew ourselves in body and spirit is to come to some relationship between ourselves and God. We find a refuge not simply in some diversion, some different activity or some different part of the country, although this may be helpful, but, much more profoundly, in God. We simply lift our heart out of all these material things that we can be overly invested in, and place it with security and confidence in God. This is the best way to get away from it all. That is to say, it is the best way to get away from things that have only limited meaning and value, which often are very shallow in reality, and get to what is fundamental and final in our lives.

Now this is especially true if, as part of our burden or conflict or difficulty that we are trying to get away from, we are in a state of anxiety. This has been called the age of anxiety. So, it is not surprising that from time to time, as individuals, we get caught up in rather anxious seizures, feelings of insecurity and threat, even fear about what our life is about and what we are doing with it.

Now when these anxieties seize us, the best place to get away, the best place to go is to God. So the Psalmist tells us: "The Lord is my light and my salvation, whom should I fear? The Lord is my life's refuge." A refuge, the dictionary tells us, is a place of protection, of shelter from danger, distress or anxiety, a place that provides security for us. We can get away to protective places of that sort. Any kind of diversion can, in a limited way, provide this. But the most effective method of all, especially when basic anxieties seize us, is to make God our refuge when we need to get away from all these things that are hounding us.

THEOLOGICAL CONCLUSION

When the need to get away hits us, and particularly when anxieties and insecurities and threats become almost too much, we must think of this line of the Psalmist: "The Lord is my life's refuge." Translated into our modern language we might say, "I go to the Lord to get away from it all. With him I am at the heart of what really matters in my life and in the world. In him I am in something much greater than my cares and fears. I have moved from shallow to deep waters, to the real meaning and significance of my life." To say this acknowledges that God is a very special refuge and security for us.

SEVENTH SUNDAY OF EASTER (SERIES A) HOMILY III

Reading II: *Rejoice, insofar as you share Christ's sufferings. When his glory is revealed you will rejoice exultantly. Happy are you when you are insulted for the sake of Christ, for then God's Spirit in its glory has come to rest on you. See to it that none of you suffers for being a murderer, a thief, a malefactor, or a destroyer of another's rights. If anyone suffers for being a Christian, however, he ought not be ashamed. He should rather glorify God in virtue of that name.* (1 Pt. 4:13-16)

ANA-GNOSIS

Our age is an age of great concern about health. Everywhere we turn, to television, radio, newspapers, magazines, we constantly hear about campaigns for better health. There's a campaign to overcome heart disease and heart attacks, another to overcome cancer, another to prevent or cure tuberculosis, and still more to promote mental health. We contribute to these too, because we see the value of medical science working to make us more healthy and to overcome those diseases which so often are the cause of early death. We feel that people should have the chance to live their lives to the fullest.

However, carried too far, these campaigns tend to give the impression that, if we could succeed in overcoming cancer or heart disease or whatever, we would never die. Yet we all know that medical science, even by curing these diseases, cannot promise immortality, and if we don't die of one thing we'll die of something else. From the time of the Psalms on, it has been acknowledged that the life span of a man is not much beyond three score and ten years. It is the rare person, even today, who lives much beyond 70 or 80 years. So while the campaigns to overcome heart disease and cancer and all those other illnesses are sensible, and we approve and support them, insofar as they seem to suggest that we will have eternal life if we overcome heart attacks and cancer, they are, of course, foolish and misleading.

One of the consequences, however, of so much emphasis upon health is that any kind of illness and any kind of suffering, particularly physical suffering, are seen as something wrong, as a punishment or an unfairness. Sometimes in tragic bitterness we find people saying, "Why did this happen to me? Why should I have this illness?" Sometimes even doctors are bitter, thinking, "Why didn't that therapy work? I worked so hard to bring about that cure. Why should this failure happen?"

But when it goes this far, this notion of health is tragically misleading. And we need to restore to ourselves the understanding that suffering can be, in its own way, a sign of God's love and a sign of God's blessings on us. Death is itself the birth of a new life. Fetal life is comparatively comfortable as far as we can judge. Possibly, given a choice, babies might never wish to be born. We might all have resisted coming into the world. But we were born into a new life.

THEOLOGICAL EXTENSION

Now the whole Christian teaching, very strongly emphasized in St. Paul, is that unless we die like the seed dies in the ground, we cannot come up and grow and blossom with new life in Christ. And suffering is a form of sharing in this life of Christ. The Epistle of St. Peter tells us this with great clarity: "Rejoice, insofar as you share Christ's sufferings." Later he says, "If anyone suffers for being a Christian, however, he ought not to be ashamed. He ought rather to glorify God in virtue of that name." So whether we are suffering for prejudice against us as Christians or, far more fundamentally, suffering in physical or psychological pain, we can attempt to see that this is the stamp of Christ on us. In a very special way, by such suffering, we can be reborn in a Christian way, reflecting in our suffering the same patience and self-giving that Christ did. For without any suffering we lack a fundamental Christ-like resemblance.

THEOLOGICAL CONCLUSION

So, despite the laudable intentions of overcoming physical illness and all the support that we rightly give this research and these projects, suffering is not going to be totally done away with. And of the suffering that we must bear, let us see it as a mark of Christ in our lives. Consequently, instead of rejecting it, or being bitter or hostile, we need to come to accept what may seem to be a strange doctrine to our age, the doctrine of Peter who says, "Rejoice!" Why should we rejoice? Because when we suffer we can do so in the Spirit of Christ.

Therefore, when we suffer, and when those very close to us suffer, let us look carefully and we should see in a very special way the face of Christ. And this is, indeed, even with all its pain, something to rejoice in. How wonderful to resemble Christ.

SEVENTH SUNDAY OF EASTER (SERIES A)
HOMILY IV

Gospel Reading: *Jesus looked up to heaven and said:*
"Father, the hour has come! Give glory to your Son that your Son may give glory to You, inasmuch as you have given him authority over all mankind, that he may bestow eternal life on those you gave

him. . . . I have given you glory on earth by finishing the work you gave me to do." (Jn. 17:1-11)

ANA-GNOSIS

We all know the feeling that the time has come, that this is the day, or this is the hour when an event that we've looked forward to and prepared for, been anxious about, perhaps, has come. We say, "This is it. This is the day. This is the hour."

A child has this feeling when, after looking forward to Christmas, his birthday, or the end of school, the day finally arrives. Adults know this too. One day we wake up and realize that this is the day we are going to be married or ordained or take vows. We may recall vividly our feeling of "this is it," when we graduated from high school or college, or the time when we sat at a table, took a pen in hand, and signed something. Just the moment before we signed we may have said to ourselves or to someone else, "Well this is it. When we sign this it's a different world." We know, too, how fundamental this feeling can be in moments of illness, that day on which we go up to surgery, perhaps, or the day when the tests come back to tell us through the doctor's interpretation just how sick we are. As the doctor walks in the room we may feel like saying, "Well, this is it."

THEOLOGICAL EXTENSION

We share this feeling of something coming to a head with Christ when he prays to his Father by saying, "Father, the hour has come." Today we commonly catch this sense of urgency and finality perhaps best of all in sports. The announcer may say, "This is the day when it will be decided who the top team is." Or he will say at a very crucial point in the game, "It looks as though it will be decided in the very last minutes," and then, "This is it. If this hitter makes an out the game is over. This decides it."

Now this is the mood of Christ. Now the hour has come. "Give glory to your Son, that your Son may give glory to you, inasmuch as you have given him glory over all mankind, that he may bestow eternal life on those you gave him . . . I have given you glory on earth by finishing the work you gave me to do."

In a sense "this is it" for us too. For as the hour has come for Christ to leave in his physical presence, the hour begins for us to take over. He has left us as his representatives, his people, to do his work. The hour has come for Christ because he has finished his work on earth that the Father has given him to do, and the hour has come for us to take over now. We must take up the work in mature, responsible discipleship, carrying on with what he gave us to do. We are his people, the people of God, whom God gave him, that he might give us and all those who through our efforts come to him, eternal life. It is an awesome responsibility which Christ bestowed upon us at our baptism. And while it may have moments when it seems that "This is it," in fact we are called upon all our lives to bring him to the world awaiting his love.

THEOLOGICAL CONCLUSION

The hour has come, then, for Christ, who has finished his work, and it has come for us to take up and carry on this work with his guidance and his direction. Let us accept this responsibility that he has given to us, knowing that every moment of our lives is important, is crucial to salvation

ASCENSION (SERIES A, B, C) HOMILY I

Reading I: . . . *"You will receive power when the Holy Spirit comes down on you; then you are to be my witnesses in Jerusalem, throughout Judea and Samaria, yes, even to the ends of the earth."* (Acts 1:1-11)

ANA-GNOSIS

We all know what a jury is. Even children, from seeing movies and television, know that the jury listens to the witnesses to an alleged crime and, at the end of the trial each juror decides whether the witnesses for or against the defendant are telling the truth. At some point they have to say, "We believe the witnesses," or "we don't believe the witnesses." On this hinges the jury's decision.

A witness, therefore, is someone who tells us something that we either do or do not believe. And we have to judge their credibility from the nature of what they have said, from their character, and also from whether they have something to gain or something to lose by their testimony.

THEOLOGICAL EXTENSION

Now in the Reading today we hear about witnesses to Christ. In a certain sense, we might be thought of as the jury, because in the person of Theophilus all of us are present. So the writer of the Acts of the Apostles says, "In the time after his suffering he showed them in many convincing ways that he was alive, appearing to them over the course of forty days, and speaking to them about the reign of God." Now a key word we hear is *convincing* ways. We know that Peter and the Apostles were not at all convinced when the women came and told them that Christ had risen. They thought it was imagination or gossip at first. But they changed their minds in the process of all the evidence that came forward, especially when they repeatedly experienced Christ. Then they could no longer deny it, no more than Thomas could as he put his hand into the wounds of our Lord. So they were convinced. But their job was not over. They were then sent as witnesses themselves.

One of the last things that Christ did was to send out witnesses not only to the immediate area and time in which they lived, but farther than that—"to the ends of the earth." Until his own return, our Lord told the apostles and disciples, "You will receive power when the Holy Spirit comes down on you. Then you are to be my witnesses. No sooner had he said this than he was lifted up before their eyes into a cloud which took him from their sight."

Now we see a double point here. First, Christ himself witnessed to his own resurrection. And then he commissioned those convinced by his evidence to go out and be witnesses for him to the ends of the earth. Now, obviously it is going to take hundreds, even thousands of years for this idea, so earth-shaking and overwhelming, of God becoming man and dwelling among us, to be explained and witnessed, demonstrated and taught all over the world. So this is, in a certain sense, the whole future delineation of the meaning of the community of the people of God, called the Church. You and I are witnesses. We cannot force people to believe or accept any more than a witness at a trial can force the jury to believe him. But we can do our very best to present what has been convincing and deeply fulfilling in our lives and faith. Just as the writer of Acts says of Jesus: "He showed them in many 'convincing' ways that he was alive," we can show in many convincing ways that our faith is rich and alive and strong in us. It is the central force and purpose of our lives. It gives our lives their meaning. We can do this, and we can do it in as effective a way as possible, almost exactly as though we were witnesses called to give evidence to a very grave trial. One might even propose that there is no other human, earthly, experience that we could be called upon to witness to which could match the responsibility and solemnity of our commission by Christ to be witnesses for him.

THEOLOGICAL CONCLUSION

This, therefore, is the point of the Ascension: that we all witness together now to the significance of Jesus Christ in our lives. Can we, by our lives and actions, be believed by those who would judge Christ? Do we give convincing testimony to him? Let us strive to do so as part of our responsibility to Christ, as a part of our Christian vocation.

ASCENSION (SERIES A, B, C)
HOMILY II

Responsorial Psalm: *God mounts his throne amid shouts of joy; the Lord, amid trumpet blasts. Sing praise; sing praise to our king, sing praise.* (Ps. 47:2-3, 6-7, 8-9)

ANA-GNOSIS

In any kind of athletic contest, play or spectacle where thousands of people are present, a major concern is how one arranges so that everyone buying a seat can see. Normally this takes two very obvious, but opposite, geometrical designs. In one instance, as in a footbabll or baseball game, the spectators are lined up in tiers, high above where the game is played. Alternately, in a theater or some place of that sort, the hundreds or even thousands of spectators are seated more or less on the same level, but the stage is high above, so they look up to see. Sometimes at a particular point of the ceremony when events center on a certain person, the main character mounts the steps very solemnly and sits, so everyone in the auditorium can clearly see that central figure. When someone is crowned or given a particular honor he or she solemnly ascends the stairs. And this becomes almost the central symbolic act or climax of the whole event. Much dignity and honor is associated with this act, as simple as it may seem, and it has come to have far greater implications than the simple act of walking up steps would at first appear to have.

THEOLOGICAL EXTENSION

The solemnity, the glory, and the dignity that go with this kind of ascent is the experience the Psalmist uses today to evoke this same feeling about God. He says, "God mounts his throne, amid shouts of joy. The Lord, amid trumpet blasts. Sing the praises to God, sing praise. Sing praise to our king, sing praise."

We can all feel the magnificence of this from our experiences of witnessing similar, far lesser spectacles. Now, if we transfer this feeling and atmosphere to our relationship with God, then we can get the sense that the Psalmist is driving at here.

In another form the Ascension of Christ doesn't mount a staircase to show the great completion of his work; his ascent in a cloud recalls another image of great honor and dignity. Clouds brought water that was so valuable, especially in the parched, dry land of the middle east. And clouds had a mysterious, undefined quality to them that always symbolized something very solemn and special. So at the Ascension we have this same glorious fulfillment when Christ ascends to his throne.

THEOLOGICAL CONCLUSION

The Ascension, then, is that Feast of the final glorification and honor of Christ as he mounts to the throne. He has completed his mission of entering the human race and giving us this life source beyond anything we could have dreamed of or imagined. Now he is going back to God, his Father, leaving us as his witnesses to carry on his work.

ASCENSION (SERIES A, B, C)
HOMILY III

Reading II: *May the God of our Lord Jesus Christ, the Father of glory, grant you a spirit of wisdom and insight to know him clearly. May he enlighten your innermost vision that you may know the great hope to which he has called you, the wealth of his glorious heritage to be distributed among the members of the church, and the immeasurable scope of his power in us who believe.* (Eph. 1-17-23)

ANA-GNOSIS

Unless one's eyesight is threatened or damaged in some way, those of us who have been blessed with sight from birth tend to take it for granted. Yet it is so basic that we who are accustomed to it would suffer tremendously trying to compensate if we lost it. It is so fundamental to our experience that we speak of sight applied not simply to physical sight, but to understanding. We say, "I see," when we mean not physical seeing, but intellectual seeing. We mean, "I understand."

Taking this meaning, then, we extend it by adding the prefix "in." We talk about having *insight*. We are no longer talking about something physical, but intellectual awareness, rather like figuring out a jagsaw puzzle in which the moment that some pieces come together, we suddenly gain an insight into what the picture is. At the moment that the pieces give us that awareness, there may still be many pieces left to fill in the picture, but we now see beyond the individual pieces to what the whole picture stands for. We sometimes say, "I get the picture." This is insight.

We also may add another word onto the front of *sight*. We talk about *oversight*. In *oversight* we fail to see, generally, because we hurry too fast and we do not pause to look carefully. If we transfer the English word *sight* to its Latin origin, which would be *to spect*, like the word *inspect*, then *respect* is simply to look repeatedly at something. *Oversight*, then, is a lack of *respect*, and we can gain *insight* by looking repeatedly and carefully at something.

THEOLOGICAL EXTENSION

Now these things having been said, let us look at the use of *sight* in St. Paul's Epistle today. He says, "May the God of our Lord Jesus Christ, the Father of glory, grant you a spirit of wisdom and *insight* to know him clearly." Now we sec this *insight* is used exactly as we use it always inside ourselves because he goes on to say, "May God enlighten your innermost vision that you may know the great hope to which he called you, the wealth of his glorious heritage to be distributed among the members of the Church, and the immeasurable scope of his power in us who believe." What a sweeping inner vision and greatness it proposes. With this insight we would see clearly, understand, and grasp, first, the greatness of our hope to which he has called us, second, our glorious inheritance of inner peace and security and direction for our lives, and finally, the immeasurable scope of God's power in us. Now, even to spell out those three categories is already to remind us that we haven't respected this enough, that we tend to "overlook" it. We obviously need to gain greater insight into this. So it is a legitimate prayer when we ask God to enlighten us, to put more light on this whole issue of our hope and our heritage and the power of Christ in us, to make us far more aware of it because we tend not to respect it, we tend to disrespect it by oversight.

THEOLOGICAL CONCLUSION

Paul's prayer is a profound one for us, one that we could never exhaust in its total meaning. There's an endless significance to exploring the great hope to which God has called us, the wealth of his glorious heritage among us, and, finally, the immeasurable scope of his power in us who believe. To dwell on these things will draw us step by step to this increased insight that Paul prays will be ours. Let us not, in our daily concerns, overlook it.

ASCENSION (SERIES A, B, C)
HOMILY IV

Gospel Reading: *The eleven disciples made their way to Galilee, to the mountain to which Jesus summoned them. At the sight of him, those who had entertained doubts fell down in homage. Jesus came forward and addressed them in these words:*

> *"Full authority has been given to me both in heaven and on earth; go therefore, and make disciples of all the nations. Baptize them in the name of the Father, and of the Son, and of the Holy Spirit. Teach them to carry out everything I have commanded you. And know that I am with you always, until the end of the world!"*

ANA-GNOSIS

We're very familiar with the idea of a man starting a business and working at it all by himself for a rather long time. But as the business gets bigger or as he gets older, he begins to delegate authority, sometimes to his children, if he's fortunate enough to have sons and daughters interested in the same work, but more commonly to people who have worked with him and whom he has carefully trained and chosen to take his place. Very large businesses, even when they were started by one man, are now run by hundreds, even thousands, of executives who act in the name of and with the authority of the original founder. But it is very common for us to know of a person, even in a very small business, finally arriving at a point where he says, "Well, I've done my work now, the store is running well, so I've turned it over to my sons and I'm taking off and going to Florida. They have the authority now."

THEOLOGICAL EXTENSION

Now this very human way of acting is exactly what Christ did too. We know that Christ could have come on earth and done things differently than he did. With God's power he could have miraculously established all sorts of things. But that was not his way. He wished to fulfill our humanity and to give it the opportunity and the occasion to develop its full potential, the innermost vision or deepening insight that St. Paul speaks about in today's second Reading. So Christ has proceeded very much as all the rest of the human race has proceeded by establishing something first by his own very hard work and effort, and then at a certain point, beginning to train others. When they reach a point where they can take over, he delegates the responsibility and the authority to them. With great institutions that have lasted through many generations, this same delegation is carried on, and as people get old and die, others take their places down through the centuries.

Now that is exactly what has happened for two thousand years. From one point of view Christ has left us. In the same way that a man might just go to the airport and take off for Florida, so that he isn't in the store any longer and his sons and daughters are in charge, Christ has gone. In another sense, though, in the way that he has delegated his authority to the Church, to the whole community of the Christian people, he is at the same time a living presence. Here we see in a special way the action of God which a man who goes to Florida can't accomplish. He cannot be present in his business; Christ can be. Having ascended into heaven physically, he has left us all the responsibility of the delegated authority. "Full authority has been given me both in heaven and on earth. Go, therefore, and make disciples of all nations," he tells us. But he gives us the assurance that no human delegator could give us, "Know that I am with you always, until the end of the world."

THEOLOGICAL CONCLUSION

We have this marvelous institution, then, the Church, sharing the delegated responsibility that Christ has given all of us. We who are committed to him share this delegation of Christ to go out and teach, and in our teaching ministry, making disciples, we have his continued presence to sustain and guide us. By his Ascension he may have left us physically, but his presence abides with us in the Spirit and in the people of God.

PENTECOST SUNDAY (SERIES A, B, C)
HOMILY I

Reading I: *And they were amazed and wondered, saying. "Are not all these who are speaking Galileans? And how is it that we hear each of us in his own native language? Parthians and Medes and Elamites and residents of Mesopotamia, Judea and Cappadocia, Pontus and Asia, Phrygia, and Pamphylia, Egypt and the parts of Libya belonging to Cyrene, and visitors from Rome, both Jews and proselytes, Cretans and Arabians, we hear them telling in our own tongues the mighty works of God."* (Acts 2:1-11)

ANA-GNOSIS

When we come to Mass now everything is in English, and the words and meanings are much more familiar to us. Understandably, then, we often look back and say, "Well, why wasn't it this way all the time?" Those of us who are older, though not by much, can remember going to Mass with a missal, and on one side there was Latin and on the other side, English. We tried to follow the Latin by paralleling it with the English meaning. Today we don't have to do that at all because the priest isn't speaking in Latin, and everything in the Church, even the inscriptions in new churches, are all in English. The question then arises: How did the Church come to use Latin for so many centuries? It used Latin officially from somewhere around the beginning of the reign of Charlemagne, about 800 AD, until the present day. Why was there 1200 years or more of focus on Latin? It seems so obvious now that each of us ought to be able to hear Mass in our own language.

THEOLOGICAL EXTENSION

Today's Reading tells us a number of obvious but easily overlooked aspects about the Church. When the Reading says that "these people were amazed . . . 'Are not all these people Galileans? How is it that we hear each of us in our own native language?' " we realize that the first public presentation in the Church was done in such a way that if we were Americans and were there at that time, we would have heard everything in English as we do now. And if we were French, we'd have heard it in French; if we were Japanese, we'd have heard it in Japanese. So from that point of view the presentation in today's Reading is a model of the Church now—if we were to go to France today we would hear Mass in French. So we could say that today's method is a very fitting way to carry out the Acts of the Apostles. Why then, wasn't it that way from the beginning? Why did we have that long period of Latin? The other side, of course, is that in the Acts of the Apostles we are witnessing a miraculous situation. They were right to wonder because, while the speaker was speaking one language, there was, miraculously, a multiple translation going on so that everyone heard his own tongue. Now if we deal with the real situation in the history of the Church, rather than this miraculous event, we see another idea for achieving this universality. If all Christians were to speak and understand the same language, then one ideal would be for the Church to accept one language as its own special one, and all Christians all over the world would learn it. That was the model for Latin, since the world was conceived, in those days, primarily as the area around the Mediterranean and Europe and Great Britain—what we now call the West. And until the Protestant Reformation, the Church was amazingly successful in having Latin understood universally by educated people all over Europe. One might propose that, had not the Reformation itself reinforced again the individual languages, or different forms of Christianity emerged, we might have witnessed down into the 20th century an astonishing extension of all Christian peoples everywhere knowing, understanding and speaking Latin.

So the justification, therefore, of the Church taking up this Roman language which is not nearly as old as Hebrew or Greek, was basically to bring about, by natural, reasonable means and education, a language common to all peoples to offset the dispersion of tongues that the Bible tells us occurred around the tower of Babel.

In modern times, then, as we hear again each our own tongue, from one point of view we see the fulfillment of the early Christion community. But we also recognize that we haven't quite the same sense of unity that we had when Latin was the common language of the Church. The advantage of Latin was that when we went to France or to Germany or to Japan, even though the priest was Japanese and the congregation was Japanese, once we heard that Latin we were surprisingly at home. So one might say, we gained and we lost. We lost the sense of common worship together that Latin gave us, all using our missals each with its different translation. We gained the much more intimate, personal sense of belonging that we now all have when we go to our celebrations and hear our own common language. Americans in America feel much more at home. But insofar as we travel across language barriers to different areas we lose that common Latin language and sense of universality that it gave us.

THEOLOGICAL CONCLUSION

We've all settled for and have seen the great advantages of having our Christian message, prayers and celebration in our own language. What we must work towards now is a deep, shared sense of unity of spirit and belonging with all Christian peoples regardless of language. Perhaps at some final point, then, a common language will emerge which all of us, as Christians, will speak and share and understand together.

PENTECOST SUNDAY (SERIES A, B, C)
HOMILY II

Responsorial Psalm: *Lord, send out your Spirit, and renew the fact of the earth.*
Bless the Lord, O my soul!
O Lord, my God, you are great indeed!
How manifold are your works, O Lord!
the earth is full of your creatures.
(Ps. 104:1, 24, 29-30, 31, 34)

ANA-GNOSIS

For the last fifteen or so years we have been hearing the term "air pollution." This is part of our almost startled realization that, with all the advantages of industrialism and new types of energy and chemistry, there are some very complicated and possibly tragic disadvantages. When we look out on the large lakes for example—Lake Michigan or Lake Erie—or even more so when we look out on the oceans, it seems inconceivable that such vast expanses of water could be poisoned and ultimately, polluted to the point that they poison fish and kill all sorts of life. Yet we know that this is true. Some parts of the lakes and northern rivers that we have thought were clean and pure are so filled with chemicals now that it is dangerous even to eat the first, or so we are told.

But even more complicatedly, we are learning that our air is polluted. Again, it is almost startling to realize that many things we now inhale may prove injurious to us because the air is unclean. And this brings forward the astonishingly obvious and yet, at the same time, startling realization that we desperately need clean air. Sometimes when an accident happens we hear someone in the center of the people gathered around the victim saying, "Step back! Give him air!" Again, here's a basic affirmation of how fundamental air—clean, pure air—is to our very life itself. And if we do not do something about the pollution of the air, and we have been doing some things in recent years with, we hope, some degree of success, we will all suffer grave illnesses of the lungs. It is theoretically possible that we will end up simply choking one another to death, poisoning one another by polluting the air.

THEOLOGICAL EXTENSION

Now if we see pure air as basic to our life, the whole Reading of today, and the whole Christian emphasis of the spirit—the pure, Holy Spirit—focus on just the same idea. The Psalmist says here: "How manifold are your works, O Lord! The earth is full of your creatures! Lord, send out your spirit and renew the face of the earth!" When we give people oxygen they rather quickly and astonishingly revive. Pure air brings life, strength, resuscitation, to all living things including ourselves. Just so, the Holy Spirit in our life with God revives us. The materialism and shortsighted goals of what might rightly be called an Unholy Spirit or a Polluted Spirit, will weaken and destroy us, as unclean air does in our actual experience of daily life. With the same anxiety that we now have about keeping our air pure and clean of those chemicals and various other elements that can injure or seriously threaten the life of individuals, we should be concerned, too, about the Holy Spirit in our lives.

If we say softly, in its Latin form, the word *spiritus,* we can hear the word "spire" in it. This gives us the word *inspire,* breathing into: *spiring* itself is breathing. The sound even imitates the way we breathe. So spirit is breath. And when we say *spiritus,* it is like the sound of breathing itself. Now there is an unpolluted *Spiritus* possible for us spiritually, as well as, we hope, unpolluted air in our material, physical life. And as we are making all these efforts to rule out those things that pollute and harm our physical air, so we must equally make sure those things that are polluting our spirit, the Holy Spirit in our lives, are also ruled out.

THEOLOGICAL CONCLUSION

Pollution, therefore, has a double meaning. We rightly want unpolluted, clean air to breathe, and we want room to breathe in our physical life. At the same time, we want unpolluted spiritual air, the air of the Holy Spirit, and room to breathe the Holy Spirit in our lives. If materiality crowds us too much and we are concerned merely with those immediate anxieties of the body and our daily physical cares, it's almost like the Spirit shouts out, "Move back! Let me breathe! Give me a little clean air! Let the Holy Spirit get to me, please!"

The Holy Spirit, therefore, is the source of our divine life, just as pure air is the source of living things around us. "When you send forth your spirit they are created and you renew the face of the earth," says the Psalmist. Give us, indeed, unpolluted air, but unpolluted air of the Holy Spirit as well as the physical spirit.

PENTECOST SUNDAY (SERIES A, B, C)
HOMILY III

Reading II: *Now there are varieties of gifts, but the same Spirit; and there are varieties of service, but the same Lord; and there are varieties of working, but it is the same God who inspires them all in every one. To each is given the manifestation of the Spirit for the common good. For just as the body is one and has many members, and all the members of the body, though many, are one body, so it is with Christ. For by one Spirit we were all baptized into one* *body—Jews or Greeks, slaves or free—and all were made to drink of one Spirit.* (1 Cor. 12:3-7, 12-13)

ANA-GNOSIS

It is very common for us now to hear the phrase, "We are number one!" Companies often claim they are "number one," and other companies rather cleverly take advantage of that and say, "Since we are not number one, we have to try harder." But the most common example of this is when a team wins a championship or tournament, it seems to have become a universal custom in recent years for the winners to shout, "We're number one!"

We know in this case that a series of tournaments in ascending steps are set up and, one team after another, they are eliminated until there are two left to play the championship game. The one who wins that is declared "number one" in whatever area we are talking about.

There is, of course, a reverse way of using this scale. So it is not uncommon to hear people say, particularly with regard to a team or competitive athletic group, "Oh, they're not much good, they're only in fourth place," or "They're in last place." That is, the emphasis on "number one" also categorizes everybody else in a descending scale down to being "no good." It's quite normal to say, "Oh, they're pretty poor because they've never seen the upper half for the last five years."

Now while these are simple phrases that we hear over and over again and possibly do not think too much about except in the context of the various athletic activities—football, soccer, baseball or whatever— they get under our skin. They become, if we're not careful, somewhat universal ways of evaluating ourselves and one another. If we let it happen this way then we are always looking for that best performance or that best performer, disregarding other people who "fail" and, in that sense, who are categorized, in greater or lesser degree, as not much good.

Now when we hear how strong that phrase is, "They're not much good," we can see that this is a very dangerous way of thinking and talking.

THEOLOGICAL EXTENSION

By contrast, the Reading of today gives us a Christian image that entirely disavows the notion that some are "number one," some are "number two," some are "number five," and some are in last place because they are no good. It totally disavows that stairstep categorization of people which accepts that the only really good people are number one. It takes a totally different form, a view which in a simpler form our Lord gave us when he gave us the story of the talents. Jesus said, of course, that some of us have one talent, and we are responsible to gain one more; some of us have two and must gain two more; some have five and have the far greater responsibility of gaining five more.

St. Paul takes that same theme but proposes that each of us in our vocation and our work for God is called in a very special way; each is given special and unique gifts. But each of us is an agent of God. So St. Paul says, "There are varieties of gifts, but the same Spirit; there are varieties of service, but the same Lord; varieties of working, but it is the same God who inspires them all in every one. To each is given the manifestation of the Spirit for the common good." Now we see this is a very different notion than some idea of "number one," or even some idea that we are "number two" and must try harder. It is certainly a long ways from saying, "They're no good because they're in last place." Rather what we see is that, in our regard for one another, we must look for that unique quality, no matter how different or how unusual, or in sort of "number one-number two" scale, how poor we may think these people perform or how inadequate they seem to us. This is a false way of rating people. They are not to be judged on a rating scale from one to ten at all. Instead we must look for what God has given uniquely to them, so that they in a special way may manifest God's activity, the activity of the Spirit in the world. By overlooking their special qualities we will miss the voice, the agency, and the direction of the Holy Spirit working uniquely in and through them.

THEOLOGICAL CONCLUSION

This is a very different picture from "number one-number two." It is almost like realizing that there are a variety of pens. Some can be bought inexpensively, others are much more costly, but each can be used to sign a check for any amount of money, and the check will be accepted with a signature written with any pen. This is St. Paul's point to us. We are all in the agency of God: "Varieties of service but the same Lord, varieties of gifts, but the same spirit." God works through each of us in our uniqueness. No "number one," or "number two," no "no good" people in last place. Not at all. We are all endowed in unique and special ways with God's gifts so that each of us can witness through them to God's message and word, and guidance for all.

PENTECOST SUNDAY (SERIES A, B, C) HOMILY IV

Gospel Reading: *On the evening of that first day of the week, even though the disciples had locked the doors of the place where they were for fear of the Jews, Jesus came and stood before them. "Peace be with you," he said. When he had said this, he showed them his hands and his side. At the sight of the Lord the disciples rejoiced. "Peace be with you," he said again.*

"As the Father has sent me, so I send you." Then he breathed on them and said: "Receive the Holy Spirit. If you forgive men's sins, they are forgiven them; if you hold them bound, they are held bound." (Jn. 20:19-23)

ANA-GNOSIS

We tend to think of things in contrasts: light and darkness, black and white, soft and hard. Among these contrasts a common one is love and hate. Not to love, then, can move in the direction of hate; and not to hate can move in the direction of love. But if we think more carefully about love, there is another contrast where it is not so much hate that opposes love, but fear. The Gospel elsewhere tells us that perfect love casts out fear.

THEOLOGICAL EXTENSION

We see this today in the Reading where the disciples show great fear. They are overwhelmed with anxiety. But then we see the coming of love—they suddenly have the presence of Christ, the presence of divine love. God is love, and Christ dwelling in God is perfect love. They are no longer afraid. And, of course, what comes with the presence of love is not only the disappearance of anxiety and the coming of security, but also a great sense of peace. The presence of love, Christ among them, brought them peace.

Now this is very relevant to our lives. We are all anxious about anxiety, we are all afraid of being afraid. This is the mood of our times. But opposite of fear and anxiety is to plunge ourselves into love, to go out and give ourselves to others, and to Another, to give ourselves in open faith and confidence to God. We see, therefore, that love is the gift of self, the antidote to anxiety and fear is love. In a very real sense, then, the opposite of love, is not hate, but fear and anxiety which can only be eradicated by love

If we hope to overcome the fear in our lives we must accept Christ's and other peoples' love for us, and we must give our love to them and to Him. Here, most totally, in the gift of ourselves to Christ we are given also love, security and peace.

THEOLOGICAL CONCLUSION

So our Lord said, "Peace be with you," and brought the disciples his love to abolish their fear. He calls on us now to make this same gift of ourselves to him and to one another so that we all share in and offer the peace of God with and to each other.

TRINITY SUNDAY (SERIES A, B, C) HOMILY I

Reading I: *Early in the morning Moses went up Mount Sinai as the Lord had commanded him, taking along the two stone tablets. Having come down in a cloud, the Lord stood with him there and proclaimed his name, "Lord." Thus the Lord passed before him and cried out, "The Lord, the Lord, a merciful and gracious God, slow to anger and rich in kindness and fidelity." Moses at once bowed down to the ground in worship. Then he said, "If I find favor with you, O Lord, do come along in our company. This is indeed a stiff-necked people; yet pardon our wickedness and sins, and receive us as your own."* (Ex. 34:4-6, 8-9)

ANA-GNOSIS

As adults some of us have been in the position of making a speech at a dinner or special occasion honoring someone and perhaps presenting them with some tribute of everyone's respect and gratitude. If we have not given the speech ourselves, we have certainly heard several in our lifetime. So we are familiar with the expressions of kindness, gentleness, graciousness and compassion that the speaker devises to convey this deep regard. By sharing incidents which demonstrate these qualities and by calling on his own witness of this person's character he presents him to everyone for acclaim.

THEOLOGICAL EXTENSION

In this Reading from Exodus we notice that these same phrases are used with regard to God. And while it may seem strange to think of God in the same way we might think of a mere person we are acclaiming, still it may help us to draw closer to him as we appreciate that he possesses even more fully these qualities we so admire in a fine, gentle, considerate person. "The Lord, the Lord, a merciful and gracious God." Mercy, compassion, sympathy, understanding. These God has. "Slow to anger." Yes, he is patient, putting up with all sorts of misunderstandings, failures and weaknesses, yet he does not burst in anger. If we were saying that of a human being, what a wonderful person he would seem. "Rich in kindness and fidelity." What would this mean if we heard it about someone? Imagine a person "rich" in kindness. He may be poor in money, but he is rich in something far greater—kindness and fidelity. He always keeps his word. He is always caring for others. What a privilege to know, to be related to, to love and be part of the family of someone honored by those terms!

THEOLOGICAL CONCLUSION

This is the description of God today in the Book of Exodus. It can help us to think of God in these human terms in order to appreciate both his greatness and his love for us. Hear it again as we would hear it about someone who loves us and someone whom we love: "The Lord, the Lord, a merciful and gracious God, slow to anger and rich in kindness and fidelity." This is the God who gives us life and to whose family we belong. He loves us more deeply than we can imagine. But perhaps by slowly considering these words we use so easily, we may come to a fuller understanding of his greatness and his love.

TRINITY SUNDAY (SERIES A, B, C)
HOMILY II

Responsorial Psalm: *Glory and praise forever! Blessed are you, O Lord, the God of our fathers, praiseworthy and exalted above all forever; And blessed is your holy and glorious name, praiseworthy and exalted above all for the ages.* (Dn. 3:52, 35, 54, 55, 56)

ANA-GNOSIS

One of the surest ways to make enemies and cause a lot of trouble for ourselves unnecessarily is to talk too much. By "talking too much," we usually also mean talking loosely and saying unwise, disrespectful things about ourselves and others. We know this is a way to alienate members of our families, particularly our in-laws who do not know us too well. It is a way of seriously threatening our job, our relationships with others in school or work, and it's a way of hindering our advancement and our making friends when otherwise people might respect our abilities and want to relate to us and work with us. To talk loosely of others, to be scornful of them, to say disrespectful things about others, to use others' names loosely and thoughtlessly are sure ways to alienate ourselves and to find ourselves having very few, if any, friends.

THEOLOGICAL EXTENSION

This being so true of the way we relate to others, it's important to think that this also applies, with all its human components, to our relationship with God. As we do not speak disrespectfully, thoughtlessly, foolishly and loosely of others, we should not speak that way about God. It's true that expletives or passing phrases where God's or Christ's name are used, are not in themselves consciously disrespectful of God. They nonetheless suggest a loose-tongued, thoughtless attitude. If we talk that way about other people, it would certainly lose us their friendship, and we must think the same as we speak about God.

The Reading today reminds us of this. "Blessed are you, O Lord, the God of our fathers, praiseworthy and exalted above all forever." We must speak always with honor and respect of him. "Blessed is your holy, glorious name, praiseworthy and exalted above all for all ages." The Jewish people in the Old Testament had such grave respect for the name of God that they seldom, if ever, pronounced God's name. In fact it was not always known exactly how God's name was pronounced so awesome did they consider it.

THEOLOGICAL CONCLUSION

We need to be reminded of this. We must realize that if we want to have friends and be respected in our families and in our work for what we are and can do, then we are very careful how we talk about others. And we must realize, too, that all these things apply even more so to the way we speak about and use God's name. It's simply applying the same politeness that we would give others to our Lord who even more richly deserves it. "Blessed is your holy and glorious name, praiseworthy and exalted above all for all ages." Let us remember that whenever we speak of God.

TRINITY SUNDAY (SERIES A, B, C)
HOMILY III

Reading II: *Brothers, mend your ways. Encourage one another. Live in harmony and peace, and the God of love and peace will be with you. Greet one another with a holy kiss. All the holy ones send greetings to you. The grace of the Lord Jesus Christ, and the love of God, and the fellowship of the Holy Spirit be with you all.* (2 Cor. 13:11-13)

ANA-GNOSIS

Nowadays, because of the different economy and the mass production of clothing, we think less and less of mending things. Sometimes the time consumed in mending is more expensive for us than buying another garment, particularly if the garment is not too expensive to begin with. But many years ago we all understood that the mother in the home often sat in the evening mending. The tears here and there were skillfully sewn together again with her needle, and socks, shirts, and other clothes were put on again with some evidence that they had been mended, but with evidence also of real skill. Certain very skilled tailors often offered to mend a cigarette burn in clothing or some tear in such a way that people couldn't see the mend. If we looked carefully though we usually could see it, but his work was extremely skillful.

In those days, too, clean clothes, well mended, though not a sign of wealth obviously still commonly pointed out children who were well taken care of, whose parents were looking after them with great concern. The mending showed that.

THEOLOGICAL EXTENSION

It is intriguing, then, to realize that we use the phrase "mend your ways" as a symbol of our changing ourselves. The evidence of the tear is going to be on us—we are not going to have a perfect garment covering ourselves—but when we change ourselves, when we overcome a weakness to become a better person, though the evidence of what we were is still there, the mending shows the care and concern that we've had in order to improve ourselves It proves that we care about ourselves because we've mended our ways. We've become, as a result, a better person.

This is the mood today in the Reading from Paul when he writes, "Brothers, mend your ways." Now how do we do this? "Encourage one another. Live in harmony and peace, and the God of love and peace will be with you." We get here a model that, while our life may be torn, we can mend what we've done wrong. When we've hurt someone else or ourselves or offended God, like we mend our clothing we can mend our ways. We possess the skill to become better persons, mended persons.

THEOLOGICAL CONCLUSION

This thought is most encouraging. God looks on us, therefore, not expecting that we be without tears—obviously we will have those in our human weakness—but he does seek evidence that we've tried to mend our ways. He wants us to care enough to try to improve and to change. He offers us hope that we can. He even tells us how: "Encourage one another. Live in harmony and peace, and the God of love and peace will be with you."

TRINITY SUNDAY (SERIES A, B, C) HOMILY IV

Gospel Reading: *Jesus said to Nicodemus: "Yes, God so loved the world that he gave his only Son, that whoever believes in him may not die but may have eternal life. God did not send the Son into the world to condemn the world, but that the world might be saved through him. Whoever believes in him avoids condemnation, but whoever does not believe is already condemned for not believing in the name of God's only Son."* (Jn. 3:16-18)

ANA-GNOSIS

Our society places considerable value on having pets, animals as friends. We particularly think of dogs as men's best friend because, we say, dogs are almost human. They have a certain quality about them that gives them an almost human personality. We can say this too about other types of animals. But we should notice that, whatever the animal, people tend to be comfortable with it in proportion to the extent to which they can read into that animal a kind of human personality—those qualities, reactions and sensitivities that we tend to associate with other human beings. Therefore we are friends with a dog because, in large measure, we have projected onto the animal qualities of faithfulness, of closeness, of affection, and of sincerity, all qualities we admire in other people.

What we are seeing here, then, is that in order to be close to an animal we must feel the animal as somewhat our equal, and to do this we must endow the animal with what we see as human qualities. Then we say, "This dog seems almost human."

THEOLOGICAL EXTENSION

While this is a very simple and primitive example, almost disrespectful to apply to God, it can perhaps be a way of understanding in our extremely limited state, the relationship of God to ourselves. Just as we need to humanize an animal and give it human characteristics in order to love that animal, so God wants to see in us some godliness. And insofar as we reflect this godliness in ourselves, we are lovable to God. He loves us, whether we deserve it or not, but just as we prefer to be friends with an animal who reflects a certain humanity, so God looks for us to develop characteristics of godliness.

This can help us, too, in understanding the Trinity. In the Gospel today, we see that God sent his Son to us not to condemn us but to bring us godliness, to redeem us, to make us worthy to be children of God, and to be with God. In the Reading from St. Paul's Epistle to the Corinthians, too, we have this all brought together in the remarkable phrase which we use at the beginning of the Mass: "The grace of our Lord, Jesus Christ, and the love of God, and the fellowship of the Holy Spirit be with you all." The Holy Spirit dwelling in us after the redemption gives us this godliness that makes us so like God. In other words, God loves in us that which is of himself. We feebly parallel this in the way we love an animal that is like us in some way. To refuse to try to become godly is to commit sin because it tries to deny what is divine in ourselves, only preferring our humanity. You can imagine an animal becoming vicious and attacking his master. That animal loses all attractiveness to humans because he has lost those things that are like warm, human friends. A vicious animal that attacks us is no longer our friend. Just so, our refusal to become like him denies that God is our friend. But through the Holy Spirit which makes us the temple of God in which the Father and Son reside with us in the mystery of the Trinity together we can learn to reflect godliness in our lives.

THEOLOGICAL CONCLUSION

By having the Holy Spirit in us we are godly and, therefore, share in the reflective love of the persons of the Trinity for one another. This is what makes us loveable to God, not anything that we draw out from ourselves.

CORPUS CHRISTI (SERIES A, B, C)
HOMILY I

Reading I: *Moses said to the people: Remember how for forty years now the Lord, your God, has directed all your journeying in the desert, so as to test you by affliction and find out whether or not it was your intention to keep his commandments. He therefore let you be afflicted with hunger, and then fed you with manna, a food unknown to you and your fathers, in order to show you that not by bread alone does man live, but by every word that comes from the mouth of the Lord.* (Deut. 8:2-3, 14-16)

ANA-GNOSIS

We've all heard many times the expression, "Experience is a good teacher." We have verified this in our own lives. There is a great difference between hearing somebody talk about something and actually experiencing it ourselves. By doing it ourselves we "know" it is so, we feel it, we are invested and engaged in it, whereas hearing someone talk about it we are still removed, still impersonal observers. So in the simplest of learning situations we are apt to say, "Show me. Let me see it or try it myself." In other words, we want to get into it and react to it ourselves.

THEOLOGICAL EXTENSION

These experiences we have in life bring us a kind of depth and wisdom and appreciation for life. Shakespeare's phrase, "He jests at scars who's never felt a wound," catches the idea well. If we have never suffered the pain, discomfort, humiliation and difficulty of something we are apt also to be rather removed and indifferent about it. So when we raise the question about why God sends difficulties, pain and afflictions to us, we find one of the answers right here: "He therefore let you be afflicted with hunger, and then he fed you with manna in order to show you that not by bread alone does man live, but by every word that comes forth from the mouth of the Lord." By allowing the Israelites this affliction God helps them to a deeper understanding of the truly important things in life, an understanding which is much more profound than that they would have had with no trials whatsoever.

So when someone talks about the importance of suffering, especially to young people or to children, speaking of how it can deepen us, we can hear them say, "Well, don't just talk about it now. Show me." And, of course, God will, in his loving kindness, show them. Suffering and difficulties will come all too soon. But if people can come to see this in the way that Moses is explaining the hunger that brought great appreciation for the manna sent by God, they can see that every act of suffering can show them more deeply the meaning and purpose of their lives.

THEOLOGICAL CONCLUSION

So while suffering can make people bitter, can make them sour and hostile, suffering rightly borne and genuinely understood in faith, hope and love can bring us great wisdom. We must turn to God and ask him to show us how to get real depth of understanding and appreciation of life. And God will show us, in his love, as he did the people of the Old Testament that Moses is speaking to. He will let us be afflicted too, perhaps with hunger, perhaps another way, in order to show us that "not by bread alone does man live, but by every word that comes forth from the mouth of the Lord."

In our greatest suffering, lying in a sick-bed, in pain, staring at the ceiling, or in any other way, often we come face to face more fully than ever before with the real meaning of life, and it is not, as we can see then, made up of a lot of the shallow things that we have been giving our energy and our efforts to. We live by every word that comes from the mouth of the Lord, but often allowing us to suffer is the only way the Lord can teach us this.

CORPUS CHRISTI (SERIES A, B, C)
HOMILY II

Responsorial Psalm: *Praise the Lord, Jerusalem. He has proclaimed* *his word to Jacob, his statutes and his ordinances to Israel. He has not done thus for any other nation; his ordinances he has not made known to them.* (Ps. 147:12-15, 19-20)

ANA-GNOSIS

In our age we have been seeking justice and equal rights for everyone. We are very conscious of those persons and groups who do not receive what they should receive, and concerned that they be recognized and be given their just due. And because this is the mood of our time, we can get so wrapped up in how equal we are that we forget or overlook how unequal we are. Thus it can come as a shock to realize how wide a variety of basic differences there are among us that laws and policies cannot resolve. It only takes a moment's thought to recognize that, whatever else we try to do with regard to education, there is, as there has always been, a distribution of people who are bright, people who are average and people who are less able. We can define this in terms of IQ or whatever else we want, but since the beginning of time people have not all had equal intelligence. There are also differences in health, in height, in weight, in appearance, in personality and in the way people respond to life around them. These are in some measure very fundamental differences. No matter how much a boy dreams of being a high school basketball star, unless nature has endowed him with above average height, he will only in a rare instance achieve this dream.

THEOLOGICAL EXTENSION

So we have to recognize that, no matter how much we strive for equality—and we should do so to gain and preserve those rights that all people should share—there will always be great differences. We see today this emphasis as it occurs throughout the Old Testament. The people of Israel were, in a very special way, chosen by God. They were favored, as so many people in all sorts of ways seem favored by birth or abilities or special characteristics.

The Psalmist says: "He has proclaimed his word to Jacob, his statutes and his ordinances to Israel. He has not done thus for any other nation. His ordinances he has not made known to them." Here Israel is in a most favored position. Other nations are not its equal. Later on we learn that the apostles of Christ are given this same "chosen people" feeling. "You have not chosen me," said Christ, "but I have chosen you." And we, too, by extension, have been specially chosen, as the people of the Old Testament of Israel were specially chosen.

Now, what do we do with this? Do we just sit in comfort and reassurance that we are the superior people and that's all that we need to think about. Unfortunately this has happened many times. The prophets constantly warned of the temptation of exaggerated security. They warned the Israelites that though all these things had been done for them, this didn't mean that they were to forget how dependent on God they were and to forget their responsibilities. In the New Testament, while Christ emphasized our being chosen, he equally emphasized our responsibilities. Perhaps nowhere is this more clearly stated than in the parable of the talents. There we see that we are not merely given gifts or favor for ourselves alone. The talents must be used for others. We are responsible in proportion to the degree that we have gifts to bring to God's light and word to others. So Israel was chosen to bring to the world the Messiah. The Messiah, in turn, gives to us, as Christians, the responsibility of bringing his redemption and his words to the whole world. Our responsibility, then, is to take up this challenge and to carry it on in our generation.

THEOLOGICAL CONCLUSION

Each of us, then, gifted in special ways, chosen as Israel was chosen, has special responsibilities. This is basically why to be gifted is not to stand superior to others in patronizing or condescending ways, but rather to be aware that, being so chosen as Christians, we have the great responsibility and privilege of bringing his message, through the use of all our gifts, to others.

CORPUS CHRISTI (SERIES A, B, C)
HOMILY III

Reading II: *Is not the cup of blessing we bless a sharing in the blood of Christ? And is not the bread we break a sharing in the body of Christ? Because the loaf of bread is one, we, many though we are, are one body for we all partake of the one loaf.* (1 Cor. 10:16-17)

ANA-GNOSIS

Sometimes life has such a subtlety about it and is, in a way, so complex, that even to teach a simple thing we sometimes must appear to be contradicting ourselves. So it often happens that our folk sayings are paradoxical or, at first hearing or first reaction, contradictory. One of these we've often heard is "The way to own something is to give it away." Stated another way, "we are never so rich as when we have given something away." We realize that this contradiction or paradox attempts to catch a far greater richness that we experience when we have shared something with others that we might simply have been tempted to keep, because we valued it, all to ourselves.

THEOLOGICAL EXTENSION

In the celebration of the Eucharist, after the peace of Christ is shared, the priest takes the host, breaks it and puts a piece in the Chalice. The host, broken then, is shortly thereafter shared by those participating. And this very act of breaking and sharing captures the essence of the paradoxical saying we've just heard. St. Paul catches this point here when he stresses that by going out to others we break something in ourselves, and then we pick up the pieces and share them together. That, in a mysterious way, Christ himself is doing as the host is broken and shared. And in our lives, too, we must break off our selfishness, our natural tendency to cleave to ourselves, and break out of that in order to become part of something far greater than ourselves. So after the breaking of the host it is very fitting that we all share the body and blood of Christ together.

St. Paul asks, "Is not the cup of blessing we bless a sharing in the blood of Christ? And is not the bread we break a sharing in the body of Christ. Because the loaf of bread is one, we, many though we are, are one body for we all partake of the one loaf." Paul gives us, therefore, this paradox: that in Christ we break the Eucharist, but, by breaking, it becomes part of each of us who gathered together are part of the greater wholeness of Christ. By initiating this and breaking ourselves, getting out of ourselves, we become something far greater than we were before. The pieces of the Eucharist in no way diminish our sharing of Christ, but magnify how all of us in these pieces of the Eucharist are one in Christ. We are more than we were before, more than we were alone.

THEOLOGICAL CONCLUSION

So whether we think of this act as giving something very valuable away or the breaking of the Eucharist, we may all share it and still be one in Christ. By breaking out of our own self-centeredness to go out to others, we gain something far greater and far beyond ourselves. We find a unity and totality far exceeding that of our own isolation.

CORPUS CHRISTI (SERIES A, B, C)
HOMILY IV

Gospel Reading: *Jesus said to the crowds of Jews: "I myself am the living bread come down from heaven. If anyone eats this bread he shall live forever; the bread I will give is my flesh, for the life of the world."* (Jn. 6:51-58)

ANA-GNOSIS

Most of us have been fortunate enough in our schooling to have had one or two very good teachers. They stand out in our memories. We can remember especially how kind they were, how patient when we didn't understand something. And we remember, too, how they always proceeded from the known to the unknown. That is, they never made a big jump in something we didn't understand, but they tried to show us from what we already knew how this was just one stage further. The next thing we needed to learn was one stage after that. We can recall, too, that we learned to trust those good teachers because we knew they wouldn't fool us. We were confident that they would take us step by step in a way that would not leave us lost, confused or humiliated. We were in good hands.

THEOLOGICAL EXTENSION

Our Lord was such a teacher. He taught one of the most difficult of all the mysteries of the Christian religion, that of the Eucharistic presence under the form of bread and wine, in just this way. He first let them learn that he had come in a very special way from God, and then slowly it emerged that he was the Son of God. Later, too, the mystery of his death and resurrection came to them gradually. None of these things was thrust upon them, but only slowly unfolded as the knowledge of a good teacher only slowly unfolds. The people believed then and gradually came to understand.

He did the same as he began to teach about his Eucharistic presence. First he was considerate of their needs. These people had followed him up into the hills and were hungry. With the very small amount of food present, he turned it into an abundance. They had seen how little food there was and they knew he had fed everyone. They had to believe then that this miracle had occurred.

Now having shared this experience with them, having given them food they could taste and enjoy, and a miracle they could believe in, he then went on to tell them that they had to believe further that: "I myself am the living bread come down from heaven. If anyone eats this bread he shall live forever." We can sense their amazement. We've all experienced this in any subject that is difficult to learn. We know one part of it, we have believed it it and understood it, but to make a further jump is very difficult no matter how kind and understanding the teacher may be. But that jump we make, and only after we've made that leap of faith in the teacher do we begin to understand what the teacher is teaching. It's only with hindsight that we grasp it at all. Now we can look back, having known the Eucharist for so many centuries and we can see more clearly what Christ was promising. But for these people it was indeed difficult. But he taught them well, moving from the known to the unknown: the food that they could taste and eat to the mysterious body of Christ nourishing them spiritually under the same appearance of this same nourishing bread.

THEOLOGICAL CONCLUSION

"I myself am the living bread come down from heaven. If anyone eats this bread he shall live forever." We have eaten the foods of the earth; we know they nourish us. We have experienced their nourishing qualities. Now we eat and experience the Eucharistic presence in us, and we know from our experience of living grace how true Christ's promise is and will be throughout all our lives.

NINTH SUNDAY OF THE YEAR (SERIES A)
HOMILY I

Reading I: *Moses told the people, "Take these words of mine into your heart and soul. Bind them at your wrist as a sign, and let them be a pendant on your forehead.* (Dt. 11:18, 26-28)

ANA-GNOSIS

We all know the practicality of having a wristwatch. We can even feel lost when we forget to have our watch on and have to ask others for the time. If we are used to wearing a wristwatch and do not have it on, we can even feel nervous and naked without it. And it is so very practical to have to remind us of the time, to guide us in getting to the appointments we have made and the places we have to be. It can warn us, when we are doing something else, that we must stop soon enough to be on time for our other appointments and duties.

THEOLOGICAL EXTENSION

Now it is this kind of common sense idea that Moses is speaking of today about the Ten Commandments. He says, "Take these words of mine into your heart and soul. *Bind them at your wrist."* That is, let us keep them as a constant reminder, much as a wristwatch is, of what our duties are and how we are to arrive at our destination, which is life with God. The Ten Commandments are most valuable guidelines for this, as they have proved from the time of Moses.

Like a wristwatch, they can remind us of what we were supposed to be doing. They can make us aware of things that otherwise we might forget about. The Ten Commandments by no means cover all our religious and spiritual relationships, obligations and responsibilities; they are primarily concerned with our relationship with God and some aspects of our relationships with others. But they are key conceptions. These ten directions for our lives are most important and basic.

THEOLOGICAL CONCLUSION

So when we look at our wristwatch to guide us in the time and to alert us to what we should do and where we should be, we can think of the Ten Commandments in much the same way. They are ten basic concerns and responsibilities that are wise guides around which we can center our lives.

As we put on a wristwatch each day to guide us in terms of time, let us put on the Ten Commandments in much the same way. Let us always keep them at hand. We need their guidance even more than we need the reminder that consulting a wristwatch can give us.

NINTH SUNDAY OF THE YEAR (SERIES A)
HOMILY II

Responsorial Psalm: *Lord, be my rock of safety . . . Let your face shine upon your servant; save me in your kindness. Take courage and be stouthearted, all you who hope in the Lord.* (Ps. 31:2-4, 17, 25)

ANA-GNOSIS

We all know the experience of waiting. Perhaps our most common experience of waiting is in a Doctor's office, or in the emergency room of a hospital, waiting for the nurses and doctors to come and take care of us. This sort of waiting is hopeful and expectant. We feel a relief at being in a safe place where in a short time the skilled hands of the medical personnel will give us care.

THEOLOGICAL EXTENSION

It is interesting that the words "to wait" and "to hope" are quite similar in many languages. For example, in Spanish it is the same word, *esperar:* to wait for and to hope for. The word "expect" is also similar. In Latin, *expectare* conveys the notion of expecting as well as of waiting. So *to hope* and *to wait* are interrelated. In the translation of the Psalm today, this is so true in the original wording that we notice one translation has the phrase, "All you who *hope* in the Lord," and the other has, "All you who *wait* in the Lord," suggesting again how hope and waiting go together.

This is our feeling with regard to God. We don't just *wait* for God, but we *hope* in our waiting, and we expect and trust and look forward to him in our waiting. But we do often wait. The nature of life does not give us immediate answers, solutions, or resolutions. We often live in mystery, in insecurity; we hope and have confidence, expecting the good that will come from the caring hands of God.

If we've been fortunate enough to have a physician whom, over a period of years, we have been able to trust, we know the positive, trusting expectancy with which we wait on his coming to take care of us when we are ill. We know how much better we feel just the moment he walks into the room because we so trust his or her knowledge of our illness. Now in that same mood and tone we wait on God. We hope and wait in the sense of the Spanish *esperar.* We expect, in the Latin sense of *expectare,* the good that will come from God no matter how long, in God's plan, we should have to wait.

THEOLOGICAL CONCLUSION

Ours is a hopeful, rich, and fulfilled waiting, encouraged and strengthened by God. So the Psalmist wisely advises us, "Take courage and be stouthearted, all of you who hope in the Lord," or alternately, "Be strong, let your heart take courage, all you who wait for the Lord."

NINTH SUNDAY OF THE YEAR (SERIES A)
HOMILY III

Reading II: *The righteousness of God has now been manifested apart from the law, although the law and the prophets bear witness to it,* *the righteousness of God through faith in Jesus Christ for all who believe . . . For we hold that a man is justified by faith apart from works of law.* (Rom. 3:21-25, 28)

ANA-GNOSIS

It is always amusing to notice how an expert does whatever he or she is good at with complete security, confidence and ease. Experts don't need to worry about following directions. Perhaps a common example of this is when a son or daughter wants to learn to make something, a pie perhaps. So they go to their mother or grandmother, whoever is the expert in the family, and ask, "How do you make an apple pie? What do you put in it?" And the expert always has that loose, easy answer: "You put some flour in, and some salt, and you make the dough. Then you put the apples in." And you can hear the young person interrupting with, "Wait a minute! How much flour do you put in? And how do you make the dough?" There's usually a look of confusion on the face of the expert when she answers, "Well, uh, you just put enough in." The young person, of course, wants a recipe, an exact measure, a rule, a law, which the really skilled, knowledgeable person no longer needs.

THEOLOGICAL EXTENSION

Obviously, in the beginning all learners use recipes as an aid to acquiring a skill. But there comes a point when one is quite skilled at something, and is able to "feel" the recipe with one's whole being, so to speak. She feels that it is right, and no longer needs the "rules." This does not mean that there are no longer rules and regulations to be followed, but rather that they are being followed in a highly personal and sensitive way. There is no longer a need to open up a recipe book and read carefully the exact instructions. The need to do this is long since past for the expert.

Now it is something of this idea that St. Paul is conveying to us today about life in Christ. He does not mean that we do not have to follow laws and directions. But he says, "The righteousness of God has now been manifested apart from the law, although the law and the prophets bear witness to it . . . that justice of God which works through faith in Jesus Christ for all who believe." That is to say, the really deeply invested, totally committed, genuine and generous Christian, living the Christ-life, does so with a spontaneity and generosity of being and action that is not necessarily in adherence to any kind of rigid rule.

As the skilled cook no longer needs to open the recipe book—although it might be dogeared from the learning process of earlier years—so the Christian who is deeply imbued with Christ's life reaches a freedom and a spontaneity of faith commitment in which he has Christ alive in him. St. Paul's phrase, "I live now not I, but Christ lives in me," catches this. He has, then, complete freedom, not to break the law or violate the conditions of Christian observance, but to be spontaneous and personal and genuine in his total commitment, rather than to have to adhere to some rigid law.

THEOLOGICAL CONCLUSION

We can see the difference when we watch the novice cook, following with her finger the directions of the recipe, in contrast to the free way that the expert puts a pie or cake together, scarcely seeming to think about it. The deeply trusting and committed Christian lives with this kind of freedom—not in any violation of the law, but beyond the law. So, St. Paul says, "For we hold that man is justified by faith, apart from the works of the law." He does his Christian work with ease and security, having the living sense of Christ in his life. He is not rigorously anxious about rules, regulations and laws. His "law" is an inner, deep sense of Christion sensibility that is wise and skillful and expert, just as a wise cook has an inner knowledge of preparing a cake or a pie for a delicious meal. The laws and rules of the recipe book are followed, indeed, in the Christian life too, but spontaneously, freely and generously in and through Christ.

NINTH SUNDAY OF THE YEAR (SERIES A) HOMILY IV

Gospel Reading: *Jesus said to his disciples, "None of those who cry out, 'Lord, Lord,' will enter the kingdom of God, but only the one who does the will of my Father in heaven. When that day comes, many will plead with me, 'Lord, Lord, have we not prophesied in your name? Have we not exorcised demons by its power? Did we not do many miracles in your name as well?' Then I will declare to them solemnly, 'I never knew you.'"* (Mt. 7:21-27)

ANA-GNOSIS

There is a constant appeal to all ages throughout history of magic, of wonderful things, things that astound and surprise us because they are so unexpected. This is not just true of the tricks of magicians, although this always remains a great attraction for every generation, but even more so of events that seem so beyond the predictions and the usual way of nature that they seem to be supernatural.

So when the Hollywood producers stumbled on the concept of exorcisms, the driving out of the devil, even in what we have thought of as a very sophisticated age of special knowledge, these stories proved to be best-sellers and successful films, illustrating again that this kind of preternatural presentation never loses its appeal.

THEOLOGICAL EXTENSION

Another supernatural experience, the miracle, always stirs up enormous public interest and challenge and excitement. Wherever and whenever we hear reports of such unusual things going on, hundreds or thousands of people quickly gather to visit the site.

Consequently, when we go back through the life of Christ and hear of similar actions, particularly of the miracles, it is understandable for us to think that this was the central message, the main thing, that Christ intended. We are apt to lose sight of the fact that he used his special powers from God only as a means to set up a greater learning and understanding atmosphere. So when all the people had gathered and had followed him up into the mountains and were hungry, he fed them in a miraculous way. But he did so especially to set the stage for their understanding of the Eucharistic Presence that would be far more overwhelming in its real meaning than simply feeding thousands from the loaves and fishes that were there.

Lest we forget this way in which Christ really dismissed miracles and their attendant reaction, we need to look carefully at his words today. Here we see why miracles or special powers in the Church are not nearly as important as popular enthusiasm or excitement might make them. Christ tells us frankly that they are by no means central to faith and will not qualify us for heaven. It is rather startling to realize this. But he says, "Even if you work miracles in my name," even if you are the most overwhelmingly successful exorcist in my name, that in itself means nothing. It is shocking to hear it stated so directly, and yet this is exactly what Christ is telling us in today's Reading from the Gospel of Matthew. "When that day comes, many will plead with me, 'Lord, have we not prophesied in your name? Have we not exorcised demons by its power? Did we not do many miracles in your name as well?' " Doesn't this sound like a claim to holiness, to special privilege, in God's Church? But our Lord answers very clearly that this is not the heart of Christian life and faith at all. He says, "Then I will declare to them solemnly, 'I never knew you. Out of my sight, you evil-doers.' "

What a surprise! He rejects those who, in a sense, pretentiously thought that by this kind of agency somehow they were confirmed in sanctity, and that there was no possible way that they could lose their state of grace, since this great thing had been done through them. This is a very clear reminder.

If we look back on the early Church with its miracles and very special happenings, we see that they were necessary because of the infantile condition of the leaders who needed the reassurance and that strength. We see now that the Church requires a life of faith, of hope and of genuine Christian love of self, neighbor, and God. This is truly the Christian life, rather than the startling, amazing miracles and other astonishing feats.

THEOLOGICAL CONCLUSION

Thus we have the words of our Lord today very clearly emphasizing that miracles and exorcisms do not cause us to gain eternal life. He reassures us that our life of faith and confidence in God, without startling and unusual things happening, is life in Christ and is truly the desirable one.

TENTH SUNDAY OF THE YEAR (SERIES A)
HOMILY I

Reading I: *"Let us strive to know the Lord; as certain as the dawn is his coming, and his judgment shines forth like the light of day! He will come to us like the rain, like the spring rain that waters the earth."* (Hos. 6:3-6)

ANA-GNOSIS

As the seasons, in recent years, seem to be undergoing a slight change so that we are experiencing longer, colder, more snow-filled winters, we can speak firsthand about what people 75 or 100 years ago talked so much about—those long, dreary, and sometimes very wearisome winters. We have been told by weather authorities that over the last 50 years or so we have had unusually mild winters and that we are now returning to what, over the centuries, seems to be more normal, namely longer, colder winters with much more snow.

But knowing that it is normal doesn't make it any less wearisome. So when someone says he is going to Florida or some other warm climate for a week or for the whole winter, we can easily look on him enviously, wishing that we, too, could escape what is beginning to become tiring and somewhat depressing.

However much we recognize that winter has its joys, beauties and excitements too, and that there is a challenge to the struggle against the cold and the snow, we can still find coping with it day to day as a tedious, discouraging prospect. Yet there have been suggestions that this is why the most successful peoples sometimes come from climates that vary a lot. A climate that is too much the same doesn't offer much challenge to people. Be that as it may, when we're in the midst of it we just want it to be over.

That is why we feel the joy and excitement after a long, hard winter when the first signs of spring come—when robins appear, the crocuses bloom, the snow starts to melt and we experience a deep sense of new life unfolding in the warmth and sunniness of the dawn of spring. It's like the passing of a long and tiresome night where we didn't get much sleep, and which we thought would never end.

THEOLOGICAL EXTENSION

Now we know this kind of description also fits our lives. Poets have constantly made this comparison—as Shakespeare does in the phrase, "the winter of our discontent"—between the harsh dreariness of winter and those periods of discontentment, worry and unrest in our lives. The challenge is also comparable. Just as we use our endurance, our intelligence and our ingenuity with God's help to survive the rigors of winter, so too through these same gifts and the grace of our faith in God will we be able to weather these trying periods in our lives. In fact our faith is made stronger by such concerns and challenges. In the passage read today, Hosea is encouraging us to have faith in God throughout our difficulties just as we, in winter, have faith that spring is coming.

It's easy to get tired walking in heavy snow. A person has to encourage himself to press on, to keep at it. It's very tempting to quit. So Hosea begins with that same idea. He says, "Let us strive to know the Lord." Another translation is, "Let us *press on* to know the Lord." Let's push ahead, get the snow out of the way, clear the way as much as we can even if it is the dead of winter. Then he gives us reassurance and hope: "As certain as the dawn is his coming, his judgment shines forth like the light of day!" Just as we will come to spring if we survive the storms of winter, just as we will see the dawn if we persevere through the night, so we will encounter the Lord if we press on even in the most difficult and discouraging times. There is no question about it. It's as inevitable as the dawn or the coming of spring. "He will come to us like the rain, the spring rain that waters the earth." And we will know the joy and excitement of his coming all the more for having struggled to meet the challenges of winter.

THEOLOGICAL CONCLUSION

Just as winter challenges us and forces us to press on, to make our way and do our work, so, too, we must press on in the midst of life's conflicts and difficulties. It is what our Lord expects of us. And he is with us, as life is with us even though masked by winter's snow, and he will be there for us at the end, just as at the end of winter we always find spring. The winter of God's love challenges us and will bring us to the happiness of his spring.

TENTH SUNDAY OF THE YEAR (SERIES A)
HOMILY II

Responsorial Psalm: *To the upright I will show the saving power of God.*
Offer to God praise as your sacrifice and fulfill your vows to the Most High; Then call upon me in time of distress; I will rescue you, and you shall glorify me. (Ps. 50:1, 8, 12-13, 14-15)

ANA-GNOSIS

When we hear, as we do so frequently, the phrase, "Praise God," or "Give praise to God," it can raise some questions in our mind. When we think of always praising other people, and especially when we think of someone who always wants to be praised, this can have a negative and pejorative effect rather than a positive one. We can feel, understandably, that if a person were constantly wanting to be praised he might be insecure and not really very admirable at all. So why should religion always keep talking about "praising God?" Doesn't it seem disrespectful to conceptualize God as someone who always needs to be praised?

THEOLOGICAL EXTENSION

Looked at simply, with one meaning of the word *praise* as we apply it to people around us, this does seem to be a somewhat disrespectful way to consider God. Yet religious homilies and discussions and the Bible itself are filled with phrases about "praising God." The line of today's Psalm, "Offer to God praise as your sacrifice, and fulfill your vows to the Most High," renews that sense that it is basic for the religious person to "praise God."

Now in order to see this praise with freshness and not simply misunderstand it or apply it narrowly to a vain, self-conscious and rather insecure person who is always seeking other people's praise, we can be helped if we look carefully at the real meaning of the word *praise*. The dictionary says that it comes from the word *preizen* in German, and we can already hear that it is the English infinitive, *to prize,* as well as *to put a price on.* It's more basic origin is from the Latin word *precare,* to value, to prize something. Thus, we can hear more clearly now that the word *appreciate* comes closer than the word *praise*. That is, this term, in its original meaning in the Psalms here and throughout the Bible, is not meant to imply that somehow or other, like an inferior or insecure person, God always needs to be praised by us. Not at all. It's much more, in its meaning, not related directly to God at all, but to ourselves. That is to say, we must *praise* God, or *appreciate* God, or put the right value or price on God in our lives. So by repeatedly putting the right value on God, we truly praise, or prize, or appreciate God.

The earlier part of the Psalm makes this clear. The custom of the Old Testament to use foodstuffs, as a source of life, to symbolize man's dependency on God, encouraged them to pick a fine animal or food and offer it as a sacrifice to God. But this was not anything God needed at all. These were simply very precious things that man needed. And by giving these precious foodstuffs to God, in the human manner of cooking them over a fire and pouring out wine on the ground rather than drinking it, people were reminded of how much they owed God, how much they needed to value and appreciate God. The Psalmist, speaking of God, makes the point clearly that it is not something God needs: "If I were hungry I would not tell you, for mine are the world and its fullness." God doesn't need somebody to sacrifice something to him. Everything came to him. "Do I eat the flesh of strong bulls, is the blood of goats my drink?" Obviously these are not things that God needs, but man eats and needs them for strength and the source of his life. Thus we can see that this kind of sacrifice or praise of God is certainly related to God, but is the source of all our life. God is the source of the foodstuffs that we receive; God is the source of the initial right to life that we have received. This is what to "praise God" really means. Another translation of the same Psalm seems to catch it a little more sharply. It says, "Offer to God a sacrifice of thanksgiving."

THEOLOGICAL CONCLUSION

Understood rightly then, to "praise God" means to appreciate him, to value him, to grasp how fundamental and necessary he is to all that we are and can be. This is "praising God"—appreciating and understanding this central, fundamental point.

TENTH SUNDAY OF THE YEAR (SERIES A)
HOMILY III

Reading II: *Abraham believed hoping against hope, and so became the father of many nations, just as it was once told him, "Numerous as this shall your descendants be." Without growing weak in faith he thought of his own body, which was as good as dead (for he was nearly a hundred years old), and of the dead womb of Sarah. Yet he never questioned or doubted God's promise; rather, he was strengthened in faith and gave glory to God, fully persuaded that God could do whatever he had promised. Thus his faith was credited to him as justice.* (Rom. 4:18-25)

ANA-GNOSIS

Like many simple words that we use and that are very basic to our lives, the word *hope* has a variety of meanings and innuendoes. Simple as the word seems, it's not simple to explain. We use it commonly in our daily exchange with one another. If we are planning a project for the next day, a picnic, going fishing or for a golf game, and someone says, "Looks like it'll be a nice day tomorrow," we answer, "I hope so." We mean that we'll get along whether it is nice or not, but it will add to the enjoyment of the day if it is sunny and pleasant. Here hope does not have a strong meaning; it's just a casual agreement and affirmation of the person's statement. It has a deeper meaning though when we think of very important issues, projects or commitments in our lives. So we think of people taking a new job as being very hopeful, or of a person entering school being hopeful of graduation, or of a person who graduates going out into life filled with hope. Beginnings are times of great hope. Here the word *hope* has much greater dimensions than the casual, "I hope so." It almost sums up in its four letters the meaning and significance that the future has for a person or a group of people. It involves their intense commitment to whatever is necessary to achieve what is hoped for.

THEOLOGICAL EXTENSION

There is a third type of hope that seems to be almost a contradiction. It is the hope of the hopeless, a hope when everything seems impossible. And this is the hope that the Reading today from the Letter to the Romans is referring to. We have the classic phrase, "Abraham believed *hoping against hope . . .*" An extreme of hope. It's a common enough situation to begin with: Abram is old, so is Sarah. All of nature would suggest that there is no way they could have a child now. It would seem to be ridiculous to think they could. It is hopeless, as we would say. Yet Abram hopes; we find a special kind of hope when in ordinary ways of thinking all hope should be gone. And this is the richest, most complete hope of all.

We encounter it most commonly in our lives related to sickness and death. There can be conditions where all hope in the ordinary medical, human sense is gone. Then we must turn to a different kind of hope—a hope, in a sense, against hope, beyond human hope. This hope is the other side of human hope, it is a leap into the hands of God and into eternity.

So Paul affirms this hope when he says, "Our faith will be credited to us also if we believe in him who raised Jesus our Lord from the dead, the Jesus who was handed over to death for our sins and raised up for our justification."

THEOLOGICAL CONCLUSION

Hope in Jesus, in his resurrection, a victory over death, is a hope against hope. It was beyond all hope. There seemed to be no way he could overcome that situation. Yet he did. Thomas Mann, the great German writer, speaks of this hope as a victory over the "sheerly irremediable." And he says it would be "a hope beyond hopelessness, the transcendence of despair, the miracle that passes belief."

This is the hope that Christ gives us. Beyond all human hope and care and remedy, we have a greater hope in the assurance of Christ's resurrection justifying all of us and those we love.

TENTH SUNDAY OF THE YEAR (SERIES A) HOMILY IV

Gospel Reading: *As Jesus moved about he saw a man named Matthew at his post where taxes were collected. He said to him, "Follow me." Matthew got up and followed him. Now it happened that,* *while Jesus was at table in Matthew's home, many tax collectors and those known as sinners came to join Jesus and his disciples at dinner. The Pharisees saw this and complained to his disciples, "What reason can the Teacher have for eating with tax collectors and those who disregard the law?" Overhearing the remark, he said, "People who are in good health do not need a doctor; sick people do. Go and learn the meaning of the word: 'It is mercy I desire and not sacrifice.' I have come to call not the self-righteous, but sinners."* (Mt. 9:9-13)

ANA-GNOSIS

We know that it is quite easy, especially when we are emotionally upset or disturbed, to overlook the obvious. We've all heard, for example, the phrase, "saving the saved." Yet this phrase is misleading in some ways and even fraudulent because none of us, in the religious sense, can know we are saved. Nonetheless, it catches the idea somewhat humorously of the priest or minister lecturing heatedly on Sunday to the people who are in church about those who failed to come. That is, we can overlook the real point of where religious concern and consideration for others really lies in our lives.

THEOLOGICAL EXTENSION

This is the point of the incident today. Because of prejudice that was as strong in the time of Christ as it is now, there was resistance to certain people, in this case tax gatherers and others labeled "sinners." Christ was being criticized for his association with these people whom prejudicial labels had called sinners and who, therefore, were not deemed worthy of his association.

But Christ reminds his critics that there is no such thing as "saving the saved." If they feel themselves above these people, they are the ones who are misled by their own prejudice and self-deception. He came for sinners and that means he came for all of us. If we fraudulently or in prejudice think ourselves saved and criticize his going to "sinners" then we have missed the whole point of why he came. A doctor, after all, goes to the sick. And even those who are well are not totally immune to disease or corruption. A doctor can be very valuable in preserving everyone's health.

THEOLOGICAL CONCLUSION

All of us, as sinners, need the ministering hand of Christ. So we should go out to others in compassion, concern and loving care, not because we are condescending, or because we feel superior to them, but because we know indeed that we, too, are sinners as well. We go out to them in loving care as Christ in mercy goes out to us.

ELEVENTH SUNDAY OF THE YEAR (SERIES A)
HOMILY I

Reading I: *The Israelites came to the desert of Sinai and pitched camp. While Israel was encamped here in front of the mountain, Moses went up the mountain to God. Then the Lord called to him and said, "Thus shall you say to the house of Jacob; tell the Israelites: 'You have seen for yourselves how I treated the Egyptians and how I bore you up on eagle wings, and brought you here myself. Therefore, if you hearken to my voice and keep my covenant, you shall be my special possession, dearer to me than all other people, though all the earth is mine. You shall be to me a kingdom of priests, a holy nation.'"* (Ex. 19:2-6)

ANA-GNOSIS

Stereotypes are perhaps the most difficult of all national and international attitudes to overcome. That is, because it is such a simple way of seeming to understand the world and its wide variety of peoples and cultures, we can stick a lot of people with one label and these labels tend, often tragically, to endure. Even though the personal achievements or, alternately, personal failures of a particular person are obvious to anyone who inquires or investigates, he still is subject to the stereotypes that tend to blur out differences which should distinguish him within his culture.

If we were to think, for example, of a common stereotype that we have of people of western Europe and the United States, at least over the last three or four centuries, we would, I think, all come up with the idea that these are a scientific people. In medicine and other sciences these people have brought to the rest of the world all the modern wisdom that they have. Scientific medicine, for example, we think had its total origin in Europe and the United States. An alternate stereotype is to assure that the tribal people of Africa a hundred years or more ago were hopelessly ignorant, inadequate, and were certainly lacking scientific and advanced medical knowledge.

Let's consider one example now that is rather startling. The innoculation for small pox has been totally accredited to western culture. Before it was used widely, small pox could wipe out a third or more of a city's population in a very short time. Everyone, including the physician, was helpless to do anything about it.

Yet Cotton Mather, one of the leading Protestant divines of the 18th century learned from some black people, who explained to him how their tribes in Africa had innoculated their members by giving them a small dose of the pox, that such prevention against small pox was possible. So here one of the great benefits to mankind came not wholly from the stereotype advanced nations of the west at all, but from African tribes.

THEOLOGICAL EXTENSION

Now this example should caution us about class or stereotypes. In today's Reading, if we make stereotypes out of what is said, then the Israelites are the "good guys" with the white hats, and the Egyptians are the "bad guys" with the black hats. But this is too simplistic a rendering of the text.

What is meant here is simply that, in the deliverance, it happened that the Israelites, chosen by God in a special way to be the source from which the Messiah would come, were freed from a group of people who held them in slavery for a time, and these people happened to be Egyptians. Egyptians by no means, as we well know, had a special priority over slavery.

Throughout the Old and New Testament, partly because of the language that is used, very few discriminations are made that should be made, so we can fall victim to classing people as stereotypes. The Jews are sometimes labeled as a class when obviously what is meant is *particular* Jews in relation to Christ. We can see how obvious this is when we realize that most of the early Christians who read this record were themselves Jews. They clearly understood that all references to Jews did not mean the whole Jewish people by any means. In Christ's own life his story of the good Samaritan not only taught neighborliness, but destroyed the notion that Samaritans were "no good."

So too today we must not forever label all Israelites as good or Egyptians as bad. What may have been true at one time does not hold true for other people at other times. And we are not following Christ's lead if we persist in this simplistic and misleading way of viewing the world. In fact in many parts of the Old Testament the prophets themselves warn the Israelites of their own evil tendencies and of how they have turned against God despite all God's goodness to them.

THEOLOGICAL CONCLUSION

So we must avoid stereotype labels and we must read the Bible in the way it is intended, that is, without reading into it whole classifications or stereotypes which only serve to distort the meaning of the story told. To do this is a terrible tragedy and a total misreading of what the Biblical message is intended to be.

ELEVENTH SUNDAY OF THE YEAR (SERIES A)
HOMILY II

Responsorial Psalm: *We are his people, the sheep of his flock. Sing joyfully to the Lord, all you lands; serve the Lord with gladness; come before him with joyful song.* (Ps. 100:1 2, 3, 5)

ANA-GNOSIS

We all know the feeling we have when we are sharing deeply with another person or group of persons. We experience an intense, and in some way indescribable, happiness or joy. There's a richness of belonging and sharing that's very deep but not easy to describe. Sometimes, to catch it, we fall back on words related to music, and so we talk about being in harmony in a group. Sometimes, too, we talk about two people having "their" song, that is, a particular song they heard when they first met or when they were going together that stands out as a common memory and catches the happiness and joy of their relationship. Sometimes to describe the opposite of this we speak of people in disharmony. All these phrases help to catch the sharpness of identity and belonging that music and a particular musical theme or sound can bring us.

Countries, for example, identify themselves by their national anthems. We all know the stirring feeling of witnessing the Olympics on television or in person when gold medals are presented and, as the winner walks up, we hear the national anthem of his country. The people of his country all have a feeling of belonging with that person. They share with him and the music brings them together. Perhaps millions of people, hearing and seeing this, share together a sense of belonging with all those who feel a part of themselves in this song. Universities do this too. Most of us can recognize quickly some of the famous songs of the large universities, and we can, if we hear ours, immediately identify with that song.

THEOLOGICAL EXTENSION

Now this idea of music is also a way of thinking about what the Psalmist has in mind today when he speaks of our relationship to God as sheep in a flock. He begins with, "Sing joyfully to the Lord, all you lands. Serve the Lord with gladness; come before him with joyful song." Now, the notion of singing is not unconnected with sheep, even though it may seem strange to us now. In the Psalmist's mind there was this connection because, as we may recall, one of the ways of identifying sheep that were all gathered together was for each shepherd to play "his" particular tune on his reed, and only his sheep would recognize it and would follow him. This was a way of easily identifying those sheep which belonged to him.

So, odd as it may seem, singing and sheep are not unrelated. Just as we recognize our national anthem, our school, or a song we share with a special person which gives us a sense of belonging so, in a very special way, a song can recall our relationship to God.

I suppose we could all pick out a favorite hymn that might do this for us. For a long time in the Church "Holy God We Praise Thy Name" was a common hymn that people could all sing together. There was an enormous sense of sharing as they sang that hymn. Hymns change however, and no doubt new hymns will come forward. But whatever the song, if we identify with it as God's song for us, then we will recall again whenever we sing it, that we belong to Christ's flock.

THEOLOGICAL CONCLUSION

Just as we feel a sense of identity and harmony in a shared song, and just as we feel harmony in a group where we belong, where we deeply share, so, by extension, we belong to God. This is our most complete and most eduring belonging. Other kinds of harmony and songs, other joys, will pass. Belonging to the Lord will endure. "The Lord is good; his kindness endures forever, and his faithfulness to all generations." There is no end to the belonging in harmony with God. His is a joyful one, sung forever. We come before him, then, with joyful song, to sing with others to the ultimate source of all the harmony in our lives.

ELEVENTH SUNDAY OF THE YEAR (SERIES A) HOMILY III

Reading II: *At the appointed time, when we were still powerless, Christ died for us godless men. It is rare that anyone should lay down his life for a just man, though it is barely possible that for a good man someone may have the courage to die. It is precisely in this that God proves his love for us: that while we were still sinners, Christ died for us. Now that we have been justified by his blood, it is all the more certain that we shall be saved by him from God's wrath. For if when we were God's enemies, we were reconciled to him by the death of his Son, it is all the more certain that we who have been reconciled will be saved by his life. Not only that; we go so far as to make God our boast through our Lord Jesus Christ, through whom we have now received reconciliation.* (Rom. 5:6-11)

ANA-GNOSIS

We all know that painful situation when two people quarrel, a father and son, a mother and daughter, close friends. We know, too, how hard it is sometimes for one or both to become reconciled. Everyone who loves them and who watches this experiences their pain. There is always great joy when such people have reconciled and everyone hears about it and is delighted.

Such a reconciliation is most commonly possible when one of the estranged people says to everyone, "Well, the door is always open. Any time he comes, he will be welcome." This is relayed back to the other person, who, sometimes in pride or stubbornness or some subtle internal difficulty that impedes him from doing what he knows he should do, will shake his head and say, "No, I just can't bring myself to do it.' Yet then finally he does. The door is open, and there's a loving embrace and reconciliation occurs. Later when we talk to that person he may well say, "I don't know why I put it off so long. There was so much unnecessary suffering. I should have believed him and just come a long time ago." This is very familiar to us all, adults and children alike.

THEOLOGICAL EXTENSION

This experience of reconciliation is St. Paul's concern in the part of the Letter to the Romans that we read today. He begins, of course, by reminding us that our worthiness was not what brought us the chance to be reconciled to God. Indeed, we were not worthy. Yet Christ, by his actions, gave us that chance. "It is rare that anyone," St. Paul says, "would lay down his life for a just man, though it is barely possible that for a good man someone may have the courage to die. It is precisely in this that God proves his love for us: that while we were still sinners, Christ died for us." That is, Christ opened the door. From the beginning of time through the anticipation of Christ's redemption, reconciliation was always potentially possible between God and man. But the door was thrown open permanently by Christ. After Christ the door is always open.

THEOLOGICAL CONCLUSION

One of the loveliest, most consoling stories of God's love that Christ himself told was that of the prodigal son. The father's arms were always extended to the son. Every night he went up the hill to look with yearning to see if his son was coming back. This is precisely the nature of reconciliation. God's arms are always extended to us. All we need to do is return, come back. We are, indeed, always welcome. The door of God's love through the sacrament of reconciliation is always open to us.

ELEVENTH SUNDAY OF THE YEAR (SERIES A)
HOMILY IV

Gospel Reading: *At the sight of the crowds, the heart of Jesus was moved with pity. They were lying prostrate from exhaustion, like sheep without a shepherd. He said to his disciples: "The harvest* *is good, but laborers are scarce. Beg the harvest master to send out laborers to gather his harvest."* (Mt. 9:36, 10:8)

ANA-GNOSIS

We know that a large crowd can evoke fear in many people. Usually we symbolize that fearful image of a crowd by calling it a "mob." And when we say "mob" we don't just mean ordinary people, we mean something unruly, something in danger of being disordered and committing serious harm, something threatening.

It is interesting that, in fact, the word "mob," which comes from the Latin *mobile* doesn't really mean anything threatening at all. It simply means "easily moved," or "easily led." And without a wise leader, of course, a mob is easily moved the wrong way. That is where the threat seems to come from.

THEOLOGICAL EXTENSION

We see here in these comments of our Lord how he understood this. He had deep sympathy and compassion, a deep sense of sharing and belonging with everyone. So he did not see a crowd of people as a mob, in the unruly, threatening sense that this word conveys to us. Rather he saw a crowd of people—all of us, if you like—who could be easily moved, easily led. And so he used the familiar image of sheep without a shepherd. He recognized how desperately these people needed good leaders, wise leaders.

Then, switching to another familiar image of the harvest, he recognized the need for laborers or else the fruit would die on the vines. Again he gave his listeners a sense of waste and loss by a harvest that wasn't fulfilled. There is potential waste in a large crowd of people; they can be a mob if they have the wrong leaders. As we well know from the recent history of Europe, at the time of World War II and later, people moved by the wrong leaders can become a tragic mob. But the people themselves are good. They simply need the right leaders. And the right leaders can indeed bring forth good fruit from the goodness of the people.

But the word "mob" does catch how easily moved a large crowd of people can be. It should recall to us, in our Christian idea of community and of leadership a sense of how desperately we need wise leaders. Even Christian people can become a mob and be easily moved to do foolish and unwise things without good leaders.

THEOLOGICAL CONCLUSION

So we pray for those who labor for Christ to be good leaders, to lead all of us who are so easily moved by emotion, feeling, and impulsiveness to those things in our lives that are for our ultimate good. These are the leaders who will make us not a mob, but wise and good through the acceptance of their understanding guidance. But these leaders are not dictators who tell us what to do and we must obey. They are ministers to us, bringing out of each of us what is uniquely good and uniquely our calling or vocation in God. These are the laborers we need to bring forth the harvest of good fruit in and through Christ.

INDEX

Agency
—of God, 61
Airplane, 28
Anxiety, 42
Ascension, 48-49
Ascent, 49
Authority, 52
—of Scripture, 8

Belonging, 57, 95
Blasphemy, 8
Breath, 59

Care, 35
Cartoons, 26
Change, 24, 39, 67
Christ, 28-29
—doctrine of, 32
—footsteps of, 22
—life in, 81
—promise of, 30, 37
Christianity, 32
Christians
—differences in, 7
Church, 39, 56
Commune, 3
Community, 2-3
—Christian, 25, 57
Contrast, 28
Courage, 10
Crucifixion, 15

Death, 19, 43
Death-wish, 19
Delegation
—of authority, 53
Differences
—between people, 73
Divinity
—of Christ, 16

Equality, 73
Equation, 12
Eucharist, 75
—Christ's presence in, 77
Evil
—suffering for, 21
Exorcism, 83
Experience, 71
—supernatural, 83

Faith, 16, 32, 82, 86
Family, 3
Fear, 10, 62 ff.
Fidelity, 65
Forgiveness, 8
Freedom
—from law, 82

Gate
—as image, 22
Gift
—of self, 63
God, 87
—as shepherd, 19
—life with, 78
—Renewal in, 41
Godliness, 69
Goodness, 27
Gravity
—law of, 19
Guilt, 7

Harmony, 95
Hate, 62
Health

—concern for, 43
Hope, 68, 79, 89
Humanity, 53

Image
—of gate, 22
Inquiry
—into faith, 35
Insight, 51
Integrity, 6

Joy, 27, 95
Jury, 47
Justice, 73

Kindness, 65

Label, 93
Language
—common, 55-57
Law, 81
Learners, 81
Life, 38
—appreciation of, 71
—communal, 2
—meaning of, 48
—quality of, 27
—urge to, 19
—with Christ, 28-29, 81
Lottery, 19
Love, 62
—of Christ, 37-38
—sign of, 43

Magic, 83
Mann, T., 90
Materialism, 58
Meaning
—of life, 48, 72
Mercy
—of God, 6
—work of, 25
Ministry, 40
—of the word, 24-25
Miracles, 32, 83
Mob, 99
Music, 96

Negation, 35-36
Nicodemus, 68

Oversight, 51

Peace, 7
Pollution, 58
Prayer, 41
—of St. Paul, 52
Prejudice, 20, 91
Presence
—Eucharistic, 76, 83
—of Christ, 53
Property
—sharing of, 2-3
Protestants, 78
Publicity, 33

Rating
—of others, 61
Reassurance
—of Christ, 30
Reconciliation, 97
—Sacrament of, 7
Redemption, 13-14
Refinement, 5-6
Refuge, 42
Relationship
—with God, 41, 50, 66, 69, 79
Renewal
—in prayer, 41
Respect, 51
Responsibility, 21, 46, 74
Resurrection
—of Christ, 48

St. Peter
—courage of, 10-11
Sacrament
—of Reconciliation, 7
Sacrifice, 88
Security
—of death, 19
Self-defeat, 19
Selfishness, 75
Shakespeare, W., 71, 86
Sheepfold, 22
Sin, 8, 92
Spiritus, 59
Stereotype, 93
Suffering, 6, 21, 43, 72

Talk
—disrespectful, 65-66
Teacher, 76
Ten Commandments, 78

Trinity, 69

Understanding, 51
Uniqueness, 61
Unity, 57, 75
Universality
—in the Church, 56
Urgency, 56

Valley
—of death, 19

Values, 2
Vatican II, 39
Vision, 51
Vocation, 25-26
—Christian, 21, 49

Waiting, 79
Wisdom, 72
Witness, 47
Women
—in early Church, 40

SECOND SERIES

Volume V-2

THE WORD BECOMES FLESH

A Psychodynamic Approach to Homiletics and Catechetics and Meditation

Homilies for the Twelfth
to the Twenty-Second Sunday of the Year

(Series A)

CHARLES A. CURRAN
Loyola University
Chicago, Illinois

APPLE RIVER PRESS
P.O. Box 3867
Apple River, Illinois 61001

NIHIL OBSTAT:

Reverend Thomas G. Doran
Censor Deputatus

IMPRIMATUR:
✠ Arthur J. O'Neill
Bishop of Rockford

May 1978

Printed in the United States of America

CONTENTS

Preface v

TWELFTH SUNDAY OF THE YEAR 1
Homily I 1
Homily II 3
Homily III 5
Homily IV 6

PETER AND PAUL, APOSTLES—JUNE 29th 9
Homily I 9
Homily II 11
Homily III 12
Homily IV 14

THIRTEENTH SUNDAY OF THE YEAR 17
Homily I 17
Homily II 19
Homily III 20
Homily IV 22

FOURTEENTH SUNDAY OF THE YEAR 25
Homily I 25
Homily II 27
Homily III 29
Homily IV 31

FIFTEENTH SUNDAY OF THE YEAR 33
Homily I 33
Homily II 34
Homily III 36
Homily IV 38

SIXTEENTH SUNDAY OF THE YEAR 41
Homily I 41
Homily II 43
Homily II 44
Homily IV 46

SEVENTEENTH SUNDAY OF THE YEAR 49
Homily I 49
Homily II 51
Homily III 52
Homily IV 54

EIGHTEENTH SUNDAY OF THE YEAR 57
Homily I 57
Homily II 58
Homily III 60
Homily IV 62

NINETEENTH SUNDAY OF THE YEAR 65
Homily I 65
Homily II 67
Homily III 68
Homily IV 70

TWENTIETH SUNDAY OF THE YEAR 73
Homily I 73
Homily II 75
Homily III 76
Homily IV 78

TWENTY-FIRST SUNDAY OF THE YEAR 81
Homily I 81
Homily II 82
Homily III 84
Homily IV 86

TWENTY-SECOND SUNDAY OF THE YEAR 88
Homily I 88
Homily II 89
Homily III 91
Homily IV 93

Index 95

PREFACE

In the following homiletic and catechetical expositions, there are at least *four* for each Sunday and feast. Each one begins with an "ana-gnosis." This is not an ana-logos. That is, it is not intended to be an analogy or simply an example. We have called them "ana-gnoses" rather than analogies, because they are aimed at involving the reader or hearer personally at the level of his own *gnosis* about himself.

Analogy, in the *logos* sense, is too intellectual and remote for what we mean here. The hope is that each person will begin to commit himself and so be talking to himself while he hears or reads. He will thus hopefully be creatively reacting and so giving a homily to himself at the level of his own personal memory and experience.

These presentations are not intended to be all-inclusive. They are only *one form* of communicating the scriptural message. Hopefully their advanced reading may stimulate the reader not simply to memorize them—he or she may do this of course, and, we hope, profitably—but rather, as a result, to move on to his own personal witness and communication with his hearers. They are, therefore, intended basically to be personal stimulants and encouragements starting the reader or hearer on his own personal quest.

One will notice here that the *immediate human meaning* is most often seized upon—not some more complicated and subtle theological conclusion. This is not to deny the latter or its importance. It is rather to draw attention to the basic and rich human elements that are so often central to the scriptural message. The intent too is to initiate a process by which the hearer, or the reader, is allowed to enter into the presentation through its immediate human meaning.

To aid in this, the speaker should simply be himself, speaking in whatever way is most comfortable to him. His natural manner

would therefore usually be more often meditative than dramatic, more conversational than theatrical, allowing for the electronic apparatus to carry his words directly into the ear of the hearer—as in an intimate communication together.

These presentations are all *short;* some are very short. People often seek a short homily or catechetical presentation. But since they are short, further doctrinal and similar material may be added to them, as fits the occasion. Or, more than one may be given.

There is also the allowance for the possibility that later dialogue will extend and develop the embryonic concepts here. In this sense, what happens after words enter the ear is more important than before. This is the "germination" process; that is, seed once entered the soil and embraced by it, germinates and grows there. The entering may be quick—as the acorn enters quickly—but slowly and mysteriously over time, a great oak with powerful branches where birds abide and sing, can result. We have described elsewhere the group dynamic process that, we feel, could aid this.[1]

The model, therefore, is not the mathematics book: problem-solving which arrives at "answers." Our model is the familiar sower who goes out to sow seed. This is our inseminational aim and hope.

These themes are based on a personal approach to homiletics and catechetics, the psychological background of which is explained in detail in a separate volume: *THE WORD BECOMES FLESH: A Psychodynamic Approach to Homelitics and Catechetics* (Theory and Practice).

1. Curran, C. A. *Religious Values in Counseling and Psychotherapy.* Apple River Press: Apple River, Illinois, 1969, pp. 231-248.

TWELFTH SUNDAY OF THE YEAR (SERIES A)
HOMILY I

Reading I: *All those who were my friends are on the watch for any misstep of mine. "Perhaps he will be trapped, then we can prevail and take our vengeance on him." But the Lord is with me like a mighty champion.* (Jer. 20:10-13)

ANA-GNOSIS

One of the great surprises in our sophisticated age of television, space travel and other fantastic achievements has been the continued success of the simple cowboy story as a form of popular entertainment. In the first stages of the film production, seventy years or so ago, someone stumbled on this simple cowboy theme. The films continued to be made when sound came, but most people thought, when television emerged in the much more sophisticated period of the fifties, that we would be far beyond that. To the surprise of many, however, the few people who preserved these films and had the copyright to them, made millions of dollars showing them again to a new generation on television.

When we ask why this phenomenon happened, what is there about the simple cowboy theme that has such perennial appeal, we can recognize almost immediately that these films deal with treachery, deception and betrayal—people who are thought to be friends betray others, and the people who draw our sympathy are left in anxiety and confusion, very much, of course, like we are sometimes. Then quickly the hero appears. He's one of these familiar people, say John Wayne, or some other familiar person, always cast as the champion. From then on we can relax and coast along because we know that the champion, no matter how many lies, distortions and maneuvers of the evil people he must survive, will win out. The good people with whom we have sympathy from the beginning, who may represent ourselves, are going to win. We can be at peace because we know that no one ever wins over John Wayne.

THEOLOGICAL EXTENSION

The reason that such simple, primitive themes in cowboy movies have been so successful for 70 years or so, despite their extreme simplicity in plot and action—people chasing one another up and down hills, and doing "dirty work at the crossroads" as we say— is that they come very close to fears and anxieties in our own lives. And this is the point of Jeremiah today. Jeremiah said, "Yes, I hear the whisperings of many, terror on every side. 'Denounce, let us denounce him.' All those who were my friends are on the watch for any misstep of mine. 'Perhaps he will be trapped, then we can prevail and take our vengeance on him.' " We, too, often feel this way. Sometimes it is exaggerated, sometimes it is, in modern psychological terms, paranoia, making up enemies and fears, but it doesn't change the anxiety and fear and insecurity we have. We look at people and it seems they are whispering about us, we have a strange feeling that something is going on behind our back. We all know this feeling so well. Often, fortunately most of the time, our fears are exaggerated: people are not as bad as we fear they are. But this doesn't change the pain, the suffering and the anxiety we feel while it is going on.

To tide us over these periods, even if they may be exaggerated, and to keep us from doing unkind or cruel things in return, we need a champion too, like the cowboy movie portrays. Jeremiah wisely reminds us, "But the Lord is with me like a mighty champion." This we hold onto, this gives us dignity and respect for ourselves. And it can help us control very often our exaggerated fears and anxieties and keep us from doing the wrong thing. Often when we have fears or suspicions it is not so much the situation that causes the ultimate difficulties or tragedies, it's what we do in retaliation, having magnified out of proportion what has been done to us. It's our reaction that can cause a far greater difficulty.

The way to keep ourselves in control when we are in those states where we fear that people are out to get us is to remember what Jeremiah reassures us of here: that God is our champion.

THEOLOGICAL CONCLUSION

So the cowboy theme has a certain truth to it. And the truth is here stated in Jeremiah, that no matter what people say and how we may feel they are hoping for us to stumble and fall and be trapped, we have God with us. When we feel people are saying, "Perhaps he will be trapped, then we can prevail and take our vengeance on him," Jeremiah says for us to hold tightly to the knowledge that, "the Lord is with me like a mighty champion." With that security we will react with balance, with reason, with control. This knowledge will help us whether our fears are justified or not because it will keep our minds focused on the Lord.

TWELFTH SUNDAY OF THE YEAR (SERIES A) HOMILY II

Responsorial Psalm: *For your sake I bear insult, and shame covers my face. I have become an outcast to my brothers, a stranger to my mother's sons.* (Ps. 69:8-35)

ANA-GNOSIS

One of the recurring experiences of the human race is that, generation after generation, we reject those who, when they are judged years later, seem clearly to be great benefactors to mankind. This is so true that we know it is almost a sign when a person is called a lunatic, a fool, when people laugh at him, reject him and in all sorts of ways, misunderstand him. Perhaps we more commonly misunderstand one another than anything else we do to each other.

This doesn't have to occur only in great historical events among important persons, even though it is often that. We know when, as children, we hear our parents or grandparents tell about certain people, or quarrels and misunderstandings among families, and we perhaps have gotten to know these people, that it is hard for us to understand how that rejection could have occurred. The people we know seem good and kind and generous. Why then, did this terrible quarrel happen between these very fine people? How could they have been labeled as harshly as they were?

THEOLOGICAL EXTENSION

All of this leads us to the theme of the Psalm today. Here we have one of God's anointed ones, specially chosen, bringing goodness, wholesomeness and gifts to the human race like all great humanitarians and benefactors have done. And here he, too, is rejected and misunderstood.

"For your sake I bear insult, and shame covers my face," the Psalmist says. "I have become an outcast to my brothers, a stranger to my mother's sons." So here it is again, long before the time of Christ, in a sense prefiguring Christ who, most of all, underwent this experience—misunderstanding and calumny and misinterpretation.

In reflecting on this passage, then, let us remind ourselves to make every attempt to understand. The only way we can prevent these tragic misunderstandings that often cause terrible suffering and pain for years, or long periods of non-communication between people, the only way we can avoid this misunderstanding is obviously to try always to understand. It's a simple word, but a difficult thing to do. But if we, in our own lives with those around us, try to understand and not quickly condemn or reject or laugh at someone because we don't understand, as is so often the impulse (the impulse that hurt the Psalmist here), but we control this, then when something very great occurs we can begin to see God's hand and help others to see also. By striving to understand and not quickly giving in to the impulse to misunderstand, to ridicule and reject what we don't understand, we will be bringing to the world God's message, God's guidance, God's gift through this person's life.

THEOLOGICAL CONCLUSION

If we do this, we at least will not be among those who misunderstand. The Psalmist says, "For your sake I bear insult and shame covers my face. I have become an outcast to my brothers, a stranger to my mother's sons." We will not be among those who, by misunderstanding, misinterpretation, distortion or ridicule bring another of these tragic misunderstandings about. It seems a small thing, " to try to understand" and yet to do so would make our lives conform so much more closely to Christ's.

TWELFTH SUNDAY OF THE YEAR (SERIES A) HOMILY III

Reading II: *Sin entered the world through one man, and through sin death, and thus has spread through the whole human race because everyone has sinned . . . Adam pre-figured the One to come, but the gift itself considerably outweighed the fall. If it is certain that through one man's fall so many died, it is even more certain that divine grace, coming through one man, Jesus Christ, came to so many as an abundant free gift.* (Rom. 5:12-15)

ANA-GNOSIS

Most children, when they are very young, go through a period of being afraid of anyone they don't know. They cling to their mothers and fathers and refuse to go into new situations where they might meet strange people. But gradually, as children grow up, they accept more and more people into their "world," and they come to see that these once fearsome people have a lot in common with them. Even among elementary school children we often hear remarks about other children or families they don't know well. They may say, "He sure talks funny. He doesn't say things the way I do," or "They really eat different food at their house." But as they get older, they begin to recognize that, for all their differences, most people have quite similar hopes and fears and wishes. Even though they live on the other side of the globe, or even if they lived two hundred years ago, these people were not very much different than the people in our families that we've known all our lives.

This sense of the "brotherhood" of mankind can be brought home to us today, in the second half of the 20th century, perhaps more easily than it could ever have been before. Through television, movies, and the wide circulation of magazines and newspapers, we know almost instantly what happens in remote parts of the globe. Earthquakes in Guatemala and 25th anniversary celebrations of British queens can be as much a part of our lives as the baseball game down the street. Mass communication systems have brought us all into closer contact with one another, giving us the most wonderful opportunity to realize fully how much a family all the people on earth actually are.

THEOLOGICAL EXTENSION

This sense of the oneness of the human family is of great importance to St. Paul in his Letter to the Romans. He says elsewhere in this Letter that God "makes no distinction between Jew and Greek: all belong to the same Lord who is rich enough, however many may ask his help, for everyone who calls on the name of the Lord will be saved." And here, in our Reading today, he stresses the common source of the fall of the human race, through Adam, and, even more remarkable, its universal redemption through one man, Jesus Christ. And so he writes, "If it is certain that through one man's fall so many died, it is even more certain that divine grace, coming through the one man, Jesus Christ, came to so many as an abundant free gift." That is to say, redemption isn't for a select few who can hug Christ's message to themselves. On the contrary, like Paul, we must accept the obligation of sharing his message of redemption with the rest of the world. We cannot simply rest secure in the notion that *we* are saved and others are not, or feel smugly superior because we are God's elect. In fact, Christ came for all people, and if we ignore or slight this fact, we are not truly Christian. Our God is not the God of a few, but Lord of the whole universe, past, present and future.

St. Paul and other disciples throughout the ages have perpetually had to combat forms of superiority or prejudice among Christians. Paul's letter to the Romans did not resolve the issue, even if the people of his time seemed to accept it. Nor, it often seems, have we accepted it. Even in the 20th century we struggle with the problems of the white being "more equal" than black, rich being "more equal" than poor, men being "more equal" than women. These are not easy issues to resolve. But because they are difficult does not mean that we ignore them. We would not be Christlike if we did so.

THEOLOGICAL CONCLUSION

St. Paul's message to us, then, is one of promise—redemption is possible for all. But it is also one of challenge—the challenge to live in such a way that we do not exult in our superiority over others who seem strange or alien to us, but rather to recognize all people as brothers and sisters in the human family and co-heirs to the ultimate redemption of Christ.

TWELFTH SUNDAY OF THE YEAR (SERIES A) HOMILY IV

Gospel Reading: *Jesus said to his Apostles, "Have no fear of men, for* *nothing is covered that will not be revealed or hidden that will not be known . . . So everyone who acknowledges me before men, I will also acknowledge before my father who is in heaven. But whoever denies me before men, I will deny before my father who is in heaven."* (Matt. 10:26-33)

ANA-GNOSIS

Perhaps many of us here, more likely many of the adults, have had the experience of being in a situation, probably a social situation, where someone came up to us whom we barely remembered or wished we didn't and attempted to force his friendship on us. Perhaps he did this in a somewhat bold, outspoken way so that we were even a little embarrassed. Once we recognized who this person was, we were suddenly almost ashamed to acknowledge that we were associated with him in the past. We perhaps recall his disloyalty to us, how he let us down, and in a very real sense we don't like to be associated with him, certainly not in public. We try to make the best of it, to put him off gently, to quiet him down as best we can, but we find it an embarrassing situation to be in.

THEOLOGICAL EXTENSION

Anyone who has ever been in this kind of circumstance can quickly get the feel of what Christ is saying to us in today's Gospel when he tells us, "So everyone who acknowledges me before men, I will also acknowledge before my Father who is in heaven. But whoever denies me before men, I will also deny before my Father who is in heaven."

We all have a tendency to profess very strongly what we believe when it is convenient and advantageous to do so. But when the going is difficult and it is not to our advantage, when it might even work against us to stand up courageously for our beliefs, then we may tend to deny them. What Christ seems to be stressing today is that loyalty, courage and faith are not at all a matter of convenience. If we truly believe what we say we believe, then we live this belief, we act on it all the time, both when it is to our advantage and when it is not.

Sometimes our Christian faith can make some very great demands on us. It can even put us in rather embarrassing situations at times. We almost continuously run into occasions when we are asked to compromise what otherwise we might very openly proclaim. We are asked to compromise it, or so we feel, because others might criticize us or ridicule us if we stood up firmly for what we believed. Our first reaction might be to belittle or play down what we know to be the truth. In doing so we end up selling ourselves out.

THEOLOGICAL CONCLUSION

It is this kind of attitude that Christ is referring to. The demands that we are faced with in our daily living of Christianity can very often force us into painful or even embarrassing situations. But if we really believe what we profess to believe, and if we really stand for what we claim to stand for, if we have the courage of our own convictions, then we don't back away from such trials. We go ahead and suffer the ridicule and criticism because we know that what we believe represents something beyond what is immediately apparent. We refuse to get caught in the lure and in the immediacy of the present situation. We recognize that while we may be immediately losing our life, in the long run we are saving it.

This is the courage and constancy that Christ will recognize on that final day when we are all called upon to stand up and be counted. When we come forward and say to Christ that we knew him he will truly recognize us and acknowledge us if we have been faithful to him.

PETER AND PAUL, APOSTLES—JUNE 29th (SERIES A, B, C)
HOMILY I

Reading I: *King Herod started to harass some of the members of the church. . . . And Peter came to himself and said, "Now I am sure that the Lord has sent his angel to rescue me from the hand of Herod and from all that the Jewish people were expecting."* (Acts 12:1-11)

ANA-GNOSIS

When a happy, but highly unexpected, occurrence takes place in a person's life, he or she may react by saying something like, "Well, I don't know why it happened to me, but I'll take it. I need all the luck that I can get." Or one may say, "I don't really feel that I deserve that, but since it's happened to me, I suppose I'd better make the most of it." Yet when this kind of event does occur to us, it may suddenly dawn on us that perhaps it was not as much by chance as we may have thought. And precisely because we were so fortunate, we now have a very real obligation to make good use of our fortune.

Very often such a surprising event can bring about a quite profound change in the life of the person to whom it happened. The person may suddenly realize that this, indeed, was not something he or she deserved because of any special virtue or merit on their part, but that they were being asked to do something for the benefit of others.

THEOLOGICAL EXTENSION

It wouldn't be especially unusual to imagine that what happened to St. Peter in today's Reading had some similar effect on him. We see him languishing in prison, surrounded by guards and locked doors. He is in an almost hopeless situation. There seems little reasan for him to expect that he might be freed from his circumstances. We know that he was deeply invested in what Christ stood for and clearly saw his obligation to carry it on. So we can readily imagine that being in prison was a rather frustrating experience because it curtailed all his hopes and expectations. But he was also resigned to it, trusting to something beyond himself. Then suddenly and completely unexpectedly he is freed from his confinement by the angel. Apparently this was so surprising to Peter that at first he could not quite realize what happened. We are told that at last "he came to himself." Apparently he did finally realize his tremendous good fortune and came to the awareness that everything he had hoped for and expected to do clearly was in the hands of God. He says, "Now I am sure that the Lord has sent his angel to rescue me from the hand of Herod."

THEOLOGICAL CONCLUSION

This fulfillment of trust and faith on the part of Peter has very significant implications for all of us. We know that Peter, once he was free, went on to become the first leader of the Church. There is no doubt that before this event he was deeply committed to the work of our Lord, but this must have deepened his conviction even more. Perhaps the lesson for all of us in this is the quiet realization that we, too, in some way or other can be instruments in the hand of God doing a share of his work. By our own deep faith and commitment we, too, will receive the necessary help and encouragement. This may come, as it did to St. Peter, in a rather surprising or unexpected way. And we also would realize that because this happened to us, it put upon us a kind of special responsibility. Like Peter we must use the gifts of the Lord, expected or unexpected, to become more like his son, Jesus Christ, and to bring Jesus' message to all people. We have received much from our Father. We must share that Good News with the whole human family.

Besides the responsibility that God entrusts to us, he gives us his love and support too. Just as his angel rescued Peter, so we will find God's help in our lives as we strive to do his will. He has not asked us to do anything that he will not give the power to accomplish if we trust him.

PETER AND PAUL, APOSTLES—JUNE 29th (SERIES A, B, C)
HOMILY II

Responsorial Psalm: *The angel of the Lord will rescue those who fear him . . . Look to him and be radiant; so your faces shall never be ashamed.* (Ps. 34:2-9)

ANA-GNOSIS

We know there are many reasons why people blush. For example, a small child who is caught taking cookies from his mother's cookie jar will often turn red in the face. Or if someone makes a slip of the tongue he will often blush as he tries to correct himself and convey the real meaning of what he had intended to say. We can readily think of many other reasons why people blush. They do so not only from guilt, embarrassment or shame, but also sometimes because they are happy and filled with joy. But most often people blush because they have been surprised by something and are suddenly disconcerted, and so it takes them a while to get their bearings again. And often, in the meantime, those around them perhaps laugh, or what is even worse, openly ridicule them. We all know how painful this experience can be. Sometimes it's so painful that the person might even say, "I just wanted to crawl in a hole."

THEOLOGICAL EXTENSION

In contrast to this shame and embarrassment that others often make us feel when we are guilty of a slip or of some other wrongdoing, in today's Liturgy we have the reassurance from the Psalmist that God will never subject us to this. He says, "Look to him and be radiant; so your face shall never be ashamed." We do, indeed, look to the Lord with radiant faces, but our radiance is of joy and hope and pleasant expectation. It is the hope that our Lord will hear us in the time of our trials, that he will respond not with reproach but in such a way that we can truly feel forgiven. He will not put us to shame, nor ridicule us, nor ignore us. As the Psalmiset says, speaking of himself, "I sought the Lord and he answered me and delivered me from all my fears."

THEOLOGICAL CONCLUSION

This is truly a most encouraging realization. When we make mistakes, when we do things that often are truly embarrassing or shameful, we are, of course, grateful when we turn to our fellow human beings and receive understanding and forgiveness, when they don't make us necessarily want to go and hide ourselves. But we cannot always depend on this from others.

God, however, is different. We can always go to him with our difficulties, our shames, our embarrassments and the many slip-ups in life that we have made. We can trust in his forgiveness. Then our faces will become radiant, not because of the shame or guilt—that has been taken away—but rather because of the joy we experience in that moment of expectation and of hope.

PETER AND PAUL, APOSTLES—JUNE 29th (SERIES A, B, C)
HOMILY III

Reading II: *I am already being poured out like a libation . . . Henceforth there is laid up for me a crown of righteousness which the Lord, the righteous judge, will award to me on that day, and not only to me but also to all who have loved his appearing.* (2 Tim. 4:6-8, 17-18)

ANA-GNOSIS

We all know the joyful experience of having worked extra hard at a certain job with no particular expectation of any recognition or reward for it, but then are given some recognition or reward anyhow. The unexpectedness of it makes the reward all the greater, and so we perhaps put all the more value on it. A baseball player, for example, after having had a particularly good season will sometimes be given a bonus by the owner of the ball club. Or even sometimes after a ball player has had one particularly outstanding game, the owner, much to the surprise of the ball player and everyone else, will tear up the contract and write out a new one for an even greater amount.

We may have had also the opposite experience, the rather painful one of looking forward to and expecting a reward for a job well done, a little extra recognition for it, and it wasn't forthcoming. This is not only disappointing to us, but it can also cause us to be bitter and mistrustful thereafter.

We've all seen the stricken face of a small child as he comes running to his mother or father in the expectation of receiving a reward for something he has just accomplished and is very proud of, and the mother or father ignoring him, not recognizing what to the child has been so significant and so meaningful. This kind of painful experience can cause a child, or anyone, to become somewhat mistrustful of others. It can cause them to lose heart, not to try as hard, to become discouraged, and often to give up without giving the task a sincere try. Either one of these reactions— either the joyful one of unexpectedly receiving an award or the discouraging one of not getting the reward we thought we deserved—are quite common. But whether or not we actually receive the award, there is seldom any guarantee that we will receive it, deservedly or otherwise.

THEOLOGICAL EXTENSION

We see none of this doubt or uncertainty in St. Paul's Letter to Timothy. He seems absolutely certain that when his work is over, when the day is done, he will receive the reward. He tells us that he has fought the good fight, he has finished the race, he has kept the faith. And then, "henceforth there is laid up for me the crown of righteousness which the Lord, the righteous judge, will award to me on that day, and not only to me but also to all who have loved his appearing." This is the statement of someone who is very sure. But we see that his sureness springs from his deep faith and trust in God. There is no doubt in Paul's mind that he will receive "the crown" for his labors.

We also have the reassurance that not only he will receive it, but anyone else who has "loved his appearing." In other words, the "crown," the award and the certainty of receiving it is open to all of us. In God we need not fear encountering the capriciousness of the inconstancy, and the subsequent disappointment, that we often find in others. We can be sure that He will recognize even the smallest efforts we put forth.

THEOLOGICAL CONCLUSION

In moments of discouragement there is in us a quite natural tendency to wonder if it's all worth it, if it makes any difference, if anybody even cares what we do, or if anybody really appreciates the extra effort that we put into what we do. These moments of discouragement can easily cause us to let up in our efforts or perhaps sometimes to even give up all together. While we may have made a good start toward our goal, we no longer see any point in finishing it, since it may seem to have no meaning.

When these moments of discouragement come to us, as they are bound to sometimes, we can look to St. Paul for reassurance. We know the tremendous obstacles that he overcame, the discouragements that he underwent, the deep physical and mental suffering he was subjected to, and yet we know that he never lost sight of the goal. He seems to have been able continually to maintain his eyes on that distant award that he knew he had coming to him and that he trusted beyond any question that God would give to him. Not only do we have St. Paul as an example, but we also have his words where he assures us that this same reward for faith and constancy and commitment is there for all of us. God, unlike the people who may fail to recognize our efforts, will not be the cause of disappointment. He really will recognize the value and importance of what we have done.

PETER AND PAUL, APOSTLES—JUNE 29th (SERIES A, B, C) HOMILY IV

Gospel Reading: *When Jesus came into the district of Caesaria Phillipi he asked his disciples, "Who do people say the Son of Man is?" And they said, "Some say John the Baptist, others say Elijah, and others Jeremiah or one of the prophets." He said to them, "But who do you say I am?" Simon Peter replied, "You are the Christ, the Son of the Living God."* (Mt. 16:13-19)

ANA-GNOSIS

There are various reasons why a person will sometimes tend to refrain from speaking out and saying what is really on his mind or what he really believes to be true. One of these reasons might be fear. He may be afraid that if he declares his position he will be the object of ridicule or even harm from others. Or perhaps one holds back because he is not really certain and he wants to wait for more evidence, but when the time comes that he is more certain he will not hesitate to speak out. Sometimes in a crowd or meeting, a person would like to speak out but feels that he would be the only one holding this opinion and would be embarrassed to stand alone in front of an entire group. And, of course, there is always the possibility that the person has no real opinion and so says nothing. So if one is confronted with a direct question such as, for example, "Where do you stand on this issue?" the answer may take various forms, depending on how invested he is in the issue, how courageous he is, or how much he knows about it.

THEOLOGICAL EXTENSION

This same situation seems to have been present among the people at the time of our Lord. In today's Gospel we see Christ directly confronting his disciples with the question, first of all, "Who do men say the Son of Man is?" As we might expect, there is a great variety of answers: some thought he was John the Baptist, others Elijah, others Jeremiah or one of the prophets, and no doubt there were many other opinions as well. But then Christ confronts them with the question, "But who do you say that I am?" We do not know how much courage was involved in Peter's unqualified reply, "You are the Christ, the Son of the Living God," because later on, on Good Friday, when Christ was about to be crucified, we see Peter vacillating. There he openly denied Christ. So whether his response to Christ in this instance was merely a sudden impulse we don't know. We do know, however, that after the resurrection Peter was among the staunchest supporters of Christ and proclaimers of his message, and he even ended his life being crucified. So there can be no question about the ultimate fidelity and courage of Peter.

THEOLOGICAL CONCLUSION

Whatever the circumstances might have been on the occasion of today's Gospel when Christ asks the disciples who they say he is and Peter replies, "The Christ, the Son of the Living God," there is for all of us a time, or several times, when we are called upon to stand up and declare ourselves. Obviously Christ recognized the sincerity of Peter's reply because it was here, as we are told, that Peter was singled out to be the future leader of the Church of Christ, the rock or foundation on which it was built. Even Peter's subsequent denial did not cause Christ to withdraw his commission to Peter.

This can be very consoling and reassuring for us. There are times in our life when things are going well and everything looks bright and it is easy to stand up and declare who we are and what we stand for. But then there are other moments when things are not going so well, when life seems bleak and dreary and we are less ready to declare who we are and what we believe. Sometimes we might even back off from a former stand we had once boldly advocated. Sometimes we may be ashamed, as St. Peter certainly was when he denied Christ, at our own sense of having betrayed a former belief or someone to whom we had previously given open support. Our consolation is that Christ doesn't hold this against us. He is not quickly disappointed in our disloyalty, in our lack of fidelity; he always gives us another chance, a chance to make good, a chance to show what we really believe in. Each day, then might be an occasion when we are called upon to declare in response to our Lord's question, "Who do you say that I am?" Hopefully each day we will respond as Peter did, "You are the Christ, the Son of the Living God." We pray that our faith will be with us both in times when things are going well and when they are not.

THIRTEENTH SUNDAY OF THE YEAR (SERIES A) HOMILY I

Reading I: *One day Elisha came to Shunem where there was a woman of influence who urged him to dine with her . . . One day he came there and turned into the chamber and rested there and he said to Gehazi his servant, "What is to be done for her?"* (2 Kings 4:8-11, 14-16)

ANA-GNOSIS

Sometimes a large company will advertise one of its unusual or exotic products as "the gift for the person who has everything." This statement catches the idea that the person is probably quite wealthy and has no real need of anything material. Not only does he have everything he needs, but he has all the luxuries besides. And so the person who is seeking to show him some token of affection or gratitude is hard pressed to know what to give him. Most of us give presents that we hope will be useful and will fill some kind of need that the recipient might have. But to achieve this goal becomes very difficult when the person already seems to have everything, and especially if the only gift that one can afford would be very small and humble. The giver may feel he would be offending or insulting the person either because he had no need of this or because it was beneath his dignity. So in this situation we may well wonder what we could possibly give this friend which would express our genuine gratitude to him. "The gift for the person who has everything" responds to this desire to give a gift when one does not know what would be suitable.

THEOLOGICAL EXTENSION

Today's Liturgy shows Elisha encountering a person who

seems already "to have everything." We are told that she is a wealthy woman, a woman of influence, so much so that she even sets up a special room for Elisha to show her hospitality to him. And Elisha, struck by her generosity and kindness, wants to do something in return to show his gratitude. But he is at a loss as to what to do. He says to his servant, Gehazi, "What is to be done for her?" From the Reading we surmise that while the woman had everything she needed in the way of physical, material possessions, yet she was not completely happy. We sense that there was something lacking in her life, some inner longing, some yearning that no material gift could satisfy. And as it turns out, Gehazi points out to Elisha that she has no son and that there is little hope of her having one since she and her husband are apparently quite old. Elisha responds by calling her to him and saying to her, "At this season, when the time comes around you will be fondling a baby son." The woman, we are told, has already recognized Elisha as "a man of God," so we can imagine the great joy she experienced on hearing from him the promise that she would be given a child. Elisha responded to her yearning in a way that was far more rewarding to her than any material gift.

THEOLOGICAL CONCLUSION

But even when we are not wealthy, and there are a lot of material comforts that we would perhaps like, even then we can sense a lack of something in ourselves that no material comfort or luxury would be able to fulfill. There is in all of us a far deeper yearning for something that would enhance our own value as persons. This is often something we can receive only from others, and it is something others can receive only from us. It is a kind of a sensitivity that we have toward others, a realization that all the material goods in the world will not bring ultimate happiness, but that there will always be something there that we seek. And we respond to this search in others by our sensitivity and understanding, much as Elisha in today's Reading responded to the yearning of the woman.

In the way that we relate to others we can fill this deeply felt but often unidentified need in them. Hopefully they will do the same for us, so that as a result of the way we relate to one another we become better persons, we have a feeling of greater worth and dignity because of the way the other person has treatd us, has been sensitive to us.

Elisha, then, can inspire us to look closely at those with whom we share our lives so that we can perhaps understand the great longings that they have and try to help fulfill them. God depends on our sensitivity to others as a means for showing *his* love for them as well as our own. If we truly care for others, being responsive to them, we will be participants in the ministry of the Lord.

THIRTEENTH SUNDAY OF THE YEAR (SERIES A) HOMILY II

Responsorial Psalm: *The favors of the Lord I will sing forever . . . For thy steadfast love was established forever by faithfulness as firm as the heavens.* (Ps. 89:2-3, 16-19)

ANA-GNOSIS

Children can often be pleasantly surprised when, after having misbehaved and then punished by their parents, they come back sometime later and find that their parents still receive them with love and kindness and concern. The child on this occasion might even express his surprise at being received back by his parents with love by saying, "They're not mad at me anymore." The child finds reassurance that, even though he may have misbehaved and done something his parents disapproved of, nevertheless their love for him still remains as strong as ever. His misbehavior did not change anything basic in his parents' attitude toward him.

Likewise it can be a very pleasant surprise for an adult to have a friend whom he has offended either inadventantly or otherwise, and to be able to go back to the friend and, after a simple apology or perhaps even without an apology, his friend accepts him back and things become much as they were before. As adults we realize the value of this kind of friendship and love. We realize how rare it is and how greatly it is to be treasured. It's very reassuring to have a friend who doesn't reject us or put any conditions on his love for us. We can go back to him again and still be his friend.

THEOLOGICAL EXTENSION

In today's Psalm we get a very personal, warm and close sense of the way the Psalmist is speaking with God. He speaks to God much as a child might speak to a parent, or you or I might speak to a close friend. We get a sense of deep trust between the Psalmist and God. He says, "For thy steadfast love was established forever by faithfulness as firm as the heavens." This clearly is a description of an unconditional love. God does not change in his attitude toward us when we "misbehave," when we sin and fall away from him. God is always there waiting, steadfast, ready to receive us back; he does not give up on us, just as the parent does not give up on the child, or as true friends do not give up on one another.

THEOLOGICAL CONCLUSION

If we can speak of the "steadfastness" of a parent in his love for his child or of one friend for another, how much more so can we speak of the steadfastness of God's love for us. We can always trust that, no matter what we've done, God will not withdraw his love. We always have another opportunity to come back to him. Those times when we feel that we have been abandoned or neglected by others, especially by those upon whom we most depended for their understanding, their consideration, their love for us, we can always go to God. He will always be there. This can be a very consoling and reassuring thought, especially so in a rapidly changing world where nothing seems to remain constant, not even the people that we expect will do so. No matter how we have been treated by them, we need only to remind ourselves that God's love, in the words of the Psalmist, was "established forever." It will not fail us.

THIRTEENTH SUNDAY OF THE YEAR (SERIES A) HOMILY III

Reading II: *Are you not aware that we who were baptized into Jesus Christ were baptized into his death? . . . But if we have died with Christ we believe that we will also live with him. For we know that Christ, being raised from the dead, will never die again. Death no longer has dominion over him. The death he died, he died for sin once for all. But the life he lives he lives to God. So you also must consider yourselves dead to sin and alive to God in Jesus Christ.* (Rom. 6:3-4, 8-11)

ANA-GNOSIS

Throughout the history of mankind, and certainly in our times, there has been a deep fascination with death. People have always wondered about and sought evidence for the continuation of life after death. And in our own time it is not unusual to read about scientific studies that would provide some kind of absolute certainty and proof that life goes on after death. There have been, of course, many incidents recorded where people who were supposedly dead momentarily have been brought back to life. These people sometimes describe the experience of death in very real and vivid images. Besides this, there have been innumerable stories of people seeing ghosts and similar apparitions which argue for a life beyond death. How real the "proof" seems, then to the person who experienced it! Yet very often most other people are left unconvinced, sceptical and unbelieving.

THEOLOGICAL EXTENSION

In today's Reading from St. Paul's Letter to the Romans we get a strong sense of urgency on the part of St. Paul to convince the people of his own time of the reality of a "new life." He says, "Just as Christ was raised from the dead by the glory of the Father, we too might live a new life." But he also tells us that we cannot have this new life unless and until we are "buried" with Christ by baptism into death.

In other words, to arrive at a new life is a very personal thing. To do it, one first must be willing to enter into death just as Christ did. This, of course, is difficult and threatening for us to do because death is associated with mystery, with the unknown. We are reluctant to let go of the life that we are living even though it might not necessarily be gratifying or pleasing to us. Still we are familiar with it, and there is security in holding onto it.

The kind of life that St. Paul speaks of is the kind that comes to us through faith. We need to be willing to make an act of faith in the new life which Christ himself achieved and which he promises to us. To achieve this life we must die to our past sinfulness through baptism, as St. Paul tells us. And for this there is no proof available that will convince anyone. This is the real nature of faith, that it cannot be proved. One can only take the risk of dying and trust that a new life truly will emerge from the death.

THEOLOGICAL CONCLUSION

But if we are looking for some real proof of life after death we look, of course, at Christ himself who, we know, arose from the dead on Easter Sunday. And having done so, Christ holds out to us the same kind of renewal of life. We would, therefore, see death not as the end of everything, not as the giving up of something, but rather we would see it more positively as opening the door through which we pass into a newer kind of life over which death no longer has dominion. And, of course, Christ is that door. In the act of faith that is required to die to the old we put our trust totally in Christ.

This is the tone of urgency that we sense in St. Paul's words today. He must be experiencing something of the frustration that you and I feel when we are really convinced of the truth of something we have experienced and yet we scarcely trust that we can convince anyone else. Yet we urgently try to explain to them, to convince them as best we can because we want them, too, to experience the same kind of joy and newness of life that we ourselves have experienced.

THIRTEENTH SUNDAY OF THE YEAR (SERIES A) HOMILY IV

Gospel Reading: *Jesus said to his Apostles, "Whoever loves father or mother, son or daughter more than me is not worthy of me . . . He who receives you receives me, and he who receives me receives him who sent me. He who receives a prophet because he is a prophet shall receive a prophet's reward, and he who receives a righteous man because he is a righteous man shall receive a righteous man's reward."* (Mt. 10:37-42)

ANA-GNOSIS

There is a story told about the famous monk, Thomas Merton, when he was living at Gethsemani Monastery in Kentucky. One weekend a group of ladies came to the monastery to make a Retreat, and when the Retreat was finished on a Sunday afternoon, as they were about to leave the monastery to go back to their home, they thanked the Monks for the fine weekend, for the opportunity to renew themselves spiritually, and for the opportunity to attend Mass each day, and then they left. As they were driving out of the monastery grounds they saw lying in the ditch a dishelved, dirty man with torn clothing and several days growth of beard. He appeared barely alive. As they drove by him one of them suggested that they stop the car and get out and see if they could offer any help. They were about to do this when one of the other ladies in the car said, "Well, we don't really have time. I have to get back. You know I have a bridge party at four o'clock this afternoon." Then another of the ladies said, "Perhaps it would be a very dangerous thing to stop. After all the man is a stranger and we don't know what he might do." So the ladies drove on.

It is said that this story somehow got back to Father Merton and his response was, "You know, these ladies received our Lord each day in the Eucharist while they were here in the monastery, and then they saw him lying in a ditch and they did not recognize him."

THEOLOGICAL EXTENSION

We don't know if this is a true story. We know how easy it is for legends to build up around famous people, some of them true, some of them false. But whether or not the incident is true, it makes a profound point. In our own involvement with ourselves, in our selfishness, we can tend to overlook the fact that Christ is truly in all of us. We are all temples of the Holy Spirit.

Christ himself makes no distinction as to whether we are wealthy or poor, whether we are well off or otherwise. He loves all of us, He is in all of us. In today's Gospel he says, "He who receives you receives me, and who receives me, receives him who sent me." This is to remind us that anyone whom we may meet in the course of our daily lives is also a child of God. That person carries Christ within him. The way we treat that person, the way we respond to him, that is the way we respond to Christ. To reject that person is to reject Christ. To receive him is to receive Christ.

THEOLOGICAL CONCLUSION

It is easy and convenient, of course, to bypass occasionally those who need us and to go directly to Christ. Often we receive Holy Communion and then turn around and ignore those who are most in need. Christ tells us in another place in the Gospels that if we have anything against our brother we should first go and make it up with him and then come and put our gift on the altar. Unless we first receive Christ in our neighbor and in those who are in need of us, we should not deceive ourselves into believing that we are worthy to receive him in the Eucharist. Christ called us to love one another, not simply to go to communion. We are his messengers. He sends us so others can receive him and his Father. It is, perhaps, an awesome responsibility to bring Christ to other people, but if we refuse to do it, who will?

FOURTEENTH SUNDAY OF THE YEAR (SERIES A) HOMILY I

Reading I: *Rejoice greatly, O daughter of Zion! Shout aloud, O daughter of Jerusalem so your king comes to you. Triumphant and victorious is he, humble and riding on an ass, on a colt, foal of an ass.* (Zech. 9:9-10)

ANA-GNOSIS

Whenever we imagine a great world leader, perhaps the first image that comes to us is a great military leader who is victorious in war; or perhaps it is a powerful, famous king who rules large numbers of people and a vast territory. In our own time, of course, kings don't have that much meaning. But even so, the leaders in our own times, whether we call them presidents or prime ministers or whatever, seem somehow very far removed from us, people with whom it would be difficult for us to relate in the ordinary, every day activities to which we are accustomed. And if by chance we ever have the opportunity to meet such a person we, of course, show them much deference and respect. Often, too, we believe that such a person has great power over our lives and, in a sense, can control our destiny.

THEOLOGICAL EXTENSION

This certainly would have been the image that the people in the time of Zechariah had of a leader. We know from the other prophets of the Old Testament how the people were looking forward to such a great leader whom they thought of as the Messiah —someone who would come and liberate them all from their afflictions. This could have been a military leader, a great king, someone rich and powerful. But in any case he would have been far above the ordinary conditions of their own lives.

So what we hear in the first Reading of today's Liturgy from the prophet Zechariah must have seemed to them a kind of contradiction. He says to them: "Lo, your king comes to you. Triumphant and victorious is he, humble and riding on an ass, on a colt, foal of an ass." The word "humble" is not one that we easily associate with great kings and military leaders. So, in a sense, the people at the time of Zechariah must have been somewhat confused by his use of humble to refer to the coming of the Messiah. Zechariah tells them that their king will indeed come triumphant and victorious, not as a conquering warrior, but rather in lowliness and in peace. He won't be like the other kings of Judah nor like the princes of old. He will come rather as someone like themselves. He will have "dominion" over them, as we are told in the Reading, but it isn't the kind of dominion that will take over their lives and determine their fate, as kings and great military leaders often seem to do. He will come "humble and riding on an ass, on a colt, foal of an ass." This is, indeed, a symbol of lowliness and humility.

This prophecy of Zechariah concerning the Messiah was, of course, fulfilled on Palm Sunday when Christ made his triumphal entry into Jerusalem. Like all great and famous leaders he was surrounded by the acclaim of the people, palms were strewn on the road as a token of deference and respect for him. In that sense he was similar to the images of the great kings people were familiar with. But this is offset by the fact that he was riding on a lowly ass. While he was a king he was unlike other kings or leaders: he did not seek his own glory or his own renown. He wanted to be someone with whom the people could identify, someone in whom they could truly hope.

THEOLOGICAL CONCLUSION

This tone of humility on the part of someone who is a leader is most encouraging for all of us. Here we see someone whom we can imitate. Instead of being someone who, like a king, is distant and for removed from us in his splendor and glory, here is someone who shares with us in the ordinary conditions of everyday life—in our suffering, our affliction, our pain, as well as in our joys and our own personal triumphs. Here we see a king very much like ourselves, someone whom we can truly follow. The king, the Messiah, holds out to all of us the promise of our own personal fulfillment, the promise of the possibility of the splendor and glory of our own individual selves, and we see this promise fulfilled in the resurrection of Christ on Easter Sunday morning. There he truly came forth as a king in all his splendor and glory. We also have that possibility open to us if we persevere in following his Way.

FOURTEENTH SUNDAY OF THE YEAR (SERIES A)
HOMILY II

Responsorial Psalm: *I will extol you, O my God and king, and I will bless your name for ever and ever . . . All thy works will give thanks to thee, O Lord, All the saints shall bless thee, They shall speak of the glory of thy kingdom and tell of thy power.* (Ps. 145: 1-2, 8-11)

ANA-GNOSIS

Of all the things that the early explorers of our American West were thrilled by, one of the most fascinating was the amazing beauty of the country, particularly in the western States and in the Rocky Mountain area. We can only guess at the tremendous thrill of the first explorer who saw, for example, the Grand Canyon or the indescribable beauty of Yellowstone National Park. In our own time we can recall a similar thrill when we first saw the picture of the earth from outer space that the astronauts took. We saw that large blue globe as it appeared to them way off in the distance, and we stood in awe as we contemplated it. Certainly each and every one of us has had some experience in perceiving remarkable beauty. Perhaps it was on a vacation trip where you saw the beauty of the country or a certain part of the world for the first time. You may remember how amazed you were. Perhaps one of the thoughts that struck you was that it was here all this time and you'd never seen it, though perhaps you'd heard about it from others. But even hearing about it, it was difficult to imagine its beauty. In trying to describe the beauty of such a scene one is often at a loss and may say to whomever he is trying describe it, "You'll just have to see it for yourself."

We can only guess at the myriad of things that have not yet even been seen and which may be of even greater beauty. But perhaps the most profound feeling we are left with when we contemplate all this is the seemingly remarkable indifference of nature. For how many eons of time have these magnificent scenes been there, and have never been known to exist? It seems as though they have been waiting for countless years only for someone to discover them and appreciate their beauty.

THEOLOGICAL EXTENSION

Something of this tone of awesomeness at the works of God we hear in the words of the Psalmist. He says, "All thy works shall give thanks to thee, O Lord, and all thy saints shall bless thee. They shall speak of the glory of thy kingdom and tell of thy power." Here we are suddenly brought to the realization that all the magnificent sights we have seen or heard about from others, to say nothing of the many others not yet discovered, have nevertheless been known by God from their beginning. The Psalmist wishes to convey that their very existence gives testimony to the greatness and the goodness of God. Their very existence gives glory to him. Whether or not the marvelous works of God have been discovered and are known by us, they bear a kind of mute witness to the power of their maker. Even more, when they are known and recognized by us, all the greater is the glory they give God, because then we share in that remarkable power, as the Psalmist says: "All thy saints shall bless thee," once we see the works of his hand.

THEOLOGICAL CONCLUSION

We are then left in deep awe and reverence of the works of God. We approach them with the utmost respect, realizing that they have come from the hand of God. And if we have this kind of reverence and respect for the beauty of God's work as seen in nature, how much more reverence should we have for one another, who, as we know, are God's crowning achievement. In this way we truly speak of the glory of his kingdom and tell of his power, just as the Psalmist does in today's Reading.

FOURTEENTH SUNDAY OF THE YEAR (SERIES A)
HOMILY III

Reading II: *You are not in the flesh, you are in the spirit, since the spirit of God dwells within you. Anyone who does not have the spirit of Christ does not belong to him.* (Rom. 8:9, 11-13)

ANA-GNOSIS

One of the first things that a new United States President does shortly after he has been elected is to choose his cabinet. It is true that he may retain some of the members of the outgoing cabinet for a while, perhaps out of courtesy or to make the transition to the new administration go more smoothly. But very quickly we see the new President attempting to surround himself with people who share the same ideals, goals and spirit as he himself cherishes. So after not too long a time he has "all his own people" in the White House, to help him and work with him. He knows that he can trust them, that they share the same spirit, and that his goals and aims are theirs too. This, of course, is the right of any new President, and it makes common sense. We elect a President on the basis of what we know about him, what he has told us he hopes to accomplish during his administration, and if he is to accomplish these things, then he has to have people he knows will support him and work with him. And whenever we read about such a person in the newspapers, or when we hear them being interviewed, we immediately recognize them as supporters or members of a particular administration.

THEOLOGICAL EXTENSION

Something of this everyday awareness is captured by St. Paul in the Letter to the Romans where he says, "Anyone who does not have the spirit of Christ does not belong to him." Obviously if we do not have the spirit of Christ, if we do not live in the manner of Christ, then how can we belong to him or have any sharing with him? How then do we become part of this spirit of Christ so that we are recognized as belonging to him?

We all, of course, have a standing invitation to join Christ, to belong to him, to become part of his spirit. But the response has to come from us. St. Paul tells us that we are to give up things of the flesh, things that seem to be of immediate value but in the long run will defeat us. He says, "For if you live according to the flesh, you will die." We may very enthusiastically start out by proclaiming our allegiance to the "spirit of Christ," but we may quickly discover that the demands this makes on us are very great. We may become quickly discouraged, deciding that this is not what we thought it was going to be or what we hoped it would be. There is always a strong temptation to abandon what we had initially advocated with zeal and enthusiasm. In this way we lose the spirit of Christ and are quickly immersed in the spirit of the flesh. We fail to see that it is only by retaining the spirit of Christ through the difficult as well as the easy times that Christ will give life to our mortal bodies. Just as Christ himself, in his body, arose from the dead, he will give us this same privilege so long as we adhere to the goals and ideals that he has espoused and to which we have committed ourselves.

THEOLOGICAL CONCLUSION

Any kind of really worthwhile endeavor requires staunch loyalty from those who profess to support it. Certainly for the members of our presidential cabinet this loyalty can become difficult. No doubt there are times when these people have their doubts and begin to question the wisdom of what they have set out to do and of their original commitment. It may seem at times that the demands that are put on them are unreasonable, and perhaps they occasionally do not even care to be identified with the President. As we have recently seen, their duty to their country and to their fellow man may require that they even disavow some of the works of their leader.

But in today's Reading we have the reassurance from St. Paul that we will never have to disavow in any way our commitment to the spirit of Christ. Once we have entered into this spirit and belong to him, we need have no concern that Christ will betray us or that his promises to us will not be fulfilled. We are told by St. Paul, "But if by the spirit you put to death the deeds of the flesh you will live." And to do this, of course, is to have the spirit of Christ. This spirit will never forsake us, it will never betray. It will never turn out to be something we need be ashamed of having identified with or having been a part of.

FOURTEENTH SUNDAY OF THE YEAR (SERIES A)
HOMILY IV

Gospel Reading: *On one occasion Jesus spoke thus: "Father, Lord of heaven and earth, to you I offer praise; for what you have hidden from the learned and clever you have revealed to the merest children . . . Take my yoke upon your shoulders and learn from me, for I am gentle and humble of heart. Your souls will find rest, for my yoke is easy and my burden light.* (Matt. 11:25-30)

ANA-GNOSIS

Whenever we are invited by someone to join them in a project or to take part in something they are involved in, among the first things we weigh is how much it is going to cost us, what will we get out of it, how much of a commitment on our part will it entail, and to what extent will we have to give up the things that we are already interested in and invested in. And after weighing the matter for some time, we may decide, if it looks sufficiently enticing to us, that we will join the person in his project. Sometimes this may require a total commitment from us. It may involve great sacrifice on our part; it may even change our whole life. In some cases our life may even become more difficult and burdensome than it was in the past. But if we decide that it is all worth it, then we agree to go ahead and join.

Or it may be that because of the circumstances of our own work and involvements, we simply cannot leave what we are doing, it simply isn't feasible to give up what we are doing and become a part of the other person's endeavor. And even if it doesn't involve the whole of our commitment or all of our time and effort, we may simply feel that we already have enough going for ourselves and we can't take on any more.

THEOLOGICAL EXTENSION

In the Gospel Reading of today's Liturgy, Christ extends to us a very gentle invitation. He knows how caught up we are, perhaps even entrapped, by all the things that life demands of us, by all the difficulties, all the anxieties, all the insecurities. But, in fact, to just those who are overburdened is his invitation extended. He says, "Come to me, all who labor and are heavily laden and I will give you rest. Take my yoke upon you and learn from me, for I am gentle and lowly of heart, and you will find rest for your souls." Who could fail to respond to such an invitation?

Perhaps the key word here is the word *yoke*. We know that at the time of Christ, slaves were required to pass beneath the yoke as a token of their submission and subjugation to their master, and in that sense the yoke was seen as a symbol of degradation. It indicated that the master was superior to the slave and, as we know, had the right of life and death over him. This kind of yoke would certainly be something to be feared and avoided if possible. But the yoke that Christ speaks of is far different from this. He asks us to learn from him, to learn from him so we can become like him, so we can become his friends. And we know Christ later told his Apostles that he now called them "friends" instead of "servants." Friendship obviously implies some kind of equality between the friends. One is not superior or inferior to the other.

THEOLOGICAL CONCLUSION

This is the kind of invitation that one would not have to weigh or consider for a long time before accepting, because Christ reassures us, "It is an easy yoke and it is a light burden." Christ certainly knows our involvements in life, all the duties, obligations and responsibilities that make endless demands on us. He is not suggesting that we abandon these. To do so would perhaps be irresponsible on our part. He is merely offering us the opportunity to rest, to refresh ourselves by learning from him. What we learn from Christ is the true value and meaning of our lives. While we are embroiled in many activities we can easily forget that all these, after all, are only temporary and will at some time pass away. This means that we can become lost in them. By his invitation to us today, Christ reminds us that there is a place of refreshment, of ease, where we can go to restore our souls and to gain a true perspective on the purpose of our life. We can go to him.

FIFTEENTH SUNDAY OF THE YEAR (SERIES A)
HOMILY I

Reading I: *Just as from the heavens the rain and snow come down and do not return there until they have watered the earth, making it fertile and fruitful, giving seed to him who sows and bread to him who eats, so shall my word be that goes forth from my mouth.* (Is. 55:10-11)

ANA-GNOSIS

At times of extreme drought or of unusual rain or snow we are made particularly aware of the vagaries of nature. Sometimes we may read in the newspaper of some part of our country, or of some other country of the world, that has been afflicted for a long time by a severe drought, and then all of a sudden the drought is over and the rains come, much to everyone's delight. The only trouble is that they often come in excess. Then we read about flooding and destruction, of homes being washed away, of dams bursting. Or we read of excessive snowfall isolating small towns from the rest of the world. When we hear about these things we cannot help but be struck with what seems to be a great waste. While before there wasn't enough rain and snow, enough moisture, now there is so much we can't use it all. We wonder perhaps what the point of it is.

THEOLOGICAL EXTENSION

In today's first Reading the prophet Isaiah, says, "Just as from heaven the rain and snow come down and do not return there until they have watered the earth, making it fertile and fruitful, giving seed to him who sows and bread to him who eats, so shall my word be that bursts forth from my mouth." We could suppose that Isaiah's words too may come to seem excessive, like too much rainfall on a saturated land. Certainly the warnings and predictions of the prophets fell often enough on deaf ears. Like the excess rain and snow, these words did not appear to do any good. Yet we know that the preaching of the Prophets was finally accomplished, and that when the Messiah did come, the people were prepared for it and aware of it. They knew it was going to happen. Where the word of God is concerned, then, we cannot claim that "too much" has been given us. It has all been given for a purpose.

THEOLOGICAL CONCLUSION

The word of God, the advice and admonitions sent through his Prophets which are so valuable and necessary, is really only a shadow of his real Word, his divine Son. But without them the people would not have been prepared for the Word to be fulfilled in the person of Christ. As Christians we are united to the Word of God who became flesh. We are members of his body. To help us to live the Christian life we have the word of God spoken through the Prophets and the writers of the Old Testament. Even more than this we have Christ himself who is the fulfillment of that Word. None of the words of God have been wasted, even if they once fell on deaf ears, if we listen to them and allow them to help us grow more deeply aware of our lives united with Christ. They prepared mankind for the coming of the Savior. Let us permit them to help us attain his salvation.

FIFTEENTH SUNDAY OF THE YEAR (SERIES A) HOMILY II

Responsorial Psalm: *You have visited the land and watered it, greatly have you enriched it. God's water courses are filled, you have prepared the grain . . . You have crowned the year with your bounty, your paths overflow with the rich harvest. The untilled meadows overflow with it, and rejoicing clothes the hills.* (Ps. 65:10-14)

ANA-GNOSIS

In the early days of the settling of our country the ability to follow the tracks of a wild animal was a highly valued skill. That skill is almost completely lost in our own time because there is so little need for it, but a century or two ago a very skilled tracker was greatly in demand. Such a person could tell a great deal about the animal he was following simply from the kind of tracks the animal made. For example, if the animal left a light impression on the earth, the tracker would surmise that the animal might be underweight or perhaps starving. If it left deep tracks the tracker would know that it was healthy and in good condition. He could tell from the size of the track a great deal about the weight or size of the animal. If the track was distorted in some way he might know the animal was lame. In a time when much of the livelihood of people depended on hunting, tracking was a highly prized skill. Depending on the nature of the animal and on its condition, the hunter could take necessary steps and precautions to prepare himself to hunt for it.

THEOLOGICAL EXTENSION

The Psalm in today's liturgy is really a hymn of praise. God is praised as one who pardons and blesses, as creator and as the one who bestows rain and fertility on the land. And in one part of the Psalm the Psalmist says, "You have crowned the year with your bounty, and your paths overflowed with the rich harvest." We are told that the literal translation of "your paths overflow with the rich harvest" is "your wagon wheel tracks drip with oil." This image of "wagon wheel tracks" would, of course, have been a very vivid one to the people at the time of the Psalmist. They symbolized the path of God as he went about making the earth fertile and productive. Just as the skillful tracker can know much about the animal that he is following from its tracks, so we can know a great deal about God from the traces that he leaves for us of prosperity and plenty. It is, of course, very easy for us to forget the source of our bounty and our wealth. Like small children we quickly tend to take things for granted. We assume that the wealth, the fertility, the productivity will always be there, and sometimes we forget its real source. But in this Psalm of praise we are reminded of what the real source is. It is, of course, God, and without God we would have nothing.

THEOLOGICAL CONCLUSION

As we look about us, it is often easy to see signs of the real source of our bounty. But only when things become difficult for us, when we are not so prosperous or well off, do we begin to remind ourselves that perhaps we should not take these things for granted. They are all given to us as gifts. And that is the point of praise in today's Psalm. The gift, however, is not just a material one—one of fruitfulness and plenty and all the joy that goes with it. It is also a spiritual gift in which God pardons and blesses us.

Just as it is easy for us to forget the source of our material bounty, so it can be easy to forget the source of our spiritual benefits and blessings. The person who is in no need of these, the person who has no need of pardon, can easily forget that ultimate pardon really comes from God himself. It comes to us from him because he is our creator, we are his creatures, and he is the ultimate source of love. And as such he is always there to pardon us.

We indeed see in the "paths" of God the sign of his bounty and of his goodness to us. We need always to follow this path, to keep our eyes on it, lest we forget it or take it for granted.

FIFTEENTH SUNDAY OF THE YEAR (SERIES A)
HOMILY III

Reading II: *I consider the sufferings of the present to be as nothing compared to the glory to be revealed to us through God. For the creation waits with eager longing for the revealing of the sons of God.* (Rom. 8:18-23)

ANA-GNOSIS

One of the common expressions that we often hear to describe a person who has been languishing in prison for a long time, perhaps even under a life sentence, is that he is "rotting away." This expression conveys, I think, the profound sense of frustration, of uselessness, for the person who is in such circumstances. He is in a kind of dead-end situation in which he has no future, and there is no longer any point or purpose to his life.

We all know from various stories or newspaper articles we've read, or movies we have watched, how true this is. In a rare instance we may hear of a person who makes the best of his situation in this confinement that seems so futile and useless. He actually may produce something worthwhile. Certainly there have been prisoners who have written books that are of great value to the human race. Some years ago there was a movie called *The Bird Man of Alcatraz* about a prisoner who did some very valuable and worthwhile research on birds which has since been of great benefit to all of us. But mostly this is an exception. The more common experience of prisoners seems to be one of languishing there or, as we say, "rotting." They experience a profound sense of lack of purpose and of despair, especially if they are there for life or there is very little hope of being released soon.

THEOLOGICAL EXTENSION

This vivid image of the wastefulness and futility in the life of the prisoner is something of the way St. Paul describes creation and the state of mankind before the coming of Christ. He says that "creation was subjected to futility," and the definition of futility contains the idea of uselessness, of lack of purpose. In his Letter to the Romans St. Paul also uses the word *decay* which would certainly catch the common image of a prisoner "rotting" in prison. Thus, before the coming of Christ mankind was indeed much like a person in prison. But St. Paul reassures us, "The creation itself will be set free from its bondage to decay, and obtain the glorious liberty of the children of God."

THEOLOGICAL CONCLUSION

One can easily imagine the tremendous sense of joy on the part of the prisoner who unexpectedly receives word that he is soon going to be free. Perhaps he has been given an official pardon by the Governor or the President. What was once, then, a sense of uselessness and waste can now become a sense of profound joy and gratitude for his release. Unfortunately we know that many prisoners, when they are released from prison, have found it to be a very embittering experience, and very often go back to their old ways of crime. But sometimes they realize their freedom and are able to take joy in it and even have a sense of gratitude for it. This latter experience would describe our condition as Christians.

We realize that without Christ we would indeed be, as St. Paul said, "subjected to futility" and "in a sense of decay." But realizing that we are now free from that, we can truly be joyful and express our sense of gratitude and our recognition of the source of our true freedom. Just as the prisoner who is unexpectedly given a pardon by a government official, even though it isn't particularly due to any merit on his part, so we rejoice in our own sense of pardon by Christ coming into the world. This was certainly not due to any merit on our part. But regardless of our merit, pardon has been granted to us. And St. Paul wants to be sure we know that. He wants to reassure us that we are no longer prisoners, that our lives are not futile and useless. We are truly free because we are "children of God" through Christ who died for us. And through his death he gave new purpose and meaning to our lives.

FIFTEENTH SUNDAY OF THE YEAR (SERIES A) HOMILY IV

Gospel Reading: *Jesus, on leaving the house on a certain day, sat down by the lakeshore . . . This is why I speak to them in parables, because seeing they do not see, and hearing they do not hear, nor do they understand.* (Matt. 13:1-23)

ANA-GNOSIS

It is not uncommon for a writer to express his or her deepest thoughts or feelings by way of an allegory or symbol. An allegory, as we know, is a kind of pictorial image containing a deeper meaning than the most obvious superficial one. As an illustration of this we have the poem of Sir Galahad in search of the Holy Grail. In this medieval poem, Sir Galahad, who is one of the Knights of the Round Table, is in search of the chalice that our Lord used at the Last Supper. Of all the Knights of the Round Table, he is the one who finally succeeds in finding it. This is the superficial story, but on a deeper level we may also find in it the story of a spiritual search, not only of Sir Galahad but of each one of us.

Stories that might be more familiar to all of us, since we all read them and heard them as children, would be the fables of Aesop. These stories usually depict an animal acting as a human being would in some kind of conflict situation which the animal then resolves either successfully or unsuccessfully. But the point of the fable is to show something of human wisdom or human folly, and it is then followed up with a moral which states its deeper meaning.

The reason for using this kind of literary form is that the writer may feel that his audience would be threatened if he were to speak more openly or more directly. He may fear that they will not understand, that they might become indifferent, or they might not be able to see themselves in what he said and that it would have no meaning if he spoke directly. So in order to soften the idea he wishes to convey he uses a story or an allegory. This has the great advantage of allowing the reader to enter into the message to whatever degree he feels capable of or secure in doing without feeling threatened.

THEOLOGICAL EXTENSION

In today's Gospel Reading we see something of this same idea on the part of Christ. He gives us here the Parable of the Sower who went out to sow seed. And after he does so, the disciples ask him, somewhat surprised, "Why do you speak to them in parables?" And Christ answers them, "This is why I speak to them in parables—for seeing they do not see, and hearing they do not hear, nor do they understand."

In his response we sense both a note of sadness because of the inability of the people to understand his true meaning and a sense of hope that perhaps by speaking in parables they might eventually come to the deeper meaning. They might begin to see themselves in it, to see that it applies to them without becoming too frightened by what he says.

In Christ's subsequent explanation of the Parable it is interesting to note that at no time does he imply that the people who misunderstand him are evil or that they maliciously attacked him. We do know that on numerous occasions the leaders of the time did openly attack Christ, and ultimately, of course, they crucified him. But here Christ doesn't seem to be accusing them of malice. Rather, in his explanation of the Parable, he says the seed that fell on rocky ground was simply snatched away from them by the evil one. There is no implication of fault on their part. And even when he speaks of the seed that failed to bear fruit because it wasn't deeply rooted he doesn't point to malice, for these people received it with joy. That which falls among the thorns, is the word spoken to those who do hear but who are overcome by the cares of the world and delight in riches and so the seed proves unfruitful for them. Here again Christ does not imply that such people are malicious or inherently evil. Perhaps they are weak, but this is entirely different. Then fortunately there is the seed that falls on the good soil—those who truly hear his word and understand it and allow it to bear fruit.

THEOLOGICAL CONCLUSION

In this Parable of the sower it is easy for us, as with any pictorial image or allegory, to see ourselves in it in whatever way we wish. We may very well see ourselves as the one who received the word, the seed, but it was snatched away from us. Or we may see ourselves as rocky ground on which the seed fell but couldn't really take root. Or we may see ourselves as thorny ground which chokes out the seed through worldly preoccupations. Or we may see ourselves as the good soil on which the seed fell and truly bore fruit. This Parable of today's Gospel gives us all the opportunity to look at ourselves openly and to take to heart the meaning of Christ's explanation in whatever way it applies to us. This of course can be difficult and frightening because in our inner hearts we cannot ignore the truth. Having heard the word, having received the seed, we are challenged by it. As the characters in the fables of Aesop, we too are faced with resolving the conflict in ourselves. It is something that only we can do. But our great consolation and encouragement for this is the realization that Christ does not imply that, however we see ourselves, we are necessarily evil. Perhaps we need to change, to view things differently. Change can sometimes be threatening. But no matter how we have viewed the word previously there is the open possibility for re-looking into it, and reincorporating it into our lives in such a way that we truly do give it space to take root, so that it can bear fruit, not only in our own lives, but in the lives of others around us.

SIXTEENTH SUNDAY OF THE YEAR (SERIES A)
HOMILY I

Reading I: *Thou who art sovereign in strength dost judge with mildness and with great forbearance thou dost govern us. For thou hast power to act whenever thou dost choose. Through such works thou hast taught thy people the righteous man must be kind.* (Wis. 12:13, 16-19)

ANA-GNOSIS

Some time ago there was a story on the news about one of our leading politicians who was campaigning for election to office. As he was giving his speech in front of a large crowd, someone attempted to assassinate him. At the time it happened the politician was not aware of the alleged attack on him, but later when he found out, he said he knew that by law the person should be prosecuted, but he hoped that the prosecutors would be lenient toward the person. He personally bore no ill will toward his attacker and completely forgave him. This incident is all the more impressive, I suppose, when we realize that the politician certainly had it in his power to prosecute the person to the fullest extent of the law. So when he forgave the person and hoped that he would not be punished severely, he evoked a great deal of admiration.

We can all think of personal incidents where perhaps someone attempted to harm us or subvert our efforts in some way or other. After we found out about it, we could have reacted angrily or in some cases even pressed charges against this person, but we did not. Instead, we forgave the person and felt it would not be in our best interests to prosecute him. We simply dismissed the whole affair. In some cases our forgiveness allows a person a chance to start over, especially if he has apologized and recognized his wrongdoing. Then we are frequently willing to give him another chance.

We all understand human fallacy and weakness in this way. So even though it may be in our power to prosecute, and in strict justice we may have the right to do so, we frequently show kindness and sympathy toward a person who has wronged us.

THEOLOGICAL EXTENSION

This is something of the image of God that we find in the Reading today taken from the Book of Wisdom. The author tells us, "Thou who are sovereign in strength dost judge with mildness, and with great forbearance thou dost govern us." There is no question here of God's *right* to punish us for our wrongdoing. We are told that he is "sovereign in strength." He can do as he will because he is not subject to any other power. Yet he chooses to judge us mildly. In this way God hopes to teach us that, as he has been kind and shown forbearance to us, we also must do so toward another. The author writes, "The righteous man must be kind." God teaches him by his own example to be kind. Even in a position of power and might, or perhaps especially so, we need to show forbearance and kindness to one another.

THEOLOGICAL CONCLUSION

Parents especially are quick to express their forgiveness and understanding to their children who have wronged them or someone else. They give them a new start, a chance to start over. And very often they do this with the conscious realization that, as they show this sort of kindness and mercy to their children, so their children may learn to do the same toward others. This example of kindness they hope will be a more powerful way of communicating the importance of forgiveness than anything they might say.

This is what God does for us also. While He is certainly in a position to treat our wrongdoing severely, he chooses instead to react mildly. In doing so he teaches us to react in the same way toward those who have hurt us. As we have been in need and mercy and forgiveness from God, so we should extend this same mercy and forgiveness to others who have injured or attempted to injure us.

SIXTEENTH SUNDAY OF THE YEAR (SERIES A)
HOMILY II

Responsorial Psalm: *You, O Lord, are good and forgiving, abounding in kindness to all who call upon you . . . Grant me a proof of your favor, that my enemies may see to their confusion that you, O Lord, have helped and comforted me.* (Ps. 86:5-6, 9-10, 15-16)

ANA-GNOSIS

Whenever the ambassador of one country travels to another country, one of the first things he does as a matter of course is to present certain documents and papers to the officials of the foreign country proving that he represents the country that he claims to represent. If there is ever any question about the authenticity of the ambassador, the authorities of the foreign country can always check with the leader of the ambassador's country. Once he is recognized as the true ambassador he is then accorded all the hospitality due his position. And, officially recognized then, he does not speak so much for himself as he speaks for the country he represents.

An illustration that might be closer to our own experience is that of the child who is sent to the corner store to buy something for his mother and is told to put it on the bill. Of course everything goes smoothly if the storekeeper knows the child. Then there are no questions asked. This, of course, would more likely happen in a small neighborhood. But if the storekeeper does not know the child, then some questions might arise and the child might be asked to give some sort of identification or evidence that he really is the child of such and such a person. The child might then show the storekeeper a note from his mother authorizing him to charge this item. Then the storekeeper would be satisfied and give the child whatever he was sent for.

THEOLOGICAL EXTENSION

These illustrations can help us get into the mood of the Psalmist today. In the final verse of his prayer to God he says, "Grant me a proof of your favor, that my enemies may see to their confusion that you, O Lord, have helped and comforted me." The Psalmist sems to be persecuted, perhaps unjustly accused, and he looks for a sign from the Lord that will confound his enemies. It's almost as though, if only he could show his enemies some proof that God was on his side, then they would stop persecuting him and would treat him with more respect. So he says to God in his prayer, "Give ear, O Lord, to my prayer. Hearken to my cry of supplication."

We have all been in positions where we felt persecuted, treated unfairly. We may have had the somewhat self-pitying feeling that if only our enemies knew who we really were, they would be a little more respectful toward us. If they only knew we had a certain powerful friend on our side to whom we could go, they would be less quick to judge us, they would not jump to make their accusations. Sometimes we may even say to them that if they keep this up we will notify someone about the unjust treatment they have given us. And as a result very often their whole attitude toward us changes. They may even say, "Oh, I didn't know you were a friend of his."

Such seems to be the nature of the Psalmist's prayer today. He knows that if he can somehow convince his enemies that God is on his side, they will treat him with greater deference. After all, they, too, realize that God is a powerful ally to have.

THEOLOGICAL CONCLUSION

This can be a very encouraging awareness for each of us. When we know we are doing God's will we can take comfort in the fact that he supports us. Just knowing that can rekindle our enthusiasm when we may have been depressed by the challenges and criticisms of others. It can enable us to carry on and live out our deepest convictions with courage. It is not an easy task to do the will of God, and our efforts will not always go unchallenged by others, but we, too, like the Psalmist, can turn to God for support and sustenance. He will not fail us.

SIXTEENTH SUNDAY OF THE YEAR (SERIES A) HOMILY III

Reading II: *The spirit, too, helps us in our weakness for we do not know how to pray as we ought. But the spirit himself makes intercession for us with groanings which cannot be expressed in speech. And he who searches the hearts of men knows what is in the mind of the spirit, for the spirit intercedes for the saints according to the will of God.* (Rom. 8:26-27)

ANA-GNOSIS

In many of the larger cities across the United States, the telephone companies offer what they call a "dial-a-prayer" service. When a person feels in need of prayer, perhaps when he is lonely or depressed or feels neglected or abandoned, he can simply pick up the telephone. The idea behind this service, or course, is that it is hoped the caller will enter into the same prayer. But the further implication is that people in a moment of crisis might not necessarily know how to pray when they suddenly felt the need of a prayer. So this need is filled by a recorded prayer which one can participate in and perhaps which will resolve the need that instigated the prayer in the first place.

THEOLOGICAL EXTENSION

One of our immediate reactions to this idea of dial-a-prayer is that it is depersonalized and mechanical. How, for example, can someone else come up with a prayer that would respond to one person's particular needs at a certain moment? And yet this idea catches a bit of what St. Paul is telling us in the second Reading of today's Liturgy. He says, ". . . we do not know how to pray as we ought." But what is it that characterizes praying "as we ought?" It is certainly more than knowing which words to say, though that, of course, helps too. It has far more to do with our attitude. Even if we are at a loss for words, if we have the right attitude God hears our prayer, for St. Paul goes on to say, "But the Spirit himself makes intercession for us with groanings which cannot be expressed in speech." God isn't looking for a polished delivery or an eloquent vocabulary. When the disciples asked Christ, "Lord, teach us to pray," he gave them that beautiful prayer that we know as The Lord's Prayer. And what characterizes the Lord's Prayer is its deep faith and trust in God. That is the way to pray—with faith and trust.

God has reassured us that he knows all of our needs and is ready to assist us in them. Yet often our tendency is to expect immediate results to our prayer rather than to allow God to respond in his own way. But to demand immediate results is to imply a lack of trust in God, a lack of faith that God really knows or understands our needs. But with a deep sense of trust we can realize that all things are present to God, and while he may not seem to be in the same hurry we're in to get the same results, we know that eventually God will respond and in a way that is far more beneficial to us than we would have thought.

THEOLOGICAL CONCLUSION

We should be reassured then that even when our prayers may seem weak or inarticulate, the very effort to pray can, in a sense, be a prayer. "The Spirit helps us in our weakness," St. Paul tells us. He knows our effort and responds to it. And he responds in a far more personal and consoling way than the telephone does when we dial a prayer. What matters is our effort to pray and the depth of our trust in the Lord. If we try and if we trust, the Holy Spirit will ensure our being understood.

SIXTEENTH SUNDAY OF THE YEAR (SERIES A)
HOMILY IV

Gospel Reading: *Jesus proposed to the crowd another parable: "The reign of God may be likened to a man who sowed seed in the field . . ." He told them another parable: "The kingdom of heaven is like leaven which a woman took and hid in three measures of meal, so it was all leaven."* (Mt. 13:24-43)

ANA-GNOSIS

When we think or change, perhaps what very often occurs to us is a dramatic or very sudden turnabout in events. Things are different than they were before, and the difference is clearly noticeable. Even when we think about change in our own life or in someone else's life, we often only perceive radical changes where it is easy to speak of a time before and a time after the change.

But of course we know that change is not always sudden and dramatic. It can be a slow, almost imperceptible process. For example, at what moment in time does one refer to a person as being old or middleaged? People most often change in a slow, almost imperceptible way.

THEOLOGICAL EXTENSION

This notion of change as a slow, gradual process seems to be more in keeping with the spirit of Christ's description of the Kingdom of Heaven in today's Gospel. In the longer form of the Gospel Christ gives us the parable where he likens the kingdom of heaven to leaven which a woman puts into the meal. The image of the Kingdom of God as leaven in meal may not be familiar to us since in our own time people are less accustomed to baking their own bread. But it certainly would have been familiar to the people at the time of Christ. As unfamiliar as we may be, however, with the process of baking bread, we know that when the leaven enters the dough nothing very perceptible or dramatic happens at once, but rather the leaven subtlety and imperceptibly pervades the entire mass of dough and gives to the baked bread a subtlety and fineness of texture that unleavened bread does not have. In a sense one could even say that the leaven doesn't change the dough at all. Bread that is unleavened has the same nourishing qualities. But when we eat it, it has a different texture, a different feel to it. It lacks a certain lightness that bread with leaven has.

THEOLOGICAL CONCLUSION

When we remark on the evil in the world, it can seem discouraging and disheartening. We can't imagine that any good could come of our particular puny efforts. Very often people say, "Well, the little good I do now will be unnoticed. It won't make any difference anyhow. So why bother? After all, I cannot bring about any dramatic change, any stirring results. Leave this for the people in power and authority."

What we may fail to realize is that all of us are part of the kingdom of God, not only those in power and authority who can effect the sudden and dramatic changes we often think are the only effective ways to get these things done. And because we are part of the kingdom we can be and are expected to be like this leaven. In each person we meet we should hope to bring about a change by the way in which we relate to them. Like the leaven that subtly but imperceptibly pervades the dough, giving it a much finer quality than it had before, so those who do the will of God should improve the quality of their own life and lives of those around them. Their efforts do make a difference.

In our over-concern with seeing sudden results or quick

changes, we can easily ignore the subtlety of the nature of the leaven and the way it enters the flour. And yet this is the way of the kingdom of heaven as Christ describes it to us. And, as Christians, each one of us has the obligation to work toward the fulfillment of that kingdom.

SEVENTEENTH SUNDAY OF THE YEAR (SERIES A)
HOMILY I

Reading I: *The Lord appeared to Solomon in a dream at night . . . And God said, "Ask what I will give." And Solomon said, "O Lord, my God, you have made your servant king in place of David, my father. I do not know how to go out or come in . . . Give your servant, therefore, and understanding heart to govern your people, that I may discern between good and evil. For who is able to govern this, your great people?"* (1 Kings 3:5, 7-12)

ANA-GNOSIS

Probably all of us at one time or another, but especially as children, have fantasized about what it would be like if we could ask for anything we wished. As we mulled over this fantasy we probably thought of many nice things we would like to have. A child might wish for a lot of toys or a meal of his favorite foods. An adult might think of a new home, ideally located, or perhaps a new car that he's dreamed of, but could never afford. Or perhaps he may dream of having a great skill, perhaps in music or art. But whenever we indulge in these fantasies, what is singularly striking about them is that they are usually centered on some material thing that will be for our own personal happiness and betterment, although we probably wouldn't rule out others being helped indirectly by whatever it is that we would ask for if given the opportunity.

THEOLOGICAL EXTENSION

In today's Reading from the first Book of Kings, Solomon is given the opportunity to ask for whatever he wants most. God says to him, "Ask what I shall give you." And Solomon's answer is quite surprising in two ways. It is surprising, first of all, in what he asks for. Instead of asking for any material goods to improve his own situation in this world, for something that would add greatly to his physical comfort, well-being and security, he asks for an understanding heart. The second thing about Solomon's request that is surprising is his reason or motivation for asking. He asks this not for himself, but so that "I may discern between good and evil. Who is able to govern this, your great people?" In his reply, then, Solomon is not thinking of himself or his own personal good, but of the good of others. He clearly recognizes his responsibility as the king to govern the people justly and wisely and with equity. And in humility he recognizes that he is very insecure about this and perhaps even unable to do it: he needs God's help if it is to be done properly.

We see that God is very pleased with this request and especially pleased with his motivation for making it. God replies, "Because you have asked this, and have not asked for yourself a long life or riches or the life of your enemies, but have asked for yourself understanding to discern what is right, behold I now do according to your word.

THEOLOGICAL CONCLUSION

There is much for us to learn in this prayer of Solomon. Especially we might learn from his motivation ". . . that I may discern between good and evil." All of us, too, while we are not kings or great leaders of people, nevertheless have responsibilities toward others—parents toward their children, teachers toward their students, employers toward those who work for them. It is, of course, often difficult to know, even with the best of good will and intentions, how to relate to them, what is truly in their best interests. Not only is this often difficult to know, it is even more difficult to carry into practice. We all need to recognize our own inadequacy and our own inability to discern what is best for others or even for ourselves. Very often because of this, perhaps even without knowing it, we are somewhat selfish in our motivation. We, too, need to share in this prayer of Solomon. Each of us has great need for an understanding mind and heart. We cannot begin to be Christian if we think only of ourselves.

SEVENTEENTH SUNDAY OF THE YEAR (SERIES A) HOMILY II

Responsorial Psalm: *I have said, O Lord, that my part is to keep your words, the law of your mouth is more precious to me than thousands of gold and silver pieces . . . Wonderful are your decrees, therefore, I observe them. The revelation of your words sheds light, giving understanding to the simple.* (Ps. 119:57, 72, 76-77, 127-130)

ANA-GNOSIS

Some time ago in the local high school of the town where I was living, the boys' physical education class would occasionally play a game they called "cave man basketball." As one of the high school students explained this to me, "It's just like regular basketball except there aren't any rules." The object of the game was the same as in regular basketball, namely, to put the ball through the basket, but there were no regulations to control the game. For example, there were no lines to indicate whether the players were in bounds or out of bounds, there were no referees, the players didn't have to dribble the ball, they could tackle one another, and so on. Fortunately the game was rather short lived: a student, in the process of being tackled, got a broken arm, and that brought a rather sudden end to the game of "cave man basketball."

But what impressed me most about this was the importance of rules and regulations in the governing of our lives. Were it not for rules and regulations, there would be no place for the most skilled athlete to exercise his skill. In the game of "cave man basketball" for example, one could be an expert dribbler, but what would be the point of his skill if at any moment someone would tackle him? In other words, the rules and regulations allowed the athlete to bring out his best self, to exercise his greatest skills. And this is true not only in sports, but in all of life. The rules and regulations, instead of restricting our freedom, give us freedom in which to exercise and demonstrate our greatest competence.

THEOLOGICAL EXTENSION

In today's Psalm we see something of this same awareness. The Psalmist says how close he is to the law of the Lord: "The law of your mouth is to me more precious than thousands of gold and silver pieces. Wonderful are your decrees. Therefore I observe them." This is the statement of a person who knows that he can fulfill himself best within the rules or decrees that God has given him instead of resisting them. He does not see them as restricting his freedom, nor does he resent them because they do not allow him to do what he wants to do. Rather he sees them in a very positive light. He knows that without the laws and decrees of God as guidelines his life perhaps would not have the meaning or purpose that it has.

THEOLOGICAL CONCLUSION

This idea of invoking some kind of rules or laws for ourselves is not to be confused with legalism. It is true sometimes that rules or regulations outlive their usefulness. Then common sense dictates that they ought to be revised or perhaps even done away with all together. We see examples of this in the changes that have taken place in the Church. Some of the rules that used to govern our behavior have been changed, some have been revoked completely. This makes good sense because they are less appropriate to our own time. But we also know that some rules or guidelines are necessary, and that our lives without them would be chaotic or directionless. There would be nothing against which to test ourselves and no limitations within which to bring out our best. This is the positive, even joyful, attitude toward laws and limitations that we hear from the Psalmist today.

We often tend to think of laws as something to take away our freedom. If we only didn't have this law or that one life would be much happier for us. But this can be very misleading by virtue of the fact that as human beings we are limited in all sorts of ways. We need to live our lives within limits. Only an infinite being is outside any kind of limits or restrictions. We are not God, we are people. And God gives us his decrees to give us direction and purpose for our life. Within them we are able to realize our potential to its fullest.

SEVENTEENTH SUNDAY OF THE YEAR (SERIES A) HOMILY III

Reading II: *We know that God makes all things work together for the good of those who love him. We have been called according to his decree (purpose).* (Rom. 8:28-30)

ANA-GNOSIS

Perhaps one of the most overworked cliches we hear, usually spoken by a person in authority to a subordinate he is correcting, is, "Well, after all, I only did it for your own good."

This is a phrase that parents use very often to their children, sometimes even apologetically, after having punished them. Of course, the child who hears this is often somewhat puzzled because he does not quite understand how this is going to help him. He doesn't understand it, at least, at this particular moment. But very often later, when he has grown up, he looks back with gratitude and affection to his parents for having corrected him or even for having punished him. He can see now the value of what his parents did, although at the time of the correction there was little possibility of that. When he grows up and understands what motivated the punishment and is capable of loving the way they love him, then he is able to appreciate what his parents did for him.

THEOLOGICAL EXTENSION

This is what St. Paul seems to be impressing on the people of Rome in the part of his letter that we read in today's Liturgy. He says, "We know that in everything God works for the good of those who love him." St. Paul here seems to be talking about a mutual relationship of love between God and man. There is no question about the unconditional love of God for us. The issue is whether we are able to return this love or not. No matter what God does for us, it cannot be of any benefit unless we respond to it in a loving and trusting way. Like a small child we might find it difficult to understand the purpose to which, as St. Paul says, "the Christian is called." It may even seem like a contradiction. But St. Paul reassures us that by a loving of God and trusting his designs, everything will work out for the good of those who love him.

THEOLOGICAL CONCLUSION

This is indeed hard for us to see at times. And perhaps only an act of complete faith in God's purpose can carry us through. God's ways, as we learn elsewhere in Scripture, are mysterious. Sometimes they seem not only to have no purpose, but even to be at cross purposes, just as it may seem to a child that his parents' disciplining of him is not for his own good at all. Then he resents it when it is given.

But we have St. Paul's reassurance that everything does indeed work through God for the good of those who love him, for those who enter into a mutual loving relationship with him. God's love is unconditional, and our duty is to return it. Then we can trust that everything will work out for our own betterment.

SEVENTEENTH SUNDAY OF THE YEAR (SERIES A)
HOMILY IV

Gospel Reading: *Jesus said to the crowd: The reign of God is like a buried treasure which a man found in a field. He hid it again, and rejoicing at his find went and sold all he had and bought that field.* (Mt. 13:44-52)

ANA-GNOSIS

It makes common sense for a person who owns a number of shares in various companies to review his investments periodically and see if they are still paying him dividends. So each year he might go to his safe deposit box, take our his various stocks and go through them and re-evaluate them. As a result of his re-evaluation he might decide that some of his stocks are not paying dividends any longer. Then he might choose to get rid of them and reinvest in other stocks that will pay him more. And he might hold onto others because they are still paying him a worthwhile dividend. A serious investor in the market might even consult with his stockbroker about the retention or the sales of the various stocks that he owns. As a result of this consultation he might come to a decision to liquidate some of his stock and to re-invest it.

Now it obviously makes good sense to do this kind of re-evaluation periodically. And on the advice of a stockbroker who knows a particularly good company in which to invest, the client would be smart to buy into that company even if it involved selling all the shares that he owned in order to make that one very worthwhile investment in that one particular company.

THEOLOGICAL EXTENSION

Something of this perhaps catches the mood of the Parable in today's Gospel where Christ compares the kingdom of God to a buried treasure which a man found in a field. The man quickly recognized the value of that treasure, and so he went and sold everything else that he had in order to invest in it, in order to make sure that he got a hold of that one possession because he realized that it alone was worth more than all the other investments he had.

All of us, in the course of our lives, have made various investments, not necessarily financial, but nevertheless investments that we considered worthwhile, that we felt gave meaning and purpose to our lives. But we may realize after a time what seemed to be, or may actually have been, a good investment, is no longer serving our needs. It is no longer a very forceful or primary value in our life, and so we tend to get rid of it. We take on another value that will serve our spiritual needs much better, will give us more fulfillment and greater purpose.

Sometimes this process of re-evaluation can be a difficult and painful one. A certain value that we have found worthwhile for a long time, perhaps our whole life, until now, we may realize is somewhat empty and doesn't give us the meaning and fulfillment that is once did. So we consider the possibility of letting go of that value, perhaps to re-invest in another value of which we are perhaps not too sure. This can be a difficult moment for us. But painful as it may be, we recognize the good sense of it and so we do what has to be done.

This process of re-evaluation is characteristic of our entire lives. There is a constant re-thinking of one's position, of one's investments, of what one sees as the real meaning, purpose and goal of life.

THEOLOGICAL CONCLUSION

In today's Gospel we have the reassurance of Christ that he is that one true value that requires our unconditional investment. Whoever discovers this value really discovers a treasure. It is worth everything that one owns, that one has, that one has previously valued, to invest in this one particular treasure, even if it involves a complete discarding of all that one has valued up to this time. Difficult though it may be to invest in this new-found treasure, it is nevertheless worthwhile.

In the Parable Christ speaks of the joy of the man who found a material treasure hidden in the field that he considered worth everything else he had in order to obtain. And if this is true of a material treasure, how much more so would it be true of a spiritual treasure, something around which the whole meaning and purpose of our life hinges. Surely it would be worth everything we treasured up until now, to get rid of all that if it meant coming into possession of this one real treasure. And this one treasure, let us constantly remember, is Christ himself.

EIGHTEENTH SUNDAY OF THE YEAR (SERIES A)
HOMILY I

Reading I: *All you who are thirsty, come to the water! . . . Why do you spend your money for that which is not bread; and your labor for that which does not satisfy?* (Is. 55:1-3)

ANA-GNOSIS

Occasionally we come across an item in the news that tells of a Company, usually of chain stores, that has built one of its stores on a certain location in a neighborhood. And while the Company generally had good business, this particular store not only failed to make a profit, but it very soon was losing a great deal of money. After a short time, perhaps after only a year, the Company decided that it couldn't stand this loss anymore, so it tore down the store or sold it. When this happens we can easily imagine the manager of that store, or the owner of the Company, saying, "What a waste of effort! What a waste of money! What a terrible investment that was!" But if he had been more careful in the first place and done a little more research, he might have made a wiser choice for the location and thus saved himself and others a lot of wasted time, effort and money.

THEOLOGICAL EXTENSION

Something of this idea of wasted effort and misspent energy we see in the Reading of Isaiah in today's Liturgy. He says, "Why do you spend your money for that which is not bread, and you labor for that which does not satisfy?" The context in which this statement is related by Isaiah is that of the Israelites running off after false gods. Isaiah is desperately struggling to have them return to the one true God. So he tells them that if they spend all this effort chasing after false gods who can give them no real satisfaction, they will not have the effort left to worship the true God who could really satisfy them. If they are going to expend all this labor and effort, he counsels them, why not extend it in the right direction, in the search for the true God rather than false gods?

But he also offers them something far more enticing: all that they receive will be free. He says, "Come, buy wine and milk without money and price." Everything that the true God has to offer them is theirs for the asking, it is a free gift to them. They are foolish to go through all this expenditure and labor for that which is theirs anyway. All that they need do is turn in the right direction and search for the true God.

THEOLOGICAL CONCLUSION

We are all seeking satisfaction and reimbursement for our labor and efforts in our own lives. But very often, like the Israelites, we expend it in the wrong direction. So what Isaiah says to the people of his time applies also to us: since we are going to use all this effort anyhow, let's use it in such a way that will give us a truly satisfying return. Then, in the end, it will not all be wasted and we will look back in sadness on our life and say, "What a waste." Let us recall, whenever we are tempted to seek false gods, the tragic words attributed to Cardinal Woolsley toward the end of his life, "If I had served my God with the same zeal with which I served my king, I would not now in my old age stand naked to mine enemies."

EIGHTEENTH SUNDAY OF THE YEAR (SERIES A) HOMILY II

Responsorial Psalm: *The Lord is gracious and merciful, slow to anger and of great kindness . . .*
The eyes of all look hopefully to you, and you give them their food in due season; you open your hand and satisfy the desire of every living thing. (Ps. 145:8-9, 15-16, 17-18)

ANA-GNOSIS

Not infrequently, newspapers will carry the pictures of starving victims of a war-torn country. Often the victims shown in the pictures are small children with distended stomachs and rickety limbs barely able to support them. They have their hands outstretched and their eyes turned upward looking to someone, apparently, to give them something to eat.

When we see such a picture we cannot help but react with a profound sympathy for these innocent victims of political strife. We would like to be there and reach out to them with the food and the nourishment that they so desperately need. There are times when we can help, but in some instances all we can do is wring our hands in anguish and lament the terrible tragedy which these children are suffering.

THEOLOGICAL EXTENSION

Something of this same picture of the starving children with their eyes looking up to someone, hoping for food, we also see in the Psalm we read today. The Psalmist says, "The eyes of all look hopefully to you, and you give them their food in due season." While the Psalmist here is not necessarily speaking of the need for material food and nourishment, there is another kind of nourishment that we all need. For this nourishment we look to the Lord that he may give it to us. And we have the reassurance of the Psalmist that God does respond to the need which is revealed in the look in our eyes as we turn toward him. He says, "You open your hand to satisfy the desire of every living thing."

Unlike the victims of a war-torn country who are desperately searching for basic physical nourishment to sustain life and who have little hope, perhaps, of receiving it, we have the assurance that in the deeper spiritual needs that we all have God will respond to us and give us what is necessary to satisfy us.

THEOLOGICAL CONCLUSION

Like malnourished children seeking food, we look to God for an inner kind of food, a deep inner fulfillment. We all need this just as much as we need physical food to sustain our bodies in good health. Our consolation is that in turning our eyes to God in hopes and expectations, we will not be deceived. That is the point of the prayer of the Psalmist today—that God does indeed satisfy the desires of every living thing. Starving children cannot always depend on the goodness of other people to feed them. But every one of us can depend on God to satisfy our inner hunger.

EIGHTEENTH SUNDAY OF THE YEAR (SERIES A) HOMILY III

Reading II: *Who will separate us from the love of Christ? . . . Yet in all this we are more than conquerors because of him who has loved us. For I am certain that neither death nor life, neither angels nor principalities, neither the present nor the future, nor powers, nor height nor depth nor any other creature, will be able to separate us from the love of God that comes to us in Christ Jesus, our Lord.* (Rom. 8:35, 37-39)

ANA-GNOSIS

Perhaps one of the people most taken for granted by all of us in our everyday life is the man or woman who delivers our mail. We have a way of simply expecting the mail to be there at its accustomed time. And on the rare occasion that it is not, we become rather irritated. Yet we all realize that there are certain days when it is indeed difficult for these people to deliver our mail. We all have images of the man or woman struggling along in the rain or snow or cold weather with the mail bag in a cart or slung across their shoulder, faithfully making their rounds to bring us the mail. And it's probably only on this occasion that we give any thought to the tremendous service that these people do us and which we usually take for granted. We know, of course, that in the United States the Post Office takes a great deal of pride in its ability to get the mail out. There is evidence of this in the Post Office's almost official model which is taken from the Greek historian, Herodotus, where he describes the messenger system throughout the kingdom of Persia in the ancient days. In this passage Herodotus says, "Nothing stops these messengers from covering their alloted stage in the quickest possible time. Neither rain, nor snow, nor heat, nor gloom of night."[1]

Our postal workers use this quotation as a kind of model for their own efficiency. They don't hesitate to put themselves out, even at times going through suffering, to accomplish their task. And they take great pride in the way that they accomplish it.

THEOLOGICAL EXTENSION

In today's second Reading from St. Paul's letter to the Romans

1. Herodotus, *The Histories.* Book VIII.

we have something of this same model held up to us for the Christion who is truly committed to his or her belief. St. Paul says to us, "For I am sure that neither death nor life, neither angels nor principalities, nor the present nor the future, nor powers, nor height nor depths nor any other creature will be able to separate us from the love of God that comes to us in Christ Jesus, our Lord." Here St. Paul tells us that nothing will get in the way of the Christian who is truly committed to his or her vocation. The committed Christian will suffer any kind of trial or tribulation, even persecution, in order to accomplish the goal that he or she has involved themselves in and committed themselves to. The Christian keeps his eye on that final goal and continually strives toward it, not allowing himself to be sidetracked, or any temporal satisfactions or comforts of life to get in the way of it. He does not allow himself to end up in a pattern of behavior that, while it might be momentarily satisfying, would ultimately defeat him. He knows what his final goal is, he knows the choice he has made for it, and he keeps it always in front of his eyes.

In last Sunday's Gospel we read the Parable about the man who found the treasure hidden in the field and who gave up all he had to obtain that treasure. This is the characteristic of a person who is single-minded in his determination. He has found something of inestimable value in his life and he allows nothing to divert him from it. The same idea occurs in St. Paul's letter to the Romans which we read today. The Christian who has committed himself to a value will not let go of it and will not let anyone stand in the way of achieving it.

THEOLOGICAL CONCLUSION

In the model which we mentioned earlier about the postal worker who, in the attempt to achieve his goal of the delivery of the mail each day efficiently and on time, undergoes the inconvenience of bad weather and other obstructions, we see the accomplishment of a very necessary and worthwhile, but nevertheless, temporary goal. They are totally committed to carrying out their task and take great pride in it, and the model they use can help us in carrying out and achieving of a goal that is more than just temporary, but that is indeed eternal.

If someone would go to that inconvenience and difficulty for a temporary goal, how much more would they willingly put up with for the accomplishment of a goal that assures them of eternal life. Like the man in last Sunday's gospel who had found a treasure of truly great worth and was willing to sell everything he had to obtain it, so we, once we have experienced the love of God in Christ Jesus, would do everything in our power to hold onto this love. We would allow nothing to separate us from it.

EIGHTEENTH SUNDAY OF THE YEAR (SERIES A)
HOMILY IV

Gospel Reading: *When Jesus heard of the death of John the Baptizer he withdrew by boat to a deserted place by himself. . . Then he ordered the crowds to sit down in the grass, and taking the five loaves and two fish he looked up to heaven and blessed and broke and gave the loaves to the disciples and the disciples gave them to the crowds. And they all ate and were satisfied.* (Mt. 14:13-21)

ANA-GNOSIS

Anyone who has been charged with the responsibility of breaking the news of the death of one of their loved ones to a person knows how very difficult this can be. A person with such a responsibility will, of course, want to break the news as gently and as easily as he can, and so he perhaps might think over beforehand, and even rehearse, different ways in which he might tell the person about the death of his loved one so that it won't be too shocking. Perhaps finally he realizes that there is not really any easy way to do this. While he may be able to ease the shock somewhat, there is no way that the pain and grief can be totally avoided. This is all the more true when such news has to be relayed to a child. How, for example, would a child be able to understand the death of his mother, father, brother or sister? Very often the adult will try to break the news by saying something like, "Well, now, your mother is with God in heaven," in the hopes that this will give a more positive tone and ease the shock somewhat. Of course often this is helpful, especially if the child is very young. He does not totally understand but he knows that something is different, something has changed in his life. But perhaps again, in the final analysis, there is no painless way to convey such tragic news to someone.

THEOLOGICAL EXTENSION

In today's Gospel we see Christ working the miracle of the loaves and fishes in order to feed the multitude that had been with him all day. This miracle, of course, was certainly a very gracious act of love and kindness on his part—people were hungry and tired and without food, so Christ responded to their need.

But as great as this physical miracle, the multiplication of the loaves and fishes was, behind it was something else, something on another level that Christ wished to convey to the people. We know that this miracle was a foreshadowing of the Eucharistic Meal, that Christ was later to give us at the Last Supper. Where this same miracle is related in the Gospel of St. John this is clearly indicated because it was the occasion for Christ's discourse on the Eucharist. But Christ surely would have known how difficult it would be for people to accept the doctrine of the Eucharist. We see this difficulty in another place in the Gospels where Christ directly tells the people that they must eat his flesh and drink his blood or they will not have life in them, and we are told there that, on hearing this, many of them left him. In other words, they were shocked and couldn't understand or accept this doctrine that Christ was proposing to them. So here we have Christ performing for them an action, the miracle of the multiplication of the loaves and fishes, which they can understand and relate to much more easily.

If we look for the deeper meaning behind the miracle then, that is, what it foreshadows, it would seem to be that what Christ is saying to the people is that just as he is able to multiply the five loaves and two fishes into enough food to feed five thousand of them, he also, in the same miraculous way, can give them his body and blood to eat and drink in the Sacrament of the Eucharist.

THEOLOGICAL CONCLUSION

Like the small child who would not be able to understand the news of the death of his father or mother, so he is told of it in as gentle a way as possible, so Christ wanted to prepare the people for a far greater miracle that he would later perform in the Eucharistic Meal. Indeed, as St. John tells us in his version of this miracle, Jesus referred to it the next day in order to introduce the promise of a heavenly bread which he would give to them.

And this, of course, was to be his own body and blood under the form of bread and wine. Our belief in this is an act of faith which each one of us makes at the Eucharistic Celebration and which we renew when we receive Christ in Holy Communion.

NINETEENTH SUNDAY OF THE YEAR (SERIES A)
HOMILY I

Reading I: *Elijah came to a cave on the mountain of God, Horeb, where he took shelter. Then the Lord said, "Go out and stand on the mountain before the Lord. The Lord will be passing by." A strong and heavy wind was rending mountains and crushing rocks before the Lord, but the Lord was not in the wind. After the wind was an earthquake, but the Lord was not in the earthquake. After the earthquake there was a fire, but the Lord was not in the fire. After the fire there was a tiny whispering sound. When he heard this, Elijah hid his face in his cloak and went and stood at the entrance of the cave.* (1 Kings 19:9, 11-13)

ANA-GNOSIS

It can often happen that a person will begin an undertaking on behalf of someone else with great enthusiasm and zeal. Such a person may be totally committed and dedicated to the goal or purpose of the other person. He or she willingly takes the other person's suggestions and advice, and abides by the methods that they have suggested; and, of course, as we all know, such auxiliary persons can be tremendously valuable. They may dedicate their entire life to the pursuits of the other person, and this they see as their vocation. It can be a very worthwhile vocation indeed. But very often after a while, if the project doesn't seem to be prospering very well and if things seem to be getting too difficult, these people may quickly become rather discouraged. And in their discouragement they may tend to use innovative methods of their own that turn out to be contrary to the original goal and purpose to which they are committed. They lose sight of the aims to which they have committed themselves on behalf of the other person, and they begin to believe and act as though the entire project depends on them. Then finally, becoming totally disconsolate, they give up all together. And when they do give up this can bring great inconvenience and hardship to the other person who has now come to depend on them. They fail to realize that he still needs their help, perhaps now more than ever.

THEOLOGICAL EXTENSION

We see something of this situation in the first Reading today from the Book of Kings. Elijah has committed himself to being the servant of God. As we know from this section previous to today's Reading, he had labored long and tirelessly in his efforts to try to persuade the Israelites of Yahweh, the true God, because they had gone astray and were beginning to follow the pagan god, Baal.

But after a while Elijah saw that all his efforts seemed to be in vain, that the people were very resistant. And so, in his discouragement, he ran away from the entire project. It seemed to him that God, Yahweh, was not the God that he expected, and that he didn't work according to the way Elijah thought he ought to work. So we are told, "A great and strong wind rent the mountain and broke in pieces the rocks before the Lord, but the Lord was not in the wind. And after the wind, an earthquake, but the Lord was not in the earthquake. And after the earthquake, a fire, but the Lord was not in the fire. And after the fire, a still small voice." In other words, Elijah expected God to be a strong, powerful, and vengeful God, and when it turned out to be otherwise, he was disappointed. But then there is the sudden revelation of God appearing in the form of a "still small voice," "a tiny whispering," we are told. And realizing this, Elijah's faith is once again renewed. He begins to realize that it is, after all, God's project for which he is working and that the whole thing doesn't totally depend on him, that as long as he does his best, God will take care of it in the long run.

THEOLOGICAL CONCLUSION

Like Elijah, we too, can easily be caught in this kind of discouraging situation where, perhaps in a momentary wavering of our faith, we lose sight of the fact that God does know what he is doing and that he will take care of things in the end. Our great consolation, then, is to realize that, having once done our best, we can trust that the rest is in the hands of God, that we only need to have faith; that, after all, we are working for a purpose and aim beyond ourselves. As long as we do not fail to remember this, in God's own way, it will work out for the best, not only for ourselves but for others for whom we are working.

NINETEENTH SUNDAY OF THE YEAR (SERIES A) HOMILY II

Responsorial Psalm: *I will hear what God proclaims; the Lord—for he proclaims peace . . .*
Near indeed is his salvation to those who fear him, glory dwelling in our Land. (Ps. 85:9, 10, 11-12, 13-14)

ANA-GNOSIS

Whenever the people of a particular country are in political or economic turmoil, they will often quickly follow anyone who rises up and offers them some kind of hope and a means of rescuing them from their difficulties. If such a rescuer truly is a leader who has the welfare of the people at heart, then those people are indeed fortunate. He offers them realistic means of repairing the situation, and promises which they not only can securely believe but which he himself truly expects will be fulfilled. Of course we all know the opposite of this kind of situation when a leader comes forth and makes all sorts of rash and unrealistic promises. Then, of course, people are tragically misled and they are worse off in the end than they were before. Such a leader was Adolph Hitler; prior to World War II, the political and economic situation in Germany was desperate. By offering them a kind of utopian existence, he got the German people to follow him, and, of course, we all know the subsequent tragedy that occurred.

THEOLOGICAL EXTENSION

In today's Psalm the theme of the Psalmist is that of salvation. The people are greatly oppressed and almost without hope. But the Psalmist attempts to reassure them that salvation is theirs. He says, "I will hear what God proclaims; the Lord—for he proclaims peace to his people and to his faithful ones, and to those who put in him their hope. Near indeed is salvation to those who fear him, glory dwelling in our land." These are, indeed, reassuring words.

If we were to ask why anyone should put any kind of trust or faith in the words of the Psalmist, because he too could turn out to be a false leader and end up betraying everyone, the answer would seem to be that the Psalmist is worthy of trust because he is not speaking for himself, nor of himself as a savior. He is only speaking what "God proclaims." He says that our salvation indeed is near, if we but have the proper fear, respect and reverence for God. In other words, if the Psalmist were seeking something for himself he might quickly become suspect; but what we read in the Psalm is the proffering of hope and salvation to those who fear God.

THEOLOGICAL CONCLUSION

We are all somewhat aware of the various promises and hopes extended to us by the different Old Testament prophets and that are contained in the Psalms. If we ask ourselves what the credentials are of those who made these promises, we would have to say that these men do not seek anything for themselves. They are clearly offering us this hope and salvation not as something they will give or that is even within their power to give, but as something coming from God. Nor do they offer it as any kind of absolute salvation, that is, that it will be absolutely fulfilled without our participation. It depends on us as well. It depends on our own attitude of respect, reverence and fear of the Lord. Salvation is possible for the Lord to give, but he asks for a response from us too.

NINETEENTH SUNDAY OF THE YEAR (SERIES A) HOMILY III

Reading II: *I speak the truth in Christ. I do not lie . . . For I could wish that I myself were accursed and cut off from Christ for the sake of my brethren, my kinsmen by race. They are Israelites, and to them belong the sonship, the glory, the covenants, the giving of the law, the worship and promises. To them belong the patriarchs, and of their race, according to the flesh, is the Christ who is God over all, blessed forever. Amen.* (Rom. 9:1-5)

ANA-GNOSIS

Not too long ago there was a story in the news to the effect that the head of the U. S. Fish and Wildlife Service had discovered a fortune in bird and animal paintings done by a renowned artist. These paintings had been stored in a vault in his office for years, but they had been ignored. And when the paintings and sketches were at last appraised they were valued at almost half a million dollars. The head of the Fish and Wildlife Service stated that he knew the paintings were there all the time, and he had been anxious to look at them, but for all these years he had never gotten around to doing so. Once they were discovered and their value made known they were appropriately distributed to different museums throughout the country where they could be appreciated by as great a number of people as possible.

Perhaps even closer to your own experience, you personally may have had the great excitement of discovering a family heirloom or some treasure, in your attic or basement. And when you discovered it, it suddenly dawned on you what a valuable possession you had that you had never realized before.

THEOLOGICAL EXTENSION

Something of this tone and mood comes through in the part of St. Paul's Letter to the Romans that we read today. He says in great sadness that, "They are Israelites, and to them belong the sonship, the glory, the covenants, the giving of the law, the worship and the promises. To them belong the patriarchs, and to their race, according to the flesh, is the Christ who is God over all, blessed forever." Here St. Paul is deeply saddened by the fact that the Israelites, his own people, his own race, had in their possession a tremendously rich heritage which they did not seem to be aware of nor were they making use of it.

So intense is he in his concern that they realize the value of their heritage that he utters the unthinkable, "For I wish that I myself were accursed and cut off from Christ for the sake of my brethren, my kinsmen by race." This is indeed a deep expression of sorrow from someone who realizes the value of what someone else has, and hopes that they will come to appreciate its value too.

THEOLOGICAL CONCLUSION

St. Paul's cry of anguish to his own people about not knowing the value of their own possessions is relevant to us as well. We, too, are the heirs of these same possessions. We are the recipients of the same promises that were made to the Jewish people. And, indeed, for us this promise has been realized in the person of Christ. But like the precious treasure of the paintings that were stored in the vault, their value is ignored, our inheritance from Christ can also be met with indifference and unconcern. We may not recognize how valuable it is.

Of course as long as we do not know the value of something we can neither appreciate it nor make proper use of it. It can be there hidden for a long time, like the paintings in the vault. But unless we at some time get around to discovering it and appreciating its worth it has no meaning or value to us. Then the whole thing is wasted. It's wasted until it's discovered.

NINETEENTH SUNDAY OF THE YEAR (SERIES A)
HOMILY IV

Gospel Reading: *Jesus made the disciples get into a boat and go before him to the other side while he dismissed the crowds. After he dismissed the crowds he went up into the hills by himself to pray. When evening came he was there alone, but the boat by this time was many furlongs distant from the land, beaten by the waves, for the wind was against them. In the fourth watch of the night he came to them walking on the sea. But when the disciples saw him walking on the sea they were terrified, saying, "It is a ghost." And they cried out for fear. But immediately he spoke to them, saying, "Take heart. It is I. Have no fear."* (Mt. 14:22-33)

ANA-GNOSIS

We all know what a shock it can be to think we are all alone somewhere and all of a sudden have someone appear in front of us or behind us whom we haven't expected. This can be very startling and momentarily disorienting. It takes a moment to get our bearings once again. For example, you might be out walking at dusk and you think you are the only one on the street when suddenly someone appears in front of you. You may be momentarily stunned until you realize that the person is an old friend you've met and that there is nothing to be afraid of. Or you might be in a room by yourself concentrating on something when someone comes in and speaks to you. Again you are momentarily startled at their presence. But once more you are reassured when you find out who they are and realize that there is nothing to be afraid of.

We all know this kind of startling experience, and if we can we usually try to prepare others instead of startling them. For example, if you are walking in a semi-dark place, like the corridor of a building, and you see someone coming toward you, and you're quite sure they don't see you, you realize that they might be startled if you do anything sudden. So as gently as you can you may call out to them, "Hi, it's just me." And of course then they recognize you and the possible shock is avoided. Ordinarily good manners and kindness dictate that we show this kind of consideration and courtesy toward others.

THEOLOGICAL EXTENSION

We see something of the same thing in the manner of Christ in the Gospel of today's Mass. The situation is this: the apostles are out on the raging sea where there's a storm. They are intent on trying to keep the boat from sinking. It's dark and, of course, they expect no one. Suddenly a figure appears to them on the waves Of course they are terrified. But Christ, recognizing their terror, calls out to them reassuringly, "Take heart. It is I. Have no fear." But even this gentle reassurance does not totally calm them. To test that it really is Christ, Peter says, "Lord, if it is really you, bid me come to you on the water." In other words, Peter wants to make absolutely certain that there is nothing to be afraid of, and so he gets out of the boat and starts walking on the water toward Jesus. But then he begins to doubt and of course he starts to sink. Christ once again has to rescue him.

THEOLOGICAL CONCLUSION

Like the men in today's Gospel we, too, often tend to seek reassurance. Our faith very often is not strong enough to save us, and so we seek repeatedly to have it reconfirmed. Like the person who is suddenly startled when someone comes upon him unexpectedly, and who then needs reassurance that the person really is a friend and there's no danger, we, too, need this kind of reassurance in the matter of our faith. And Christ gives us that reassurance when he says to the disciples, and therefore, to all of us: "Take heart. It is I. Have no fear."

What could be more reassuring than to hear the statement, "Take heart. It is I," from someone whom we know and have known for a long time? Once we realize who it is we may, in fact, be slightly embarrassed at having been alarmed in the first place. We may apologize and say, "I'm sorry; I didn't know it was you." If we have this kind of faith and trust in the reassurance of someone whom we've known for a long time, how much more so can we have faith and trust in Christ himself, who, as he did to St. Peter, also bids us to come toward him. He reassures us there that there is no danger, that he will save us, that he will protect us. As he consoled and reassured Peter, so Christ encourages us to take heart, that it is he. If we trust him then we, indeed, have nothing to fear.

TWENTIETH SUNDAY OF THE YEAR (SERIES A) HOMILY I

Reading I: *Thus says the Lord: Observe what is right, do what is just. . . . The foreigners who join themselves to the Lord, ministering to him, Loving the name of the Lord, and becoming his servants— All who keep the sabbath free from profanation and hold to my covenant, Them I will bring to my holy mountain and make joyful in my house of prayer; Their holocausts and sacrifices will be acceptable on my altar, For my house shall be called a house of prayer for all peoples.* (Is. 56:1, 6-7)

ANA-GNOSIS

At the end of the Civil War, Abraham Lincoln was greatly concerned that the rights and principles embodied in the American Constitution be extended to all peoples. So, for example, he was quick to give amnesty to all the soldiers in the Conferedate Army. Rather than imprison or punish them in any way, he wanted to give them equal status with all other citizens of the United States. The same was true with all those people who had previously been slaves. He was very anxious that the principle of equality be applied to them as well. And we know that, in attempting to implement these rights, Lincoln was met with great opposition, not only from some of the other political leaders of the time, but also from a great many of the ordinary citizens of the country. While many of these people were insistent, of course, on their own rights as given them by the Constitution, they were less quick to see that these rights should apply to all the people of our country. We are all somewhat familiar with the difficult era called the "Reconstruction of the South" when, in an attempt to heal the wounds of the country, Lincoln wanted to give everyone an equal opportunity and to make sure that everyone enjoyed the benefits and privileges that were theirs.

We know how easy it can be for a country or an individual to lose sight of their destiny and to become victimized by a rather narrow and selfish outlook. They can begin to assume that some rights are theirs alone as the destined person or nation, and they refuse to extend these same rights to others.

THEOLOGICAL EXTENSION

In today's first Reading we see Isaiah inveighing against the people of Israel, apparently for just such kind of narrow-sightedness.

As a prophet he knows that God's love extends to all peoples, not just to the Israelites. But he also sees that the Israelites are apparently caught in a rather narrow view of things where they have, as the chosen people, appropriated special rights to themselves alone that they would deny to other nations. While it is true that they were the chosen people of God and, therefore, a nation destined to bring salvation to all the world, and they did have a special covenant with God, they failed to see that this covenant in some way extended to all peoples who accepted it. So Isaiah says to them, "Foreigners who join themselves to the Lord, ministering to him and loving the name of the Lord, becoming his servants—all who keep the sabbath free from profanation and hold to my covenant, them I will bring to my holy mountain and make joyful in my house of prayer." Here Isaiah wishes to remind the Israelites that if they are truly to fulfill their destiny of the chosen people of God of bringing salvation to the entire world, then they must open up and extend the covenant to all peoples. God truly is a father to everyone because he is the maker of everyone. And so anyone who, in the words of Isaiah, "keeps the Sabbath free from profanation and holds to God's covenant" is also included in the destiny of the Israelites as the chosen people.

THEOLOGICAL CONCLUSION

In our personal life we, too, can get caught in a somewhat narrow view of things, and we can tend to think that the way we see things is the way God sees them. When we do, we can sometimes feel a kind of a resentment toward others who are given the same advantages, the same privileges, the same honors that we claim for ourselves by some special right. And so, like the Isrealites in today's Reading, we fail to see that God is the father of all and that God loves all of us, that we are all his children. This realization of God as the father of everyone and not simply of the chosen few is a great consolation for us. No matter how neglected or rejected we might feel, no matter how much we may feel that we are outsiders and on the fringe of things, we always have this reassurance from Isaiah that everyone is acceptable to God who keeps his covenant.

TWENTIETH SUNDAY OF THE YEAR (SERIES A) HOMILY II

Responsorial Psalm: *May God have pity on us and bless us; may he let his face shine upon us.*
So may your way be known upon earth; among the nations, your salvation . . . The earth has yielded its fruits, may God, our God, bless us, and may all the ends of the earth fear him. (Ps. 67:2-3, 5-6, 8)

ANA-GNOSIS

After long and toilsome striving at some task a person may look back on his efforts and see mixed results. While he may clearly see, by hindsight, all his mistakes and failures, he may also see a lot of good results in what he was working at. So in the final evaluation of his effort he may say, "Well, I must have done something right," or "Somebody up there likes me."

These and other similar popular expressions capture the person's awareness that he was not alone in what he was trying to do; that, while he did make a lot of mistakes and in some sense failed, there was a power beyond himself that was somehow overseeing and guiding his efforts. In the long run, then, everything did not necessarily depend on him.

THEOLOGICAL EXTENSION

This same awareness of a dependence on someone beyond ourselves is illustrated in the Psalm of today's Liturgy. The remarkable thing about this Psalm is how God's blessing on Israel is taken as a sign of his salvation for the nations and how all the nations who fear God are filled with his blessing. The Psalmist says, "The earth has yielded its fruits. God, our God, has blessed us. May God bless us and all the ends of the earth fear him." God's blessing can be depended on to come to those who fear him, who have a proper reverence and respect for him. This prayer of the Psalmist is a profound act of faith expressing a dependence on God and not relying completely on his own strength. He recognizes that all things come from God, and to all those who show a proper recognition and humility, God's blessings are forthcoming. So he implores all the people to praise God as the source of their blessings.

THEOLOGICAL CONCLUSION

Oftentimes in the face of our mistakes and failures we can easily become discouraged and give up, thereby defeating ourselves. This happens when we fail to recognize the source of our blessings and when we forget that, in the final analysis, all things come from God. We need always to put forth our best effort in what we do, but having put forth our best effort even though we may fail, we can be encouraged by the fact that, after all, God perhaps wanted it this way though we may not totally understand why. If we remember that God is present in our efforts and we alone are not solely responsible then we can renew our courage. We can continue to work confident that God's blessings will once again be showered on us.

TWENTIETH SUNDAY OF THE YEAR (SERIES A)
HOMILY III

Reading II: *I say this now to you Gentiles: Inasmuch then as I am the apostle of the Gentiles, I magnify my ministry in order to make my fellow Jews jealous and thus save some of them. For if their rejection means the reconciliation of the world, what will their acceptance mean but life from the dead!* (Rom. 11:13-15, 29-32)

ANA-GNOSIS

As children, probably most of us heard or read the Fable of Aesop in which the fox tries to grab a bunch of grapes that are just out of reach. Try as he might though, the fox does not succeed in getting the grapes and so, in disgust and discouragement, he walks away saying, "Well, they were probably sour anyway."

This is a feeling that we, as adults, have probably had from time to time too. We even use the phrase "sour grapes" to describe the attitude of a person who, when he wants something that he can't have, dismisses it as not being worth having anyway.

The danger and difficulty with this attitude is that it can be self-defeating because it can cause us to refuse to make any further effort to gain something which in itself is a great good and which, with a little more or a little different effort we could actually have. And if we get into a similar situation with people, we may close all doors on any further communication with whoever is involved. We may walk away from them and never wish to speak to them again.

THEOLOGICAL EXTENSION

We can easily see how St. Paul might have been faced with this same potentially self-defeating situation. He saw that his own people, the Jews, had rejected the agent of reconciliation of the world, the long awaited Messiah, and that there wasn't much that he could do for them. So he went off to work among the Gentiles and to bring to them all the promised blessings and the redemption that had been intended for his own people. One might easily imagine here a kind of "sour grapes" attitude on the part of St. Paul. He could have felt that his own people were not worthy of his efforts and that there was no use in trying. He would simply reject them altogether. But we see in today's second Reading from St. Paul's Letter to the Romans that he does not get caught in this kind of self-defeating attitude. On the contrary, he keeps the door open to some future reconciliation to the Messiah by his own people, the Jews. Instead of writing them off as lost, he says, "I magnify my ministry to the Gentiles in order to make my fellow Jews jealous and thus save some of them."

While in a sense this may sound like a strange procedure on St. Paul's part it nevertheless reveals a man who deeply loves and cares for his own people and holds open the possibility of future acceptance. He says, "For if their rejection means the reconciliation of the world, what will their acceptance mean but life from the dead!" Instead of seeing their rejection as an offense beyond the forgiveness and mercy of God, St. Paul, on the contrary, says,

"The gifts and the call of God are irrevocable." In other words, the invitation to them is always open; God does not close the door to them and neither does he. In fact St. Paul implies that it is precisely because of their disobedience that the greater mercy of God and the greater forgiveness is due to them.

THEOLOGICAL CONCLUSION

We, too, can easily "write people off" in our frustration and discouragement with them. But like St. Paul we need to realize that their rejection of us puts on us all the greater challenge to remain open to them, not to close the door, to trust in the future possibility of reconciliation with them. Just as we ourselves are always in need of God's mercy and forgiveness, so are those who reject us. Perhaps they have all the greater need of it. And for this reason they may need us as an instrument of their future reconciliation. We must be willing to be that instrument, remaining open to them, willing to welcome them whenever they may return. To react in a "sour grapes" fashion is to give up on someone, and God, even though he may be disappointed in people at times, never gives up on them. Neither should we.

TWENTIETH SUNDAY OF THE YEAR (SERIES A) HOMILY IV

Gospel Reading: *Jesus withdrew to the district of Tyre and Sidon . . . But he answered, "It is not right to take the food of sons and daughters and throw it to the dogs." "Please," she insisted, "even the dogs eat the leaving that fall from their masters' tables." Jesus then answered her, "Woman, great is your faith! Be it done for you as you desire."* (Mt. 15:21-28)

ANA-GNOSIS

The expression "knotholer" is a term usually associated with the game of baseball. It has its origins in the early days of baseball when the playing field and the bleachers were surrounded by a wooden fence. Of course the boards in the fence had knotholes in them, and people, most often youngsters who could not afford to pay to get in to see the game, would watch it through these various knotholes. People who did this, then, were called "knotholers."

Such youngsters who watched the game this way were obviously on the fringe of things. They were not really a part of it, and perhaps they even had a vague feeling that they were doing something illegal or wrong. But, in any case, they were considered, and considered themselves, "outsiders," although usually the owners of the teams were quite considerate of them. An incident is related in which one of the owners of a baseball team in the early days, being told about all the knotholers watching the game, invited them all in to see the game without charge. We can imagine their joy and delight at suddenly becoming a part of something that at first they were merely on the fringe of and even feeling somewhat guilty about.

THEOLOGICAL EXTENSION

In the incident about the knotholers we see a parallel to today's Gospel story about the Canaanite woman. As a Canaanite she was, of course, a foreigner and not among the chosen people. So in a sense she could be thought to have had no right to hear the words of Christ and to benefit from his miracles. She was clearly an outsider, very much on the fringe of things. And yet she so persisted in her begging that Christ responded to her plea. He obviously recognized in her someone who understood very clearly what he was about. So he says to her, "O woman, great is your faith! Let it be done for you as you desire." Christ's miracle on behalf of the Canaanite woman is all the more remarkable when we realize that only in one other instance did our Lord's dealings with Gentiles involve the working of a miracle, namely that of the healing of the Centurion's servant at Capernaum.

But like the youngsters who were invited by the owner of the baseball team to enter the stadium and see the game properly, we can imagine the even more tremendous joy of this woman when Christ performed the miracle of healing her daughter. Through her persistence in prayer and through her great faith, she received what she had asked for.

THEOLOGICAL CONCLUSION

From the example of this Canaanite woman we can learn a great deal. She offers us in her deep and unquestioning faith much that we can imitate. Although she was an outsider she did not cease in her prayer, in the prayer that her own deep faith prompted in her. And our encouragement from this example is that no matter how much we see ourselves as "outsiders" at one time or another, due to our many faults, failings, and sins, if we persevere in our prayer Christ will hear us. We can trust that, as he did with the Canaanite woman, he will always recognize the faith that is behind our prayer and he will unfailingly answer that prayer.

TWENTY-FIRST SUNDAY OF THE YEAR (SERIES A)
HOMILY I

Reading I: *Thus says the Lord, the God of hosts: Up, go to that official, Shebna, master of the palace:*
"I will thrust you from your office and pull you down from your station . . . I will place the key of the house of David on his shoulder; when he opens, no one shall shut, when he shuts no one shall open." (Is. 22:15, 19-23)

ANA-GNOSIS

There is a proverb which states, "If you wish to know what a man is, place him in authority." This proverb, of course, implies that when a person is in a position of authority and responsibility he is also in a position to do either good or harm to others. We all know people, whether in politics, in business, or in other walks of life—perhaps in some instances people very close to us—who were suddently put into a position of responsibility and the position brought out the best in them. They responded in a manner which redounded to their own honor and to the good of those who were under them. But, of course, we also know the opposite of this. We know people who have been in positions of authority where they tragically abused it. They forgot the purpose for which they were put in that position in the first place and they become high-handed and devious, autocratic toward others under them. Fortnuately for everyone concerned they were finally removed from their position or forced to resign, sometimes in terrible disgrace and embarrassment to themselves and to others who were close to them.

THEOLOGICAL EXTENSION

In today's Reading from Isaiah we have just this example of

the abuse of power. The steward of the household whose name was Shebna, apparently exceeded his authority by urging the king Hezakiah to revolt against Assyria and call Egypt to his aid. Isaiah was really opposed to this idea because it implied the Israelites' failure to trust in their own God by calling in pagan help from the outside. So through the prophet Isaiah God says, "I will thrust you from your office and pull you down from your station . . . I will place the key of the house of David on his shoulder. When he opens, no one shall shut; when he shuts, no one shall open."

In the exercise of his authority, the steward was thwarting the plan of God by calling in outside help in the Israelites' revolt against Assyria. Anyone who would be disloyal to God's plan would, of course, need to be deposed, and this is what happened to the steward in today's Reading. He became so filled with worldly ambition that he failed to see the ultimate end of God's plan.

THEOLOGICAL CONCLUSION

Like the steward, we sometimes forget our own eternal interests through our single-minded pursuit of the goods of this world. Often when we are in a position of authority or responsibility to others we seek our security in temporal goods, goals and aims. And in doing this, we fail to realize that there is an ultimate purpose, a purpose to God's plan, and unless we exercise our position of authority in a responsible way, we too, instead of being an instrument for the furtherance of that plan, are an instrument in blocking it. So, like the steward, we too would need to be deposed.

Whether we are in a position of authority as Christians or not, we have an obligation to others; especially we have the obligation to them of being a good example. By being overzealous for temporal things, although not wrong in themselves, we are in danger of misleading others and causing them to place their ultimate faith in these temporary things. In this sense each of us is subject to abusing authority which we all possess as Christians.

TWENTY-FIRST SUNDAY OF THE YEAR (SERIES A) HOMILY II

Responsorial Psalm: *I will give thanks to you, O Lord, with all my heart, for you have heard the words of my mouth . . . The Lord is* *exalted, yet the lowly he sees, and the proud he knows from afar.* (Ps. 138:1-2, 2-3, 6, 8)

ANA-GNOSIS

One of the popularly understood meanings of the word charisma—apart from its theological meaning—is a kind of quality that certain people, especially leaders, possess. A person who has a touch of "charisma" seems to be able to establish immediately a kind of identity or rapport with another person or even with very large groups. The person, or even an entire group feels a personal relationship to the charismatic person.

Various people come to mind who had this quality. Pope John XXIII would be one of them. Exalted though his position was, when he was with large groups of people everyone immediately felt a very personal kind of relationship to him. Every person in his presence felt that they mattered as individuals, that Pope John saw them in a special way. Other such people were Martin Luther King or John Kennedy. Many of us can remember that at the death of Kennedy, people all over the world wept. Even though they had never met him or talked to him they felt a personal loss. They had lost a friend.

THEOLOGICAL EXTENSION

Such is the nature of the prayer of the Psalmist today. He says, "The Lord is exalted, yet the lowly he sees." Sometimes, because of the notion that God is so exalted and so far above us, we think he is also removed, distant and impersonal. How could such a distant and remote figure have any personal relationship with you or me in our lowly condition? How can he touch us in any direct, immediate way? Yet in spite of our lowly condition we are persons of worth in his eyes. The Psalmist gives us the reassurance that this is so. As lowly as we may see ourselves in relationship to God, God nevertheless has a personal relationship with us and we can trust in this relationship. The Psalmist says, "When I called you, you answered me. You built up strength within me." This is, indeed, a very personal response from God. Anyone of us can call on God in sincerity and humility and be reassured that he will answer. This is the point of today's Psalm.

THEOLOGICAL CONCLUSION

Just as we often feel this kind of personal closeness to a great leader or great figure of our own time, even though he may have a very exalted position and be far removed from us, all the more so is this true of our relationship with God. God sees all of us, and we are his children. He has personal warmth and relationship to us. It is a great consolation that we find in the Psalm today: contrary to our image of God as removed, distant and possibly frightening, he is a very warm and personal father who truly cares about each of us. He assures us all that he hears and will answer our prayers.

TWENTY-FIRST SUNDAY OF THE YEAR (SERIES A) HOMILY III

Reading II: *O the depth of the riches, the wisdom and knowledge of God! How unsearchable are his judgments, and how inscrutible his ways! For "who has known the mind of the Lord? Or who has been his counselor? Who has given a gift to him that he might be repaid?* (Rom. 11:33-36)

ANA-GNOSIS

Sometimes when a person receives a valuable and expensive gift from someone, his immediate reaction might be a reluctance to accept it. He may fear that there is no way he could ever repay the person for such a gift or even thank him adeuqately for it, and so he hesitates about taking it. He might even say, "Well, you know I can never repay you for this. You realize that, don't you?" This kind of reaction on the part of the recipient might stem from the fact that he feels himself unworthy of it, or that it puts him under some kind of obligation to repay in some manner the person who gave the gift, instead of seeing it as a true gift. It's almost as if he feels he is entering into a kind of bargain, a "quid pro quo," even though the thing was intended strictly as a gift. So not wanting to put himself under obligation because he realizes the impossibility of his repaying it, he refuses it or at least attempts to make sure that the other person understands his situation.

THEOLOGICAL EXTENSION

This kind of reluctance that we may have with one another to put ourselves under obligation to them by accepting some extremely valuable thing, or the tendency we might even have to enter into a bargain with them, is something, of course, that we cannot do with God. St. Paul says to us, "For who has known the mind of the Lord? Or who has been his counselor? Or who has given a gift to him that he might be repaid?" This statement expresses our complete dependency on God. And as we often do with one another, we might tend to feel the same way with God, namely, how can we possibly repay him for what he has given us? And knowing that we cannot possibly repay him, we might feel a little reluctance to be too dependent on him. But this dependency on God and the acknowledgement of him as the source of all we have is the whole idea of worship. We know from elsewhere in the Scripture that we, of ourselves, are nothing, that everything that we are and have comes from God. But instead of this knowledge putting us in a negative relationship with God, through the virtue of worship it gives us worth, dignity and meaning for our existence.

Calvin Coolidge once said, "It is only when men begin to worship that they begin to grow." That is, it is only when we begin to recognize God as the source of all that we have and all that we are that we move toward a deeper understanding of the infinite wisdom and goodness of God.

THEOLOGICAL CONCLUSION

A person who gives us a very valuable and expensive gift realizing that we cannot repay them, does not expect any kind of repayment or bargain. Most often they are just grateful when we offer them some sign or recognition of what they have done. This is all that they wanted in the first place. They didn't want to put us under any kind of negative obligation to them or imply that we had to pay them back. What would be the point of that kind of gift?

Certainly this is all the more true with God. He surely knows that we cannot pay him back, and so he puts us under no obligation to repay. The only obligation that we all have is to worship him, that is, to recognize and acknowledge him as the source of our whole being, our whole life and all that we are depends on him. And the acknowledgement of this is, of course, what worship is all about.

TWENTY-FIRST SUNDAY OF THE YEAR (SERIES A) HOMILY IV

Gospel Reading: *When Jesus came to the neighbourhood of Caesarea Philippi, he asked his disciples this question: "Who do people say the Son of Man is?" And they said, "Some say John the Baptist, others Elijah, and others Jeremiah or one of the prophets." He said to them: "But who do you say that I am?" Simon Peter replied: "You are the Christ, the Son of the Living God."* (Mt. 16:13-20)

ANA-GNOSIS

It is common for people in public life to spend a great deal of energy and effort to create a certain image of themselves in the minds of other people. This is true, for example, of politicians who attempt to cultivate in the minds of their constituents a certain image that they would like to represent. We might think, too, of movie stars who even change their names in order to create a certain image of themselves as public figures. Such persons are very careful to control as much as they can the circumstances of any public appearance that they make. If they appear on television, for example, they want to make sure their appearance is just so, and that they say things that will not antagonize others or will not destroy the image that they hope others will have of them. Of course we know how devastating it can be when such a person actually does lose his public image. Very often it can destroy his entire career and he may even end up in disgrace because people find out "who he really is," and are then disillusioned with him.

THEOLOGICAL EXTENSION

This kind of developing of a public image is something that Christ might easily have done, but which he very clearly avoided. The people's idea of what the Messiah should be took different forms; some of them thought he would be a great military leader or some other kind of great temporal ruler who would free them from the bondage of the Romans. But, of course, this was not the image that Christ had of himself at all. In fact, he did many things that actually antagonized the religious leaders of the time and violated their notions of who the Messiah ought to be. Instead of falling for or being trapped by the popular image of the Messiah, Christ constantly holds very profoundly to his own integrity in explaining who the Messiah was—not a temporal ruler at all, but someone who represents to the people eternal values. Christ did not have one public and another private image. He was, as we say in popular language, "himself" all the time. He always let people know who he was, and so there could be no disillusionment on the part of the people.

In his humanity, Christ also had a need to know that at least some people understood him for who he was. And so he asks his disciples, "But who do you say that I am?" And the response is Peter's spontaneous outburst, "You are the Christ, the Son of the Living God." Jesus then appointed him as the leader of the future church.

THEOLOGICAL CONCLUSION

There are many and often strong temptations in all our lives to be someone that we are not, to create a certain image of ourselves that we would like others to believe. But we all know that this can sometimes be a very difficult image to uphold; all of our energy and efforts are concentrated on trying to keep it intact. And there's always the danger that when the image doesn't hold, people will be disillusioned with us and sometimes even embittered.

The great lesson for us from Christ in today's Gospel is that, apart from this being the occasion on which he appointed Peter as the head of his Church, he gives us an example of personal integrity. We cannot escape who we are no matter what image we might attempt to portray to others. But rather, by firmly holding to and respecting who we are with whatever talents and abilities we have, with no need to defend them or pretend that they are more than they really are, we are true to ourselves, and we can trust that at some point some people will recognize this and respect us for it. If other people will do this, so much more will God himself do this as he knows us completely as our maker. This is a great consolation from the example of Christ. We can trust that even if no one else understands or knows who we are, God does. And in the end we will be recognized for who we are.

TWENTY-SECOND SUNDAY OF THE YEAR (SERIES A)
HOMILY I

Reading I: *You duped me, O Lord, and I let myself be duped . . .*
All the day I am an object of laughter; everyone mocks me.
Whenever I speak, I must cry out,
Violence and outrage is my message;
The word of the Lord has brought me derision and reproach all the day. (Jer. 20:7-9)

ANA-GNOSIS

Throughout the history of mankind there has never been a lack of people who claimed to be prophets and did, in fact, make various prophesies. Different religious denominations, for example, from time to time have predicted the end of the world. Then, of course, when their prediction didn't come true they were ridiculed by people and lost many of their followers. But usually they were able to come up with some kind of reason why the prediction didn't come true. Even in our own time a number of people who claim to see into the future and foretell events come to mind. Sometimes these people are correct in their predictions. That is, the event that they foretold does, in fact, happen. But many times, of course, it fails to come true, and then they are held up to derision, mockery and ridicule by others, and people tend to lose faith in them.

THEOLOGICAL EXTENSION

Whether any of our modern day prophets are true prophets or not, we need not consider here. In any case, our familiarity with them can give us some feeling and sense of the situation of which Jeremiah speaks in today's Reading. We accept the fact that Jeremiah was a true prophet, a true mouthpiece for the word of God. Jeremiah was by nature a gentle and peaceable man, and so it was a great torture to him to have to foretell to his own people their own impending destruction that would follow their plan of revolt against the power of Babylon. At the time of Jeremiah's prophecy about the destruction of his own people this seemed far off and unreal. Everything at the present moment seemed prosperous, and the dire things Jeremiah was predicting seemed impossible. They had not happened, and so he was ridiculed by his people. Then, in bearing the anguish of a true prophet, he cries out, "All the day I am an object of laughter. Everyone mocks me. Whenever I speak I must cry out, violence and outrage is my message. The word of the Lord has brought me derision and reproach all the day."

In spite of Jeremiah's reluctance to carry out the burden that God had imposed on him, he nevertheless found the courage and strength to do it, even in the face of the scorn and mockery of his own people.

THEOLOGICAL CONCLUSION

The sufferings of Jeremiah can serve as an encouragement to us to bear whatever sufferings our own Christian faith might entail for us. At times we, too, may be called on to take a courageous stand for what we believe in, knowing that others will not understand us. In doing so we leave ourselves open to their mockery and ridicule. Yet like Jeremiah we are not prevented because of this from carrying out our Christian duty whether others understand it or not. We trust that in the long run God's plan will be carried out and that good will come out of it, that the suffering and anguish we have endured will not be in vain. Then we have the satisfaction of knowing that, difficult as it was, we have done our part as Christians.

TWENTY-SECOND SUNDAY OF THE YEAR (SERIES A) HOMILY II

Responsorial Psalm: *O God, you are my God whom I seek; for you my flesh pines and my soul thirsts like the earth, parched, lifeless and without water . . .* (Ps. 63:2, 3-4, 5-6, 8-9)

ANA-GNOSIS

The folklore saying, "You don't miss the water 'til the well runs dry," is one of those expressions whose origin has been lost over time. But it obviously goes back a rather long time to when people customarily drew their water from a well either by pumping it out with a hand pump or by drawing it out with a winch. Of course in some countries people still do that. In small villages especially there is a well in the center of town where people go to draw water. Naturally they take it for granted that the water is going to be there—they depend on it being there—until some tragic incident, such as a prolonged drought, causes the well to dry up. Then, of course, people realize how blessed they were when they had water.

In modern times we wouldn't usually speak of the "well going dry" in industrial countries, but we do have something of the same experience, for example, when the electric lights go off or when the water system in town breaks down and people are temporarily without water. In recent years in our own country where there have been prolonged spells without rain, people have been asked to conserve water, and in some places it was even rationed. These people would certainly have a very vivid experience of the value of water and of its place in their life. It is not something that can be taken for granted. When they do have it they treasure it and acknowledge its source.

THEOLOGICAL EXTENSION

This experience of lack of water and of intense thirst is the image that the Psalmist uses today to portray for us what life would be like without God. Intensely as we miss the water that quenches our thirst and waters our crops, even more intensely would we miss the presence of God. So the Psalmist says, "O God, you are my God whom I seek; For you my flesh pines and my soul thirsts like the earth, parched, lifeless, and without water."

We all know how desolate and foreboding the earth can be in those areas that are afflicted by drought. The crops are burnt, and there is often nothing but dust and useless dead shrubbery. So also with our spiritual needs. Without God as a fountain and a source of life, we thirst, we are parched. We are barren and dusty like the land that has not had rain for a long time.

The Psalmist's prayer here today is a prayer of thanksgiving.

He recognizes God's presence in the sanctuary for him. He recognizes the value and the meaning of God and what his life would be like without God. He says, "For your kindness is a greater good than life."

THEOLOGICAL CONCLUSION

Just as we often take for granted those things which seem to be abundant and always there, such as water, and we do not miss it until we are in need of it and it is gone, so too with God. We all need to be constantly aware of a need of God's presence in our life. Like the water which is necessary, he sustains and supports our whole being. Without him, indeed, we would be like the earth, "parched, lifeless, and without water."

TWENTY-SECOND SUNDAY OF THE YEAR (SERIES A) HOMILY III

Reading II: *Brothers, I beg you through the mercy of God to offer your bodies as a living sacrifice holy and acceptable to God, your spiritual worship. Do not conform yourselves to this age, but be transformed by the renewal of your mind, so that you may judge what is God's will, what is good, pleasing and perfect.* (Rom. 12:1-2)

ANA-GNOSIS

One of the words quite popularly used in recent years is *uniqueness.* By *uniqueness* we understand that quality or that characteristic which makes a person whatever he or she is, whatever causes that person to stand out, to be an individual, to be distinct from other people. Now our uniqueness is something that, of course, we are all very proud of and which we insist on maintaining. One expression of this was heard in a song that was recently popular. The opening lyric was, "I gotta be me." The lyrics expressed the idea that each person wants to be himself and resists any kind of imposing on that self or someone trying to make him to be something he is not. To be unique is something that we want very much to hold on to.

But the idea of uniqueness is also somewhat paradoxical because to be unique also presents a kind of a threat. In other words, to be myself, to be different from others, to express my uniqueness means to stand out, to somehow be different. The threat of this is that in being different from others, I may appear as a kind of an oddball, and as such I am open to ridicule and condemnation. To prevent this, my natural tendency is to conform quickly to what others want or to be what I think others would want me to be. So in conforming I deny, in a way, my own uniqueness. This then is the paradox of uniqueness: that while we are all very proud of it, at the same time we are somewhat threatened by it.

THEOLOGICAL EXTENSION

Now something of this paradox is what St. Paul confronts in his Letter to the Romans in today's Liturgy. There is the strong natural tendency on the part of the people to conform to the present age. That present age was, of course, very materialistic in the sense that it had weak spiritual values and, much like in our own time, everyone was expected to conform to the values of the age. Anyone who did not conform immediately stood out as someone being different, and because they were different they were open to ridicule and rejection of others. So it would take a great deal of courage for anyone not to conform, not to "be like everyone else." And yet this is what St. Paul is asking the people of Rome at that time to do.

In other words, to be a true Christian means to exert one's uniqueness, to stand out, to take the risk of being different. So, St. Paul says, "Do not conform yourselves to this age," but rather, be transformed by the renewal of your mind." The dictionary definition of the word *transformed* equates it with the idea of change, even a change in one's basic nature. That would be the meaning St. Paul is exhorting here. He wants them to make a basic change in their way of looking at things, a change from a materialistic viewpoint to one that is more spiritual.

THEOLOGICAL CONCLUSION

Much of what St. Paul says in his Letter to the Romans here is relevant to our own time. We all know from our own personal experience the strong temptation to conform to the materialism of our own time. It is much easier to go along with it and be allowed to be "at peace" rather than to be different, and to live in the danger of rejection by others. So we go along with what others expect of us.

But this, according to St. Paul, is not the meaning of the Christian way of living. The true Christian is one who takes the risk of a complete about-face, a complete change in the very nature of his way of seeing things, a "transformation," as he calls it. And it is only by making this kind of change, this transformation, this renewal of our mind, that we are then able to truly judge "what is God's will, what is good, pleasing and perfect."

TWENTY-SECOND SUNDAY OF THE YEAR (SERIES A)
HOMILY IV

Gospel Reading: *From then on Jesus the Messiah started to indicate to his disciples that he must go to Jerusalem to suffer greatly there at the hands of the elders, the chief priests and the scribes, and to be put to death and be raised up on the third day. And Peter took him, and began to rebuke him saying, "God forbid, Lord, that this should ever happen to you." But he turned and said to Peter, "Get behind me Satan. You are a hindrance to me, for you are not on the side of God but of man."* (Mt. 16:21-27)

ANA-GNOSIS

There is a natural expectation in all of us that those whom we look up to as leaders should in some special way be dignified—more dignified than the ordinary people. And thus we surround the office of our presidency with a great deal of respect and dignity and awe. We accord willingly certain privileges to our leaders that we would perhaps even resent in ordinary people. For example, we have no difficulty in allowing them to have their own special chauffeurs and cars to go places in, their own bodyguards to protect them, and people to look after them and see to their needs in a special way. We accept all this because we look to them as our leaders, and as such, we willingly give them privileges that we would not expect others to have and which we would not expect for ourselves. This also applies to their personal appearance. We would all probably be quite shocked if our President appeared in public on television wearing, say, at T-shirt and a pair of blue jeans. We would expect greater dignity than this and would be offended at this apparent lowering of the status of all our leaders.

THEOLOGICAL EXTENSION

People at the time of Christ obviously had these same expectations of their own leaders. And inasmuch as the disciples saw Christ as a leader, as a Messiah, they had these expectations of him. So when Christ tells the disciples that he is about to be subjected to an outrageous indignity, they are shocked. As we see in today's Gospel, "Peter took him and began to rebuke him, saying, 'God forbid, Lord. This shall never happen to you.'" The shock on Peter's part came from the fact that this was a violation of his natural expectation that, as a leader, Christ should not be subjected to this kind of indignity; and if Christ were subjected to it, it would somehow, by implication, be an indignity to Peter. Now while we can understand and respect this kind of concern on Peter's part for Christ, nevertheless his action here seems to indicate that he had not yet grasped the spiritual nature of the kingdom that Christ was establishing, so Christ says back to him, "Get behind me Satan. You are a hindrance to me." That is, Christ was saying to Peter that he was, for all his good intentions, nevertheless impeding God's plan. If Christ did not suffer and die, submitting to the horrible outrage of the crucifixion, then eternal life could not be earned for us. It was in God's plan that it should happen this way. In a sense Christ was saying that because his kingdom was spiritual and not concerned with material values, that Peter and the other disciples had to see it from a whole different perspective.

THEOLOGICAL CONCLUSION

In the second Reading of today's Liutrgy, in the letter to the Romans, we saw there St. Paul's concern was for a change in the outlook of people, that they begin to see things on the spiritual side. Here, too, Christ asks for the disciples to change their perspective and realize that unless Christ submitted to the cross the salvation of all mankind would be thwarted. And this is what we are called upon to do ourselves. We are asked to see in greater depth the real plan of our salvation. And if we do, we will not be shocked at what seems to be the great indignity that Christ suffered, because it was out of this indignity that God brought salvation for us.

INDEX

Agent
—of reconciliation, 77
Allegory, 38
Ambassador, 43
Anxiety, 2
Attitude
—of prayer, 45
Authority, 81
Awesomeness, 28

Baptism, 21
Blessing
—of God, 76
Blushing, 11
Bounty
—source of, 36
Brotherhood, 5

Champion, 2
Change, 40, 46, 92
Charisma, 83
Christ
—as a door, 22
—Spirit of, 29
Commitment, 10, 31
Convenience, 7
Conviction
—courage of, 8
Coolidge, C., 85
Covenant, 74

Death, 21
Decay, 37
Dependence, 75, 85
Discouragement, 13, 66
Doubt, 13
Drought, 33, 90

Effort
—wasted, 57
Entertainment, 1
Equality, 73
Eucharist, 63
Evidence, 43
Evil, 39, 47
Expectations, 93-94

Fables
—of Aesop, 38, 76
Faith, 21, 64, 71
—demands of, 7, 30
Fantasy, 49
Fear, 14, 71
Flesh
spirit of, 30
Forbearance, 42
Forgiveness, 12, 41
Freedom, 37, 51
Friendship, 19, 32
Futility
—of life, 37

Gift, 17-18, 36, 84
Goal
—Final, 61
God
—as father, 74
—awesomeness of, 28
—forgiveness of, 12
—love for us, 20, 53
—plan of, 82
—word of, 34

Heart
—understanding, 50

Hero
—theme of, 1
Herod, 10
Herodotus, 60
Hitler, A., 67
Hope, 68
—of Christ, 39
Humanity
—of Christ, 87
Humility, 26, 50

Image, 86
Instrument
—of God, 10
Investment, 55
Invitation, 31

Joy, 37, 39

Kindness, 42
Kingdom
—of God, 47, 55
"Knotholer," 78

Law, 51
Leader, 25, 67, 93
Leaven, 46-47
Life
—according to flesh, 30
—new, 21
—value of, 32
—without God, 90
Limitations, 52
Love
—between God and man, 53
—source of, 36
Loyalty, 30

Mail, 60
Malice, 39
Merit, 38
Merton, T., 22
Miracle
—of loaves and fishes, 62-63
Misunderstanding, 3
Model
—of suffering, 60-61
Motivation, 50

Nature, 28, 33
Needs, 45

Nourishment
—spiritual, 59

Oneness, 5
Outsider, 79

Parable
—of the sower, 39
Paranoia, 2
Pardon
—from God, 36
Path, 35
Power
—abuse of, 82
Praise
—hymn of, 35
Prayer, 45, 80
—of Solomon, 50
Predictions, 88
Prejudice, 6
Prison, 36
Promise, 70
Purpose, 52, 55, 82
—lack of, 37

Reassurance, 14
Reconciliation, 77
Redemption, 6
Rejection, 3, 77
Relationship
—to God, 83
Responsibility, 10, 50
Reward, 12
Rules, 51

St. Peter
—courage of, 15
Salvation, 67
Sir Galahad, 38
Solomon, 49
Spirit
—of Christ, 29-30
Symbol, 38

Terror, 71
Tracking, 35
Transformation, 93
Treasure
—buried, 55
Trust
—fulfillment of, 10
Truth, 40

Uncertainty, 13
Understanding, 3-4, 42
—heart, 50
Uniqueness, 91

Value, 55, 87
Victims
—of war, 58
Vocation, 61

Wastefulness
—of life, 37
Water, 90
Word
—of God, 34
Worship, 85

Yearning, 18
Yoke
—of Christ, 31

SECOND SERIES

Volume VI-2

THE WORD BECOMES FLESH

A Psychodynamic Approach to Homiletics and Catechetics and Meditation

Homilies for the Twenty-Third
to the Thirty-Fourth Sunday of the Year

(Series A)

CHARLES A. CURRAN
Loyola University
Chicago, Illinois

APPLE RIVER PRESS
P.O. Box 3867
Apple River, Illinois 61001

NIHIL OBSTAT:

Reverend Thomas G. Doran
Censor Deputatus

IMPRIMATUR:

✠ Arthur J. O'Neill
Bishop of Rockford

August 1978

Printed in the United States of America

CONTENTS

Preface vii

TWENTY-THIRD SUNDAY OF THE YEAR 1
Homily I 1
Homily II 2
Homily III 4
Homily IV 5

TWENTY-FOURTH SUNDAY OF THE YEAR 8
Homily I 8
Homily II 9
Homily III 11
Homily IV 12

TWENTY-FIFTH SUNDAY OF THE YEAR 14
Homily I 14
Homily II 15
Homily III 17
Homily IV 18

TWENTY-SIXTH SUNDAY OF THE YEAR 21
Homily I 21
Homily II 22
Homily III 24
Homily IV 25

TWENTY-SEVENTH SUNDAY OF THE YEAR 28
Homily I 28
Homily II 30
Homily III 31
Homily IV 33

TWENTY-EIGHTH SUNDAY OF THE YEAR 36
Homily I 36
Homily II 37
Homily III 39
Homily IV 40

TWENTY-NINTH SUNDAY OF THE YEAR 43
Homily I 43
Homily II 45
Homily III 46
Homily IV 48

THIRTIETH SUNDAY OF THE YEAR 50
Homily I 50
Homily II 51
Homily III 53
Homily IV 55

THIRTY-FIRST SUNDAY OF THE YEAR 57
Homily I 57
Homily II 58
Homily III 60
Homily IV 62

THIRTY-SECOND SUNDAY OF THE YEAR 64
Homily I 64
Homily II 65
Homily III 67
Homily IV 68

THIRTY-THIRD SUNDAY OF THE YEAR 70
Homily I 70
Homily II 72
Homily III 73
Homily IV 75

THIRTY-FOURTH SUNDAY OF THE YEAR and
FEAST OF CHRIST THE KING 78
Homily I 78
Homily II 79
Homily III 81
Homily IV 82

Index 85

THE HOMILIES IN THIS BOOK HAVE BEEN WRITTEN BY

REV. DANIEL D. TRANEL, Ph.D.

ACCORDING TO THE INSEMINATIONAL MODEL

DEVELOPED BY

Rev. Charles A. Curran, Ph. D.
of Loyola University, Chicago

PREFACE

In the following homiletic and catechetical expositions, there are at least *four* for each Sunday and feast. Each one begins with an "ana-gnosis." This is not an ana-logos. That is, it is not intended to be an analogy or simply an example. We have called them "ana-gnoses" rather than analogies, because they are aimed at involving the reader or hearer personally at the level of his own *gnosis* about himself.

Analogy, in the *logos* sense, is too intellectual and remote for what we mean here. The hope is that each person will begin to commit himself and so be talking to himself while he hears or reads. He will thus hopefully be creatively reacting and so giving a homily to himself at the level of his own personal memory and experience.

These presentations are not intended to be all-inclusive. They are only *one form* of communicating the scriptural message. Hopefully their advanced reading may stimulate the reader not simply to memorize them—he or she may do this of course, and, we hope, profitably—but rather, as a result, to move on to his own personal witness and communication with his hearers. They are, therefore, intended basically to be personal stimulants and encouragements starting the reader or hearer on his own personal quest.

One will notice here that the *immediate human meaning* is most often seized upon—not some more complicated and subtle theological conclusion. This is not to deny the latter or its importance. It is rather to draw attention to the basic and rich human elements that are so often central to the scriptural message. The intent too is to initiate a process by which the hearer, or the reader, is allowed to enter into the presentation through its immediate human meaning.

To aid in this, the speaker should simply be himself, speaking in whatever way is most comfortable to him. His natural manner

would therefore usually be more often meditative than dramatic, more conversational than theatrical, allowing for the electronic apparatus to carry his words directly into the ear of the hearer—as in an intimate communication together.

These presentations are all *short;* some are very short. People often seek a short homily or catechetical presentation. But since they are short, further doctrinal and similar material may be added to them, as fits the occasion. Or, more than one may be given.

There is also the allowance for the possibility that later dialogue will extend and develop the embryonic concepts here. In this sense, what happens after words enter the ear is more important than before. This is the "germination" process; that is, seed once entered the soil and embraced by it, germinates and grows there. The entering may be quick—as the acorn enters quickly—but slowly and mysteriously over time, a great oak with powerful branches where birds abide and sing, can result. We have described elsewhere the group dynamic process that, we feel, could aid this.[1]

The model, therefore, is not the mathematics book: problem-solving which arrives at "answers." Our model is the familiar sower who goes out to sow seed. This is our inseminational aim and hope.

These themes are based on a personal approach to homiletics and catechetics, the psychological background of which is explained in detail in a separate volume: *THE WORD BECOMES FLESH: A Psychodynamic Approach to Homelitics and Catechetics* (Theory and Practice).

1. Curran, C. A. *Religious Values in Counseling and Psychotherapy.* Apple River Press: Apple River, Illinois, 1969, pp. 231-248.

TWENTY-THIRD SUNDAY OF THE YEAR (SERIES A)
HOMILY I

Reading I: *You, Son of Man, I have appointed watchman for the house of Israel . . . . . . If I say to the wicked, "Wicked man, you shall surely die, and you do not speak to warn the wicked to turn from his way, that wicked man shall remain in his iniquity, but his guilt I will require at your hands."* (Ez. 33:7-9)

ANA-GNOSIS

One of the difficult and often painful duties a responsible adult has to perform from time to time is that of warning others of their mistakes or shortcomings. Parents, for example, must point out the occasional wrongfulness of their children, teachers must do the same for their students, and employers for those who work for them. It would be much easier simply to close an eye to the evil and mistakes that we see around us or to rationalize it by saying that to correct someone "won't do any good anyhow." So we are strongly tempted not to say anything because we might cause a ruckus, but rather to ignore the situation and hope that it will soon go away.

We all know how much courage it takes to point out to someone the erroneous path they have taken. Yet, because we recognize our responsibility to them and also because we care for them, we must take the risk of warning them of the wrongfulness of their action even though they might interpret our speaking out as interference in their affairs.

THEOLOGICAL EXTENSION

This is the same situation that the prophet Ezekiel seems to have found himself in in today's first Reading. He is charged by God to point out to the Israelites the wrongfulness of their ways and to warn them to desist from their wrongdoings. As God's prophet, he has a grave responsibility for the salvation of his people. And in having this serious responsibility placed on him by God, Ezekiel must have felt much of the same fear and anxiety that you or I would feel when we take the risk of pointing out to someone the falsity of their ways. But in spite of all the misgivings he must have felt, we see that Ezekiel had the courage to carry out the task God had imposed on him. He obviously trusted to some power, in some strength, beyond himself and realized that, of himself, he could not possibly undertake thie great task.

THEOLOGICAL CONCLUSION

As Christians, we are all, in a sense, God's prophets. We all have the obligation of letting the light of our own faith shine before others. Oftentimes this entails great risk. We are never certain how well we will be received by those for whom we intend the best. They might misunderstand us, they might ridicule us, they might reject us. And yet, in today's Reading we are given a great consolation for taking this risk. While we will be required to give an account of how well we have carried out our responsibility to others, we are reassured that, having done this, the rest is in the hands of God. God says, "If you warn the wicked to turn from his way, and he does not turn from his way, he will die in his iniquity, but you will save your life." We are here called on to do our Christian duty, and once having done it, we can rest secure in the knowledge that we have "saved our life."

TWENTY-THIRD SUNDAY OF THE YEAR (SERIES A) HOMILY II

Responsorial Psalm: *Oh come, let us worship and bow down, let us kneel before the Lord, our Maker. For he is our God, and we are the people of his pasture, and the sheep of his hand.* (Ps. 95:1-1, 6-9)

ANA-GNOSIS

Any responsible writer of a book tries to be very careful when he quotes an authority to document his position; he gives proper recognition to that authority in his work. Consequently he makes sure he gives the proper references and footnotes so that due credit is given to the person whom he is quoting, and so there is no mistake on the part of the reader about where the statement came from. This is one of the reasons, for example, for our copyright laws. They are to protect the originator of an idea against plagiarism by others who might use that idea without acknowledging its originator. Occassionally we hear of an instance where someone is sued because he failed to give proper recognition to the true discoverer of a new idea. We can all understand how the originator of an idea would truly like to be recognized as the authority and as the one who discovered it. This is not a matter of simple pride; rather it is the proper recognition that is due to that person. It is true that there may be elements of jealousy and false pride in the author or the originator of something new, but on the whole we willingly overlook this, or allow the person to have these feelings, often out of gratitude to him or her because we recognize the significance of their accomplishment.

THEOLOGICAL EXTENSION

While we do not attribute to God human feelings, passions, and such, we can nevertheless see something of this very human element in the Psalm today. The Psalmist exhorts us, "Let us worship and bow down, let us kneel before the Lord, our Master." Here we are being called back to a recognition of the true source of not only all that we have, but of our very existence. In this Psalm of praise God is recognized as our Maker, as the one to whom true worship is due. The people for whom this Psalm was originally written were constantly in danger of attributing all their blessings and all the things they had to a false source, even sometimes to themselves. So they needed to be reminded of the true source of their salvation, of the one true God who is their Maker.

THEOLOGICAL CONCLUSION

Just as the author of a book takes time to credit the sources from which he draws his material, so we, the Psalmist says, should take the time and make the effort to acknowledge God as the source of our being. Even more than the limited contributions of a few talented people should deserve our recognition, the creative work of God should cause us to stop and reflect on the power and goodness of our Creator. He is the source of us all and we must never forget it.

TWENTY-THIRD SUNDAY OF THE YEAR (SERIES A) HOMILY III

Reading II: *Owe no one anything, except to love one another, for he who loves his neighbor has fulfilled the law.* (Rom. 13:8-10)

ANA-GNOSIS

Anyone who has ever been in debt knows, perhaps after years and years of struggle to pay off the debt, the good feeling of making that final payment. Perhaps it was the final payment on a house, or on a car, or some other possession. After the final payment was made, perhaps even a little celebration was held. The person might have said, "Now I will be able to sleep better at night." Even if the debt is still there, anyone who has been making continued payments knows how he anticipates the joy of finally getting that debt paid off. He looks forward to the feeling of relief that from now on he won't have to worry about those monthly payments, and that perhaps he can even save a little from time to time. It's a wonderful feeling of security to know we don't owe anyone anything. We feel free and in the clear, and from now on no one can make any further demands on us because we owe them nothing.

THEOLOGICAL EXTENSION

While this obviously is a wonderful feeling to have, it can be also somewhat misleading. It can cause a person to have a sense of smugness, or a feeling that he or she no longer has anyone who can make some kind of a claim on them. So it can be a bit startling to read in St. Paul's Letter to the Romans that, in another sense, while we may have paid off our temporal debts, we are never really out of debt. St. Paul says, "Owe no one anything, except to love one another." This is a kind of debt that no matter how much or how often we pay on it we are never free of it. Or if, as St. John tells us, God is love, then to be free of the obligation to love, in other words to stop loving, is to cut oneself off from the source of love and, therefore, of life. It is to stop living. Like a quiet lake that is fed deep down by the flow of hidden springs which no one can see, so a person's love is grounded in God's love. To stop loving is to stop living, to stagnate. This is why St. Paul tells us we can never get out of the debt of loving one another.

THEOLOGICAL CONCLUSION

None of us would ever think of stopping our payments on a temporal debt that we might be under until the final payment was made. When we hear of people who do that sort of thing they strike us as being quite irresponsible people whom we could not really trust. But when we have finally made the last payment, we rightly feel a sense of relief. For the true Christian there is one debt from which there cannot be that sense of relief until the moment when we are reunited with God who is love itself. This is the debt of loving one another as ourselves and God above all. We can never fully pay this debt, and it is also one we would never want to be fully paid off or come to an end. For through our loving one another and our Lord our lives have meaning and we draw nearer to the source of all love, God.

TWENTY-THIRD SUNDAY OF THE YEAR (SERIES A) HOMILY IV

Gospel Reading: *"Where two or three are gathered in my name, I am in their midst."* (Mt. 18:15-20)

ANA-GNOSIS

One statement that we are all familiar with is, "With friends like these, who needs enemies?" This expression is intended to catch the idea that a person can be often victimized by well-intentioned, but naive, friends. Such people are not malicious, nor do they consciously intend to harm one, but very often this is the effect that comes about because of their lack of full understanding about what one stands for; because of their untempered enthusiasm, or maybe because of some need of their own that is being met in their association with the person, they end up harming him or her. Sometimes the association can become so painful for the person that he or she may at some time have to disavow it and thereafter avoid these people.

THEOLOGICAL EXTENSION

Something of this same eventuality can occur in our relationship to Christ. In today's Gospel Christ says to us, "For where two or three are gathered in my name, there am I in the midst of them." The presence of Christ in the midst of those who are gathered together in his name is, of course, very reassuring and consoling, but the difficulty is how to know if we are truly gathered together "in my name" or if we are gathered together in our own name. A person may, in all sincerity, believe that he is performing a great good or doing something for the sake of someone else and for the sake of Christ, when in fact, upon a little closer inspection, it might appear that he is not in it for the other person at all, as he might think he is, nor is he in it for the sake of Christ. He is in it perhaps only because, whatever the involvement might be, it meets some personal need. Such a person might say, "You know I'm really not getting anything out of this. It's not for myself that I'm doing this, it's only for your good." But that's not always true. It is difficult to determine sometimes whether or not our actions are truly for the other person or if they are not actually for ourselves. We all have many selfish needs that without realizing it, we seek to fulfill by the sometimes unjust use of others. When we do this there is no question but that Christ cannot be present among us, for it is not in his name that we are doing this or that thing, but in our own.

THEOLOGICAL CONCLUSION

So while it is very encouraging to realize the presence of Christ among us where we are gathered together "in his name," we need to take sometimes a very vigorous look at our motives and our reasons for being gathered together. We need to ask ourselves constantly whether we are acting for ourselves or for the other person, as we claim to be. If we find that our true motive is selfish then what we are doing becomes distorted and merely caricatures of Christ's presence. To avoid this takes a constant vigilance and self-examination. But in the end, then, we will turn out to be true friends of Christ and not someone who has used him for selfish gains and with whom he was never really present.

TWENTY-FOURTH SUNDAY OF THE YEAR (SERIES A) HOMILY I

Reading I: *Anger and wrath, these are abominations, and the sinful man will suffer vengeance from the Lord, and he will firmly establish his sins. Forgive your neighbor the wrong he has done, and your sins will be pardoned when you pay.* (Sir. 27:30, 28:7)

ANA-GNOSIS

We can all remember a time in our life, perhaps many times, when we have offended someone or hurt them physically, and we could not be at peace with ourselves until we had received forgiveness. We can recall our relief then when the person sincerely forgave us and the wounds were once again healed and we were restored to their friendship. Since the forgiveness of others is something we all need, one might think that the most natural thing in the world would be that when one person has hurt another, the other would very naturally be ready and willing to forgive. Yet, as natural as this kind of forgiving one another would seem to be, we know in fact that the opposite is true. To forgive someone is no easy thing. A much more natural tendency is to hold a grudge against the person or to seek revenge rather than to forgive. To forgive someone, then, since it is not natural, requires a conscious effort or choice on the part of each one of us whenever someone has injured us or seeks revenge on us. It seems to constitute a kind of contradiction: namely, that while we all need forgiveness, we find it very difficult and unnatural to grant forgiveness to others.

THEOLOGICAL EXTENSION

This contradiction is something that we read about in today's first Reading from the book of Sirach. We read, "Does a man harbor anger against another and yet seek for healing from the Lord?" Just as it would be a contradiction for us to seek forgiveness from others without offering to them the same forgiveness, even more so would it be a contradiction to seek forgiveness from the Lord, to expect him to hear our prayers, when we harbor vengeance against our neighbor.

THEOLOGICAL CONCLUSION

The natural impulse to seek vengeance on those who have hurt us, who have insulted us or offended us in some way can be difficult to overcome. Forgiveness is not natural. It is something that we must make a special effort to do. But our consolation from today's Reading is knowing that ultimately God will see that justice is done. For ourselves to seek vengeance is, in a way, to pretend that we are God. It is taking onto ourselves a prerogative that God claims for himself. We need to trust that he will accomplish justice. In the Lord's prayer Christ tells us we must "forgive those who trespass against us." It is only in this way that we can expect the forgiveness of others, and also the forgiveness of God.

TWENTY-FOURTH SUNDAY OF THE YEAR (SERIES A) HOMILY II

Responsorial Psalm: *Bless the Lord, O my soul, And all my being, bless his holy name . . . He will not always chide, nor will he keep his anger forever. He does not deal with us according to our sins, nor requite us according to our iniquities.* (Ps. 103:1-4, 9-12)

ANA-GNOSIS

Whenever we hear of a criminal who has been sentenced in a court of law to a term in prison for the crime he has committed, one of our first thoughts is whether or not the punishment is suitable. If we feel that the punishment was not stringent enough we might comment that the criminal "got off too easy." This question arises, too, in issues of a much less serious nature. Parents, for example, are often faced with the responsibility of punishing their children, and naturally they want to choose a punishment that is appropriate to the misbehavior of the child. If the misbehavior is not too serious, then of course the punishment will not be too great either.

Whether it is the judge passing sentence on the criminal or the parent punishing the child, it can sometimes be difficult to know if the punishment does, in fact, fit the crime. Sometimes there is no real way of knowing this. When a person commits murder, for example, is it right that he should be given the death penalty? Should he spend the rest of his life in prison or should he be given a certain number of years in prison? Perhaps in some unusual case, he should be left off without any punishment at all. These are difficult questions to answer, and, of course, there is much disagreement about this issue. It sometimes may appear that whatever the punishment, it was, at best, somewhat arbitrary.

THEOLOGICAL EXTENSION

This issue of "whether the punishment fits the crime" is one that can also be raised in regard to our relationship to God. We may ask, "What punishment really would be suitable for our sins and the wrong-doings we have committed against him?" As we know, any sin is fundamentally a rebellion against God, a refusal to recognize him as our creator. We who are guilty of such acts of rebellion would seem, by our own choice to merit a very severe punishment. But in today's Psalm we are reminded of God's mercy. The Psalmist tells us, "He does not deal with us according to our iniquities." The punishment obviously, if it were given, should be a very severe one. Yet we are reassured that it is tempered with God's mercy. Because of God's mercy he does not really deal with us as he ought, he does not punish us as we truly deserve.

THEOLOGICAL CONCLUSION

In spite of the overwhelming guilt that we may feel for the sins we have committed, we can always be reassured of God's mercy and forgiveness. Unlike our human tendency to be satisfied only if the punishment is suitable to the crime, God does not seem to be concerned about the punishment. He is concerned about our own sense of sorrow and of our return to him. When we return to him in sorrow he is there to forgive us and he overlooks the real punishment we deserve.

TWENTY-FOURTH SUNDAY OF THE YEAR (SERIES A) HOMILY III

Reading II: *None of us lives as his own master, none of us dies as his own master. While we live we are responsible to the Lord, when we die we die as his servants. Both in life and in death we are the Lord's. That is why Christ died and came to life again that he might be Lord of both the dead and the living.* (Rom. 14:7-9)

ANA-GNOSIS

Perhaps one of the greatest fears that all of us have is that of being alone. This concern is expressed, for example, when people talk about their fear of old age. Much of their anxiety centers around their realization that most of their friends will have preceded them in death and they will be left alone, perhaps uncared for and with no sense of belonging. We also see this anxiety expressed in the deeply human need we all have to join different clubs or organizations. We all need to belong to someone, to have some identity so that we will not be left with that horrible sense of being alone and lonely. This concern that all of us have about loneliness is perhaps also at the basis of our natural fear of death. What could be more anxiety provoking than the feeling that after death we will be all alone!

THEOLOGICAL EXTENSION

In his Letter to the Romans St. Paul addresses himself directly to this issue. He says, "Both in life and in death we are the Lord's." For the true Christian, there is really no need to fear being cut off from others, to have this sense of alienation and of non-belonging. The Christian always belongs to Christ. We know from another place in his Letters that St. Paul tells us Christ has taken "the sting" from death. This is what he means: that in this life, as long as we belong to Christ, we are not alone. Death, far from changing this, brings us even closer to Christ. For the Christian who dies there is an even greater sense of intimacy and communion with Christ. Whether living or dead we are one in Christ.

THEOLOGICAL CONCLUSION

This can be a very comforting awareness for all of us. While we all have a natural fear of being left alone, perhaps in our old age, or an even greater fear of loneliness and isolation after death, our faith reassures us that once we belong to Christ we are not at all alone. We can begin to see that there is not a very dramatic difference between life and death. Death for the Christian is more of a transition from this life to the next life. It is a means to a more intense unity and sense of belonging with Christ. For the one who has been baptized into Christ the fear of death has truly been removed. Death is not "the enemy" but a step toward closer life with Christ.

TWENTY-FOURTH SUNDAY OF THE YEAR (SERIES A)
HOMILY IV

Gospel Reading: *Peter came up and asked Jesus, "Lord, when my brother wrongs me, how often must I forgive him?" . . . So the servant fell on his knees imploring him, "Lord, have patience with me, and I will pay you everything," And out of pity for him the Lord of that servant released him and forgave him the debt.* (Mat. 18:21-25)

ANA-GNOSIS

When a person goes to a bank for a loan, he borrows money for a definite period of time. It might be for six months or a year or maybe longer. But there is a definite agreement between the person borrowing and the bank that the money will be paid back at the end of the agreed upon time, along with any interest that might have accrued. Most often the person borrowing feels fairly certain that, given the present economic circumstances of the country, it is not unreasonable to hope that he will be able to pay back the debt in whatever time was agreed upon. But if, at the end of that time, he finds himself unable to pay back all of the loan, he will go to the banker and try to arrange for an extension. He might say, "I'll just need a little more time and I'll be able to pay the whole thing off." So they arrange for an extension, and naturally when he is given the extension, he is very grateful.

THEOLOGICAL EXTENSION

Something of a parallel to this situation exists in the Parable of today's Gospel. The man in the Parable was deeply in debt to his master and so he says, "Lord, have patience with me and I will pay you everything." The master very generously does more than give the servant additional time in which to pay off the debt; he simply writes off the whole thing.

One would naturally expect that, having been the recipient of such generosity, the servant would be generous to those who were in debt to him, that he would be very lenient with them since his master had been lenient with him. But we see that the opposite occurs. Instead of passing on the generosity, the servant is all the more harsh toward those who owe him money. When the master hears about the servant's cruelty, he punishes him all the more severely.

THEOLOGICAL CONCLUSION

Christ uses this very powerful Parable to impress upon us the importance of forgiving one another. We have all been the recipients of enormous gifts from God, some of which perhaps we are not even aware of, and many which we probably do not even deserve. What Christ seems to be saying to us in the Parable is that, just as we have been the beneficiaries of God's generosity, so we should pass on the same forgiveness and love to others. We should have the same readiness as God to forgive and love those around us. Unlike the servant in this Parable we must pass on the generosity shown to us. Only then will we truly be sharing in God's Kingdom and doing the work of Christ on earth.

TWENTY-FIFTH SUNDAY OF THE YEAR (SERIES A) HOMILY I

Reading I: *Seek the Lord while he may be found; call Him while he is near . . . for My thoughts are not your thoughts, nor are your ways My ways, say the Lord.* (Is. 55:6-9)

ANA-GNOSIS

Psychologists use the term "projection" to describe a particular phenomenon. This occurs when one person "projects onto" or attributes to another person his own thoughts or feelings. It is the assumption, in other words, that another person or other people feel and see and think about things the same way as oneself. Obviously this kind of thing can be the cause of great misunderstanding and eventually of hurt and pain. The person who does the "projecting" can often be quite surprised when someone else replies, "Well, you know that's not at all the way I feel about it or the way I see it." So while a person may derive a great deal of security and reassurance by imagining that others think and feel the same as he does, he can leave himself open to misunderstandings. Such a person fails to realize that other people are separate and distinct human beings—that they are unique in their own person and so they have their own particular way of seeing things and of viewing them.

THEOLOGICAL EXTENSION

If this is a mistake we often make with one another, failing to recognize each person's separateness and uniqueness, how much greater would be the falsity and misunderstanding if we were to do this same thing with God who is infinitely above us and totally distinct and separate from us. Even though God made us to his own image and likeness, he is nevertheless not like us in the sense that he is infinitely above us and so we do not have the capacity to understand the workings of his mind. That is why Isaiah quotes God in today's Reading, as saying, "For my thoughts are not your thoughts, neither are your ways my ways."

At the time of Isaiah there were people among the Israelites who thought their sins were so great that not even God could forgive them. But our Lord says this is not necessarily so, for his mercy, understanding and love are infinite in comparison to our own mercy and love and understanding. So, when we imagine that God sees the same as we do, we make the mistake of denying his infiniteness. While we might find it extremely difficult, for example, to forgive another person for something he has done, because to us it appears too evil, we need to realize that God does not necessarily see it this way. In his infinite mercy God has the capacity to forgive every sin, no matter how great it might be.

THEOLOGICAL CONCLUSION

By projecting onto God the feelings, the thoughts, the ideas that we ourselves have, and by imagining that God sees everything in the same way, we show a lack of trust in God. It is as though we don't really believe his mercy and love are infinite, and that he does not get caught in the same narrow view of things that sometimes can trap us and cause us to defeat ourselves. When we imagine God in this limited way we set up a kind of false god. Instead of doing this we need to accept our own separateness from one another and also from God. In this way we allow God to be who he is and to do things in his own way. Just as we cannot presume to know how others think, we cannot presume to know about the thoughts of God.

TWENTY-FIFTH SUNDAY OF THE YEAR (SERIES A) HOMILY II

Responsorial Psalm: *The Lord is near to all who call upon Him . . . . the Lord is good to all, and His compassion is over all that He has made.* (Ps. 145:2-3, 8-9, 17-18)

ANA-GNOSIS

There is a tendency in people that causes them to seek security in belonging to a select or chosen group. Sometimes such a group is referred to as a clique, and those who belong to the clique may tend to see themselves as superior and in some ways "better" than those who are on the outside. Many of us, perhaps as adolescents in high school, have experienced the painful situation of not belonging to one of these cliques. The person who didn't belong saw himself or herself as an outsider with no real sense of being a part of things. The popular students in the high school belonged to the clique and were in on the running of things. And while they personally had a sense of security and belonging, those on the "outside" often had a very difficult and painful experience.

THEOLOGICAL EXTENSION

Such a feeling of being on the fringe of things, of never quite being a part of what's going on, can be true of adults as well. But in today's Psalm we are reassured that "the Lord is good to all, and His compassion is over all that He has made." As the creator of all of us, God is equal in his kindness and in his compassion to each one of us. For God there are no "outsiders." We all belong to Him, for as His creatures, we are part of Him. The "arms" of God are open to all of us, and no matter how cruelly we may seem rejected by others in this or that particular group, God does not exclude us. His love and mercy and compassion extend to everyone.

THEOLOGICAL CONCLUSION

No matter how cruelly we may be made to feel by not belonging, we can be reassured of always being able to go to God. He will never turn us away. As the mercy and love of God are extended to all of us, so we, too, need to reach out to and include others in our own kindness and compassion. As Christians we follow the example of Christ. This means that we reject no one, turn no one away. He wanted to bring God's love to all people, and it is part of our Christian vocation to help him however we can.

TWENTY-FIFTH SUNDAY OF THE YEAR (SERIES A) HOMILY III

Reading II: *Christ will be exalted through me whether I live or die. For to me "life" means Christ. Hence, dying is so much gain. If, on the other hand, I am to go on living in the flesh, that means productive toil for me and I do not know which to prefer. I am strongly attracted by both for I long to be freed from this life and to be with Christ for that is the far better thing, yet it is more urgent that I remain alive for your sake.* (Phil. 120-24, 27)

ANA-GNOSIS

It can be amusing to watch a small child faced with several different kinds of candy to choose from. Usually he ends up trying all of them, sometimes with the unfortunate result of getting a stomach ache. And, as adults, we, too, know what it is to be faced with several conflicting goals, all of which appear to be equally attractive. Unlike the small child, we want all of them, but we usually have to decide in favor of only one. If there is no immediate need to make a decision, however, we usually put off our choice as long as we can, hoping that something will develop to help us decide on one or the other. In the end though, helped by the movement of events or not, we finally have to make a choice.

THEOLOGICAL EXTENSION

We see something of this conflict between two equally desirable goals facing St. Paul in the Reading today. St. Paul is torn between "life in the flesh," that is, earthly existence, which he sees as very valuable in aiding those over whom he has responsibility, and death, which would give him life in Christ. He says, "I long to be freed from this life and to be with Christ for that is the far better thing. Yet it is more urgent that I remain alive for your sakes." We see here in the words of St. Paul a magnificent willingness to be used as an instrument in the hands of God. So free is St. Paul that he no longer claims dominion over his own life; rather he leaves it in the hands of God. If God wants to take him to himself, that is a great good, but if, in his plan, God has more work for St. Paul to do, he equally accepts that. In either event he is totally willing to go along with what God's plan for him is.

THEOLOGICAL CONCLUSION

One might say that the child, faced with the large selection of candies, all of which appear equally attractive to him, is not really free. He finds himself in a conflicting situation. But as we grow in Christian maturity, like St. Paul, we could become more and more free and more open to God's plan for us. This does not mean, of course, that we never make decisions, sometime even painful decisions. We are all many times faced with conflicts wherein we must make a choice, but in making the choice we recall that ultimately all is in the hands of God. Then, like St. Paul, whatever best suits that plan we would allow to happen so that we could effectively further his kingdom.

TWENTY-FIFTH SUNDAY OF THE YEAR (SERIES A) HOMILY IV

Gospel Reading: *Jesus told his disciples this parable: "The reign of God is like the case of the owner of an estate who went out at dawn to hire workmen for his vineyard . . . . "I am free to do as I please with my money, am I not? Or are you envious because I am generous? Thus the last shall be first and the first shall be last."* (Mt. 20:1-16)

ANA-GNOSIS

It is not uncommon for a motorist who has been stopped by the Highway Patrol for speeding to protest his innocence by saying that he was not driving any faster than any of the other drivers. In fact, he may say that many other motorists were going even faster than he was. While such an excuse is usually to no avail, it does make the point that if, in fact, the motorist was stopped for speeding when other cars were passing him, what disturbs him more than anything is the seeming injustice of it. While the speeder may even admit that he was in violation of the traffic laws, he wants to see others receive the same punishment that he is going to receive. He wants to see the law applied equally to everyone.

This, of course, is the nature of all human law. If it were not applied, at least in some measure of equality to everyone, then it would lose its purpose and its meaning. We know, for example, that even our judges, legislators, and high officials of government are not supposed to be exempt from the law. If they break the law they are subject to the same punishments as we are. So while at times we may resist the law or consider a particular law to be outmoded, useless or even unjust, at least we have the consolation of knowing that it will be applied equally to everyone.

THEOLOGICAL EXTENSION

We would all agree that even though some of our laws have their limitations, they are the best that human ingenuity can devise to insure some kind of justice and equality. They aim to treat everyone equally and fairly. In the Parable of today's gospel about the laborers in the vineyard, strictly speaking, there was no law applicable. But we nevertheless see a situation quite different from the one we try to establish with our human laws. We see here that what applies to man may not necessarily apply to God. Not only is God above the law, but he is above any human way of seeing things.

In the first Reading of today's Liturgy from the Prophet Isaiah, we read, "For my thoughts are not your thoughts." This is to say, it can be difficult for us at times to understand God's plan for us. This is the reason for the "grumbling" that we read about in this Parable. Those who worked the entire day considered themselves treated unjustly by the master since they did much more work than the ones who started at the last hour. But the master says to them, "Do you begrudge my generosity?" The master obviously sees things differently than the laborers. For his own reasons he chooses to give the last as much as the first.

THEOLOGICAL CONCLUSION

From a human point of view this seems unfair or even cruel. Just as we all expect to be treated equally before the law, so we also expect to be given a fair return for what we have done and to be treated equally when we are recipients of someone else's generosity. But this is only from a human point of view. We do not know God's design, so we must trust that whatever he does for us is ultimately working for the fulfillment of his plan.

Instead of ourselves being the judge of what is right and equitable, we must learn to leave this judgment to the mystery and wisdom of God. For it is God who sees our inner hearts and knows our true value, and it is he who rewards us accordingly.

TWENTY-SIXTH SUNDAY OF THE YEAR (SERIES A)
HOMILY I

Reading I: *"You say, The Lord's way is not fair. Hear now, House of Israel, is it my way that is unfair or rather are not your ways unfair."* (Ez. 18:25-28)

ANA-GNOSIS

A person in public life who is responsible for the successful outcome of a specific project or task that involves the public welfare will often have others assisting him or her in the project. If one or several of the people who are thus engaged makes a slip-up and the whole task fails, usually one of the first things that the journalists will do will be to look to the person "at the top." In other words, they try to find the person who is responsible for the overall outcome and demand an explanation from him or her as to why it failed. There is an understandable tendency on the part of the person in the responsible position to disavow any connection to the failure. He or she may tend to offer the excuse that a subordinate made a slip-up and that is what caused the entire endeavor to go awry, but that he or she had nothing to do with it. Even though this may, in fact, be true, generally we have very little patience with what appears to be merely an alibi. It seems to us that the person is trying to disclaim any responsibility for the failure by putting the blame on someone in a less responsible position.

In contrast to this, we all admire the person who, even though the fault was not directly his own, steps forward and takes responsibility for it instead of making excuses or seeking someone to blame. This would be one of the true characteristics of maturity —to be responsible for whatever one has invested in or taken on.

THEOLOGICAL EXTENSION

The prophet Ezekiel in today's first Reading is attempting to impress this fact upon the people of his own time. At that time there was a notion prevalent among the Israelites that the sins of the parents were punished in their children. What Ezekiel wanted to point out was that each person, because of his own free will, was responsible for his own actions. Each person was directly answerable to God for whatever he did; it was false to think that misfortunes befalling someone are the result of his parent's sinfulness. Much later on, Christ had to remind the Apostles of this when they asked him, "Who sinned, this man or his parents?" because the man was blind (John 9:1-2). The mission of the prophet in today's Reading, then, is to disabuse the people of the notion that they could easily project their own faults, failings or misfortunes onto someone else. Each one of them had to take personal responsibility.

THEOLOGICAL CONCLUSION

Like the mature and responsible public official who openly accepts responsibility for a task to which he is committed instead of looking around for others to blame for its failure, we, too, need to look at our own tendency to blame others. Instead of pointing to others as the cause of our faults and failures, we must realize that we all have our own sins, and it is for these that we will be held responsible.

This can be both disturbing and reassuring at the same time—disturbing in the sense that, as Christians, we can no longer "pin the blame" on someone else, but reassuring in the sense that we are not the victim's of someone else's failings and shortcomings. The outcome of our life is determined by our own free will in cooperation with the grace of God.

TWENTY-SIXTH SUNDAY OF THE YEAR (SERIES A) HOMILY II

Responsorial Psalm: *Remember your mercies, O Lord . . . . . . Good and upright is the Lord, therefore he instructs sinners in the way. He leads the humble in what is right, He teaches the humble the way.* (Ps. 25:4-9)

ANA-GNOSIS

There is an ancient saying, the origin of which is lost in time, to the effect that a person who knows that he does not know is open to being taught. From this it would seem to follow that the first requirement for learning anything is the admission that one does not know it in the first place. If one thinks he already knows something, obviously it is impossible to teach him. Parents and teachers, for example, know the frustration of trying to teach someone who continually repeats the same mistake and yet will not admit that he doesn't know where the mistake lies. It is so much easier and more pleasant to teach a child or a student who openly acknowledges that he does not know something and is willing to be taught. Then the parent or teacher will particularly respond to whatever it is that the learner wishes to know. Any teacher knows the joy of teaching a student or a class of students who have that kind of openness.

THEOLOGICAL EXTENSION

This same kind of openness of learning seems to characterize the notion of humility of which the Psalmist speaks in the Liturgy today. He says, speaking of God, "He leads the humble in what is right, and teaches the humble his ways." The humble person, because of his right knowledge of himself, willingly admits when he doesn't know something. It is possible, then, to teach him. The arrogant person, by contrast, the one who keeps insisting that he is right even though he may be making the same mistakes time and again, is incapable of learning. It is only when he will admit his ignorance that he can begin to find out what he doesn't know. Similarly we need to acknowledge our own sinfulness before we are capable of acquiring virtue. The Psalmist reassures us that "God will lead the humble in what is right," and basic to being "humble" is the acknowledgement of our own sinfulness.

THEOLOGICAL CONCLUSION

Even with the best of intentions people may make many mistakes and do many things that are contrary to God's will. But to persist in them because we don't want to admit we were wrong or have something to learn is to compound the evil. We all need to be open to be instructed "in his way."

This kind of humility can be difficult to arrive at. The more deeply a person is invested in a particular way of life the more difficult it can be to change. For in order to change, one would have to admit that what he was doing in the past was not correct. To avoid facing this somewhat painful admission, the person may choose to continue in his own wrongdoing, to prove to himself that he has been right all along. Such a person, as long as he maintains this attitude, can never be humble enough to follow in God's way. Once he is willing to accept his own ignorance and sinfulness though, he can begin to learn from the Lord and grow in what is right and conform more closely to "the Way."

TWENTY-SIXTH SUNDAY OF THE YEAR (SERIES A) HOMILY III

Reading II: *In the name of the encouragement you owe me in Christ, in the name of the solace that love can give, fellowship and spirit, compassion and pity, I beg you . . . . have this in mind among yourselves which was in Christ Jesus, who, though he was in the form of God, did not count equality with God a thing to be grasped, but emptied himself taking the form of a servant, being born in the likeness of men and being found in human form, humbled himself and became obedient unto death, death on a cross.* (Phil. 2:1-11)

ANA-GNOSIS

A friend or associate of someone who is especially renowned, talented or important, such as a movie star or a president, will sometimes seek for themselves vicarious privileges and honors because of the association. Such a person may not have any particular ability, talent or claim to fame on his own, but he can derive a great deal of satisfaction in seeking the same honors and privileges that are the right of his famous friend. Such a person can often make himself obnoxious by his arrogant and demanding behavior in the name of the person he claims to represent, and if challenged he may say, "Don't you realize that I am a friend of So-and-so?" While this is perhaps true, it does not mean that the person "really is somebody"; there is a note of falsity about his identity. He is trying, it seems, to claim more than he has a right to.

THEOLOGICAL EXTENSION

In today's Reading from the letter to the Philippians, St. Paul gives us an opposite example of this from Christ. He says, "Though he was in the form of God, he did not count equality with God a thing to be grasped, but emptied himself out, taking the form of a servant, being born in the likeness of man." Certainly if anyone could have claimed vicarious honors and privileges because of his association with someone much greater, it would have been Christ. After all he was the Son of God, and as such, he would have been in a position to set himself up as superior to all other people. Had he done so, it would not have been false, because truly he was superior. But instead of doing all that, he took on a human form and became like us in all things "save sin," as St. Paul says elsewhere. As an example to us he even became obedient to death.

THEOLOGICAL CONCLUSION

It is because of this humility on the part of Christ that he was "exalted" above every name. By taking on equality with us Christ becomes someone with whom we can readily identify. His life, then, is a model to which we can look for inspiration and guidance. He is not so removed from us, he does not choose to be so superior in his claims, that we must look elsewhere for help in living our lives. And just as he has taken on humanity to encourage and help us, so we, too, must help each other. We owe each other solace and love, compassion and pity, fellowship and spirit, as St. Paul reminds us. He chose to empty himself for our sakes. We also must learn from his example and begin to empty ourselves for others.

TWENTY-SIXTH SUNDAY OF THE YEAR (SERIES A)
HOMILY IV

Gospel Reading: *Jesus said to the chief priests and elders of the people, "Let me make clear that tax collectors and prostitutes are entering the kingdom of heaven before you."* (Matt. 21:28-32)

ANA-GNOSIS

Perhaps one of the greatest insults that one person can offer to another is to suggest that that person is closed- or narrow-minded. Most of us like to pride ourselves on how open- and broad-minded we are. We like to insist that we are eager for new ideas, new ways of looking at things, and even new ways to invest our effort and our energy. So when someone implies that this is not true of us, we tend quickly to become defensive and point to evidence that will prove how open-minded we are. But this very defending of our "open-mindedness," as we all know, can itself be an indication of a kind of inner blindness and unwillingness to truly keep an open mind and hear what others are saying to us.

THEOLOGICAL EXTENSION

We see something of this kind of blindness on the part of the religious leaders of the time of Christ in today's Gospel passage. To jar these men out of their fixed notions, Christ said something that would be shocking to them, "Let me make it clear that tax collectors and prostitutes are entering the Kingdom of God before you." The religious leaders of that time were very sure that right was on their side. They continually pointed out their own very minute observances of the Law of Moses and that others, such as the tax collectors, failed to keep these observances. These rigid practices, in their own eyes at least, made them better than others who failed to observe the minituae of the Law. By thus setting themselves up as superior to others, they were, by that very fact, negating the virtue that they claimed for themselves. Because they were so insistent on their own self-righteousness, they were unable to see any other view, and that is why Christ told them that the tax collectors and the prostitutes were entering heaven before them. Christ was not condoning sinfulness here. Rather he was suggesting that because the sinners focused less on their own goodness and their own sense of righteousness, they were more open to being taught, open to changing their ways. In contrast to this, the religious leaders of the time, because they were so fixed and rigid in their ways, were almost totally closed to even the consideration that there might be some other way, that they too, had something to learn.

THEOLOGICAL CONCLUSION

There is a danger that we, too, can be so intently focused on our way of doing things or seeing things, or on the notion that we have the right way, that we become just as blind as the people Christ addressed in today's Gospel. This reminds us of St. Paul elsewhere, where he tells us that we need to work out our salvation in "fear and trembling." Who of us can claim, with any kind of absolute certainty, that we are right and others are wrong? Without an honest and almost continual self-examination we can become trapped in a kind of blindness that ultimately will lead to a dead end. We can never totally know God's ways; but our reassurance is that through our effort to hold open God will see our willingness to learn his ways, and through his grace we will be able to work out our salvation.

TWENTY-SEVENTH SUNDAY OF THE YEAR (SERIES A)
HOMILY I

Reading I: *Let me now sing of my friends, my friend's song concerning his vineyard. My friend had a vineyard on a fertile hillside. . . . . . what more was there to do for my vineyard that I had not done in it? When I looked for it to yield grapes, why did it yield wild grapes?* (Is. 5.1-7)

ANA-GNOSIS

When parents receive the disturbing news that one of their children has run afoul of the law or in some way has not lived up to their expectations, their first reaction is often to examine themselves. They may say in anguish, "What did we do wrong? Where have we failed? We gave him or her everything that they wanted. I don't know what else we could have done." Instead of quickly blaming their child for the wrongdoing or the failure, rather they first ask if they themselves have perhaps failed in some way, if it might not be their fault. But later they may come to the conclusion that, whatever may have caused their child to fail or to fall into the hands of the law, there was really nothing more that they could have done. They realize at some point that it is out of their hands and any further effort on their part would be an unfair intrusion into the life and on the freedom of their child. So they may sadly shake their heads and say, "Well, I guess everyone has to make his own mistakes."

All of us, regardless of what our position of responsibility may be, know and understand this kind of disappointment. Teachers know it with respect to students on whom they have placed great expectations; employers know it in regard to those who are under their employment; religious leaders feel it about those who are under their spiritual care. But there is a kind of relief in the realization that there isn't really anything different that one could have done, once one has carefully looked at their responsibility toward the other person.

This, of course, does not necessarily mean that one ceases any longer to care for the other person; rather it means one is at peace knowing that to do anything more might have been equally disastrous. It is the realization that the other person also has a certain obligation to respond and that this cannot be forced, for if it were it would be devoid of any real value.

THEOLOGICAL EXTENSION

In today's first Reading we see a vivid portrayal of this kind of experience between God and the chosen people. The "friend" to whom the Prophet refers is, of course, God. Out of love and concern for the people whom he had chosen, God made sure that they had everything they needed in order to follow him. He had done his part. Like the planter of the vineyard, once it is planted, he has done his job.

The point of the story is that it is not enough simply for God to hold out to his chosen people all the opportunities they need. Nothing will happen unless there is free cooperation and response on their part. In order for anything productive and creative to come about, loving interaction and mutual response is required from both parties. For God to force this kind of response and cooperation from his people would be to deny their freedom. He could, of course, have forced, in some way or other, the results he had hoped for. But love is not something that people have forced from them. It must be freely given to be real and responsive. God wished to show a far greater respect for the freedom he had given to his people so he left the response in their hands.

THEOLOGICAL CONCLUSION

Just as parents or teachers or employers arrive at the awareness that there is nothing further they can do, that those under them must be respectfully allowed the full exercise of their freedom, so also God is toward us.

One of the greatest acts of love and care for another person is to allow them the use of their freedom, knowing that they may abuse it. Very often one is forced to suffer along with this abuse.

To interfere with it is, in a far deeper sense, to disrespect the person. So, too, in our own relationship to God, he respects our freedom. Unless our response is willingly given it loses its real value. It ceases to become a gesture made by a creature of God exercising his freedom.

TWENTY-SEVENTH SUNDAY OF THE YEAR (SERIES A) HOMILY II

Responsorial Psalm: *The vine from Egypt you transplanted; You drove away the nations and transplanted it. Why have you broken down its walls? Once again, O Lord of hosts, look down from heaven and see; Give us new life and we will call upon your name.* (Ps. 80:9, 12-16, 19-20)

ANA-GNOSIS

In traveling throughout our country, a driver often goes along smoothly on a four-lane highway, the traffic moving rapidly and without delay. At such times he may momentarily reflect on what a marvelous thing it is to have these wonderful expressways on which traffic moves so efficiently. Then, very much to his disappointment, he looks ahead to see the traffic beginning to slow down. Pretty soon it becomes a kind of stop-and-go situation, and after a while he finally realizes what the problem it—the four-lane highway has ended and it has become a two-lane highway, creating what we call a "bottleneck." If this occurs on a road that one travels frequently, on the way to work or school every day, after putting up with this "bottleneck" for a while, a person might try to think of a different route that he might take. And in his exasperation he might wonder, "When is the Highway Department going to get that four-lane highway finished? His frustration at this situation can go on for a long time, perhaps even years, usually because the Highway Commission has run out of money and cannot afford to complete the highway for a long time to come. Yet eventually it will be finished and when it is those who were frustrated for so long feel a tremendous relief. In fact, in a very short time they quickly forget what a difficult drive it was when the "bottleneck" existed. It is almost as though the beautiful four-lane highway were always there.

THEOLOGICAL EXTENSION

We see something of this in the prayer of the Psalmist today. The Psalmist is reminding God of the work that God himself has begun. He says, "The vine from Egypt you transplanted; you drove away the nations and transplanted it." It's as though the Psalmist is reminding God that God has begun a good work, and the Psalmist is disappointed that God seems to be neglecting it now. This Psalm is very reassuring because it reminds us that even when we are concerned because God seems to have forgotten us, he will not let us down. God does not abandon what he has started, he does not give up on it. No matter how guilty we may feel for many of our past actions, we must realize that our own life is a work begun by God. God cares about what we are doing and he will not abandon us or forget us.

THEOLOGICAL CONCLUSION

With a good deal more dependability than the Highway Department, God, too, brings to completion and fruition whatever he has begun. To our limited vision it may seem like God has completely forgotten about us, just as in our frustration about the highway we might think that the State has completely given up completing the four lanes. Our consolation in the prayer of the Psalmist is to recall that God knows our needs and while momentarily it may seem as if he has turned away, he is nevertheless there. We may not always understand his plan or what seems like neglect on his part, but we must trust that, in the long run, he has a purpose and we know that what he has begun he will see through to completion.

TWENTY-SEVENTH SUNDAY OF THE YEAR (SERIES A) HOMILY III

Reading II: *Dismiss all anxiety from your minds, present your needs to God in every form of prayer and in petitions full of gratitude. Then God's own peace which is beyond all understanding will stand guard over your hearts and minds in Christ Jesus.* (Phil. 4:6-9)

ANA-GNOSIS

Swimming instructors often begin by telling their students that they must first of learn to abandon themselves to the water.

They point out to beginning swimmers that the water will actually support their bodies if they but learn how to relax and allow the water to do it. But if they fight the water and struggle against it, they will only wear themselves out and they could find themselves in danger of drowning. This may at first sound rather strange and mysterious to the beginners in their anxiety and fear of the water. Their first reaction often is to see it as a kind of an enemy that must be overcome. But once they conquer this attitude, once they see the water as something that actually supports them, they quickly become at ease and relaxed. They now experience a kind of peacefulness in the water and an enjoyment of it. Naturally, they are still aware that one can drown in deep water and so they respect it. But now, instead of being afraid of it, they are at ease with it, comfortable in it, and are able to enjoy it.

THEOLOGICAL EXTENSION

This experience of the beginning swimmer who finally achieves a relaxed attitude toward water and finds peace with it can give us some idea of what St. Paul is telling us in the letter to the Philippians about our attitude toward God in prayer. There is no end to the cares and concerns and anxieties of life. No sooner do we resolve one difficulty or concern than others keep cropping up; life is a kind of continual round of seeking peace but never finding it. This, of course, is what life is about—any kind of real investment in something, any concern and care about it, naturally has its concomittant anxieties. When St. Paul tells us, then, to "dismiss all anxiety from your minds" he is obviously not suggesting that we stop caring about anything or stop becoming involved with or invested with the real values of our life. Rather he is saying that these anxieties will always be there, but if we can abandon ourselves to God in prayer we will find a peace that, in his words, "passes all understanding." We are to present our needs and cares and anxieties to God in the form of prayer and petition, trusting that God will acknowledge all these needs and that he will support us in filling them. In this kind of prayer we come to see God not as someone against whom we must struggle, but as someone from whom we derive encouragement, aid, and support. In this way, then, we arrive at the peacefulness of which St. Paul speaks.

THEOLOGICAL CONCLUSION

Just as the water will support swimmers once they abandon

themselves to it, so God will support us also, once we abandon ourselves to him. It is in this abandonment that we eventually find real peace. We recognize that life is full of risks and of anxieties and that for the committed Christian there is no way around these. To avoid them would be, in a sense, to stop loving. But in our faith and trust in prayer we find peace amid all these anxieties because we take them to God and we abandon ourselves to him.

TWENTY-SEVENTH SUNDAY OF THE YEAR (SERIES A) HOMILY IV

Gospel Reading: *Jesus said to the chief priests and elders of the people, "Listen to another parable. There was a property owner who planted a vineyard. He put a hedge around it, dug out a vat, and erected a tower. Then he leased it out to tenant farmers and went on a journey . . . . What do you suppose the owner of the vineyard will do to those tenants when he comes?" They replied, "He will bring that wicked crowd to a bad end and lease his vineyard out to others who will see to it that he has grapes at vintage time."* (Mt. 21:33-43)

ANA-GNOSIS

In the early days of our American west there were vast tracts of land that were not owned by any particular individual. Instead they were owned by the United States Government and were under its administration. The government would lease this unoccupied land, usually for little or nothing, to various ranchers who would then use it for grazing their cattle and other livestock. After a number of years of using the land in this way, the ranchers understandably came to see it as their own land. This possessiveness on the part of the ranchers gave rise to many incidents which we've all read about or seen on television where homesteaders, who in good faith would set up a homestead on this land they bought from the government, would be attacked or harrassed by the rancher who had been using it because he had come to think of it as his own. In the ensuing fight, then, between the rancher and homesteader, often there was a great deal of bloodshed and tragedy. These fights came to be known popularly as the "range wars." Sometimes the homesteaders would try to stay and fight it out with the rancher, as he had the legal right to do, but very often, in discouragement he would pack up his family and move on to another place where he hoped he would not find so much distress and trouble.

THEOLOGICAL EXTENSION

We see a parallel to this situation in today's Gospel. The owner of the vineyard let his vineyard out to tenants and then went away on a journey. Apparently he was gone for quite a long time because the tenants came to think of the vineyard as their own. When the owner finally returned and tried to reclaim his property through his servants he ran into a great deal of trouble. We are told that the tenants beat one, killed another, and stoned a third, until finally the owner sent out his son in the hope that they would acknowledge him as the rightful heir. But, as we also learn, they killed the son as well. The point, it seems, that Christ wishes to make to the religious leaders of his time is that ultimately everything that we have and all that we are belongs to God, and at some time we must make an accounting for it. Even our very life in this world is only temporary, and eventually we must give that, too, back to God. So whatever we possess in this life must be used respectfully and with the proper end in view, because really it does not belong to us; it is only ours on loan from God. At any time God can step in and demand it all back. If we are like the tenants in today's Gospel, then we are in danger of forfeiting any claim to eternal possessions as well. We are told, "He will put those wretches to a miserable death, and let out the vineyard to other tenants who will give him the fruits in their season."

THEOLOGICAL CONCLUSION

Like the early ranchers, it is easy for us to become so attached to the things of this life that we can readily forget their real source and their true owner. So we often end up claiming ownership to something which is really not ours in the first place, or acting disrespectfully or abusively of a talent we have. What Christ wishes to remind us of today is that eventually we will be accountable for the way we have used the things that are given to us and the trust that has been put in us. Everything we have, including our own life, has been given to us in tenancy. This, in itself, is a very great act of trust on the part of God. We must remember not to abuse the freedom that goes along with the use and the enjoyment of what we have. We must use our talents to the best of our ability and for their greatest productivity knowing that in the end that their use is not to achieve our goals, but God's. If we remember the rightful owner of what we have we will not make the mistake that the vineyard tenants made and, instead of being cast out, we will be pleasing to God.

TWENTY-EIGHTH SUNDAY OF THE YEAR (SERIES A)
HOMILY I

Reading I: *On this mountain the Lord of hosts will provide for all peoples. A feast of rich food and choice wines, juicy rich foods and pure, choice wines . . . . . He will destroy death forever. The Lord God will wipe away the tears from all faces.* (Is. 25:6-10)

ANA-GNOSIS

One of the joys of life that perhaps all of us can share is the anticipation of a happy event or experience. Certainly all of us anticipate the joy of a vacation. We often plan long ahead of time what route we will take, what sights we will stop to see, and so on. Just the idea of getting away from the daily routine of work can bring a very keen sense of anticipation. We may also anticipate a good meal. We all know, for example, how excitedly small children look forward to a picnic with its variety of foods and games, or a birthday party they will be having.

It has been said, however, that what we anticipate seldom occurs. This statement, I suppose, is intended to capture the fact that the actual experience of the anticipated event often falls short of what we hope it will be. Perhaps the vacation doesn't turn out as we have hoped; maybe there is a lot of trouble with the car or in making connections with the airplane. Perhaps the meal doesn't live up to our expectations. Something may have occurred to make the day a negative or painful experience instead of the joyful one we'd looked forward to.

THEOLOGICAL EXTENSION

This idea of anticipation is in the theme of today's Reading from the prophet Isaiah. God says through the prophet that while things are difficult, laborious and painful now, at some time this will all come to an end. The people, Isaiah writes, have something very pleasant to look forward to if only they can make the best of the present situation.

In describing what is to be anticipated the prophet uses the image of a meal. He says, "A feast of rich food and choice wines, juicy rich food and pure, choice wines, well-refined" awaits them. The prophet, of course, is referring here to the final stage of the Messianic Kingdom. He uses this very common image of a banquet or a meal so that the people can readily understand and relate to what he is saying: their present labors and sufferings are all worthwhile because in the end they will have this total, unending joy.

THEOLOGICAL CONCLUSION

Unlike our anticipation of coming events in our lives which may or may not turn out to be happy experiences, which very often let us down, we have God's reassurance in the Reading today that what we can anticipate hereafter will not disappoint us. The prophet says, "He will destroy death forever. The Lord God will wipe away the tears from all faces." This thought can be most consoling in our own present difficulties, turmoils and sufferings for it is God's own promise. Here, even if the things we anticipate turn out well for us, they nevertheless come to an end. After the vacation is over, for example, we have to go back to the routine of daily work and living. The meal that we may have anticipated with so much enthusiasm provides a very limited kind of fulfillment. This is true of all earthly things we look forward to. But in today's Reading we hear that we may look forward with great joy to a happiness that is complete and that never ends. It is this that makes everything in our present circumstances worthwhile.

TWENTY-EIGHTH SUNDAY OF THE YEAR (SERIES A) HOMILY II

Responsorial Psalm: *The Lord is my shepherd, I shall not want. In verdant pastures he gives me repose . . . . For even though I walk through the valley of the shadow of death, I fear no evil. For thou art with me, thy rod and thy staff, they comfort me.* (Ps. 23:1-6)

ANA-GNOSIS

We have all seen small children cling to their parents or to some other older person for strength and protection. They may clutch the clothes of their mother or father or nestle snugly in their arms, and from this position they seem to look out upon the world with a great sense of confidence and security because they know that their parents will protect them. This is especially common when children are among a crowd of strangers. But even as adults we know a sense of security in being around someone who seems to know what he is doing and seems to be in charge of the situation. We know, for example, the sense of relief and security we have when a crowd of people are standing around a person who has been injured in an accident and no one seems quite sure what to do, and then someone comes to the crowd and says, "Stand back and let me through, I'm a doctor." The people then willingly stand aside and let the person take charge. They even seem to derive a vicarious strength from the sureness and the stability of the person who has taken charge.

THEOLOGICAL EXTENSION

This same theme of security that comes from trusting someone who knows what he is doing and who is in charge of things is found in this well-known Psalm that we read in today's Liturgy. The Lord is depicted as a shepherd and, like a good shepherd, he knows what is best for his sheep, for those who follow him. They can trust that wherever he leads, they can follow without the fear or anxiety that they will be misled or will be exposed in insurmountable dangers or difficulties. Although life is fraught with risk and uncertainty, he gives us the reassurance that by trusting in God we can come through unscathed. The Psalmist tells us "Even though I walk through the valley of the shadow of death, I fear no evil." No matter how difficult and dangerous things may seem at times, no matter how overwhelming the burdens of life may appear, we can trust that God, as our shepherd, will bring us through in the end.

THEOLOGICAL CONCLUSION

The image of God as shepherd leading the sheep to safety and protection would have been a very vivid one for the people at the time of the Psalmist. By understanding the relationship of the sheep and the shepherd, we, too, can derive the same sense of security and reassurance that the Israelites felt. Just as God cared for the sheep, he cared for them. And so he cares for us.

We can follow him unfailingly in whatever direction he leads us. Even death itself is no cause for fear. For we know that, in the end, we will be brought home safely from the risks and dangers and uncertainties of life because we have a true shepherd, our God.

TWENTY-EIGHTH SUNDAY OF THE YEAR (SERIES A)
HOMILY III

Reading II: *I am experienced in being brought low, and I know what it is to have an abundance . . . . In him who is the source of my strength I have strength for everything. Nonetheless it was kind of you to share in my hardships.* (Phil. 4:21-14, 19-20)

ANA-GNOSIS

At the beginning of the great Depression in 1929 many people, literally overnight, went from wealth to poverty. Perhaps some of you here even remember that or experienced it. But even if you didn't, you certainly have read about it or heard of it from those who did experience it. You know how people lost their whole life's savings when banks closed, and others lost enormous fortunes in the stock market. For many people this was so painful that they committed suicide. We also know of the reverse experience where a person goes from poverty to wealth in a very short time. We have all read, for example, of people who discovered oil on their property or who came into a very large inheritance, and their whole life changed from hardship and deprivation to great abundance and leisure.

In either instance a challenge is presented to the person. Whether he or she goes from wealth to poverty, as in the Depression, or from poverty to wealth, as in the good fortune of the person who discovered oil or inherited great wealth, the challenge is one of adjustment to a new and wholly different way of living and of coping with life.

THEOLOGICAL EXTENSION

St. Paul, in his letter to the Philippians, speaks of this same kind of challenge. He tells us that he has experienced both want and abundance and that he has "learned the secret" of facing both. In times of plenty he does not allow himself to forget the source of the good things that he has; he recognizes them as coming from God and is thankful for them. And in times of want and hunger he likewise does not allow himself to become unduly discouraged. Rather, he trusts in God and in God's plan. He says, "I can do all things in him who strengthens me."

THEOLOGICAL CONCLUSION

There are many circumstances in life over which we may not have control. Among these circumstances often is whether or not we have wealth or are instead poor or deprived. We may not be personally responsible for either one of these. But we are challenged in times of abundance not to allow ourselves to forget the source of this bounty and become proud and conceited. In times of want and lack we try not to become discouraged and depressed to the point where we lose trust in the ultimate goodness of God.

St. Paul's example to us today shows that he did not put an undue amount of significance on whether he had a lot or a little. Rather he faced up to the challenge of both and kept his eyes fixed on whatever it was that God wanted of him. He trusted that, in either circumstance, God had certain plans for him and that he must carry these out. In carrying out our Christian responsibility we, too, must keep our eyes fixed on eternal values, on those which will last rather than on the circumstances of life which are subject to the whims of uncertain fortune.

TWENTY-EIGHTH SUNDAY OF THE YEAR (SERIES A) HOMILY IV

Gospel Reading: *Jesus began to address the chief priests and elders of the people once more using parables. "The reign of God may be likened to a king who gave a wedding banquet for his son..... At this the king grew furious and sent his army to destroy those murderers and to burn their city."* (Mt. 22:1-14)

ANA-GNOSIS

We are all familiar with the duplicating process called xeroxing, but when it was new people were not certain it would work. At that time one could have bought shares in the Xerox Corporation for a very small sum of money. In fact, it is said that if one had bought ten shares in Xerox thirty years ago, today one would be a millionaire. Now shares are obviously expensive because it has become such a good investment. So today one might look back and say regretfully, "If I had only known what that company was going to come to, I would have bought stocks in the beginning. If I had, now I'd be a millionaire." This kind of statement, of course, represents what many of us perhaps have experienced ourselves—a lost opportunity. There is an old expression that we are all familiar with, "Opportunity knocks but once." Of course we know that this is very often true. Unless we take advantage of the moment we may forfeit forever the tremendous benefit or advantage that could have been ours.

THEOLOGICAL EXTENSION

This is something of the theme of the Parable in today's Gospel. The people at the time of Christ, the Chosen People, were the ones who were invited to the "wedding feast" that we read about. They were the selected guests who were asked to come. But instead of taking advantage of the opportunity they began, one after the other, to make excuses about why they could not attend. Some of the excuses may have been valid, but some may have been simple rationalizations. They were caught up in the immediacy of their lives and could not see the long-range goals. For the sake of a momentary satisfaction or pleasure, they gave up a far greater and more enduring prospect for themselves. So, as we are told in the Gospel, "They lost everything."

In their daily busy-ness they didn't recognize that, by seizing the opportunity of this invitation, they would be laying up for themselves a far greater good in the long run. So what could have been theirs was then given to someone else.

THEOLOGICAL CONCLUSION

While Christ spoke this Parable to the people of his own time, it could also be the story of all of us. When we think back, how many lost opportunities are there in our own lives? In our preoccupation with an immediate good we often lose sight of the far greater good which, if we recognized, we would invest everything in order to gain. Like those people in the early days invested in the Xerox Corporation, taking advantage of the low cost of its shares, and became millionaires, so we, too, by putting off the lure and attractiveness of immediate goals can become "billionaires" in the spiritual sense by holding out for the long range goal.

We know that God's generosity, his forgiveness and his love are always there, and that with God we always have another opportunity. But we need to remind ourselves that God in his goodness can react to our obstinacy with a very genuine kind of indignation. Who knows whether or when we will be given the opportunity again. So we need, from time to time, to take a look at the things we are invested in, and to honestly ask whether this is a short term value in which we have invested ourselves or whether it will serve us well in the long run. This kind of self-examination may involve us in a new and different investment in a long-range goal, one that may not produce any immediate satisfaction, but ultimately can make us wealthy in the eyes of God.

TWENTY-NINTH SUNDAY OF THE YEAR (SERIES A)
HOMILY I

Reading I: *Thus says the Lord to his anointed . . I surname you, though you do not know me. I am the Lord and there is no other. Beside me there is no God.* (Is. 45-4-6)

ANA-GNOSIS

History is replete with instances of people who came from insignificant and oftentimes poverty-stricken backgrounds and who made a very significant contribution to the human race. One thinks of someone like Abraham Lincoln, Booker T. Washington, or Charlie Chaplin, to name but a few. Of course we can all think of many other people whose background was impoverished, not only economically, but also socially and culturally, who would have seemed to be most unlikely candidates for some lasting and widely known contribution to mankind. One can easily imagine that the people who lived near and knew such people as Lincoln or Chaplin or Booker T. Washington would hardly have seen them as marked in any special way to make a great contribution. So later on, when these people rose to fame, it must have struck early friends and acquaintances as very strange that these people were such a powerful agent for good and for furthering the general progress of civilization.

THEOLOGICAL EXTENSION

In much the same way it can seem strange to us when God chooses people as his agents who, to us, would seem most unlikely to further his plan and his design. We see just such a situation in today's first Reading from Isaiah. At the time of the writing the

Jews were captives in exile in Babylonia under the subjugation of Cyrus, king of the Medes and of the Persians. Such a person, in a position of authority as Cyrus was, would seem most unlikely to be chosen as one to contribute to and to further the plans of God with his Chosen People. After all, Cyrus was not even an Israelite, and he had nothing in common with the Israelites religiously, politically or economically except that he found them useful as his slaves. So he would seem to be the last person that we would think of as someone who would be an agent of God in his plans for his Chosen People. Yet we see that God chose Cyrus. God says of King Cyrus, through the prophet Isaiah, "I surname you, though you do not know me. I am the Lord and there is no other. Beside me there is no God. I gird you, though you do not know me, that men may know from the rising of the sun that there is no other beside me." We know, historically, that unusual as it must have seemed to the Israelites of that time, God nevertheless used Cyrus as the agent for the liberation of the Jews. It was through Cyrus that they were set free and were given permission to rebuild their temple. So God's plans for his own Incarnation eventually were enabled to come to fulfillment.

THEOLOGICAL CONCLUSION

Sometimes, in our limited view of things, we tend to limit God as well. But, of course, God is God, not only of a select chosen few, but of everyone, and his plans are intended for everyone. So he can choose whomever he will to carry out those plans, even though his choice may seem somewhat strange or unlikely to us. We might tend to think that only those who belong to our own religious group ought to be chosen to be the agents of God's design for the world. But this is, of course, putting limits on God and restricting him. He may choose whomsoever he will because we all belong to him and he is the final goal of all of us.

There is a wonderful consolation in this thought. Sometimes you or I might feel that we are, after all, just ordinary people and God has no particular place for us in his plans, in his design for the world and for the human race. But our consolation as well as our responsibility is that each of us can see ourselves in some way as an instrument in the hands of God, to be used in whatever way he sees fit to carry out the salvation he has intended for everyone. For most of us this usually doesn't take a very dramatic form; perhaps it often goes unnoticed. But the fact is that each of us is significant in God's eyes, and we are all important in the overall fulfillment of God's plan.

TWENTY-NINTH SUNDAY OF THE YEAR (SERIES A) HOMILY II

Responsorial Psalm: *Sing to the Lord a new song. Sing to the Lord, all you lands . . . . . . Worship the Lord in holy array. Tremble before him all the earth. Say among the nations, "The Lord reigns; He will judge the peoples with equity."* (Ps. 96:1, 3-5, 7-8, 9-10)

ANA-GNOSIS

Whenever people attend a special celebration or event, such as a wedding or a party, they put on their best clothes and try to show the best side of themselves. This is true not only of people who go out or who go to visit someone, but also if people expect visitors themselves. One of the first things they do is check the mirror to see if their hair is in order, and maybe then put on a nicer suit of clothes and make their appearance generally more presentable. The reason for doing this, of course, is that it shows honor and respect to the people who are visiting or whom they will visit.

We also do this when we go to church on Sunday. People even speak of their "Sunday clothes," meaning that these are special clothes, somewhat better than the ones they wear during the week. These are clothes that they come to Church in not only to appear a little more attractive to other people, but also to honor God whom they have come to worship by their appearance.

THEOLOGICAL EXTENSION

This idea of putting on our "Sunday best" in order to show respect, reverence and honor not only to other people but to God as well, is one of the themes of today's Psalm. Recognizing that God is infinitely great and that glory, praise and honor are due him, the Psalmist exhorts us, "Worship the Lord in holy array. Tremble before him all the earth." This statement of the Psalmist suggests that we must acknowledge God in a very special way, that we must honor him above all creatures and give to him a certain deference and respect that we give to no creature. One of the symbols of respect, deference and worship to God is the outward appearance of the people in the act of worship. It symbolizes their acknowledgement of God as above all creatures.

THEOLOGICAL CONCLUSION

We know, of course, that true and sincere worship and respect for God comes from the heart—it is an internal thing. So no matter how radiantly one may be adorned externally, if this inner sincerity is lacking then the act of reverence and worship is not worth much. But the external adornment, if it goes along with an interior sincerity of respect and honor, is complete. It's an external way of expressing what we feel internally.

If we appeared before our friends in tattered and soiled clothing when, in fact, we had something better to wear, understandably they might be offended, and might feel that we didn't respect them enough to bother dressing up for them. In a similar way, our appearance, as the Psalmist suggests today, is an external sign of how we feel inside toward God as we come in his presence to worship him.

TWENTY-NINTH SUNDAY OF THE YEAR (SERIES A) HOMILY III

Reading II: *Paul, Sylanus and Timothy, to the Church of the Thessalonians who belong to God the Father and the Lord Jesus Christ. Grace to you and peace. We give thanks to God always for you all, constantly mentioning you in our prayers, remembering before our God and Father your work of faith, and labor of love, in steadfastness of hope in our Lord Jesus Christ.* (1 Thes. 1:1-5)

ANA-GNOSIS

Oftentimes someone who has been invited to an event at which many of his friends will be gathered, and he knows that he, because of some prior commitment, will be unable to attend, will say to the person who invited him, "Well, I'll be with you in spirit." This statement can express a deep and sincere feeling, especially if it is said to someone with whom the person feels rather close. Indeed, the other person often feels that, even though his friend is unable to be present physically, he is there in another way.

We have other expressions that convey this same idea when we have to be away from someone for awhile. For example, we say, "I'll remember you in my prayers," or "I'll be thinking of you as you take your examination," or "I'll be thinking of you during your surgery." All these expressions convey a sense of caring for a person, as well as a desire to be close to him and to support him, to share in his joys if it's a joyous occasion, or in his suffering if that is the situation.

THEOLOGICAL EXTENSION

St. Paul's letter to the Thessalonians opens in just such a reassuring and consoling way. He says, "We give thanks to God always for you all, constantly mentioning you in our prayers." We know, of course, that prayers of any spiritual thoughts are not subject to the bounds of time and space. So here St. Paul is speaking of, among other things, the value of praying for one another, of remembering each other in his or her efforts before God. God hears not only our own prayers, but he hears the prayers of others for us. Obviously St. Paul felt very close to the people to whom he addressed these words because they had been recent converts to Christianity. So he reassures them that while he is unable to be present to them physically, they have not been forgotten—he is still supporting them by his prayers.

THEOLOGICAL CONCLUSION

We have all experienced loneliness and a feeling of being neglected by others. We may often have wondered perhaps if anyone really cared or if anyone really understood what we were going through, or the value of what we were trying to accomplish. But whenever someone tells us that we are being remembered in his prayers and he says this sincerely and from the heart, it can be very reassuring. We know that people cannot always be present physically to encourage us and support us, but when we know they would like to be and are keeping us before the Lord in their prayers we can feel very reassured and no longer lonely. For we know that "in spirit" they are with us, and that God hears their prayers for us and that we truly do matter both to them and to God.

TWENTY-NINTH SUNDAY OF THE YEAR (SERIES A) HOMILY IV

Gospel Reading: *The Pharisees went off and began to plot how they might trap Jesus in his speech . . . . "Who's head is this and whose inscription?" "Caesar's," they replied. At that he said to them, "Then give to Caesar what is Caesar's, but give to God what is God's."* (Mt. 22:15-21)

ANA-GNOSIS

Nearly everyone at one time or another has been in the painful position of having to choose between two or more equally difficult or undesirable options. Faced with such a situation a person might react by saying, "This is the same as no choice at all," or he might say, "I'm between a rock and a hard place," or "I'm damned if I do and damned if I don't." What can be similarly painful is when a person is asked a question to which a yes or no answer is required and no matter which answer one gives he will be condemning himself. An example that comes to mind is the one that we've all heard: "Have you stopped beating your wife?" No matter how the person answers this question he is open to condemnation.

THEOLOGICAL EXTENSION

In today's Gospel we see where Christ was put deliberately by the religious leaders of his time in that kind of an impossible situation. Their question of him, "Is it lawful to pay taxes to Caesar or not?" was unanswerable. If Christ had said yes, it is lawful, he would have, of course, brought upon himself the wrath of the Jewish population for his seeming loyalty to the Romans. If he had said no, it's not lawful, he would have been accused of disloyalty and disobedience to the Roman emperor. The answer that Christ actually gave to this question contains a profound religious and Christian doctrine. He says simply, "Then give to Caesar what is Caesar's, but give to God what is God's." In this reply we see that there is no conflict between religious and political authority. Both are necessary; each one has its proper place. We all benefit from the taxes that are paid, we need civil government to perform tasks we, as individuals, cannot do. But there is also another dimension of our lives: the non-material, spiritual element. And this, too, has its own peculiar claims and prerogatives that must not be neglected. It is this spiritual side that Christ came among us to highlight.

THEOLOGICAL CONCLUSION

We can sometimes get so entangled in the immediacy of our everyday concerns and difficulties, in the immediacy of political concerns that we forget the spiritual order of existence that is equally or even more important and necessary for our complete and ultimate happiness and fulfillment. So we see Christ as almost dismissing the question the Pharisees put to him, not because he thought government was unimportant or unnecessary in the life of everyday existence, but rather because he was here for another reason. He came to teach something else. This "something else" is, of course, the business of his Father in heaven, and his first obligation is to accomplish its fulfillment. It is the first priority of his Incarnation.

Unless we are reminded of this from time to time we, too, can lose sight of the real priorities in life. We can spend so much time, effort and energy on the achievement of goals that do not last that we fail to follow through on the goal of eternal fulfillment and satisfaction. As Christ stood so profoundly for this goal that he reminds us of in today's Gospel, we, too, need to stand for something beyond immediate goals. We also should be a reminded to others of the ultimate, eternal goal of life.

THIRTIETH SUNDAY OF THE YEAR (SERIES A) HOMILY I

Reading I: *Thus says the Lord, "You shall not wrong stranger or oppress him, for you were strangers in the land of Egypt."* (Ex. 22:20-26)

ANA-GNOSIS

People who have lived through a time of trial, distress or difficulty can have widely differing actions when the period of suffering is over. One person might come out of it feeling very bitter toward his experience and toward other people. He may say, "I went through all that suffering, worry and anxiety. Now let others go through it and find out what it's like." Such a person might say this even though in his time of distress others were quite helpful and sympathetic toward him. Perhaps there was nothing they could really do. But another person might react to a very difficult experience in a rather positive way. His reaction might be, "I've been through that and I know exactly what it's like. I can empathize with people in that position, and they deserve my help." This person might spend much time and effort or, in unusual cases, devote his life to helping others who are in the same circumstances that he too experienced.

THEOLOGICAL EXTENSION

This second reaction, the positive one of the person who, instead of being embittered by his experience after it is all over, extends himself to other people, is the one we are exhorted to adopt in today's Reading. God tells us through the prophet, "You shall not wrong a stranger or oppress him, for you were strangers in the land of Egypt." Here the people were reminded that they, too, were in difficult circumstances when they were enslaved in Egypt. But now that their enslavement is over, they should not forget the source of their present good fortune. As God helped them out of their slavery and into the Promised Land, as goodness and kindness were shown to them at the time of their distress, they must now turn and show that same goodness and sympathy to others around them who are in distress. They must help strangers without homes, widows, orphans, those who are poor, helpless or otherwise in need.

Whatever good fortune people have is a very tenuous thing; they acquired it not necessarily through any merit of their own, but through the goodness of God. Just as it was given to them, so it can be taken away and given to someone else. One person is not necessarily more meritorious or deserving than another.

THEOLOGICAL CONCLUSION

There is both a lesson and a consolation for us in this Reading. The lesson is that, instead of allowing whatever past, negative experiences we might have had to embitter us toward life and toward people, now that we are in a happier position we need to help others arrive there also. We need to keep in mind where all of our good fortune has come from and share it with others. The consolation is that God shows his love and compassion especially to those who do as he does and love their neighbors, be they strangers or friends.

THIRTIETH SUNDAY OF THE YEAR (SERIES A)
HOMILY II

Responsorial Psalm: *I love you, O Lord, my strength. Lord, my rock, my fortress, my deliverer.*
My God, my rock in whom I take refuge, my shield and the horn of my salvation, my stronghold. (Ps. 18:2-4, 47, 51)

ANA-GNOSIS

We've all read or seen on television stories of people who have been shipwrecked at sea. If they are fortunate, the survivors of such a disaster end up in a lifeboat with a large number of other people and a limited amount of food and water. Often in the small boat they are tossed about on the sea for many days until someone comes to rescue them. Perhaps they are seen by a passing ship which then takes them aboard. But in less fortunate instances some of the survivors may not be able to reach a lifeboat and so they'll clutch onto anything available, perhaps a board or some remnant of the sinking ship just to try to stay afloat. In this precarious situation they desperately hope for someone to come to their rescue, to deliver them, to take them out of their plight. They may even be further imperiled if the waters are infested with sharks. So we can imagine their enormous relief when they see someone coming in a boat from a passing ship to take them aboard. Such a person is obviously filled with enormous relief and, of course, gratitude to his or her rescuer.

THEOLOGICAL EXTENSION

This image of someone being adrift at sea and surrounded by numerous dangers, and then someone coming to his rescue is a parallel to the one we have of ourselves being rescued by God in today's Psalm. The Psalmist refers to God as "my rock, my fortress, my deliverer." Any attempt to describe God is, of course, inadequate and falls far short of what God really is, but to speak of God as a "rock" or a "fortress" or a "deliverer" conveys to us a sense of someone who really supports us, someone to whom we can go in time of distress and whom we can depend on to take us in, to deliver us. All of our lives, at times at least, are surrounded by uncertainties, by dangers, and by the anxiety that comes from the unknown. We all know a sense of loneliness, of being cut off from others, and of needing to go somewhere to be once again restored and given security and hope. The Psalmist today gives that profound sense of reassurance that God is that person of hope, of deliverance for us. Through all difficult and perhaps perilous adventures through life God is always there to bring us home.

THEOLOGICAL CONCLUSION

A shipwrecked person, lost and adrift at sea, while he strongly hopes for rescue and deliverance, cannot always depend on this. We all know this. Many people do drown and are never recovered.

Our reassurance today is that, unlike this situation, we can always depend on God. We can always go to him in our times of trouble, anxiety and despair. He is there to give us relief and restore us again. God is the source of our strength and all that we are. He cares about each of us, and he will come to our aid in our time of need.

THIRTIETH SUNDAY OF THE YEAR (SERIES A)
HOMILY III

Reading II: *You know as well as we do what we proved to be like when, while still among you, we acted on your behalf. You, in turn, became imitators of us in the Lord receiving the word despite great trials with the joy that comes from the spirit.* (1 Thess. 1:5-10)

ANA-GNOSIS

One summer during the baseball season the newspapers were full of stories about Los Angeles Dodger pitcher Tommy John who was on his way to winning more than 20 games after having been told that he would most likely never pitch again. John had ruptured the ligament of his pitching arm midway through the previous season and later underwent surgery which replaced the torn ligament with a tendon taken from his other arm. His recuperation was slow; doctors said he would use the arm again but doubted he would be able to pitch effectively. The outlook was clearly not promising. But John did not give up. He persevered, exercising, running, working out, and the following year was back in the starting rotation full time. In fact, he won the "comeback" award of the year.

One can readily think of other heroic people who overcame great difficulties to go on to significant achievements. Such people, as we know, stand out as examples to all of us. Parents are quick to point out to their children how So-and-so overcame enormous obstacles, and the child can use that person as a source of encouragement when he has to overcome difficulties of a much lesser nature.

Perhaps even closer to our own experience would be that of knowing a person who has had a stroke or some sort of paralysis. Some people, instead of succumbing morosely to their afflictions, do all sorts of exercises and work out to regain the use of those muscles that had been paralyzed. When we see this overcoming of a personal obstacle we are all greatly impressed and even inspired by it. We might say, "He really must have believed in himself," or "He really must have wanted it awfully badly to pay that kind of a price."

THEOLOGICAL EXTENSION

In today's second Reading St. Paul is full of the same kind of praise for the people of Thessalonia who had to overcome enormous difficulties, trials and sufferings in accepting the word of God. They became converts from Judaism and suffered a great deal at the hands of the Jewish community. In fact they were eventually driven from their own city, but their suffering for their belief did not go unnoticed. Their faith in God went forth to others who, inspired by their suffering and strong belief, then also became converts to Christianity. As they had imitated St. Paul in the beginning, seeing his example, now others, seeing their example, imitated them in turn. In this way the word of God was spread among the people of that area.

THEOLOGICAL CONCLUSION

At times we may feel that people are against us and that we are all alone in what we believe and what we stand for. Even more discouraging is feeling that no one understands or recognizes the "price we are paying" to hold onto what we believe, and so we become discouraged and even give up if the trials and sufferings are too great. If some people actually do take notice of us and are inspired by our good example, we often don't know about it so it isn't much encouragement for us. We feel that we have to suffer in silence for what we believe in.

The pitcher who was told he would likely never pitch again had only his own strong faith and conviction to hold onto. This strong faith is a characteristic of the true Christian who, in times of trials and difficulty, holds onto his belief and convictions. Christ suffered ridicule and lack of understanding as well. This remembrance should give us all courage. Even though others do not understand, God does. He knows our faith and he knows the price we are paying to exercise it. And in exercising it we are examples, just as Tommy John and other courageous people have been, to encourage and inspire those around us to persevere even when the going gets rough.

THIRTIETH SUNDAY OF THE YEAR (SERIES A) HOMILY IV

Gospel Reading: *When the Pharisees heard that Jesus had silenced the Saducees they assembled in a body and one of them, a lawyer, in an attempt to trip him up, asked, "Teacher, which commandment of the law is the greatest?" . . . . . "You shall love your neighbor as yourself."*

ANA-GNOSIS

One of the remarkable things about the Constitution of the United States is that it is a very simple and uncomplicated document. Beyond laying down some basic principles providing for the respect of individual rights and guaranteeing that these rights be upheld, it has amazingly little detail to it. The details are left up to the interpretation of the Supreme Court to spell out later on. We know that, since the writing of the Constitution, innumerable volumes of law have been written about its various statutes and how they are to be interpreted and carried out in practice. But in the interpretation it all comes back to the essential question of whether or not such a law is constitutional or not. Every subsequent law since the writing of the Constitution *depends* on the Constitution itself, and if that law does not correspond to the spirit of the Constitution then, as we know, it is often declared "unconstitutional." The noteworthy thing about the Constitution is that it assures us of some kind of integrity; in our own personal life, no matter how poor or how much of an outcast we may seem to be, we have the same rights as everyone else, guaranteed by it.

THEOLOGICAL EXTENSION

This realization helps us to understand better Christ's reply to the man in the Gospel today who asked him which was the greatest of the laws. Christ responded that we were to love the Lord with all our heart and with all our soul and with all our mind and our neighbor as ourselves. Then he said, "On these two commandments *depend* the Law and the Prophets." Instead of going into a detailed enumeration of the various laws and regulations that we are to follow, Christ took us to the core of all Law, the substance on which all other laws depend, namely love of God and of our neighbor. If one does not keep these two commandments, then all the other laws and commandments, however strictly one might abide by them, have no meaning. Because they don't spring from a basic love out of which they must come to be truly valid, they are like "unconstitutional" laws. They are laws for their own sake—part of a cold, removed, skeletal structure with little relation to the human condition. The other side of this is, if we do keep these two commandments, loving God above all else and our neighbor as ourselves, then we will, by definition, also be keeping all the other laws. If one has love of God and of one's neighbor at heart then it will be impossible for that person to violate any other laws.

THEOLOGICAL CONCLUSION

Just as all the laws of our country are invalid unless they are based on the Constitution and so can be overthrown or repealed, so also are the laws of our Christian life. If our life is not based upon the love of God and of others, then all the other things that we do become suspect. They are subject to challenge and questioning by others around us. So whatever we do, if to the question "is it based on love of God and one's neighbor" we can answer, "Yes," then we can be assured that we are truly keeping all of God's commandments and that our life has meaning because it respects love which is the root of human life.

THIRTY-FIRST SUNDAY OF THE YEAR (SERIES A)
HOMILY I

Reading I: *I am a great king, says the Lord of hosts and my name is feared among the nations . . . . . you have turned aside from the way, you have caused many to stumble by your instructions, you have corrupted the covenant of Levi, says the Lord of Hosts, and so I make you despised and abased before all the people inasmuch as you have not kept my ways but have shown partiality in your instruction.* (Malachi 1:14, 2:2, 8-10)

ANA-GNOSIS

Whenever several members, or even one member, of a highly respected profession becomes corrupt in the practice of that profession, it is in danger of falling into disrepute and of losing its credibility, especially among those people whom that profession is intended to serve. Occasionally we read about a lawyer, a doctor, or a psychologist who has been removed from the practice of the profession because he or she has been exercising it unjustly or unethically. Sometimes the people who are paying for the services are seriously hurt and it becomes known that this person was practicing only for material gain and took advantage and misused the people that he was supposed to be helping. To try to prevent this kind of corruption most professions have set up a code of ethics by which all their members are expected to abide. This is a protection for the people who make use of their services. It gives them a feeling of trust and the assurance that they will get an honest return for the fee they are paying.

THEOLOGICAL EXTENSION

In today's Reading from the prophet Malachi we see just such an instance of the abuse of power that goes with a certain profession or standing in the community. At that time many of the religious leaders were corrupt. They had been remiss in adhering to the celebration of the liturgical services and they were misleading people in various other ways. So we are told about them by Malachi, "You have turned aside from the way, you have caused many to stumble by your instruction, you have corrupted the covenant of Levi, says the Lord of hosts." As representatives of God to the people, the religious leaders had an obligation to uphold the Mosaic Law, to carry out the proper observances of the religious celebrations, and to instruct the people properly in the ways of God. But they themselves had become so corrupt and had strayed so far from the right path, that now they had become totally ineffective in carrying out the plan of God. So unless they changed their ways they invited God's condemnation upon them: "They will be punished, despised, and abased before all the people."

THEOLOGICAL CONCLUSION

We all know what a terrible thing it is to see innocent people taken advantage of by those in positions of power. It is even more tragic when such people have no platform from which to proclaim the injustice and the abuse that is done to them. They may, in fact, not even realize that it is happening. How, for example, can a patient know whether a doctor is applying the proper medication or charging the appropriate fee for his services. How does a client know if his lawyer is doing all he can in a trial? How does the untutored student know that the instructions he receives are accurate? All persons, then, who have power and authority in any form have awesome responsibilities. Christians have the same responsibility to others. At times we are all in the position of abusing the innocence of others, particularly our children. So we must heed Malachi's warning and remember always our obligation to set a good example to others. If we do not we are in danger of inviting the condemnation of God upon ourselves.

THIRTY-FIRST SUNDAY OF THE YEAR (SERIES A)
HOMILY II

Responsorial Psalm: *In you, Lord, I have found my peace . . . .*
O Lord, my heart is not lifted up, my eyes are not raised too high;

I do not occupy myself with things too great and marvelous for me.
(Ps. 131:1-2, 3)

ANA-GNOSIS

One of the areas of research in which there is great controversy is genetic engineering. Significant breakthroughs have been made in genetics in recent years, and it seems that now scientists are on the edge of making even greater advances. By various manipulations of the substance called DNA, scientists can bring about all sorts of changes in the structure of the cell and, through that, eventually they may be able to produce new and different forms of life. Through the process known as cloning, it is said that scientists may be able to produce an exact duplicate of any other human being.

The fear that we all have of this is that, in addition to the good that could come from it, it might get out of control and all sorts of "monsters" would be produced and would reproduce. In our anxiety about this, the normal reaction of many people is to say, "They ought to leave these things in the hands of God. They have no right to tamper in these areas."

One can think of many other instances where man seems to be overstepping his limits and intruding on the domain of God. It has been thought that a kind of arrogance exists in this kind of overstepping of one's proper bounds. One seems to be in danger of inviting God's wrath and punishment on oneself and on the whole human race.

THEOLOGICAL EXTENSION

The real danger here, I suppose, in this kind of adventurism is that one can forget that, after all, one is not God. God truly is in control of things; we are not. Today the Psalmist is reminding us that there is a right knowledge and understanding of one's own limitations. He says, "I do not occupy myself with things too great and too marvelous for me." This is a prayer of trust in God, and an acknowledgement of God as the creator of everything.

We all, of course, have the responsibility to use our God-given talents to the utmost of our ability. If we fail to do this we will be answerable to God also. But we can become too haughty and arrogant and forget that, after all, everything depends on God. We need to be reminded, as the Psalmist recalls, that ultimately our satisfaction and fulfillment is to be found in God alone. As long as we hold this awareness and dependency on God and keep our trust in him, then there can be no real danger of our overstepping our bounds.

THEOLOGICAL CONCLUSION

In each of our lives we need to strike a proper balance in the exercise of our talents, abilities and gifts that have been given to us. We must use these talents to their fullest extent, for if we don't we will be answerable to God for their neglect. But we must not feel so arrogant about them that we believe they did not come from God but are due to ourselves. As we deal with such controversial issues as genetic engineering now and in the future we must always keep in mind that we are not God but that we must use responsibly the talents and intelligence he has given us. With this in mind and asking for his guidance we can hope to make the right decisions.

THIRTY-FIRST SUNDAY OF THE YEAR (SERIES A) HOMILY III

Reading II: *We were gentle among you, like a nurse taking care of her children . . . . . We also thank God constantly for this, that when you received the word of God which you heard from us, you accepted it not as the word of men, but for what it really is—the word of God which is at work in you who believes.* (1 Thess. 2:7-9, 13)

ANA-GNOSIS

One of the duties of the Presidential press secretary is to speak in behalf of the President. So when the Secretary holds a press conference regarding a certain Presidential policy, everyone understands that he is not speaking for himself, but for the President. Such a person obviously has to have the trust and confidence of the President to convey properly his thinking and not to distort it. This is true of any person who claims to represent someone else—he or she would have to be true to the authentic policy or plans of the person he or she claims to represent. We can all understand how tempting it might be to claim for one's own what is really the thought of the represented person or how tempting to put one's own words into the mouth of the person one claimed to represent. In either case the representative is unfaithful to the person he represents and through his deception can mislead and confuse people.

THEOLOGICAL EXTENSION

In today's Reading we see that St. Paul did not succumb to such temptations. On the contrary, he gloried in the fact that the people accepted his word and saw it "not as the word of men, but as what it really is—the word of God." St. Paul clearly sees his task of bringing others to Christ. He never claims God's word as his own for then people would be in danger of stopping there—at St. Paul, the person—and not getting beyond him to Christ.

Elsewhere in his writing we find St. Paul continually insisting that what he says is not his own, but that it comes from Christ, and that those who reject him are, in fact, rejecting Christ; but that those who hear him also hear Christ. He does not speak in his own name, then, but on behalf of Christ. And he personally is so imbued with the teachings of Christ that he would go to any lengths, through any sufferings, to make Christ known among the people so that all could share in and benefit from his love.

THEOLOGICAL CONCLUSION

Unless it is clearly known that someone who acts as a spokesperson for someone else is speaking on behalf of the other person, we can become confused and even misled. We don't know for certain whether the spokesperson is speaking for himself or if he is authentically conveying the thoughts of the other person. In today's Reading St. Paul leaves no doubt in our mind for whom he is speaking. As an agent of God he does not claim any personal glory or renown for himself. On the contrary, he rejoices that the people see his words as coming from a source beyond him.

In this same way we must relate to one another. We must not simply bring people to ourselves, achieving their admiration through our good example. That, at best, is only a first step. We must allow them to see through us and beyond us to the real source of the Christian message and what it has to offer to them. If their response to us stops just with us, then we are not Christ's true followers; we represent only ourselves. We must do as Paul and become such effective agents of God that the people who know us know Christ and realize his love for them through us.

THIRTY-FIRST SUNDAY OF THE YEAR (SERIES A)
HOMILY IV

Gospel Reading: *Jesus said to the crowds and to his disciples, "The scribes and the pharisees sit on Moses' seat. Practice and observe whatever they tell you, but not what they do, for they preach but do not practice.* (Mt. 23:1-12)

ANA-GNOSIS

Recently there was an account in the news about the President of the United States considering taking a voluntary cut in his annual salary. He was also suggesting this same voluntary action to his cabinet. He hoped that if everyone saw that the President was taking a cut in his salary then they would be less insistent on increases in their own pay, and the result would be, hopefully, a lessening of the rising spiral of inflation. Rather than simply talk about a need to hold down an increase in wages and prices he thought this action would serve as an example that everyone might follow, and it might be conceivably more effective than a lot of talk.

Another illustration of effective behavior by a leader came in a recent story about the Governor of one of the States who was stopped by the Highway Patrol for speeding. What many people found impressive was that the Governor, instead of "pulling strings" because of his position, insisted on paying the fine just like anyone else. People respected him because he did not abuse his authority to avoid paying the fine. He accepted his responsibility for obeying the law just the same as everyone else.

Not everyone does this. In recent years the phrase "the credibility gap" has become popular. This phrase, as we know, is used to describe a situation in which a person, usually someone in a position of leadership, tells people to do one thing, but does not do it himself. The result is that the people are left confused and skeptical about that person's sincerity. They don't feel that they can trust or depend on him.

THEOLOGICAL EXTENSION

This latter situation is the one we find in the Gospel today among many leaders at the time of Christ. To use a modern expression, there was obviously a "credibility gap" between the Pharisees, the leaders, and the people. According to the Gospel, the Pharisees "preach but do not practice." Understandably, seeing this, the people grew skeptical about the seriousness of their obligation to obey the Mosaic Law. But Christ does not downgrade the Law or say that it is unimportant to observe it. On the contrary, he upholds the Law and insists that it ought to be observed. He says "Practice and observe whatever they tell you, but not what they do." The Law in itself at that time was valid, it was given to the Jewish people by Moses, and ultimately it came from God, so in no way was it to be disrespected or disregarded regardless of the behavior of the Pharisees.

THEOLOGICAL CONCLUSION

We can all understand how difficult it is to observe a law when we see those in positions of authority and power disrespecting it. We expect to see them subject to the same rules and regulations that we take seriously and observe. When the Governor paid his fine for breaking the speed laws we all respected his integrity. The people of Christ's time had difficulty respecting people who didn't seem to practice what they preached. In fact they began to wonder if what they preached was really true or worthwhile. Christ assures them that it is. And he tells them that even though their leaders are not acting responsibly, they must continue to do so. They cannot shirk their obligations just because they see someone else doing so. Their own integrity is still involved.

Christ says the same thing to each of us. We are each responsible for doing the decent and respectful thing. In the final analysis each of us has his own honor and integrity to uphold and to answer for. Just because others give us a bad example we are not excused. He honors us by expecting us to be capable of giving a loving response even when we see others who should know better turning away.

THIRTY-SECOND SUNDAY OF THE YEAR (SERIES A)
HOMILY I

Reading I: *Wisdom is radiant and unfading. She is easily discerned by those who love her and is found by those who seek her . . . . . For he will find her sitting at his gates . . . . . . because she goes about seeking those worthy of her, she graciously appears to them in their paths and meets them in every thought.* (Wis. 6:12-16)

ANA-GNOSIS

Perhaps one of the greatest causes of disappointment in the lives of many people is putting greater expectations on another person or another thing than that person or thing is able to provide. One may look forward for a long time with keen anticipation to a vacation that he or she is going to take, and when the time comes for the vacation and the person goes on the trip, he finds that it falls far short of what he had hoped it would be. This can often take a more serious and even tragic form. The alcoholic looks forward to his next drink in the vague expectation that it will somehow resolve all his difficulties; the dope addict looks forward to the next "high" with the false hope that it will give perfect and complete fulfillment. Very often the result of such unrealistic expectations is that the person ends up back where he was, let down and even more empty and unfulfilled than he was in the first place, and oftentimes far worse off than before.

The opposite of this, of course, can also be true. Sometimes a person is unexpectedly but pleasantly surprised with the joy and happiness he finds in something or someone that seems in itself to be very simple.

THEOLOGICAL EXTENSION

This second experience, of finding happiness in something

quite simple where one did not expect it, is closer to the theme of today's first Reading from the Book of Wisdom. We often think of a wise person as one who is highly intellectual or well-educated. While this may or may not be so, it does not necessarily characterize real wisdom. In today's Reading we learn that real wisdom is "found by those who seek her," and that it is "found sitting at one's gates." Wisdom, according to these statements, then, would not necessarily be associated with great knowledge or a complicated intellectual understanding of things. Rather, it is something rather simple. What is very reassuring to us is that it is open to everyone who seeks it in simplicity.

We have all met people who have had little formal education but whom we recognize immediately as being very wise. Such people radiate simplicity and graciousness; they make people feel secure in their presence. We recognize such a person as having a wisdom that comes from a simple acceptance of one's own limits and of doing all that one can within these limits. Having done this, such a person is at peace with himself and the rest of the world. This is the kind of person, as we are told in today's Reading, who is "worthy of wisdom," and to whom "she graciously appears."

THEOLOGICAL CONCLUSION

It is the kind of wisdom that comes from the simple recognition of one's limits and the acceptance of working within those limits to the utmost of one's ability that we are exhorted to in the Reading today. At times we can all be victimized by expecting too much of others and of ourselves. Eventually we see that this is not only unrealistic but it can also be unfair to whomever we expect these things from. Instead of this, real wisdom asks us to see people and things as they are. In this way we will find true contentment and peace.

THIRTY-SECOND SUNDAY OF THE YEAR (SERIES A) HOMILY II

Responsorial Psalm: *Oh God, You are my God whom I seek . . . Thus have I gazed toward you in the sanctuary . . . . .*
As with the riches of a banquet shall my soul be satisfied . . . . . I will remember you upon my couch, and through the night watches I will meditate upon you. You are my help, and in the shadow of your wings, I shout for joy. (Ps. 63:2-8)

ANA-GNOSIS

In a recent newspaper interview one of the civilian prisoners of war held for five years during the Viet Nam War said, "It still isn't safe for me to go into a store just to buy a loaf of bread." He meant that he was now a compulsive shopper, that, faced again with an abundance of food after enduring such scarcity during his captivity, he could not just buy one item, but felt compelled to buy a whole cartload of groceries. He had fantasized again and again about marvelous foods and extensive banquets while he was a prisoner. It was one of the visions that kept him going.

THEOLOGICAL EXTENSION

Today the Psalmist speaks of God as the one who satisfies all of our needs and desires, and he uses the image of a banquet with all its abundance and riches. He says, "With the riches of a banquet shall my soul be satisfied." This analogy of God to a banquet or elaborate meal that can satisfy all our desires, while it obviously falls far short of any real description of God, gives us some sense of God being the true source of our ultimate satisfaction and fulfillment. While a banquet can only satisfy our immediate physical craving for food, God, of course, does much more than this. He fulfills that longing that we all have for something beyond the immediate. Inadequate as the image of a banquet may be, it nevertheless was very meaningful to people who were often without the abundance that we have. It presented them with a promise of fulfillment, even though this fulfillment would only be physical and temporary.

THEOLOGICAL CONCLUSION

We know that even when our hunger is satisfied we are not wholly fulfilled. No matter how glorious a banquet may be, no matter how many material comforts we may have, they are not by themselves enough. Our lack can never be satisfied by any material thing. Only God can completely satisfy the deepest longings and desires of our hearts. It is the vision of our satisfaction in him which must keep us going through our daily lives. If we keep our gaze fixed on him then we will find the ultimate happiness which is only slightly foreshadowed in such material comforts as banquets. We will find God capable of completely fulfilling our hopes and expectations, of rounding out our lives.

THIRTY-SECOND SUNDAY OF THE YEAR (SERIES A) HOMILY III

Reading II: *We would have you be clear about those who sleep in death, brothers. Otherwise you might yield to grief like those who have no hope. For we believe that Jesus died and rose. God will bring forth from the dead those also who have fallen asleep believing in him. Henceforth they will be with the Lord unceasingly. Console one another with this message.* (1 Thess. 4:13-17)

ANA-GNOSIS

By the time most of us have reached middle age we don't usually object if someone calls us pessimistic. After all, we have very little trouble believing in inflation, in the likelihood of a worsening economic outlook, and even that it will probably rain tomorrow (unless we are farmers who would like it to, in which case we believe equally firm that it won't).

All of these things, of course, may be quite true. But even if they turn out not to be, we go right on expecting them to be anyway. The fact is that we don't look at very many things with much optimism, and since we've grown up, most of us have simply gotten out of the habit of it. It's so much more sensible somehow to always anticipate the worst that we bring this tendency to every aspect of our lives—even ultimately to our faith in and our relationship with God.

THEOLOGICAL EXTENSION

In his first Letter to the Thessalonians St. Paul is protesting vigorously against this pessimistic tendency. He is worried that they will approach death with the same pessimism that most people approach other things. And he assures them that they do not need to. He says, "We would have you be clear about those who sleep in death, brothers. Otherwise you might yield to grief like those who have no hope. For we believe that Jesus died and rose. God will bring forth from the dead those also who have fallen asleep believing in him." In other words, they have no reason to expect the worst after death. Instead, through their belief in Christ, they will enjoy eternal life with their Lord. No matter how discouraging every other future event might look to them, and no matter how right they might be in anticipating the worst in many of their everyday affairs, they would be totally wrong if they yielded to grief and to despair when they encountered death.

THEOLOGICAL CONCLUSION

St. Paul's words, intended to give strength and consolation to the people of Thessalonia, should also strengthen and console all of us. For we, too, live in the hope that Christ gave us. We, too, facing death, face not annihilation but eternal life. This is the Good News that we should be living with every day. And because we would appear to anticipate the bad far more readily than we anticipate the good, we must be careful that we do not obscure or forget this very positive, optimistic, joyful truth. Because Jesus died and rose from the dead, God will bring forth all who believe in him. This is better news than we will likely ever hear again, so let us do as St. Paul counsels and remember it always and "console one another with this message."

THIRTY-SECOND SUNDAY OF THE YEAR (SERIES A) HOMILY IV

Gospel Reading: *Jesus told this parable to his disciples: "The reign of God can be likened to ten bridesmaids who took their torches and went out to welcome the groom. The foolish ones, in taking their torches, brought no oil along."* (Mt. 25:1-13)

ANA-GNOSIS

One of the standard pieces of equipment in an automobile is a spare tire. The reason for this is, of course, most obvious. It is a common sense precaution to take one along so that one is not left stranded if he has a flat tire. It is not uncommon, however, for a person to have a flat tire and then discover to his chagrin that for some reason there is no spare tire in the trunk of the car, or that the one there is also flat. This can be even more upsetting if it happens at night or out on a remote road with very little traffic and no houses in sight. What one usually has to do then is walk a long distance to the nearest farmhouse and call for help. The ensuing delay usually causes the person to be late to wherever he is going, if indeed he is able to get there at all.

When he finally does get the tire fixed, someone might say, "Well, why didn't you check beforehand to see if you had a spare, or to see if the one you had was any good? You should always check the spare tire from time to time." Everyone already knows this, of course. But sometimes we just take things for granted. We assume that the tire is there, and we frankly doubt that there will be any need for it.

THEOLOGICAL EXTENSION

This habit of taking things for granted as regards our spiritual and eternal values and our need to be constantly vigilant about them is the point of the Parable that Christ uses in today's Reading about the ten bridesmaids who went out to meet the groom. Those who had the foresight to take extra oil along with them were not victimized by the unexpected late arrival of the groom. Those, on the other hand, who understandably, assumed that the bridegroom would come on time and so did not take extra oil along, were unprepared. Christ tells us that this is what the kingdom of heaven is like: we don't know how much time we will have; we don't know "when the bridegroom will come." So we need to be always vigilant and alert. Our whole life should be one of vigilance and preparedness so that in the end we are not caught like the foolish maidens, unprepared.

THEOLOGICAL CONCLUSION

When we are caught out on a lonely road at night with a flat tire and no spare, we are extremely annoyed and inconvenienced. We may miss an important appointment or some function that others are depending on us to be there for. Understandably, then, we are upset and even angry at ourselves for not having thought a long time ago to see if the spare was in serviceable condition. If we had, we wouldn't be in our present predicament.

THIRTY-THIRD SUNDAY OF THE YEAR (SERIES A) HOMILY I

Reading I: *When one finds a worthy wife her value is far beyond Pearls . . . . Charm is deceptive and beauty fleeting . . . Give her the reward of her labors. And let her works praise her at the city gates.* (Pro. 31:10-13, 19-20, 30-31)

ANA-GNOSIS

Throughout the history of any relatively stable society there is usually a fairly well-defined set of norms and guidelines by which different classes and groups within that society are to relate to one another and to conduct themselves with one another. In Europe, for example, where up until at least relatively recently there was a fairly rigid heirarchial structure, those of the lower rank of nobility showed a certain deference to those in the rank above them. In ancient Greece and Rome there were slaves who related to their masters in a certain way, and freed men who related in another way. But when the society changes and the old structures are broken down there is a period of time in which there is considerable confusion and uncertainty about one's identity. At the end of our own Civil War when black people were freed from slavery, while intellectually they knew they were freed and theoretically had the same rights as everyone else, it took a long time for this awareness to become internalized in both blacks and whites, until it was something that they could act on and integrate into their lives. We know, for example, that some of the black people had a difficult time adjusting to their newly won freedom and often they had difficulties relating to whites other than slaves. Slavery was a way of life that society had imposed on them for such a long time that they were unsure of any other way of life. So in any change in society there is such a period of turmoil before people can adjust to and internalize the new way of relating to one another and of conducting themselves with one another.

In our own time such conflict and confusion centers around women's rights. Throughout the history of our own society it had been pretty well established what the place of women was. Until recently, with several exceptions of course, it was not seriously or extensively challenged. But now this is all changing. Women are coming forth and demanding recognition for the uniqueness of their persons and for the contributions they have made and are making to society. And that leaves many of us in a state of confusion and uncertainty. Many women themselves do not seem to know exactly how to respond to this change in circumstances.

THEOLOGICAL EXTENSION

The author of the Book of Proverbs, from which we have a selection today in the first Reading, probably would not have understood what we are talking about when we are so concerned with women's rights and the Equal Rights Amendment. In his time the role of women in society was clearly defined and that definition very often prescribed a position of inferiority—their relationships to men and their position in society was decidedly inferior.

Yet he does make a strong point about the contribution in his society that women make: He says that as the husband is dependent upon his wife so we are all dependent upon one another. The issue becomes, then, not so much one of whether a person is a man or woman, but of each person's own uniquencss and the particular contribution that he or she can make to the welfare of another. One might say that it took us a long time to come to this awareness, yet we know that even in St. Paul's time there was something of this. St. Paul tells us that in the true Christian community there is "neither male nor female, all are one in Christ." This would surely bear out the idea that is expressed in the Book of Proverbs, that seeing ourselves in terms of our inferiority or our superiority to one another is not correct. We must see each other as unique individuals, each in a way responsible for the others.

In the true Christian community, then, no one would be seen as superior or inferior to any other, but rather we would see one another as equal in the eyes of God and each of us answerable to God for the use of our talents and gifts in the mutual redemption and convalidation of one another. That is perhaps one of the most exciting things about our present age—that at long last we are beginning to adopt this attitude toward women.

THEOLOGICAL CONCLUSION

Exciting as it is, this idea is nevertheless accompanied by a great deal of confusion, mistrust and questioning of our own identity that happens whenever a radical change takes place in the structure of a society. It took a long time after the Civil War for both whites and blacks to begin to adjust to seeing blacks as truly equal and valuable citizens. We are confronting the same thing in our time regarding women, but there is a growing awareness of the equality of all of us.

There should be no real divisions among persons, and certainly God does not see any divisions in terms of our worth as persons. Perhaps this awareness is not coming about as rapidly as many of us might hope. In the meantime it will require great patience and understanding of one another. Old attitudes do not die easily, and without some resistance. But to establish a true Christian community we must see all persons as equally worthy. We must begin to see one another, whether man or woman, as unique and of infinite worth in the eyes of God.

THIRTY-THIRD SUNDAY OF THE YEAR (SERIES A)
HOMILY II

Responsorial Psalm: *Happy are those who fear the Lord . . . . . Blessed is everyone who fears the Lord Who walks in his ways. You shall eat the fruit of the labor of your hands, You will be happy and it will be well with you.* (Ps. 128:1-2,3,4-5)

ANA-GNOSIS

Short cuts are supposed to help us get some place faster, do something quicker or generally save us time in whatever we're trying to do. Sometimes they work, if we know what we are doing, and sometimes they don't. Sometimes, if we aren't sure where we're going or exactly what we're doing, "short cuts" can be disastrous and end up being "long cuts." Then we eventually have to go back where we began to start again because we've become so lost or confused.

If a person begins, however, with a clear idea of where he is going and with good directions in the way of advice, instructions, road maps or whatever, he is unlikely to try any foolish short cuts. He knows he stands a good chance of getting lost and, in fact, losing time and wasting effort if he ignores the clear cut instructions he should follow.

THEOLOGICAL EXTENSION

This analogy of the person getting lost, sometimes foolishly, and wasting a lot of time and effort is applicable to what the Psalmist tells us today about God. He says, "Blessed is everyone who fears the Lord, and walks in his ways," The "ways" of God are clear and well marked, but because they don't always correspond with our own particular wishes and desires, we can be tempted sometimes to abandon them. We think perhaps that we know a better, easier or shorter way to get there and like a foolish driver we thoughtlessly head off in our own direction. Because we do this thoughtlessly we often have to come back to where we began and start all over.

This is the very thing that St. Augustine bewails in his *Confessions:* the great loss of time and the waste of a good part of his life. We know that St. Augustine spent the last part of his life in an intense effort to make up for all that he considered lost in his early life when he went his own way, in his own search.

THEOLOGICAL CONCLUSION

Seeking the "short cut" is characteristic of many of us, if not always, perhaps at least at one time or another. Sometimes, seeking our own selfish designs, we get off the true way. Fortunately, most of us realize it after much frustration and anxiety or error, and we come back and start again.

The Psalmist exhorts us today to know the ways of the Lord and to follow in them. He cautions us not to go off on our own, thinking that we can achieve the kingdom of heaven "our own way." He reassures us, too, that those who do follow in the ways of the Lord, "eat the fruits of the labor of your hands. You shall be happy and it shall be well with you."

THIRTY-THIRD SUNDAY OF THE YEAR (SERIES A) HOMILY III

Reading II: *As to the times and the seasons, brethren, you have no need to have anything written to you . . . When people say "there is peace and security," then sudden destruction will come upon you. But you are not in darkness, brethren, for that day to surprise you like a* *thief, for you are all sons of light and sons of the day . . . So then let us not sleep as others do, but let us keep awake and be sober.* (1 Thess. 5:1-6)

ANA-GNOSIS

Recently there was a movie about a flood resulting from a burst dam that washed away an entire town. The town was situated some distance below the dam and there had been some indications that the dam might be weakening; there had been a number of leaks in it, and the officials of the town were somewhat concerned. They called in a number of engineering experts and received their reports. The engineers, after making an inspection of the dam, assured the officials of the town that the dam was perfectly safe. They said that the few leaks in it would not affect the basic structure of the dam and could be very easily repaired.

Reassured by this report, the officials and all the people in the town once more forgot about the dam and went about their daily life. As it turned out, the engineers' report about the stability and strength of the dam was faulty, and some time later, totally unexpectedly, the dam burst. The town was totally destroyed and many of the inhabitants were washed away and drowned.

It is generally true that in times of serenity and plenty people are lulled into a sense of security and relaxation. If a disaster then occurs, all the more harm results. If the people had been a little more on guard they could have warded off much of the disaster if not all of it. For this reason, the Weather Bureau issues warnings about storms, tornadoes and hurricanes. The warning gives people a chance to take shelter and to protect not only their lives but often their property as well.

THEOLOGICAL EXTENSION

This preparedness or lack of it is what St. Paul is speaking of today in his first Letter to the Thessalonians. They are curious about when the end of the world will come, and after St. Paul tells them that he knows no more about that than they do, he then says, "As to the times and the seasons, brethren, you have no need to have anything written to you." He tells them that "the day of the Lord will come like a thief in the night." St. Paul exhorts them to a state of continual preparedness—living their lives as though the

Lord may appear at any moment. The fact that the moment is hidden from them, however, need not frighten them, because they are living their Christian faith every day.

Some of us might ask why God does not reveal to us more clearly when his coming will take place so we will be better prepared without knowing this. Each of us has certain talents and abilities given to us, a life's work allotted to us. If with these talents and abilities and in the time allotted, we carry out the responsibilities of the task that we have, we can be reassured that when God comes, we will be prepared.

THEOLOGICAL CONCLUSION

In times of prosperity or good health we can easily be lulled into a sense of security that things will always remain this way. Perhaps we may have in the back of our minds that there will always be some kind of warning given to us so we can take the necessary precautions to make ready. But like the people of the town that was flooded and totally destroyed, we, too, can be deceived by a false sense of security. We can have no stronger warning than that of St. Paul today, that we are always to be on our toes and not "sleep as others do." The true Christian is always alert, and when the Lord appears he will find him or her carrying out his or her assigned life's work. This is the best preparation that we can have, namely to go about our work in the most responsible way we know how.

THIRTY-THIRD SUNDAY OF THE YEAR (SERIES A) HOMILY IV

Gospel Reading: *Jesus spoke this parable to his disciples: "The kingdom of heaven will be as when a man going on a journey called his servants and entrusted to them his property. To one he gave five talents, to another, two, to another, one, each according to his ability . . . He who had received five talents went at once and traded them, and he made five talents more. And also he who had two talents, made two talents more. But he who had received one talent went and dug in the ground and hid his master's money."* (Mt. 25: 14-30)

ANA-GNOSIS

Whenever we hear about a person who has done a good deed

for someone else at some risk to himself, we all admire him very much. We realize that he didn't have to take the risk of assisting the other person, "sticking his neck out," and that, by doing so, he had much to lose. Yet knowing that he had a lot at stake, he went ahead and did it anyway without counting the cost to himself or even considering what the outcome might be.

In contrast to this we have also heard of people who do see someone in difficulty and to whom they could be of genuine assistance, and yet they refuse to become "involved." Such a person may have witnessed a crime but when called on to give testimony to the police, he may refuse to do so, either because it is too much trouble or because it might entail some kind of risk or inconvenience for himself. So he denies having seen anything.

THEOLOGICAL EXTENSION

This idea of risk is, among others, one of the keys to today's Parable about the Talents. One man was given five talents and another two talents, and they went out and invested their money and doubled it. They were praised by their master. He says, "Well done, good and faithful servant, you have been faithful over a little. I will set you over much. Enter into the joy of your master." But the man who was given the one talent "played it safe"—he hid his master's money in his fear of losing it. He is the one who is condemned. One might rightly ask here, "But what if the man who had received the five talents and the one who had received the two talents had invested their money and lost? What then? Would not the master perhaps have condemned them also?"

We are obviously not talking about taking foolish risks. Whatever we do must be thought out and arrived at through our prudential judgment. But even after this judgment, one still cannot be absolutely certain. Life is fraught with risks and uncertainties, and to hold back totally from them is to misuse the talents that God has given us. There is a risk in everything we do. We can never know absolutely the outcome of each action upon which we embark. At some point we must realize that there is no way around an element of this risk. To wait until we are absolutely sure about what we must do would be to remain inactive, to be paralyzed by fear. If we are, then we allow our talents to be wasted.

THEOLOGICAL CONCLUSION

Because there is no way around all risk in life, even after one has weighed all the alternatives under the virtue of prudence, the true Christian does not ask the question, "What if I take a risk and lose? Wouldn't that be far worse than if I played it safe and didn't take any risk at all?" Rather, he or she asks, "Is this the decent thing to do?" or "Does this need to be done?" And if the answer is "Yes," then one goes ahead and does it without counting the cost to oneself or considering the results.

This is the challenge we are all faced with from time to time. In responding actively to the challenge, we, too, like the men given the five talents and the two talents, will hear the master say to us, "Well done, good and faithful servant . . . Enter into the joy of your master."

THIRTY-FOURTH SUNDAY OF THE YEAR (SERIES A)
FEAST OF CHRIST THE KING
HOMILY I

Reading I: *Thus says the Lord God, "I myself will look after and tend my sheep. As the shepherd seeks out his flock when some of his sheep have been scattered abroad, so will I seek out my sheep, and I will rescue them from all the places where they have been scattered on a day of clouds and thick darkness. I myself will be the shepherd of my sheep and I will make them lie down," says the Lord God.* (Ez 34:11-12, 15-17)

ANA-GNOSIS

Oftentimes an organization will engage the services of a speaker, usually someone famous or renowned, to come and give a talk to their group. If the speaker is well known, he will have a busy schedule, and perhaps it will be necessary to engage him a long time in advance of his appearance. Sometimes it happens though that, shortly after the person is to appear, he becomes ill or for some reason is unable to keep the engagement. What he may often do then is to call and say that he personally cannot come, but he will send someone in his place. Understandably this will cause some disappointment and letdown, but generally the group will go through with it because everyone has been notified and all the plans made. Also they understand that usually the substitute speaker can be trusted to represent adequately the thoughts and ideas of the person who couldn't come. It may happen though that the substitute who comes does not truly represent the original speaker's viewpoint. People then are left even more disappointed or hurt by the misrepresentation because it is not at all what they have been led to believe.

THEOLOGICAL EXTENSION

We see something of this substitution idea in today's Reading from the prophet Ezekiel. The people had definitely been "let down" by God's substitutes. The prophet was called upon to comfort and console as well as instruct the Jews who were exiles in Babylonia. The exile itself and all its related hardships were caused by the peoples' infidelity and disloyalty to God on the part of the kings and leaders. They were supposed to be the "shepherds of Israel" and care for the flock God entrusted to them. They were to be God's representatives. But instead of being true to the task given them, they misled the people, disappointed them, and caused them increased difficulties and sufferings. So in the Reading today, God, through the prophet Ezekiel, says that he himself will be their shepherd, that he will come and there will be no substitutes for him. He says, "I myself will be the shepherd of my sheep." From now on the people could look for the real, authentic shepherd who would not mislead or deceive them.

THEOLOGICAL CONCLUSION

We know, of course, that this prophecy was fulfilled in the person of Christ who became incarnate among us. Christ came as the "real shepherd" whom we could trust and follow with confidence. There is no fear with him that we will be misled, deceived or tricked in any way. Unlike the substitute speaker whom we may or may not be able to depend on to represent the authentic position of someone else, we do not have that anxiety with Christ.

This is a great consolation. No matter how lost we may feel, we can depend on it that God truly cares for us. Like the true shepherd, he goes after the lost sheep. We see this theme in the New Testamnt in the Parable of the Lost Sheep (Luke 15:10) where Christ, as the true shepherd, comes to gather us together and to bring us home. This is our reassurance and consolation of the first Reading of today's Liturgy.

THIRTY-FOURTH SUNDAY OF THE YEAR (SERIES A) FEAST OF CHRIST THE KING HOMILY II

Responsorial Psalm: *The Lord is my shepherd, I shall not want. In verdant pastures he gives me repose. Beside restful waters he*

leads me. He refreshes my soul. He guides me in right paths for his name's sake.
You spread the table before me in the sight of my foes. You anoint my head with oil. My cup overflows. Only goodness and kindness follow me all the days of my life. And I will dwell in the house of the Lord for years to come. (Ps. 23, 1-3, 5-6)

ANA-GNOSIS

We all know what a delightful experience it can be to visit in the home of a gracious and charming host and hostess. When we arrive at the door, our coats are taken and we are made to feel welcome and comfortable. Often there is a period of easy conversation and perhaps a glass of wine or a cocktail before the host or hostess announces that the meal is ready. When we sit up at the table everything is deliciously prepared and elegantly served. Something of the same pleasure of being cared for and served well can occur when we go out to a good restaurant. Here we experience relaxation and a lack of responsibility simply from having someone else wait on us and do all those things we ordinarily have to do at home. It is nice to be able to leave these things in the hands of someone else and to be able to depend on them giving us what we need and to do their best to try to please us.

THEOLOGICAL EXTENSION

This is the theme of the Psalm today, that famous Psalm 23. There are vivid images derived from shepherding and from the agrarian way of life that cover all the contingencies of human life. But most vivid is the image of God as the host who waits on his guests with graciousness and consideration.

THEOLOGICAL CONCLUSION

This image of God as the gracious host at the meal is one we can all clearly identify with. In the anxiety and stress of life, we can be reassured that at the end God is there, as our host, waiting to welcome us. He does for us all those things that the host at a lovely dinner would do.

While these are all human images they allow us to grasp something of the idea of what it means to be in the presence of God—all our worries cease, and all our sorrows and sufferings are given meaning. We are at ease in the house of the Lord.

THIRTY-FOURTH SUNDAY OF THE YEAR (SERIES A) FEAST OF CHRIST THE KING HOMILY III

Reading II: *Christ has been raised from the dead, the first fruits of those who have fallen asleep.* (1 Cor. 15, 20-26, 28)

ANA-GNOSIS

It is often customary for young baseball players who are just beginning their careers in the major leagues to keep as a souvenir the baseball they hit for their first home run. While they hope to hit many others, the first has a special significance for them. It has a particular value and meaning.

In football the ball that was used in the game is often awarded to whatever player is selected as Player of the Game. Here again, this football, while not different from any other, has a special and sentimental value for the person who has won it. It indicates a special achievement on the part of that player and is something which he will cherish for a long time.

THEOLOGICAL EXTENSION

At the time when St. Paul was writing today's Letter to the Corinthians, there was also a special custom of setting aside something that had particular meaning and significance to the people. This is what they called "the first fruits." The term refers to the Jews' offering to God the first fruits of the harvest as a symbol of the dedication of the entire harvest to him.

St. Paul uses this same term in reference to Christ. He calls him "the first fruits of those who have fallen asleep." But in referring to Christ this way, St. Paul intends something far more than a mere symbolization of Christ. This is indeed something very real; for through the intervention of God we have all been raised up to sonship with Christ, who atoned for our sins. We are all in a very real sense in union with Christ and the citizens of God's kingdom on earth. And he promises that, following this, we are to have citizenship in the eternal kingdom.

On this feast day of Christ the King, which honors Christ as man, it is fitting that we give him the highest title that mankind can bestow on someone. As the "first fruits" of the Resurrection, Christ truly is our King.

THEOLOGICAL CONCLUSION

In our everyday activities with one another we choose some symbolic object such as the football or the first ball we hit as a home run to recall some special event. And, of course, this does have special significance for us. But while Christ has that symbolic significance, he has more. In being referred to as the "first fruits of our redemption," he holds out to us, through his own resurrection, the real and living hope of our own resurrection. Unlike the football or baseball that is bestowed upon the player and can only be given to one person, there is, in Christ, as the "first fruits," the real possibility of redemption for all of us. We all share in and benefit from Christ as the "first fruits of our redemption."

THIRTY-FOURTH SUNDAY OF THE YEAR (SERIES A)
FEAST OF CHRIST THE KING
HOMILY IV

Gospel Reading: *Jesus said to his disciples, "When the Son of Man comes in glory, and all the angels with him, then he will sit on his glorious throne . . . . Then he will answer them, "Truly I say to you, as you did it not to one of the least of these, you did it not to me." And they will go away into eternal punishment, but the righteous into eternal life."* (Mt. 13:31-36)

ANA-GNOSIS

At one time or another we have all been the recipients of an act of kindness and charity. This could have been something quite simple, such as someone giving us directions when we were lost in a strange city. Perhaps it was simply an understanding word or look or gesture. Or it may have been arriving at the home of someone late at night and being given a place to sleep. We may have been stranded along the highway with our car broken down and someone stopped and offered to assist us. But whether the act of charity was a simple or a more complicated one, we all remember with great warmth the person who bestowed that kindness on us.

At the same time we have all been the donors of kind and charitable deeds. Doubtless we have all reached out, perhaps even at some cost to ourselves, to assist others, to be of help to them in whatever way we could, knowing there would be no monetary return. Of course, we did not begrudge the person the kindness we were able to do for them.

Sometimes, however, the opposite occurs. We have all been in need and have been passed by by someone who might have helped us. At some time we might have ignored someone else when we didn't want to bother. Perhaps we felt we didn't "have the time," or something else was more important. So we were able to justify our ignoring the other person in a moment of need.

THEOLOGICAL EXTENSION

If someone were to have accused us of having passed a person by or ignored them when they needed our time and our charity, we might, from one point of view, have justifiably replied, "There is no law saying that I had to do that." And of course, technically, we would have been right. There is no state official or authority who could have arrested us because we ignored someone in his moment of need. No one can justifiably accuse us of any wrongdoin. What this brings home to us is that the most important of all laws is an unwritten law of charity toward one another.

We are all familiar with the laws that regulate our lives, and we generally admit the necessity of these laws. But what we perhaps sometimes forget is that without the unwritten law of charity, while life would not exactly stop, it would lose a great deal of its meaning. We all know the tremendous reward, not only of receiving something from someone else, but also of giving it. The act of giving someone something that we are not strictly obliged to give them, is an act above and beyond the ordinary written laws.

All these laws, of course, we arc bound to keep. In fact Christ tells us elsewhere in the Gospel that he did not come to destroy the Law but to fulfill it. But in addition to this, he gives us another command that supercedes all the other laws, and that is the command of charity to our neighbor as ourselves and to God above all.

So we can indulge in an act of self-deception if we think that by keeping all of the written laws we are beyond reproach and blame. This is the least we must do. There is an added dimension which, if it is lacking, makes all of our keeping of the laws empty and meaningless. And this is the dimension of love or charity.

THEOLOGICAL CONCLUSION

What we see in today's Gospel is that we will not be judged

so much on whether we have kept all of the laws and regulations that enter into our lives, but whether or not we have lived up to that unwritten command to which no one can technically hold us bound. The scene in today's Gospel is that of the final coming before the judgment seat of God. Some people will claim they are innocent of any offense, and yet it is these whom Christ will accuse because they are not even aware of the most important law of all—the law of charity. It is the most binding on a Christian, and it is on this law that we shall be judged.

Because we have all been the recipients of charity as well as the donors of charitable deeds, we know the importance of charity in our lives. Charity adds an extra, enriching element in the life of the Christian. Even those without faith keep the laws, but the Christian is required to do something above and beyond this. He or she must keep the law of love of neighbor as oneself, and God above all.

INDEX

Abandonment, 32
Abundance, 39
Acceptance
—of God's will, 17
—of present circumstances, 36
Accountability, 21, 34
Adjustment, 39
Alienation, 11, 16
Alibi, 21
Aloneness, 11, 16, 54
American West, 33
Anger, 8
Anticipation, 36
Anxiety, 31
Appearance
—physical, 46
Arrogance, 23, 24, 59
Authority, 58

Banquet, 37, 66
Belonging
—need for, 11, 16
Blame, 21, 28
Blindness
—inner, 26
Borrowing
—money, 12
"Bottleneck", 30
Broad-mindedness, 26
"busy-ness", 41

Certainty, 27, 76
Challenge, 40
Change, 22, 39, 70
Charity, 9, 82
Children, 28, 37
Choice, 17, 48
Christ
—as a model, 25
—identification with, 25
—intimacy with, 11
—presence of, 6
Christian
—challenge, 77
—committed, 33
—faith, 54
—maturity, 18, 21
—responsibility, 1, 40, 58
Cliques, 16
Cloning, 59
Closed-mindedness, 25
"Comeback", 53
Commandments
—greatest, 4, 55, 83
Compassion, 15, 25
Conceit, 40
Confidence, 38
Conflicts, 17, 70
Confusion, 70
Conscious choice, 8
Constitution, 55
Contradictions, 8
Converts, 54
Cooperation, 29
Copyright laws, 3
Corruption, 57
Courage, 54
"Credibility gap", 62
Criminal, 9
Cyrus, 44

Death, 11, 67, 81
—fear of, 11
—obedience to, 25
—security in facing, 39

Debt, 4, 13
Decisions, 17, 48, 60
Depression
—of 1929, 39
Difficulties
—overcoming, 54
Disappointment, 28, 66
Disasters, 74
Discouragement, 40, 67
Disrespect, 30
Distress, 50
DNA, 59

Employers, 28
Enthusiasm
—untempered, 6
Equality, 18, 24, 71
ERA, 71
Evil, 23
Exemption
—from the law, 19
Expectations, 28, 36, 64
Expressways, 30

Failure, 22, 28
Fairness, 21
Fear
—of aloneness, 11
—of old age, 11
—of the Lord, 72
Feelings
—of neglect, 47
"First fruits", 81
Forgiveness, 8, 13, 15
—not natural, 9
Fraternal correction, 1
Free will, 22, 28
Freedom
—human, 29, 34
Friends
—famous, 24
—of Christ, 7
Frustration, 30

Genetic engineering, 59
Generosity, 13, 19
Goals
—immediate, long range, 40, 49, 66
God
—above the law, 19
—as gracious Host, 80
—as our Master, 3
—attitude toward, 32
—goodness of, 51
—honoring, 45
—is hope, 52
—is love, 5
—rescued by, 52
—return to, 10
—source of our being, 3, 11
God's
—agents, 43, 62, 79
—care, 31
—compassion, 16, 51
—condemnation, 58
—grace, 22
—mercy, 10, 15, 16
—neglect, 31
—plan, 19, 31, 39, 44
—promise, 37
—will, 17
—wisdom, 20
Graciousness, 65, 80
Gratitude, 52
Grief, 68
Grudge, 8
Grumbling, 19
Guilt, 10

Happiness, 37, 64, 66
Honor, 45
Honors
—vicarious, 24
Hope, 68
Humanity
—of Christ, 25
Humility, 23, 26

Identity, 24, 70
Ignorance, 23
Immediacies, 41, 49, 66
Impossible situation, 48
Indignation, 42
Infiniteness
—of God, 15
Injustice, 18, 58
Instrument
—of God, 17, 44, 62
Integrity, 63
Isaiah, 15, 19, 36, 43

John, Tommy, 53

Joy, 36
Judgment
—final, 82
Justice, 9, 18

Kindness, 82
Knowledge
—of oneself, 23

Law
—human, 18
—of charity, 56, 82
—unconstitutional, 56
—written, 83
Learning
—openness to, 23
Leisure, 39
Life
—a place of risk, 32
—immediacies of, 41
Limitations, 59, 65
Limiting God, 44
Loan, 12, 34
Loneliness, 11, 47
Love
—a free gift, 29
—of self, neighbor, God, 56, 83

Malachi, 57
Maliciousness, 5
Maturity, 21
Messianic Kingdom, 37
Misbehavior, 10
Misrepresentation, 78
Mistakes, 1, 21, 23, 28
—admission of, 23, 24
Misunderstandings, 14
Money, 12
Motives, 6
Motorist, 18

Narrow-mindedness, 25
Need
—moment of, 82
—personal, 6
—selfish, 6

Obligation, 62
Obstinacy, 42
Openness, 23, 26
Opportunity
—a lost, 41
Optimism, 67
Options, 48
Outsider, 16
Ownership, 34

Parable
—of foolish bridesmaids, 68
—of property owner, 33
—of talents, 75
—of vineyard owner, 18
—of wedding banquent, 40
Parents, 23, 28, 37
Patience, 13
Peace, 29, 32, 65
Pessimism, 67
Pharisees
—behavior of, 63
Pity, 25
Plagiarism, 3
Possessiveness, 34
Poverty, 39
Power, 58
Priorities
—of life, 49
Prayer, 32, 47
Preparedness, 69, 74
Presence
—of God, 6, 80
Pride, 40
Prisoners of war, 66
Privileges
—vicarious, 24
Projection, 14, 22
Protection, 38
Prostitutes, 25
Prudential judgment, 76
Psalm 23, 37, 80
Public officials, 21
Punishment, 9, 19
—just, 10

"Range Wars", 33
Rationalizations, 41
Rebellion
—against God, 10
Religious leaders, 26, 48, 58, 63
Representative, 60
Respect, 28

Responsibility, 1, 21, 29, 40, 58
Responsiveness, 29
Resurrection, 81
Revenge, 8
Risk-taking, 76

St. Augustine's Confessions, 73
St. Paul
—challenge of change, 39
—Christ as servant, 25
—death, 11, 17
—representative of Christ, 61
—salvation, 27
Salvation, 26
Security, 4, 16, 38, 74
Self-examination, 7, 27, 28, 42
Self-righteousness, 26
Separateness, 15
Shepherd
—Lord as, 38, 79, 80
Shipwreck, 51
Shortcomings, 1
Shortcuts, 72
Significance
—of each person, 44
Simplicity, 65
Sin, 10, 22, 23
—condoning, 26
Sinners, 22, 25
Smugness, 4
Sorrow, 10
Spare tire, 68
Stewardship, 34
Strangers
—love of, 51
Structures
—societal, 70
—in transition, 70
Suffering
—for beliefs, 54
Superiority, 24, 26
Swimming, 31
Sympathy, 50

Taking for granted, 69
Talents, 34, 60, 71, 75
Tax Collector, 25
Teachableness, 23
Teachers, 23, 28
Teaching
—frustration in, 23
—the humble, 22
Tenancy, 34
Traffic jam, 30
Trust, 15, 19, 31, 34, 38, 39, 59

Uncertainty, 71, 76
Unexpected
—victimized by, 69, 74
Unfairness, 21
Uniqueness, 14, 71

Vacations, 36
Values
—eternal, 40, 49
Vengeance, 9
Viet Nam War, 66
Vigilance, 69
Virtue, 23
Vocation
—Christian, 16

"Way, The", 24
Wealth, 39
Wedding feast, 41
Wisdom, 64
Women's rights, 70
Worthy wife, 70

Xeroxing, 40